Sir
Walter
SCOTT

---

a reference guide

A
Reference
Publication
in
Literature

Marilyn Gaull
Editor

Sir
Walter
SCOTT

---

a reference guide

JILL RUBENSTEIN

G.K.HALL&CO.
70 LINCOLN STREET, BOSTON, MA

Library of Congress Cataloging in Publication Data
Rubeinstein, Jill.
  Sir Walter Scott : a reference guide.

  (Reference publications in literature)
  Bibliography : p.
  Includes index.
  1. Scott, Walter, Sir, bart., 1771–1832 — Bibliography.
I. Title.   II. Series.
Z8802.R82   [PR5332]   016.828'7'09   77-26785
ISBN 0-8161-7868-2

This publication is printed on permanent/durable acid-free paper
MANUFACTURED IN THE UNITED STATES OF AMERICA

in memory of
Earl R. Wasserman

Contents

Contents

Introduction

> I would also like to force them all [the Brahmins of
> Eng. Lit.] to read straight through the works of Sir
> Walter Scott, or at least up to that point when they
> were ready to stand in sackcloth and ashes in front of
> their own blackboards and admit what any honest person
> knows; namely, that Scott stinks.[1]

This uncompromising condemnation makes the devoted Scott reader
wince, but it is a fairly safe guess that Scott would not have been
unduly pained. His supposed indifference to his art and his supposed
or real indifference to the critics' view have long been notorious
and have resulted, particularly in the twentieth century, in a tradition of cavalier treatment or vilification of this peculiar writer
who persisted in his refusal to regard art as either a sacred calling
or even a way of life. Other critics have chosen the opposite extreme, mindless adulation which often fails to distinguish between
the exemplary character of the man and the shortcomings of his work.
Praise of Scott's sterling virtues began during his lifetime; even
Lord Cockburn and Francis Jeffrey, both Whigs and hence political
opponents of Scott in a fiercely partisan time and place, repeatedly
affirmed their high estimation of his character. This trend continued through the early 1950's and ranged from puerile discussions
of his love for animals and peasants to the more thoughtful considera-
tions in Grierson's biography and an honest admiration for the man
who emerges sadder but wiser from the pages of Scott's Journal.

Born in 1771 to a moderately prosperous Writer to the Signet,
Scott grew up in the waning years of Edinburgh's Golden Age and
learned from some of her greatest thinkers. When an early case of
polio left him lame and delicate, he was sent to his grandparents'
farm at Sandyknowe in the Border country to recuperate. There he
first heard the traditional ballads and folktales that molded the
romantic side of his ambivalent and paradoxical sensibility. As a
young man he was educated in the law, but he regarded legal duties
as rather onerous distractions from literary pursuits. Nevertheless,
the unique ambience of the Edinburgh Parliament House left an in-
delible mark on his fiction, and he continued to serve the Scottish

---

[1] Aubrey Menen, "Party of One," Holiday, July, 1959, p. 11.

legal establishment as Sheriff of Selkirk and Clerk of Session during his phenomenally successful progress as the Author of Waverley. It was a remarkably multi-faceted career. In addition to writing the narrative poems and the seemingly endless series of novels, Scott collected ballads, wrote histories, edited Swift and Dryden, and contributed regularly to the periodical press. He enjoyed a busy social life, dabbled in politics, and actively supervised the affairs of Abbotsford.

This Tweedside estate which Scott purchased in 1811 quickly became a consuming passion. He envisioned a Gothic castle fitted with all the modern conveniences and invested vast sums to realize his vision. To support the continuing expansion and improvement of Abbotsford, Scott inextricably entangled himself with his publishers, entering into financial arrangements which have been variously regarded as naive, indiscreet, or unscrupulous. The intricate structure finally collapsed, and in 1826 Scott went bankrupt. Although he acknowledged that he would have advised a client to rid himself of the debt by a petition of sequestration (i.e., legal bankruptcy), Scott promised to "dig in the mine of my imagination and find diamonds (or what may sell for such) to make good my engagements, not to enrich myself."[2] As a result of this honorable resolution, he worked himself to death in six years. After a series of debilitating strokes, he traveled to Rome in an unavailing attempt to regain his health. He finally fulfilled his last wish by returning to Scotland to die at Abbotsford in September, 1832.

Scott's death was widely mourned, and one pernicious tendency of Scott criticism surfaced almost immediately, the portrayal of bluff Sir Walter as a wholesome, healthy, and manly exception to his self-indulgent and effeminate contemporaries. Carlyle initiated this deplorable tradition in what he must have regarded as a touch of magnanimity amid his otherwise phlegmatic review of Lockhart's Life of Scott. Carlyle labeled Scott "one of the healthiest of men" and linked him with Cobbett, "the pattern John Bull of his century":

> So bounteous was Nature to us; in the sickliest of recorded ages, when British literature lay all puking and sprawling in Wertherism, Byronism, and other Sentimentalism tearful or spasmodic (fruit of internal wind), Nature was kind enough to send us two healthy Men, of whom she might still say, not without pride, "These also were made in England; such limbs do I still make there!"[3]

Subsequent critics have imitated Carlyle in proposing Scott's works as a healthy alternative to whatever sickly, decadent literary school they wish to deplore. In 1933 Edward Wagenknecht offered Scott as a

---

[2] The Journal of Sir Walter Scott, ed. W. E. K. Anderson (Oxford: Clarendon Press, 1972), p. 68.

[3] London and Westminster Review, 28 (January, 1838), 306-307.

suitable antidote to the neurotic tendencies of post-World War I
literature, and in the same year Arthur Fox found Scott objectionable
only to "the not over-fastidious students of sex problems." As late
as 1952 Alfred Noyes praised Scott for that "splendid objectivity"
that provides a refreshing alternative to "the tangled psychiatrics
of modernity." Like the diseased culture of the Romantic period, our
own could benefit, Noyes suggested, from the healthy influence of
Scott's poems.

This kind of anti-intellectual or anti-literary favor necessarily
created an opposite and equally extreme reaction, the revisionist
view of Scott's deeply flawed character. Amid the chorus of praise
stimulated by the 1932 centenary, Donald Carswell raised a dissenting
voice. In an acerbic article he attributed the neglect of Scott to
the "Scottolaters" who resist all criticism of their idol, a man of
high genius who lacked artistic integrity. This view, of course,
also echoed Carlyle, who pithily summarized Scott's career "of writing
impromptu novels to buy farms with." The tradition has been capably
perpetuated by Eric Quayle, who published The Ruin of Sir Walter
Scott in 1968 as a corrective to Lockhart's attempt to exonerate
Scott in the Ballantyne affair. Quayle portrayed his subject as a
status seeking snob, whose aloof attitude toward business, coupled
with his desire to become a landed aristocrat, brought him to ruin.

The 1932 centenary set the fashions in Scott criticism for the
next twenty years. The celebration provoked an enormous outpouring
of notices, most of them totally useless for the serious student of
Scott. A good deal of regional self-congratulation centered in Edinburgh and the Border country. The S. M. T. Magazine (published by
Scottish Motor Traction, the Edinburgh bus company) lauded Scott as
founder and best promoter of the Scottish tourist industry. Moray
McLaren wondered "Would Scott Be a Nationalist Today?" and answered
positively on the basis of some very conjectural evidence. J. A.
Falconer argued somewhat more convincingly that only a Scot can fully
appreciate the Waverley Novels, and several Border towns rushed to
claim Sir Walter as their very own. Various writers dramatized
Scott's life and works in plays and stories, most of them glaringly
deficient in literary merit.

However, the centenary year did bring forth some very important
contributions to Scott scholarship. Both John Buchan's Life and the
first volume of Grierson's Letters appeared in 1932. Pope-Hennessey
also provided a biography, but her theory of the revised chronology
of the Waverley Novels did not appear until the following year. Two
useful volumes of critical essays were published in 1932, Grierson's
Sir Walter Scott Today and the Scott Centenary Articles, collected
from earlier numbers of the Times Literary Supplement.

Among the tributes, both British and international, arose a recurring question: why is Scott no longer read? The critical consensus converged on two answers, the changing standards of literary

critics and the changing expectations of the general public. To un-
ravel "The Riddle of His Lost Reputation" David Cecil cited Scott's
deficiencies in "the qualities of craft." Unlike the Victorians who
sought edification, modern critics who prize form, structure, and
stylistic fine points, find Scott disappointing. The demands of the
reading public have similarly shifted. John Buchan worried that
Scott's respect for law, order, and universal purpose are uncongenial
to "an era of dilapidation and disintegration," and M. W. Wallace attributed Scott's declining reputation to his conservative temperament
and detachment from psychological minutiae. Hugh Walpole also suggested the inevitable reaction to Scott's enormous nineteenth century
popularity as one reason for the disinterest of the modern reader.

After the centenary, Scott criticism reached its twentieth century
nadir in the late thirties and forties. The bulk of the entries con-
stitutes what can only be classed as trivia, short notices in the
Times Literary Supplement and endless questions and answers in Notes
and Queries. The student of Scott finds surprisingly little work of
enduring value in this period. Grierson completed the twelve volume
Centenary Edition of the letters by 1937, and Tait's three volume
edition of the Journal appeared in 1939, 1941, and 1946. The latter
achievement, however, was somewhat compromised by a minimum of critical apparatus and the editor's rather querulous attitude expressed in
his pamphlets of 1936 and 1938. The best interpretive work came from
Edwin Muir, whose attitude toward Scott, ambivalent throughout, seems
to have mellowed as he wrote about him sporadically from 1932 to
1945. Muir defined Scott's essential artistic flaw as the division
in his works between the romantic and the practical, the feeling and
the thinking man. He attributed this split to two causes, the "imperfectly integrated society" in which Scott lived, symbolized by
the tradition which made Scots the language of feeling and English
the language of thought; and Scott's unrequited love for Williamina
Belsches, which rendered him incapable of dealing with love realis-
tically in the novels. The remainder of the critical work in the
thirties and forties is either insignificant or idiosyncratic. Coleman Parsons' studies of Scott's use of the supernatural are fascin-
ating but uneven; his Witchcraft and Demonology in Scott's Fiction
(1964) synthesized his earlier work into a highly readable and much
more useful form. Christabel Fiske in Epic Suggestion in the Imagery
of the Waverley Novels (1940) identified Scott as an epic writer on
the basis of his "bardic" traits, nationalism, and recurring rhetori-
cal patterns; but her techniques of classification have made little
impact on subsequent studies. Finally in 1948 Una Pope-Hennessey
published an expanded version of her theory of Scott's fictional apprenticeship which was promptly refuted in the same year by Robert
Mayo's defense of the orthodox view of Waverley chronology.

The 1950's witnessed the beginning of meaningful criticism of
Scott as thinker and artist. Perhaps most encouraging was the relative lack of frivolity of the subjects under discussion. Writers
began to treat Scott seriously as a systematic thinker, an historical

theorist, a conscientious artist, and an influence on the development of fiction. In a seminal essay (1953) Duncan Forbes placed Scott in his intellectual context and showed him to be a product of the intellectual burgeoning of Enlightenment Edinburgh, a disciple of the speculative philosophers and "philosophical" historians. In 1957 Patrick Cruttwell followed Forbes' lead in arguing that the intellectual constrictions inherent in Scott's personality and milieu formed his creative power. Their work provided the base for further development of the subject in the seventies by Avrom Fleishman and Peter Garside.

In 1951 David Daiches published his pioneering two-part study of "Scott's Achievement as a Novelist." Daiches had three purposes: to combat the prevailing view of Scott as an "ultra-Romantic" whose fiction is best suited for children; to distinguish the excellencies of the Scottish novels from the rest of the corpus; and to identify the essential ambivalence of Scott's attitude toward historical change and progress, which Daiches elaborated in his essay on Redgauntlet in 1958. Daiches' willingness to take Scott seriously as an historical thinker greatly stimulated the revival of interest in Scott, and much of the work which followed Daiches' for the next twenty-five years was designed either to elaborate, qualify, or refute his view of Scott as an anti-Romantic who reluctantly affirms the values of prudence and progress. Daiches' cogent argument soon provoked several carefully drafted rejoinders, most notably Robert C. Gordon's on The Bride of Lammermoor in 1957 and Mary Lascelles' on "Scott and the Sense of Time" in 1961.

Other defenders of Scott as an historical thinker emphasized his grasp of the movement of history and his vision of how historical processes form and interact with individuals and communities. David Cecil, Walter Allen, and J. A. Bramley offered several versions of this thesis throughout the 1950's, and Donald Davie in The Heyday of Walter Scott (1961) demonstrated how Scott's concern with the formative tensions of history influenced several other novelists. In 1962 the English translation of Georg Lukács' The Historical Novel reinforced the defense of Scott as an historical theorist. Lukács located Scott's great contribution in two insights: that the dynamics of history are manifested in average, simple people rather than in great historical figures; and that the roots of historical necessity lie in the social and economic bases of daily life. Lukács treated Scott with absolutely no condescension, a salutary change that heralded the critical resurgence of the sixties and seventies.

The defense of Scott as a systematic thinker and as a conscious historical novelist was accompanied somewhat later by a relatively feeble defense of Scott's artistry. The standard charges of sloppy craftsmanship, ramshackle plots, and tedious prose had been levelled at the Waverley Novels since their publication. Both Hillhouse (The Waverley Novels and Their Critics, 1936) and Hayden (Scott: The Critical Heritage, 1970) emphasized that Scott's contemporaries were

as cognizant as modern critics of his weakness in these areas. In
his essay on "Waverley and the 'Unified Design'" S. Stewart Gordon
began a rescue effort in arguing for the novel as a well ordered,
logically structured, and unified whole. In the same year, 1951,
Robert K. Gordon attempted a similar resuscitation of Scott's prose
style. However, the defense of Scott as an artist met with consider-
ably less success than the defense of his intellectual respectability.

The critical discussions of The Heart of Midlothian offer a microcosm of the writings about Scott in the fifties. Dorothy Van Ghent
opened the attack in 1953. She linked incoherencies in the novel's
structure to incoherencies in its intellectual foundation and in
Scott's world view. Two years later P. F. Fisher disagreed, arguing
effectively that Scott's belief in the Providential order of history
gives the novel a consistent intellectual framework. In 1956 Robin
Mayhead addressed the question of Scott's artistic slackness and de-
clared the first half of the novel "a piece of concentrated and sus-
tained art" unequalled elsewhere in the Waverley Novels. Even Mayhead, however, found himself unable to defend the second half of The
Heart of Midlothian. By 1960 Winifred Lynskey entered the breach,
rejecting the judgment of the last ten chapters as extraneous and
deeming them wholly consistent with the Calvinist doctrine which provides the novel's moral structure. Finally, in the next year
William H. Marshall identified Jeanie Deans's point of view as the
unifying device of the novel. These discussions of The Heart of Midlothian treated the novel strictly as a literary document; the writers
were not interested in Scott's life, or his business affairs, or his
religion, or his dogs. Scott criticism had finally escaped the
"Scottolaters" of the thirties and forties.

The rehabilitation of Scott's reputation continued into the
sixties. Cultural historians began to use Scott and his works as a
document in the history of thought and taste. In an impressively
thorough examination (1963), John Henry Raleigh demonstrated how attitudes toward Scott reflect changing Victorian values, and other
scholars published an increasing number of comparative studies relating Scott to writers as diverse as Shakespeare, Byron, Emerson,
Hawthorne, Burns, Dickens, Pushkin, and Twain. This period also witnessed several important critical efforts to identify connections
among the Waverleys and to establish causal links among narrative
methods, treatment of historical material, political philosophy,
characterization, and other aspects of the novels. In Romantic Narrative Art (1960) Karl Kroeber cited parallels between Scott's mode
of sequential narration and his evolutionary view of history, and
Alexander Welsh explored a similar connection between Scott's passive
heroes and his socio-political morality in The Hero of the Waverley
Novels (1963). The critical indictment of Scott abated but did not
disappear, and the more censorious judges also traced connections
among Scott's beliefs, techniques, and recurring themes. Frederick
Karl (1964) pronounced the novels totally devoid of literary merit
and attributed Scott's clumsy romanticism, rigid characterization,

and simplistic morality to his Tory politics. Emilio Cecchi (1961) also aimed at this vulnerable spot in Scott's character, finding his escapist medievalism a product of his inability to grasp the significance of early nineteenth century revolutionary forces.

Although John Lauber dismissed Scott in 1966 as "a purely historical figure" who is "no longer part of the living novel," the development of Scott studies in the last decade has proven this a premature burial. By the later sixties, the battle for Scott's critical revivification had been won, and the six years before the bicentenary celebration brought forth an increasing number of items of skillful literary criticism. With the sometimes jovial and always reverent exception of the annual Sir Walter Scott dinner addresses, very few of these paid any attention to Scott as a man or bothered to praise his character. However, after the publication of the Anderson edition of the Journal in 1972, the personal focus briefly reappeared. Daiches' ideas continued to influence the work of this period. Several important books (Cockshut's and Gordon's, both in 1969) and articles expanded or refuted them. The best of these, Francis Hart's Scott's Novels (1966) incorporated Daiches, but Hart commendably insisted on going beyond the formulaic implications of Daiches' basic dichotomy of tradition and progress. Hart argued that Scott was concerned not only with historical transition but also with its impact on individual integrity and cultural continuity. To demonstrate this thesis, he expanded his scope to include the non-Scottish novels, which had been largely ignored by recent critical consensus. James Anderson's six-part study of "Sir Walter Scott as Historical Novelist" (1966-1968) was also influenced by Daiches, but Anderson's consideration of Scott's theory and practice, use of sources, and attitudes toward the past expanded and specified Daiches' more theoretical approach.

The writers of the sixties continued the retrospective studies of Scott's place in intellectual history, in his own period, and in the development of the historical novel. Critics oriented toward cultural and intellectual history placed Scott in various traditions. Alice Chandler (1965) portrayed him as both a product of the eighteenth century medieval revival and an impetus to Victorian medievalism, especially in his influence on the social philosophies of Ruskin, Carlyle, and Disraeli. William Madden (1966) described The Heart of Midlothian as a typical nineteenth century novel in its concern with religious forgiveness, and Max Schulz (1968) maintained that Scott's passive hero anticipates the modern angst of Pynchon and the black humorists.

In locating Scott in the literary milieu of the Romantic period, John Hayden's work (The Romantic Reviewers, 1968 and Scott: The Critical Heritage, 1970) demonstrated that despite his enormous popularity in his own time, Scott's early reviewers found the same faults we recognize, but they were willing to overlook them. Richard French, in considering "Sir Walter Scott and His Literary Contemporaries"

(1968), concluded that although Scott was familiar with the work of
most of his contemporaries, he preferred to ignore the literary
fashions set by others and create his own.

In surveying Scott and his imitators in the historical novel,
the retrospective critics generally acknowledged Scott not only as
the originator but as the master of the genre. Thus Robert Donovan
(1966) judged Redgauntlet superior to Henry Esmond in the ability to
integrate historical and fictive elements; Erwin Wolff (1967) se-
conded this appraisal of the two novels. In a 1968 article followed
by a book in 1973, James Simmons surveyed the rapid degeneration of
the nineteenth century historical novel after Scott, while A. Serdyukov (1968) offered one explanation of the failure of the German historical novel to approximate Scott's achievement.

Perhaps the most significant sign of the rehabilitation of
Scott's critical reputation is that by the late sixties he was finally
being widely accepted as a knowledgeable literary artist and critic.
Writers of this period began to question the heretofore unassailable
assumption that Scott wrote carelessly, never revised, and held stylistic niceties in contempt. Mary Lascelles examined the proof sheets
of "Wandering Willie's Tale" from Redgauntlet and determined in 1968
that, although Scott probably reposed too much trust in the editing
of James Ballantyne, Scott's own best revisions worked to create that
equilibrium between natural and supernatural which accounts for so
much of the story's success. Lascelles' work has been expanded by
G. A. M. Wood. Additional writers have demonstrated Scott's careful
attention to other aspects of form. Frank Jordan (1968) and D. W.
Jefferson (1969) examined the strategic uses of dialogue and the
variety of styles and idioms used for deliberate purposes in the
novels. Scott's reputation as critic and editor also rose from the
depths during the later sixties. Although he has generally been
deemed a careless textual editor according to modern standards, Scott
gained some high praise as biographer, historian, and literary critic.
George Falle (1967) conjectured that Scott's empathic talents as a
novelist helped him to recreate the lives and milieux of Swift and
Dryden, and Charles Zug (1970 and 1976) even offered a tentative defense of Scott's editorial liberties with the ballad material of the
Minstrelsy. In his usefully arranged and annotated collection of introductions and reviews, Sir Walter Scott on Novelists and Fiction
(1968), Ioan Williams defined Scott as a practical rather than a theoretical critic who resisted prescribed rules and, like a good romantic, sought to judge a work according to its own most appropriate
principles.

Another indication of the increasing interest in Scott during the
six years before the bicentenary was the appearance of at least four
new biographies. Each, however, was limited or specialized in some
way. Arthur Melville Clark's Sir Walter Scott: The Formative Years
(1969) raised again the question of Scott's birth date and stressed
the importance of the late eighteenth century Edinburgh ambience to

his intellectual and imaginative development. In Sir Walter Scott: The Man and the Patriot (1970) Moray McLaren also emphasized this influence of the "Golden Age" and discussed Scott's impact abroad. Other lives by Schultz (1967) and MacNalty (1969) lacked critical orientation. The biographical renewal culminated in Edgar Johnson's monumental Sir Walter Scott: The Great Unknown (1970), which combined perceptive criticism of the works with a respectful but never sentimentalized presentation of the man. Invaluable to the student of Scott, Johnson's biography should remain the definitive life for the foreseeable future.

The 1971 bicentenary prompted a flurry of activities, conferences, and exhibits as well as literary criticism. To a certain inevitable extent, the celebration resembled its 1932 counterpart; there was much praise of Scott's character and courage, citing particularly his last years so affectingly documented by the Journal. Publishers issued several commemorative volumes: Allan Frazer's selection of the Edinburgh Sir Walter Scott Club annual dinner speeches, David Daiches' liberally illustrated Sir Walter Scott and His World, and Alan Bell's Scott Bicentenary Essays, not published until 1973 but including selected papers read at the Edinburgh Bicentenary Conference in the summer of 1971. As in 1932, there was wide international notice of the event. The Russians sought to find common ground between Marxism and Scott's profound conservatism, but essays by Mikhal'skaya and Rogov praising Scott as a people's ideologue are not totally convincing. A few new topics appeared in 1971 and following. The Johnson biography stimulated a revaluation of Lockhart's principles and methods in his Life; Francis Hart explained Lockhart's manipulations of source material as an attempt to resolve the paradoxes inherent in his "Romantic" conception of his role, and Robert Speaight judged Lockhart rather more harshly for avoiding the obligations of a literary critic. In 1971 scholars evinced some renewal of interest in the poetry, which had been generally neglected by serious writers on Scott, and several articles dealt with Scott and various aspects of the visual arts, another subject virtually unexplored before 1971.

The work since the 1971 celebration has continued the best tendencies of scholarship and criticism of the previous decade. W. E. K. Anderson's fully annotated and indexed edition of The Journal of Sir Walter Scott in 1972 contributed the single most important publication of the post-bicentenary period. The newer genre studies of the historical novel have subsumed Lukács' and Daiches' insights and have concentrated more on the ontological questions which arise from the coexistence of historical and fictive materials within a single framework: how can the novelist transform reality into illusion without sacrificing credibility, and what kind of verisimilitude should be demanded from the historical novelist? These questions are not new, but they have been treated with a new degree of philosophical sophistication, most notably in the work of Wolfgang Iser (1964 and 1974) and Avrom Fleishman (1971).

Scott criticism, then, during the last forty-five years has markedly improved in the quality of its questions, in the variety of tools it employs, and in its willingness to respect Scott on his own terms without condescension. One recalls, however, those apparent paradoxes implicit in Scott's introductory remarks on history and human nature at the beginning of Waverley; because despite the apparent progress, a number of themes and value judgments recur repeatedly through this period. The critics almost unanimously agree that Scott's best novels deal with Scotland of the seventeenth and eighteenth centuries, because these novels concern people and material he knew intimately, and consequently they express his deep devotion to region and country. Scott is deemed weakest, as in Anne of Geierstein, when writing about a culture and/or period completely strange to him, for knowledge of which he must rely on books rather than on his own or someone else's personal memories. Another almost unanimous judgment defines Scott's best characters as those of low degree, particularly comic characters such as Edie Ochiltree, Dandie Dinmont, and Peter Peebles. Conversely, Scott's heroes and heroines are almost universally considered insipid, passive, and stereotyped, with occasional exemptions granted to Jeanie Deans and Diana Vernon. With the exception of the most blindly devoted partisans, writers on Scott acknowledge that he fails miserably in delineating the psychological and sexual complexities of love.

In terms of structure and craftsmanship, the critics tend to concur that Scott's novels begin too slowly and often end incredibly. The short stories such as "Wandering Willie's Tale" and "The Two Drovers" excel because they avoid this organizational sloppiness. Scott generally receives high praise for his portrayal of manners and milieux. His natural language is the Lowland Scots dialect, in which he is unmatched, but some critics feel he writes English as awkwardly as a foreign language. When he indulges in the "tushery" or "Wardour Street English" of Ivanhoe or in what he himself called the "Big Bow wow strain," Scott receives almost total condemnation. His use of dialogue surpasses his narration and description, which too often lean toward the clumsy and prolix. The relatively few critics who have written on Scott's poetry find his best work not in the long verse narratives which were so popular in his own time, but in the ballads, songs, and fragments interpolated into the longer poems and novels. Scott as a poet is often differentiated from his Romantic contemporaries because his best verse is dramatic and objective rather than personal. In general Scott's critics admire his life as much as (and sometimes more than) his works and find that both as a man and as a writer his quintessential genius was for harmonious reconciliation.

There are still more areas of criticism and scholarship besides those which show a chronological pattern. One finds an astoundingly enormous range of writers, subjects, approaches, and degrees of skill, even in a period when supposedly Scott's reputation is at a low point and no one reads him. Since 1932 there have been close to

a hundred comparisons of Scott to other writers, most frequently
Shakespeare, Goethe, Balzac, and Poe. Scott has also been compared
to almost every nineteenth century American novelist and to at least
a dozen foreign writers ranging from Livy to Pushkin. Another favorite topic in the thirties, Scott's religion, has lost much of its attraction for later critics. Most of the studies of his religious
principles affirm that although Scott was uninterested in theological
details and doctrinal distinctions, his works celebrate and his life
exemplifies the Christian virtues of benevolence, forgiveness, and
acceptance of God's will. Scott's personal sectarian preference between Presbyterian and Episcopalian has been disputed, and his attitude toward Catholicism seems to vary in the eyes of the beholder.
Although Cardinal Newman and others have identified him as a formative
influence on the Oxford Movement, some scholars (for example Richard
French in 1964) see in the novels negative feelings toward Catholicism
and an attempt to link it with superstition and fanaticism. One
other kind of study, the survey of Scott's changing reputation, has
appeared five times since 1932. These studies usually take into account Scott's enormous popularity and offer some explanation for its
subsequent decline. James Hillhouse (1936), Paul Landis (1937), and
S. C. Roberts (1948) agree in attributing it to changes in the sensibility of readers and in the aesthetic demands of critics. Raleigh
(1963) uses Scott as an index of these changes in the Victorian
period, and Coleman Parsons (1972) divides Scott scholarship into six
phases, culminating optimistically in the present revaluation.

The overall impression derived from a survey of these last forty-
five years of Scott scholarship is one of infinite variety blended
with amazement that a writer who has been supposedly relegated to the
status of "the great unread" can stimulate such continuing notice.
A survey of this kind also offers sound encouragement to the serious
student of literature as he sees the paeans of the thirties and the
endless notes, queries, and jottings of the forties give way to the
much more judicious criticism of the last twenty-five years. One
hopes that Scott would be pleased, since he frequently expressed
contempt for the writer's need for constant commendation:

> When I first saw that a literary profession was to be
> my fate I endeavour by all efforts of stoicism to di-
> vest myself of that irritable degree of sensibility--
> or to speak plainly of Vanity--which makes the poetical
> race miserable and ridiculous. The anxiety of a poet
> for praise and for compliments I have always en-
> dea[vourd to avoid].[4]

Praise and compliments have been lavishly bestowed upon Scott since
the publication of The Lay of the Last Minstrel, and the 1971 bicentenary celebration affirmed that the tradition has not died. However, in good Waverley fashion, progress has accompanied and assimilated tradition, and Scott studies today treat their subject with

---

[4]Journal, p. 51.

respect rather than awe. The size of the corpus combined with the
years of neglect leave much still to be accomplished; and if future
critics follow the examples of their recent predecessors, we shall
gain an increasingly perceptive understanding of the Author of Waverley and his works.

I have begun the selections in this volume with the centenary year
of 1932. Corson's definitive bibliography covers material through
1940; while it seemed pointless to repeat the bulk of his work, I
wanted to provide some overlap. In addition, the vast outpouring of
Scott material in 1932 offers a recapitulation of the critical trends
of the early twentieth century. The chronological arrangement emphasizes the dramatic contrast between the 1932 and 1971 commemora-
tions, which emerged as an almost inevitable byproduct of the steady
changes in Scott scholarship during the intervening years. I have
tried to include in the list for each year everything written on
Scott with only a few exceptions. These include study guides, editions of Scott's works, newspaper articles, and reviews. I have,
however, included significant introductions or prefaces to editions
of Scott's works, special commemorative numbers of regular newspapers,
and longer review articles which survey several works or identify
critical trends. I have placed dissertations in the year in which
they were written; most of these are not directly annotated, but the
reader is referred to the dissertation writer's own abstract whenever
it is available. Reprints have not been included unless the original
was written in 1932 or later. Some foreign language material has been
impossible to have translated; where this is the case, I have attempted to include as much source information as possible. Material
which I was unable to locate is identified by an asterisk and a source
statement is provided. With these exceptions, the endeavor has been
for completeness. Where the endeavor has failed, I offer apologies
to any author who has been inadvertently overlooked.

To the Research Council of the University of Cincinnati and to
the Charles Phelps Taft Memorial Fund I am grateful for grants-in-aid
of research which facilitated work on this project. I am also indebted to the staffs of the National Library of Scotland and the University of Cincinnati Library, especially Bonnie Arthur and her
intrepid inter-library loan department. Arthur Melville Clark, S.
Stewart Gordon, Mark Weinstein, and Richard Dunn generously provided
copies of their work, and Frank Jordan offered valuable advice on
Romantic bibliography. I have received extensive assistance on
foreign language material from Lydia Kuniavsky and Jamie Lamb, and
without the indefatigable help of Joan O. Shevchik, the very paragon
of research assistants, this project could never have been completed.

Sir Walter Scott's Major Poems and Fiction

1802–1803	Minstrelsy of the Scottish Border
1805	The Lay of the Last Minstrel
1808	Marmion
1810	The Lady of the Lake
1811	The Vision of Don Roderick
1813	The Bridal of Triermain and Rokeby
1814	Waverley
1815	Guy Mannering, The Lord of the Isles and The Field of Waterloo
1816	The Antiquary, Old Mortality, and The Black Dwarf
1817	Harold the Dauntless
1818	Rob Roy and The Heart of Midlothian
1819	The Bride of Lammermoor and A Legend of Montrose
1820	Ivanhoe, The Monastery, and The Abbot
1821	Kenilworth
1822	The Pirate, The Fortunes of Nigel, Halidon Hill, and Peveril of the Peak
1823	Quentin Durward
1824	St. Ronan's Well and Redgauntlet
1825	The Betrothed and The Talisman
1826	Woodstock
1827	"The Two Drovers," "The Highland Widow," and "The Surgeon's Daughter"
1828	The Fair Maid of Perth
1829	Anne of Geierstein
1831	Count Robert of Paris and Castle Dangerous

A Selected List of Reference Books for Scott Studies

CORSON, J. C. <u>A Bibliography of Sir Walter Scott: A Classified and Annotated List of Books and Articles Relating to His Life and Works, 1797-1940</u>. Edinburgh: Oliver and Boyd, 1943.

ELKINS, A. C. and L. J. FORSTNER. <u>The Romantic Movement Bibliography, 1936-1970: A Master Cumulation</u>. 7 vols. Ann Arbor, Michigan: Pierian Press, 1973.

HAYDEN, JOHN O. <u>The Romantic Reviewers: 1802-1824</u>. Chicago: University of Chicago Press, 1968.

_____. <u>Scott: The Critical Heritage</u>. New York: Barnes and Noble, 1970.

HILLHOUSE, JAMES T. and ALEXANDER WELSH. "Sir Walter Scott," in <u>The English Romantic Poets and Essayists</u>. Edited by Carolyn Washburn Houtchens and Lawrence Huston Houtchens. Revised edition. New York: Modern Language Association, 1966, pp. 115-54.

WARD, WILLIAM SMITH. <u>Literary Reviews in British Periodicals, 1798-1820</u>. 2 vols. New York: Garland, 1972.

Writings about Sir Walter Scott, 1932-1977

1932 A BOOKS

1   ALLAN, JOHN. <u>Sir Walter Scott. A Centenary Memento in Scene and Story</u>. Dundee and London: Valentine and Sons, 34pp.
     Scott had a great soul which gloried in nature and tradition. His pen revealed the picturesque grandeur of Scotland. Includes several "gems" of description quoted from the poems. <u>See</u> 1932.A2.

2   [ALLAN, JUNIOR]. <u>Sir Walter Scott. A Centenary Memento in Scene and Story</u>.
     Pseudonym for John Allen. <u>See</u> 1932.A1.

3   ANON. <u>Old Kelso Days With Scott</u>. Kelso: Border Minstrelsy Press, 52pp.
     An evocation of memories of Scott associated with Kelso and its vicinity.

4   BARNSLEY, ENGLAND. "Scott Centenary Exhibition, 1932," organized by Davidson Cook. Barnsley, Yorkshire: Wombwell, Taylor, 56pp.
     The catalogue, which includes 500 items, is divided into I. Writings of Sir Walter Scott; II. Manuscripts (original holographs and facsimiles); III. Biographies of Scott; and IV. Scottiania. There is an Appendix of "Special Rarities from the Collection of the Rev. W. S. Crockett, D.D."

5   BAXTER, PETER. <u>Perth and Sir Walter Scott</u>. Perth: Thomas Hunter & Sons.
     Covers the connections between Scott and the city of Perth, both actual and fictional, with emphasis on background of <u>The Fair Maid of Perth</u> and Scott's visits to the city. Includes survey of the present reputation of the novel, of its editions in French and in Braille, and of its dramatizations.

6   BOS, KLAAS. <u>Religious Creeds and Philosophies as Represented by Characters in Sir Walter Scott's Works and Biography</u>. Amsterdam: H. J. Paris, 304pp.

1932

Scott refers frequently to both pagan and Christian religions and generously shows the best aspects of each. He
admires Christianity's beneficial effects on society, although he tends to equate profuse religious emotion with
fanaticism. Although he was reserved about his own religion, he lived a life of Christian charity and reverenced
divine revelation. Includes chapters on branches of
Christianity with which Scott came in contact as well as
his views on ancient religions and philosophies.

7 BUCHAN, JOHN. Life of Sir Walter Scott. London: Cassell;
New York: Coward McCann, 387pp.
A biography which contains some critical assessments of
the works but concentrates on an analysis of Scott's character as "the normal man raised to the highest power."
Scott's imagination inhabited a "secret domain" of fantasy
and vision. His Toryism developed from his distrust of re-
form and his unspeculative frame of mind. Scott's Christian
faith coexisted with the "common sense" of eighteenth
century Scottish philosophy, but it remained firm.

8 COOK, DAVIDSON, ed. New Love Poems by Sir Walter Scott,
Discovered in the Narrative of an Unknown Love Episode with
Jessie ----- ----- of Kelso. Oxford: Basil Blackwell,
48pp.
Publishes an excerpt from a MS volume entitled "Sir
Walter Scott and His Contemporaries" found in the Library
of the South Kensington Museum. The four letters and fifteen poems are addressed to "Jessie," the Kelso sweetheart
of the young Scott. Also includes the connecting narrative
of the unknown biographer.

9 CORFIELD, MARY H. Sir Walter Scott: A Sketch. London:
Elliot Stock, 22pp.
Although Scott's appeal is universal, only Scotsmen can
fully appreciate his character and his novels. He was
deeply patriotic and anti-revolutionary but not narrow-
minded. He honored the peasants of the country but feared
the proletariat of the towns. His socialism and his Christianity were practical, based on a love of the old
simplicities.

10 Edinburgh. National Gallery of Scotland. "Catalogue of the
Sir Walter Scott Exhibition in the National Gallery of
Scotland, Edinburgh, July 1 to September 30, 1932."
Edinburgh: Constable, 77pp.
The catalogue is divided into I. Original Portraits;
II. Engravings; and III. Books, Manuscripts and Relics.

2

It lists 291 items and includes Notes on the Exhibits by
Sir James Caw, Kenneth Sanderson, and W. K. Dickson.

11   Edinburgh. National Library of Scotland. "Scott Exhibition—
      1932," compiled by W. K. Dickson.
         A scrapbook compiled by the Convener of the Sir Walter
      Scott Centenary Exhibition in the National Gallery, Edin-
      burgh. Contains newspaper clippings, photographs, letters,
      and other documents relating mainly to this exhibition.

12   GRANT, ISABEL FRANCES. A Masque of Sir Walter Scott: A
      Series of Episodes from his Life and Works. Edinburgh:
      Grant and Murray, 172pp.
         Dramatized episodes from the novels are interwoven with
      Scott's own words, those of his family and friends and of
      the presiding "Spirit of the Masque" to celebrate Scott's
      patriotism and "the seemingly inexhaustible treasury of
      his imagination."

13   GRAY, WILLIAM FORBES. The Scott Centenary Handbook: A Guide
      to Edinburgh, Abbotsford, and the 'Rob Roy' Country.
      Edinburgh: Grant and Murray, 136pp.
         A traveler's guide to those places of the Borders, Edin-
      burgh and the vicinity of Glasgow most intimately associated
      with Scott. The narrative is interspersed with quotations
      from the poems.

14   GRIERSON, HERBERT JOHN CLIFFORD, assisted by DAVIDSON COOK,
      W. M. PARKER, and others. The Letters of Sir Walter Scott,
      1787-1807. Volume I. London: Constable, 531pp.
         The letters are annotated from correspondence to Scott,
      from Lockhart, and from other sources to provide information
      on events, people, and other necessary references. Each
      volume includes a list of correspondents, lenders of MS
      letters, and printed sources of letters. Volume I includes
      as an appendix business letters to John and James Ballan-
      tyne, 1807-1818. See also 1932.A15, A16; 1933.A4, A5;
      1934.A2, A3; 1935.A3, A4; 1936.A2, A3; 1937.A1.

15   _____. The Letters of Sir Walter Scott, 1808-1811. Volume II.
      London: Constable, 544pp.
         Includes letters through 11 September, 1811. See also
      1932.A14, A16; 1933.A4, A5; 1934.A2, A3; 1935.A3, A4;
      1936.A2, A3; 1937.A1.

16   _____. The Letters of Sir Walter Scott, 1811-1814.
      Volume III. London: Constable, 542pp.

Includes letters through 11 September, 1814. <u>See also</u>
1932.A14, A15; 1933.A4, A5; 1934.A2, A3; 1935.A3, A4;
1936.A2, A3; 1937.A1.

17 GRIERSON, HERBERT JOHN CLIFFORD. <u>Sir Walter Scott:</u>
<u>Broadcast Lectures to the Young</u>. Edinburgh: Oliver and
Boyd, 145pp.
A chronological account of Scott's life and literary
career interspersed with paraphrases and quotations from
his works designed to illustrate his insights into human
nature and the Scottish character.

18 _____, ed. <u>Sir Walter Scott Today: Some Retrospective</u>
<u>Essays and Studies</u>. London: Constable, 206pp.
A collection of essays whose purpose is to discover how
"Scott's work as antiquarian, historian, poet, historical
novelist" appeared after a hundred years and to consider
his influence on his successors.

19 GUNN, W. E. <u>Scott of Abbotsford</u>: or, <u>The Moving Hand: a</u>
<u>Dramatic Presentation of the Man</u> (in 3 acts, with prologue).
London: Constable, 78pp.
A dramatized version (with fictional liberties) of the
events of Scott's life from 1796, when he lost Williamina
Belsches, to 1827, when he acknowledged his authorship of
the Waverley Novels. Some of the speeches are adapted from
the novels and from the <u>Journal</u>.

20 Leeds, England. Brotherton Library. "Sir Walter Scott
Centenary Exhibition, October, 1932," compiled by John
Alexander Symington. Oxford: Basil Blackwell, 17pp.
The catalogue is divided into 1) Autograph Letters and
Manuscripts; 2) First Editions of Poems and Waverley
Novels; 3) Miscellaneous Prose Works; 4) Biographies of
Sir Walter Scott; 5) Song Sheets.

21 MACKIE, DAVID. <u>"The Shirra" o' the Forest</u>. Selkirk: R. G.
Mann, 80pp.
Celebrates Scott's association with Ettrick Forest and
its ancient capital, Selkirk. Includes anecdotes of
Scott's judgments as sheriff, his local friendships, his
popularity among the "Souters of Selkirk" and his partici-
pation in local ceremonies. There are still many memorabilia of Scott in Selkirk, especially in and around the
Old Court House.

22. MacNALTY, ARTHUR SALUSBURY. <u>The Great Unknown: A Short Life</u>
<u>of Sir Walter Scott, Bart</u>. Epsom: Birch and Wittington,
96pp.

An anecdotal biography. Scott was an epic poet whose gifts include his power of narration and his descriptions of battles. His poetry was influenced by Celtic love of nature and fervent patriotism. Under the inspiration of genius, he wrote rapidly but not carelessly. Although he remained a poet at heart, he elevated the novel form and increased its influence on human life. Partially incorporated into 1969.A7.

23 MARSHALL, DAVID. <u>Sir Walter Scott and Scots Law</u>. Edinburgh: William Hodge, 144pp.

Scott used legal material extensively from <u>Waverley</u> through <u>The Heart of Midlothian</u>, but legal references become less important in the later novels. Technical terminology creates verisimilitude, and antiquated legal phrases suggest a feudal atmosphere. Includes detailed chapters on <u>Waverley</u>, <u>Guy Mannering</u> and <u>The Antiquary</u>; shorter examinations of legal references in <u>The Black Dwarf</u>, <u>Old Mortality</u> and <u>Rob Roy</u>; and a study of <u>The Heart of Midlothian</u> focusing on Bartoline Saddletree. Partially reprinted in <u>Scottish Law Review</u>, vols. 46-50, 1930-1934.

24 MUDIE, P. LAURENCE K. <u>Scott and the Lure of the Road</u>. London: James Clarke, 189pp.

Relates seventeen novels to their local legends and topography and demonstrates the profound influence of actual surroundings on Scott's imagination. Scott was also a spiritual teacher who advocated "a faith of acceptance." His works show religion to be "the only key to the locked door of experience."

25 New York. Columbia University Library, Avery Hall. "Sir Walter Scott, Author of the Waverley Novels. List of the Autograph Manuscripts and the Editions of His Works in a Commemorative Exhibition. 1832-1932." New York: Columbia University Press, 19pp.

Catalogue of the Exhibition includes eighty-three items, including a large number of original manuscripts.

26 PARTINGTON, WILFRED. <u>Sir Walter's Post-Bag: More Stories and Sidelights from His Unpublished Letter-Books</u>, with a foreword by Hugh Walpole. London: John Murray, 419pp.

Selections from correspondence to Scott from 1796 to 1831 with generous interspersed narrative and notes by Partington. The letters are arranged chronologically, but they do not provide a complete record of Scott's biography for this period. They offer a survey of his wide acquaintanceship and many-faceted activities. Most of the letters are extracts.

1932

27   PATTEN, JOHN A. <u>Sir Walter Scott: A Character Study</u>.
     London: James Clarke, 192pp.
          Part I offers a biographical account of Scott's last
     years, stressing his natural benevolence and religion.
     Part II surveys Scott's critics from his own time through
     the early twentieth century and defends him from his at-
     tackers. Part III considers the "Genius of Scott" and af-
     firms that the Waverley Novels teach indirectly "the great
     and imperishable truths of Christianity."

28   POPE-HENNESSY, UNA. <u>The Laird of Abbotsford. An Informal</u>
     <u>Presentation of Sir Walter Scott</u>. London: Putnam's, 310pp.
          A biography which draws heavily on Lockhart but empha-
     sizes Scott's "shrewd instinct for self-protection" in his
     legal career, his search for official favor, his anonymity
     and his business affairs. Lockhart's explanation of the
     Ballantyne controversy was "fantastically unfair"; Scott
     used company funds for private expenditures and sheltered
     his own questionable dealings behind the name of the firm.

29   <u>The Romance of Scott: His Home, His Work, His Country. Sir</u>
     <u>Walter Scott Centenary 1832-1932</u>. Edinburgh: Travel
     Press and Publicity.
          A reprint of the June, 1932 (volume 8, no. 6) issue of
     <u>The S. M. T. Magazine</u>, the "Sir Walter Scott Centenary
     Number," in book form without the advertisements. Reprint
     of 1932.B1, B5, B6, B12, B18, B20, B21, B43, B54, B56,
     B59, B69, B83, B110, B112, B114, B117, B119, B120, B127,
     B140, B170, B173, B176, and B179.

30   SECCOMBE, THOMAS, et al. <u>Scott Centenary Articles</u>. London:
     Oxford University Press, 202pp.
          A series of eighteen essays from the <u>Times Literary</u>
     <u>Supplement</u> which appeared on the centenaries of the various
     novels. They are originally dated from 9 July, 1914 to
     12 April, 1928. Includes an index.

31   SMELLIE, PETER. "Address on the Centenary of the Death of
     Bro. Sir Walter Scott." Delivered in Lodge St. David,
     No. 36, on the Centenary of the Death of Sir Walter Scott,
     8pp.
          A commemorative address which reviews Scott's life,
     praises the humanity of his character and summarizes his
     connection with Freemasonry. He was initiated a member of
     the Lodge St. David on 2 March 1801. However, he was not
     a prominent Mason, and his Masonry did not significantly
     influence his writing.

32 SYMINGTON, JOHN ALEXANDER. "Introduction" to <u>Some Unpublished</u>
    <u>Letters of Sir Walter Scott from the Collection in the</u>
    <u>Brotherton Library</u>. Compiled by John Alexander Symington.
    Oxford: Basil Blackwell, pp. xi-xix.
        The volume includes letters dating from 1809 to 1832 and
    continues with correspondence relating to the erection of
    the Scott monument in 1840. Introduction provides back-
    ground for the letters in the volume, which also includes
    facsimile MSS of "MacRimmon's Lament" and of a portion of
    <u>The Seige of Malta</u>.

33 VAN ANTWERP, WILLIAM CLARKSON. <u>A Collector's Comment on His</u>
    <u>First Editions of the Works of Sir Walter Scott</u>. San Fran-
    cisco: Gelber, Lilienthal, 156pp.
        Provides detailed descriptions and histories of editions
    in the author's possession as well as information on loca-
    tion of proofsheets and manuscripts. Also provides inci-
    dental notes on the reception of the works and the identi-
    ties of persons who received them as presentation copies.
    An appreciative essay on "Scott and the Waverley Novels"
    (pp. 71-78) argues that the Waverley Novels appeared at the
    right time; people were looking for something new after a
    victorious war, and the age welcomed Scott's "sturdy manli-
    ness" and his vision of life.

34 WALPOLE, HUGH. <u>The Waverley Pageant: The Best Passages from</u>
    <u>the Novels of Sir Walter Scott</u>, with notes by Wilfred
    Partington. London: Eyre and Spottiswoode, 661pp.
        A selection of passages from the novels. For introduc-
    tion <u>see</u> 1932.B183.

35 WRIGHT, S. FOWLER. <u>The Life of Sir Walter Scott</u>. London:
    The Poetry League, 739pp.
        A biography which concentrates on Scott's financial af-
    fairs. Lockhart's exculpation of Scott as a helpless
    sleeping partner is inadequate. Scott took an active in-
    terest in the affairs of the Ballantyne firm and cannot be
    absolved of responsibility. Lady Scott has been neglected
    in other biographies; she was a great inspiration to her
    husband's work and provided the model for Diana Vernon.
    Includes close analysis of Scott's poetic techniques in
    chapter 43; Scott's poetry is among the greatest in English.
    Reprinted: 1971.A22.

1932 B SHORTER WRITINGS

1   ABERDEEN AND TEMAIR, MARQUESS OF. "A Tribute. Memories of
    Seventy Years." <u>The S. M. T. Magazine</u>, 8, no. 6 (June),
    54-56.

1932

Scott gives a many-sided interpretation of Scottish life
and character, which is especially well illustrated in The
Antiquary. Agrees with John Buchan that Scott's treatment
of the poor lifts them to the "sublime." Reprinted:
1932.A29.

2   ADAMS, LADY. "Scott and His Visitors." Scots Magazine, N.S.
17, no. 6 (September), 443–47.
John James Audubon journeyed to England and Scotland in
1826 in search of an engraver willing to publish his bird
drawings. He was very eager to see Scott, and visited
twice at Abbotsford.

3   AITCHISON, CRAIGIE MASON. "Sir Walter Scott Centenary: The
Lord Advocate's Speech at the Dinner of the Scottish Bench
and Bar." Juridical Review, 44, 374–85.
The Parliament House was as important an influence on
Scott as the Borders. He was steeped in legal lore and in
its connections to the history and traditions of Scotland.

4   ANON. "The Scott Centenary." The Jacobite (New Zealand),
4, no. 8 (12 March), 175–76.
Although he harbored some admiration for Jacobitism and
founded the Jacobite novel, Scott actually "stabbed the
Jacobite cause in the back" when he acknowledged George IV
as heir of the House of Stuart. Scott's attitude was "a
gross perversion of the truth," since he should have known
that the rights of the exiled male Stuarts would pass to
their female descendants.

5   ANON. "Editorial." The S. M. T. Magazine, 8, no. 6 (June),
43–45.
Scott's life was informed by humanity, generosity and
courage. His humble characters demonstrate his conviction
in the brotherhood of all men and his respect for the Scottish peasantry. He was a romanticist with a deep sense of
responsibility. Reprinted: 1932.A29.

6   ANON. "Seeing the Scott Country: A Land of Minstrelsy and
Song." The S. M. T. Magazine, 8, no. 6 (June), 143–48.
A tour guide for travellers who wish to seek out spots
particularly associated with Scott. He has "cast a spell"
over the entire region from Edinburgh to Liddesdale and
knew the history and legends of every crumbling tower and
pathway in the area. Reprinted: 1932.A29.

7   ANON. "Scott Centenary Number." Border Magazine, 37, no. 441
(September).

Most of the material in this centenary number consists of commemorative speeches delivered to various organizations or reprinted with acknowledgements from other sources.

8 ANON. "Waverley Revisited." The Times Literary Supplement
(15 September), pp. 629–30.
    Scott was the last great novelist of the eighteenth century, not the first great novelist of the nineteenth. He was a Romantic of the school of Horace Walpole, not of Byron or Chateaubriand.

9 ANON. "Who Reads Scott's Novels?" Literary Digest, 114,
no. 15 (8 October), 18–19.
    A series of excerpts from several centenary notices, mainly from American newspapers. The question of the title is not answered.

10 ANON. "A Scott Exhibition." Times Literary Supplement
(27 October), p. 796.
    Describes the exhibition of books, manuscripts, and portraits relating to Scott in the rooms of Messrs. J. and E. Bumpus. It includes a representative selection of manuscripts and letters addressed to Mackenzie, Byron and others, and a display of books ranging from first editions to modern sets of the Waverley Novels.

11 BARCLAY, JOHN B. "The Scott Monument. A World Famous
Memorial." The S. M. T. Magazine, 9, no. 3 (September),
22–26.
    The foundation stone of the Scott monument in Princes Street (Edinburgh) was laid on 15 August, 1840. The architect was George Meikle Kemp, and Sir John Steell was the sculptor of the marble statue. The monument is adorned with representations of Scottish poets and of characters from the Waverley Novels.

12 BARNETT, T. RATCLIFFE. "The Humanity of Scott. 'True gentleman, heart, blood and bone.'" The S. M. T. Magazine, 8,
no. 6 (June), 122–26.
    Scott possessed an extensive understanding of human nature and liked people regardless of rank. He loved children, horses, and dogs, and he treated his servants respectfully. His Journal demonstrates his heroism under misfortune. Reprinted: 1932.A29.

13 BATHO, EDITH. "Scott as a Medievalist," in Sir Walter Scott
Today. Edited by H. J. C. Grierson. London: Constable,
pp. 133–57.
    The artist usually triumphed over the antiquary in Scott. He regarded facts as important only as they contributed to

human understanding. He collected miscellaneous facts to
form the picture of an historical period, and he did not
always verify his references. However, in the novels and
essays his fundamental knowledge compensates for occasional
inaccuracies. Includes discussion of Scott's knowledge of
Old Norse sagas and their possible influence on the Waverley
Novels.

14   BELL, AUBREY. "Scott and Cervantes," in Sir Walter Scott
     Today. Edited by H. J. C. Grierson. London: Constable,
     pp. 69-90.
         Scott read Cervantes in the original and admired him for
     his "genuine Spanishness" and treatment of the peasantry.
     He preferred the humanity of Cervantes to the satiric tone
     of other Spanish picaresque novelists. Scott learned from
     Cervantes how to include in a novel a vast amount of ma-
     terial. Includes some commentary on Scott's influence on
     the Spanish historical/regional novel.

15   BENSLY, EDWARD. "Walter Scott: Classical Allusion." Notes
     and Queries, 162 (23 April), 301.
         Scott's source for "Axylus" was Pope's version of the
     Iliad. He is "a wealthy and hospitable Trojan killed in
     battle by Diomede." The accent in Greek makes the meaning
     "without wood" impossible. See 1932.B92.

16   BLUNDEN, EDMUND. "The Poetry of Scott." Queen's Quarterly,
     39 (November), 593-602.
         Scott wrote poetry "at too great a rate to be embarrassed
     by details." His poems constitute a "mechanical pageant of
     antiquarian verse." They are fluent but ungrammatical, ex-
     citing but not very profound. The short poems are superior
     to the narratives, which are merely "journalism in verse."

17   BOLTON, J. R. GLORNEY. "The Influence of Scott." Bookman, 82
     (April), 13-14.
         Scott was a conservative, concerned more with social
     status than with literature. He was uninterested in sex
     and untroubled by passion. He never understood Reform and
     opposed progress. Although he was a good novelist, the
     novel has progressed far beyond what he could ever hope to
     accomplish.

18   BOYD, HALBERT J. "A Friend in Need." The S. M. T. Magazine,
     8, no. 6 (June), 91-95.
         A fictionalized account of Scott's meeting with Tom
     Purdie, the poacher whom Scott refrained from punishing and
     who later became Scott's devoted shepherd for twenty-two
     years. Reprinted: 1932.A29.

19   BOYD, JAMES. "Sir Walter Scott," in his <u>Goethe's Knowledge</u>
      <u>of English Literature</u>. Oxford Studies in Modern Languages
      and Literature. Oxford: Oxford University Press,
      Clarendon Press, pp. 212–30.
          Although Goethe and Scott admired each other's works,
      their correspondence never developed much intimacy. Goethe
      regarded <u>Waverley</u> as Scott's greatest work and read the
      <u>Life of Napoleon</u> for the English point of view he felt it
      embodied. Goethe also read <u>Kenilworth</u>, the <u>Letters on De-</u>
      <u>monology and Witchcraft</u>, <u>Rob Roy</u>, <u>The Fair Maid of Perth</u>,
      <u>Ivanhoe</u>, and <u>The Abbot</u>. He noted his reactions to them in
      his diary. Goethe acknowledged the flaws in Scott's work
      but admired his great gift as a storyteller.

20   BROWN, IVOR. "Salute to Sir Walter. An Appeal for Libera-
      tion." <u>The S. M. T. Magazine</u>, 8, no. 6 (June), 82–83.
          Scott's books should not be forced on school children.
      They will delight in the Scottish novels (but not the
      chivalric romances) if they are not required to read them
      for examination. Reprinted: 1932.A29.

21   BUCHAN, JOHN. "Scott: Some Centenary Reflections." <u>The</u>
      <u>S. M. T. Magazine</u>, 8, no. 6 (June), 51–53.
          Present critics see Scott as dated, conventional, and
      irrelevant. He believed in order, law and universal pur-
      pose, ideas which are uncongenial to "an era of dilapida-
      tion and disintegration." Expresses the hope that Scott
      may be judged by the Scottish novels, and that in a newly
      constructive world he will once again be taken seriously.
      Reprinted: 1932.A29.

22   _____. "The Scott that Remains." <u>Listener</u>, 8 (21 September),
      407–10.
          Scott's particular genius was the transformation of re-
      ality into a world of romance and beauty. He juxtaposes
      the splendid with the prosaic, comedy with tragedy. He
      recognizes "the tragic dualism of life," and his purpose is
      always reconciliation.

23   _____. "Sir Walter Scott, 1832–1932: A Centenary Address."
      Bound with "A Forgotten Antiquary" by William C. Van An-
      twerp. San Francisco: The Book Club of California,
      pp. 1–8.
          Scott's personality is as precious a legacy as his works.
      He loved the countryside and the people among whom he lived.
      The local people respected him primarily as Sheriff and
      Laird and did not care much about his writing. As "a plain
      man among plain men," Scott learned insight and sympathy.

1932

24   BUCHAN, SUSAN. "Sir Walter Scott," in <u>Lady Louisa Stuart:</u>
      <u>Her Memories and Portraits</u>. London: Hodder & Stoughton,
      pp. 190–217.
           The correspondence between Scott and Lady Louisa Stuart
      was remarkably frank on both sides. She offered honest
      criticism of his works, and he complained about the proces-
      sion of guests at Abbotsford. Scott's letters to Lady
      Louisa show none of the usual condescension of a masculine
      author to a woman; he admired her both as a person and as
      a writer.

25   BULLOUGH, GEOFFREY. "A Letter of Crabbe to Scott." <u>Times</u>
      <u>Literary Supplement</u> (22 September), p. 666.
           Publishes a letter of June, 1815 in which Crabbe ac-
      knowledges receipt of Scott's <u>Lord of the Isles</u> and hints
      that he suspects Scott's authorship of <u>Waverley</u> and <u>Guy</u>
      <u>Mannering</u>.

26   BURDETT, OSBERT. "Goethe and Scott." <u>Bookman</u>, 82 (April),
      15–17.
           Goethe was fascinated by Scott's novelistic technique,
      and Scott was inspired by Goethe's <u>Götz von Verlichingen</u> to
      invent the stories of the Waverley Novels. However, Goethe
      was more modern and complex than Scott, who lived in an in-
      nocent, healthy, and properly proportioned world.

27   BURNETT, GEORGE. "Sir Walter Scott and Tweed." <u>Listener</u>, 8
      (10 August), 208–209.
           The River Tweed, its natural beauty and the many ballads
      and legends connected with it, were closely intertwined with
      all the phases of Scott's life.

28   BURRILL, KATHARINE. "A Bunch of Bluebells." <u>Chambers'</u>
      <u>Journal</u>, 8th ser. 1 (September), 662–64.
           Scott's novels should not be forced on children as holi-
      day tasks. Readers who object to extended descriptions
      should feel free to skip what bores them. With the excep-
      tion of Die Vernon, Scott's heroes and heroines are inferior
      to the idiosyncratic characters.

29   CARSWELL, DONALD. "The Legend of Abbotsford." <u>Nineteenth</u>
      <u>Century</u>, 112 (September), 374–84.
           Although Lockhart's <u>Life</u> lacks affection for Scott, over
      the years the harshness of its image has blurred into "the
      Abbotsford Legend" of Scott's exemplary life. This needs
      to be corrected in several respects, including the character
      of Lady Scott, the chronology of the novels, Scott's finan-
      cial ethics, and his lack of artistic conscience.

30   ____. "Sir Walter Scott." <u>Scottish Country Life</u>, 21, no. 9 (September), 261-63.
      Scott would be surprised to find his centenary celebrated, because he mocked the idea of artistic immortality. Although he admitted that he wrote for money, he wrote only what he wished. He was an artist in spite of himself who "created modern fiction and never knew it."

31   ____. "Why Scott is Neglected," in "Sir Walter Scott: A Centenary Commentary by Various Writers," <u>The Modern Scot</u>, 3 (August), 111-13.
      Present critics acknowledge Scott's importance but refuse to read him. This neglect is partly due to the adherents of the Scott cult who regard criticism as heresy. A more significant reason is Scott's character; he was a man of genius who lacked artistic integrity and was corrupted by popularity.

32   CECIL, DAVID. "Sir Walter Scott. I. A Study in Genius." <u>Atlantic Monthly</u>, 150, no. 3 (September), 277-87.
      Because Scott's primary interest is in the connections of human life to its past, his subjects and themes are limited and do not include private life. His strengths lie in his powers of narration, description, and character creation. "He combines the substance of the realist with the fantasy of the romantic." Reprinted: 1932.B34 and slightly revised 1933.A2.

33   ____. "Sir Walter Scott. II. The Riddle of His Lost Reputation." <u>Atlantic Monthly</u>, 105, no. 4 (October), 485-94.
      Scott gains tragic effects through his semi-humorous characters and vernacular dialogue. However, he was deficient in "the qualities of craft" and lacked a sense of form. His novels tend to be anti-climactic and lacking in proportion. Although no single novel is completely successful, even his worst work shows "the hint of careless greatness." Reprinted: 1932.B34 and slightly revised 1933.A2.

34   ____. "Sir Walter Scott." <u>Life and Letters</u>, 8 (June), 142-83.
      Reprint of 1932.B32, B33 and slightly revised 1933.A2.

35   CHARTERIS, ARCHIBALD HAMILTON. "Walter Scott," in his <u>When the Scot Smiles in Literature and Life</u>. London: Alexander Maclehose, pp. 91-118.
      Scott had an unerring ear for the vernacular and for narrating through dialogue. His humor was genial, never mocking, and drawn from his wide observation of human types.

1932

> Although he failed in the spoken "English of the books," in the Journal he wrote easily and gracefully in his own natural English.

36   CLARK, ARTHUR MELVILLE. "Scott and the University." Univer-
      sity of Edinburgh Journal, 5, no. 1 (Summer), 8-22.
           Scott's formal education at the University of Edinburgh
      left little influence on his true genius. He had to educate
      himself in his real interests, the medieval and Romantic,
      which were ignored by the University with its classical ori-
      entation. Although he worked hard on his courses in Civil
      and Scots law, in all that went to form his writing he was
      self-educated. This article marks the first appearance of
      the author's conjectures on Scott's correct birthdate. See
      1969.A2 and 1970.A2.

37   COLLOCOT, T. C. "Scott and John Richardson." Chambers'
      Journal, 8th ser. 1 (July), 538-42.
           Anecdotal account of the warm friendship between Scott
      and Richardson, an Edinburgh and London lawyer. Their
      friendship began in 1800 and continued until Scott's death.

38   COOK, DAVIDSON. "Scott First Editions." Times Literary
      Supplement (18 August), p. 584.
           Offers two corrections to errors in Van Antwerp's A Col-
      lector's Comment on His First Edition of the Works of Sir
      Walter Scott. The "Two Letters on Scottish Affairs, from
      Edward Bradwardine Waverley, Esq., to Malachi Malagrowther,
      Esq." were written by Croker in response to Scott's Mala-
      growther letters. The 1824 edition of "Memorials of the
      Haliburtons" is actually a second, not a first edition.
      See 1932.B46, B146.

39   CRÉPET, JACQUES. "Edgar Poe et Anne de Geierstein." Figaro
      (14 December), pp. 4-5.
           In his "Bérénice" Poe alludes several times to Anne of
      Geierstein. Scott stimulated Poe's imagination and his
      works suggested images, descriptive techniques, and plot
      outlines.

40   CRICHTON, GEORGE. "Sir Walter Scott and Galashiels." Transac-
      tions of the Hawick Archaeological Society, Session 1932,
      ix-xiii.
           The entire Borderland has a right to claim Scott as a
      son, but unlike most of the other towns, Galashiels honored
      him during his lifetime. Includes accounts of Scott's at-
      tendance at the town's annual festival in 1821, his lending
      his piper to the Galashiels weavers for an 1819 celebration,
      and his purchase of Cartley Hole.

14

41 _____, ed. "Sir Walter Scott Centenary Commemoration."
Supplement to the Galashiels Border Telegraph (27 September),
8pp.
Includes a detailed account of the "more than passing
intimacy between Scott and the Galashiels people." He had
many friends at Galashiels and attended several celebrations
there in his honor. Also includes: a series of quoted
"pen pictures" of Scott from his Journal; an account of the
dedication of the Galashiels memorial to Scott; and "A Gala
Man's Reminiscences" by Walter Scott of Crieff, who reviews
Sir Walter's associations with Northern England, the Borders
and the fringe of the Highlands.

42 CROCKETT, W. S. "Sir Walter's Country." Edinburgh Scotsman:
Sir Walter Scott Centenary Supplement (21 September),
p. iii.
Scott was a product of his forebearers who gave the Border country its distinctive character. He has made this
region "Sir Walter Scott's Land," and his grave at Dryburgh
is "a Scottish Mecca."

43 _____. "Some Waverley Prototypes." The S. M. T. Magazine, 8,
no. 6 (June), 117–21.
Scott worked in composites and never created a character
as an actual counterpart of a particular individual. Summarizes The Scott Originals (1912) and adds the correction
that Williamina Belsches rather than Jane Anne Cranstoun
was the prototype of Diana Vernon. Reprinted: 1932.A29.

44 CUNNINGHAME, A. T. "Scott in 1932," in "Sir Walter Scott:
A Centenary Commentary by Various Writers." The Modern
Scot, 3 (August), 114–18.
Scott is no longer an active literary influence. He appeals neither to those who seek the fusion of religious-
emotional-intellectual experience with art nor to those who
seek in art the perfection of form. The novels are inade-
quate representations of human nature. They provide only
"boyish thrills" and escapist refuges from modernity.

45 CURLE, JAMES. "The Scott Country--1800-1832." Scottish
Country Life, 21, no. 9 (September), 263–64.
Describes the appearance of the Border country and the
ways of life of its people in Scott's time.

46 _____. "Scott First Editions." Times Literary Supplement
(29 September), p. 696.
Conjectures that the "Memorials of the Haliburtons" was
printed in 1819, but the Preliminary Notice was not set and
the book was not issued before March, 1820. See 1932.B38,
B146.

1932

47   DIGEON, A. "Sir Walter Scott." France–Grande Bretagne;
      bulletin des relations franco–brittaniques (November),
      pp. 287-90.
            It is unfair to compare Scott disparagingly to Balzac in
      terms of what Scott did not do. He taught Balzac and all
      other subsequent novelists how to portray a society in its
      totality and to analyze not only people but an epoch. Scott
      is less popular now than he was in the nineteenth century,
      because this is an age that seeks to emancipate itself from
      history. But fashions will change, and his faithful readers
      will return.

48   DIMNET, ERNEST. "Sir Walter Scott in France." Listener, 8
      (21 September), 410-12.
            The French never regarded Scott as a foreign writer, and
      he deeply influenced French literature--Vigny, Hugo, Lamar-
      tine, Thierry and especially Balzac. Although he is no
      longer widely read, many French people still feel a strong
      bond of affection for Scott and the Scottish people.

49   DIXON, W. MACNEILE. "Address to the Thirty-second Annual
      Dinner of the Edinburgh Sir Walter Scott Club." Edinburgh
      Sir Walter Scott Club Annual Report, pp. 20-33.
            Scott was a Romantic who admired heroism and had faith
      in human nature, in contrast to modern writers who dwell on
      gloom and ugliness. He judged people by what they did and
      things by how they appeared; he eschewed unintelligibility
      and psychoanalysis. He discovered "the human values of his-
      tory" and drew attention to Scotland's native genius. Re-
      printed: 1932.B50 and 1944.B4.

50   _____. "Our Debt to Scott Today." Queen's Quarterly, 39
      (November), 581-92.
            Reprint of 1932.B49. Reprinted: 1944.B4.

*51   DOTTIN, PAUL. "Le Centenaire de W. Scott." L'Européen
      (26 August).
            Cited in the Annual Bibliography of English Language and
      Literature (Cambridge: Modern Humanities Research Associa-
      tion, 1933), XIII, 199, item #3211.

52   DOUGLAS, GEORGE. "The Minstrel of Romance." Edinburgh
      Scotsman: Sir Walter Scott Centenary Supplement
      (21 September), p. vi.
            Although the novels are the greatest part of his work,
      Scott's verse has a valid claim to genius. His lyrics come
      from his gift for storytelling and not from his own life.
      The Lay of the Last Minstrel, Marmion, and The Lady of the
      Lake excel, but the later poems are inferior and tend to
      become monotonous.

53   _____. "Scott Among the Immortals." Everyman, 8 (22 September), 269 and 280.
     Scott's poems reconstruct a past life by eliminating archaism and using a rich knowledge of history. His gift for narrative surpassed both Coleridge's and Byron's. The novels gave him the scope he required, especially for his comic creations.

54   _____. "Sportsman and Country Gentleman." The S. M. T. Magazine, 8, no. 6 (June), 61–64.
     Although he was an Edinburgh man and a lawyer, Scott made himself welcome among the shepherds and hill-folk of his district. He delighted in simple sports and maintained cordial relations with those who served him. Reprinted: 1932.A29.

55   DROUGHT, J. B. "Pepper and Mustard: The Dandie Dinmont Terrier." Scottish Country Life, 21, no. 10 (October), 298.
     A history of the Dandie Dinmont Terrier, popularized by Scott in Guy Mannering. He saw the fearless, scrappy dogs as typifying the Border yeomen who bred and hunted with them.

56   DUKE, WINIFRED. "Poet, Romancer, and Man of Law. A Famous Clerk of Session." The S. M. T. Magazine, 8, no. 6 (June), 65–67.
     Scott's legal training and experience gave him opportunity to meet a wide variety of personalities who stimulated his literary imagination. Although his duties as Clerk of Session were monotonous, he found the Edinburgh legal society highly entertaining. Reprinted: 1932.A29.

57   ELIOT, CHARLES W. "President Eliot on Sir Walter Scott: An Unpublished Address of the Late President of Harvard." More Books, 7 (November), 336–39.
     Reprints the address of 17 May, 1899 on the unveiling of the bust of Scott in the Boston Public Library. Scott appeals to children because of his descriptions of fighting and adventure, his local patriotism, his love of prosperity, and his happy endings. He seems unconscious of the many instances of cruelty in his work.

58   ELLIS, S. M. "Followers of Sir Walter." Bookman, 82 (April), 10–12.
     Scott worried that his imitators--Ainsworth, James, and Hesiltine--would spoil his audience. But he realized that he had the advantage of a strong memory, which released him from dependence on scholarly sources. James became Scott's

1932

personal friend and visited at Abbotsford during the last
eighteen months of Scott's life. Includes text of a letter
from Scott to Archibald Trail, dated 20 March, 1827.

59   EYRE-TODD, GEORGE. "The Power of a Magic Pen. Scotland's
         Greatest Publicist." The S. M. T. Magazine, 8, no. 6
         (June), 103-105.
              Scott's stimulus to tourism has changed the appearance
         and economy of many regions of Scotland. He brought back
         to life many of the half-forgotten names of Scottish his-
         tory, and his own tragic life helped to ennoble the Scottish
         character. Reprinted: 1932.A29.

60   FALCONER, J. A. "Sir Walter Scott: What He Means to Scot-
         land." English Studies (Amsterdam), 14 (August), 145-54.
              Scott's best poetry and fiction are connected with Scot-
         tish history. His masterpieces, the novels of Lowland life,
         can be fully appreciated only by a Scotsman because the dia-
         lect creates a problem for other readers. His sanity,
         sweetness of character, and materialism are the values which
         make him congenial to his countrymen.

61   FERRANDO, GUIDO. "Sir Walter Scott: Nel Primo Centenario
         Della Morte." Pegaso, 4 (October), 483-87.
              Although Scott's writing style is not perfect, it is
         natural and organic. His prose is best when relating
         something great or heroic. He is weak in psychological
         exploration, and so his characters lack depth and soul.
         Nevertheless, he enriched English and world literature.

62   FRASER, W. C. "Oral Tradition About Sir Walter Scott, Col-
         lected in Ettrick and Yarrow." Transactions of the Hawick
         Archaeological Society, Session 1932, 26-33.
              A series of anecdotes, collected in and around Selkirk,
         from old people who had known or seen Scott. Most of these
         are related in dialect.

63   GAULD, H. DRUMMOND. "In the Land of Guy Mannering. The
         Cruives of the Cree." The S. M. T. Magazine, 9, no. 6
         (December), 23-30.
              A travel guide to the Galloway region, setting of Guy
         Mannering, which speculates on prototypes of Ellangowan and
         identifies other features in the landscape connected with
         the novel.

64   GLAESENER, HENRI. "Walter Scott et son influence." Le
         Flambeau, 15 (August), 159-80.
              Scott's popularity among French readers has derived from
         his contact with his French wife's sensibility, his love of

18

the past and his use of French historical figures. His descriptive technique influenced Prosper Mérimée, and Quentin Durward deeply influenced Prosper de Barante, a Belgian historian and author of L'Histoire des ducs de Bourgogne.

65   GLEN, JAMES. "Sir Walter Scott's Financial Transactions," in The Letters of Sir Walter Scott. Edited by H. J. C. Grierson. Volume I. London: Constable, lxxx-xcv.
     The failure of James Ballantyne & Co. was immediately due to the failure in London of Hurst, Robinson & Co. The large number of bill transactions which then led to the collapse of Ballantyne was partly due to Scott's large expenditures for lands and buildings and partly to the business having been run with insufficient capital. Scott accepted his responsibility for the large number of accommodation bills, "both an expensive and hazardous system of borrowing."

66   GORDON, GEORGE. "The Chronicles of the Canongate," in Scott Centenary Articles. London: Oxford University Press, pp. 174–84.
     Scott's decision to write the Chronicles of the Canongate was prompted by his acknowledgement in 1827 that he was the Author of Waverley and by his desire to depart from the demands of the three-volume novel while finishing Napoleon. The Journal entries of this period reflect his sense of lost youth and friends and his determination to persevere. Although he still used the habitual device of a mask, in many ways Scott resembles Chrystal Croftangry. First published 12 April, 1928 in the Times Literary Supplement. Reprinted, slightly revised: 1950.B4.

67   _____. "Redgauntlet," in Scott Centenary Articles. London: Oxford University Press, pp. 137–49.
     Despite its defects of structure and method and the copious apologies, the novel has "a vitality of creation" that compensates for defects. The proof-sheets reveal Scott's early uncertainty about names and show minor changes in other details. The third letter, in which Darsie describes night and tempest on the Solway sands, shows Scott at his descriptive best. First published 4 September, 1924 in the Times Literary Supplement.

68   GORDON, ROBERT KAY. "Scott and the Comédie Humaine," in Sir Walter Scott Today. Edited by H. J. C. Grierson. London: Constable, pp. 93–108.
     Balzac deeply admired the Waverley Novels and regarded Scott as his worthy rival. In the general preface to the

Comédie Humaine he acknowledges his debt to Scott in the
plan to portray the private life of a nation. Balzac
learned from Scott the importance of detail in describing
the social life of a period. However, Balzac criticized
Scott's heroines as devoid of passion and believed that
Scott withdrew from the evil in human nature.

69   GORDON, SETON. "The Wizard and the Misty Isle." The S. M. T.
     Magazine, 8, no. 6 (June), 78–81.
         Scott visited Skye in 1814. Quotes his letter of 3
     March, 1815 to his hostess, Mrs. MacLeod of Dunvegan Castle.
     Also includes a letter to the Highland Society, in which
     Scott introduces his piper, John of Skye. The scenery of
     Skye inspired Scott to write The Lord of the Isles. Re-
     printed: 1932.A29.

70   GRAEME, ALAN. "Scott and 'The Scots Magazine': Sir Walter's
     Works and Contemporary Reviews." Scots Magazine, N.S. 17,
     no. 6 (September), 401–407.
         The Scots Magazine reviewers wrote favorably on Scott's
     poems, and the notices of the novels continued even more
     flatteringly until 1826, when the first series of the maga-
     zine ceased publication. It was a victim of the fall of
     Constable that also led to Scott's bankruptcy.

71   GRAY, WILLIAM FORBES. "Early 'Lives' of Scott." Edinburgh
     Scotsman: Sir Walter Scott Centenary Supplement
     (21 September), p. vii.
         Deals with several pre-Lockhart memoirs and biographies
     of Scott by Robert Chambers (1832), David Vedder (1832)
     and George Allan (1834). These biographers either knew
     Scott himself or his acquaintances and could write with a
     freedom Lockhart denied himself. They provide information,
     particularly on Scott's earlier life, that Lockhart does
     not include.

72   _____. "Friends of Sir Walter: Unpublished Letters."
     Cornhill Magazine, N.S. 73 (September), 257–65.
         Includes passages quoted from letters in the unbound cor-
     respondence at Abbotsford. Two letters from J. B. S.
     Morritt of Rokeby concern Byron. A letter from Lady Louisa
     Stuart (2 July, 1825) expresses her first impressions of
     The Talisman and The Betrothed. A letter from Mrs. Hughes
     of Uffington (23 August, 1824) offers to be of assistance
     to Charles Scott at Oxford.

73   _____. "The Religion of Sir Walter Scott." Hibbert Journal,
     31, no. 1 (October), 47–60.

Scott was uninterested in doctrine and indifferent toward church-going. His religious history was "outward conformity without inward conviction." He retained a sentimental attachment to Presbyterianism, but his mind was more in sympathy with the Episcopal Church. He based his own religion on natural rather than supernatural virtue, "a kind of stoicism tinctured with Christianity."

74 _____. "Some Unpublished Letters to Sir Walter Scott."
National Review and English Review, 99 (July), 80-88.
A selection of passages with annotations from a group of letters, discovered at Abbotsford in 1931, written to Scott from 1806 to 1820. The collection includes letters from Wordsworth, Sir George Beaumont, Allan Cunningham, Robert Southey, the Duchess of Wellington, the Duke of Somerset, Daniel Terry, Lady Louisa Stuart, and John Graham.

75 GRIEG, DAVID M. "The Cephalic Features of Sir Walter Scott."
Edinburgh Medical Journal, 39, no. 8 (August), 497-506.
Scott was "craniometrically though not clinically megacephalic": i.e., he had an unusually long skull with a sloping but not broad forehead. The shape of his skull and the size of his head were not responsible for his talent. However, his infantile paralysis may have increased the circulation of blood to his brain and thus stimulated his genius. There may have been a similar relationship between Byron's lameness and his literary genius.

76 GRIERSON, HERBERT JOHN CLIFFORD. "His Many-Sided Character."
Edinburgh Scotsman: Sir Walter Scott Centenary Supplement (21 September), pp. i-ii.
Scott lived several separate lives--as writer, lawyer, laird and businessman. Disagrees with Pope-Hennessey's thesis that Scott began as a realist and developed into a romance writer. On the contrary, he found his proper task in writing about real life and manners with an historical background that provided scope for his vast knowledge. Although he wrote for money, the novels glorify not worldly values but the affections and resignation to God's will.

77 _____. "Scott, Shelley and Crabbe." Times Literary Supplement (15 September), p. 643.
A letter thought to have been written by Scott to the young Shelley was actually to James Dusautoy. A letter written by Crabbe to Scott shows Crabbe did not know who wrote "The Rime of the Ancient Mariner."

1932

78   ____. "Scott's Letters: A Correction." <u>Times Literary</u>
<u>Supplement</u> (29 September), p. 691.
The story of Scott's early warning that Constable had
"thrown up his book" and of Scott's midnight ride to get
assurance from him is more myth than fact. Lockhart's date
for Scott's first reading of "English Bards and Scotch Reviewers" is inaccurate.

79   ____. "Sir Walter Scott in His Letters," in <u>The Letters of</u>
<u>Sir Walter Scott</u>. Volume I. London: Constable, xxvii-
lxxix.
Scott's letters reveal faults and errors but show that
he remained a generous man throughout his life. His business affairs and lavish expenditures were motivated by his
imaginative nature; in both business and literature he
blended the dreamer and the practical man. His character
was dutiful and kind, but his "sanguine and impatient temperament" led to his disappointment in love. He possessed
no illusions about life but nevertheless managed to remain
happy most of the time.

80   GUNDOLF, FRIEDRICH. "Scott and Goethe." Translated by Frank
Nicholson, in <u>Sir Walter Scott Today</u>. Edited by H. J. C.
Grierson. London: Constable, pp. 41–65.
Although Goethe's <u>Gotz von Berlichingen</u> inspired Scott,
he never understood Goethe's genius or finer qualities as
an artist. Goethe admired Scott's work, especially the
mythologizing of history in the <u>Life of Napoleon</u>, but his
admiration lessened in his last years. Goethe and Scott
exerted no significant influence on each other: "Their two
worlds did not touch." Reprinted and translated from
1932.B81.

81   ____. "Scott und Goethe." <u>Die Neue Rundschau</u>, 43, no. 1
(April), 490–504.
Reprinted and translated: 1932.B80.

82   GUNN, W. E. "A Christian Stoic." <u>Border Magazine</u>, 37
(September), 140.
Scott was not interested in sectarian differences, but
he was angered by all forms of religious fanaticism. The
Stoic virtues of Christianity appealed to him, and his moral
code gave equal weight to courage and kindness.

83   GWYNN, STEPHEN. "Scott and Ireland." <u>The S. M. T. Magazine</u>,
8, no. 6 (June), 74–77.

The Irish were even more foreign to Scott than the Highlanders, and he rarely wrote of them. He acknowledged his
literary debt to Maria Edgeworth, but he had two advantages
she did not possess: his Lowland characters speak in their
native Scotch, not in a foreign tongue; and he felt loyalty
to <u>all</u> his countrymen, and when he mocks them it is without
condescension or venom. Reprinted: 1932.A29.

84 H., O. E. "Sir Walter Scott and Douce." <u>Bodleian Quarterly</u>
<u>Record</u>, 7 (October), 99–102.
   Prints three letters from Scott to the antiquary Francis
Douce. The letter of 12 May, 1808 introduces Henry Weber,
the impoverished German scholar and Scott's amanuensis.
The second letter (11 March, 1815) introduces J. C. Dunlop.
The third letter, undated but probably written in 1817, ac-
knowledges Scott's reception of a work by the Abbé de la Rue
sent to him by Douce.

85 HARPER, GEORGE McLEAN. "Scott's Novels: an American View."
<u>Quarterly Review</u>, 259 (October), 344–51.
   Scott's novels appeal to our interest in history and
human characters. Their strong point is the portrayal of
Scottish manners and dialect. Unlike the works of Hardy,
Galsworthy, Dreiser and Bennett, Scott's novels are "free
from sordidness." They teach the "ethics of honour plus
charity." As a novelist he is equalled only by Thackeray
and Dickens. Reprinted: 1937.B10.

86 HENRY-BORDEAUX, PAULE. "The Laird of Abbotsford," in her
<u>Fântomes d'Écosse</u>. Paris: Librairie Plon, pp. 121–45.
   The Border country ("Quel terrain merveilleux pour un
poète.") stimulated Scott's interest in ballad and romance,
which in turn made him poet, novelist and historian. He
built Abbotsford from a desire to live the life of his
heroes and to found a distinct branch of the Scott family.
Although he created many vigorous male figures, he constantly repeated one type of passionless heroine. This may
have been partly due to the weak feminine psychology traditional in Anglo-Saxon literature. Includes an account of
visits to Abbotsford and Melrose.

87 HERON, F. W. "Scott in San Francisco." <u>Times Literary Supple-</u>
<u>ment</u> (1 September), p. 607.
   An account of the Centenary celebration sponsored by the
Literary Anniversary Club. The exhibit includes two sets of
the Waverley Novels in original boards and an 1816 autograph
letter from Scott to Joseph Train (partially reprinted) in
which Scott discusses the publication of <u>Old Mortality</u> but
does not acknowledge his authorship.

1932

88 HILL, MURIEL. "Scott and Lyric Poetry." Scots Magazine,
    N.S. 17, no. 6 (September), 431–39.
        Scott believed that poetry should be popular and should
    appeal to commonly held emotions. He mocked poets who took
    themselves and their art too solemnly. He treated his sub-
    jects objectively and possessed a natural facility for
    metre. Nature holds a relatively unimportant place in his
    lyric poetry. Scott distrusted revision, and spontaneity
    is one of the distinctions of his poetry.

89 _____. "Sir Walter Scott and the Jacobites." Scots Magazine,
    N.S. 18, no. 2 (November), 97–107.
        Scott sympathized with the Jacobite cause throughout his
    life, but this sympathy did not influence his practical
    politics. In the Tales of a Grandfather he emphasizes the
    glamorous features of Prince Charles while playing down his
    faults. However, the three Jacobite novels draw a sharp
    distinction between sentiment and reason; the thinking char-
    acters disdain Jacobitism and undercut the enthusiasts with
    their good judgment.

90 HUTCHISON, ROBERT. "The Medical History of Sir Walter Scott."
    Edinburgh Medical Journal, 39, no. 8 (August), 461–85.
        Scott's medical history includes the polio which left him
    lame, a mysterious illness at age fourteen, severe attacks
    of gall stone colic, high blood pressure, and the series of
    strokes which finally killed him. He also suffered occa-
    sionally from a skin rash, a urinary complaint, and a nerv-
    ous disturbance. Although he died at the beginning of his
    sixty-second year, he spoke of himself as aged for the last
    ten years of his life. He met all his illnesses with
    courage and good humor and was undaunted by pain or fear
    of death.

91 HUTTON, W. H. "Tales of the Crusaders," in Scott Centenary
    Articles. London: Oxford University Press, pp. 150–61.
        The strength of The Talisman lies in its mingling of ro-
    mance with common human life. Despite some historical er-
    rors, Scott's image of the Holy Land is successful and
    basically accurate. He regarded chivalry almost as a reli-
    gion and was fascinated by military life, but he never
    thought of himself as a hero. First published 25 June,
    1925 in the Times Literary Supplement.

92 J., W. H. "Walter Scott: Classical Allusion." Notes and
    Queries, 162 (9 April), 261.
        In The Fortunes of Nigel, chapter XVII, Reginald Lowe-
    stoffe calls Duke Hildebrod "this second Axylus." Queries
    who was Axylus, and could Scott have written "Astylus," as
    in Ovid's Metamorphoses? See 1932.B15.

93   JACKSON, MRS. NEVILL. "The Shadow of Scott." Connoisseur, 90
     (September), 169-71.
          Augustin Edouart assembled a gallery of silhouette por-
     traits of Edinburgh notables including Scott and many of
     his associates. Article includes five plates.

94   JALOUX, EDMOND. "Le Centenaire de Walter Scott." Le Temps
     (16 September), p. 3.
          Scott made Scotland universal and was the first British
     writer to gain worldwide popularity. His physical infirmity
     prevented him from becoming a man of action but led him in-
     stead to celebrate the traditions of war and heroism in his
     work. Scott's women seem a bit bloodless to the modern
     reader, but they are of the ethereal type that the English
     have always loved. His heroes are conventional and unin-
     teresting, but in his more realistic secondary characters
     he forms a bridge between Shakespeare and Dickens. Scott's
     influence has been enormous, especially on Balzac, Barbey
     d'Aurevilly and Dumas père.

95   JAMIESON, M. E. "The Dumb Friends of Sir Walter Scott."
     Scottish Field, 60 (October), 132.
          Scott's fondness for animals continued throughout his
     entire lifetime. Includes anecdotal accounts of his horses,
     dogs and cat.

96   JOHNSTON, REGINALD F. "The Lay of the Last Minstrel." Times
     Literary Supplement (11 August), p. 569.
          Stanzas x-xii of the fourth canto are missing in the
     first edition. Author's edition is autographed by Scott,
     as it was a gift to Skene of Rubislaw. See 1932.B172.

97   KEITH, CHRISTINA. "Scott the Novelist." Edinburgh Scotsman:
     Sir Walter Scott Centenary Supplement (21 September), p. ii.
          Scott's vital and very human characters compensate the
     reader for his dry introductions and unlikely conclusions.
     He draws his characters from all strata of society and
     gives a simple eloquence and good sense to the poor, unedu-
     cated ones. Every novel includes a wide variety of scenes
     and subjects. Scott's was a wholesome world in which
     laughter was more important than passion or introspection.

98   KENT, W. "Sir Walter Scott's London." Everyman, 8
     (22 September), 279-80.
          In The Fortunes of Nigel Scott provided a "vivid and in-
     spired picture" of seventeenth century London, especially
     "Alsatia," the area between Whitefriars Street and the
     Temple. London also appears in most of the other Waverley

1932

novels; Scott usually concentrated on the City rather than
the West End.

99   KER, J. INGLIS. "The Land of Scott." Everyman, 8
      (15 September), 246-48.
          The Borderland was "Scott's spiritual home," and his love
      of this area pervades all his work. Provides a suggested
      itinerary for touring the Scott country.

100   KER, W. P. "The Fortunes of Nigel and Peveril of the Peak,"
      in Scott Centenary Articles. London: Oxford University
      Press, pp. 123-27.
          Scott's introductory discussions with "the Author of
      Waverley" in Nigel and Peveril indicate he was uncertain of
      the future direction of his work and of his continuing popu-
      larity. Peveril is ill-proportioned, tedious at the be-
      ginning and devoid of local color. Nigel, however, is
      closely unified, with every paragraph contributing to the
      development of the story. First published 25 January, 1923
      in the Times Literary Supplement.

101   _____. "Quentin Durward and St. Ronan's Well," in Scott
      Centenary Articles. London: Oxford University Press,
      pp. 128-36.
          Quentin Durward inaugurated Scott's popularity abroad and
      provided the pattern for his imitators. The portrait of
      Louis XI incorporates traditional touches but has a vitality
      beyond them. The love story, a version of a traditional ro-
      mance plot, bears traces of "the author's own early rever-
      ies." St. Ronan's Well, designed as a story of real life
      in the present day, has different kinds of merits. Balzac
      admired its realism. In compliance with the wishes of Bal-
      lantyne, Scott censored the love affair between Clara and
      Tyrrel and substituted melodrama for tragedy. First pub-
      lished 14 June, 1923 in the Times Literary Supplement.

102   KERR, JAMES. "A Memorable Meeting--Burns and Scott."
      Canadian Bookman, 14 (September), 93.
          An account of Scott's only meeting with Burns, which took
      place at Professor Ferguson's when Scott was fifteen, re-
      counted mostly in Scott's own words written to Lockhart.

*103 KOSKIMIES, RAFAEL. "Walter Scott novellistina." Valvoja-Aika
      (Helsingfors) (September), 447-52.
          Cited in the Annual Bibliography of English Language and
      Literature (Cambridge: Modern Humanities Research Associa-
      tion, 1933), XIII, 200, item #3227.

104   L., J. T. "Scott and Music." The Choir and Musical Journal,
       23 (September), 175–77.
       Scott regretted his lack of musical knowledge, but many
       of his characters have natural musical talent. His greatest
       achievement was in stimulating reader enthusiasm for the
       days of chivalry and troubadors. Includes accounts of the
       visits of Moscheles and Mendelssohn to Abbotsford.

105   LANG, JEAN. "Bygone Days. In the Time of Scott." The
       S. M. T. Magazine, 9, no. 1 (July), 34–38.
       An evocation of colorful Border superstitions and oddi-
       ties in Scott's day, including gypsy life, body snatchers,
       accusations of witchcraft, and the effects on the region of
       the French war.

106   LANOIRE, MAURICE. "Walter Scott." Revue de Paris
       (15 September), pp. 393–410.
       Scott's ability to tell stories that hold the reader's
       attention, to create memorable characters like Louis XI,
       and to use dialogue were responsible for his success. His
       works synthesized theatre and novel. Scott's works have
       declined in popularity because readers are less tolerant of
       digressions than in his day, and because our fascination
       with man's relation to his time has passed.

107   LYND, ROBERT. "I. Scott and His Critics." John O'London's
       Weekly, 27 (25 June), 443 and 445.
       Although Scott had some detractors during his lifetime,
       including Lamb and Carlyle, the general praise overwhelmed
       the occasional dissent. Although literary critics have
       altered their idea of what makes good fiction, recent
       writers such as Saintsbury and Elton have commended his
       understanding of human nature.

108   _____. "II. Walter Scott the Man." John O'London's Weekly,
       27 (16 July), 559.
       Scott's character was not flawless and included a strain
       of recklessness. His love of land came not from worldliness
       but from romanticism. He should be given the benefit of the
       doubt in his business ventures, since he redeemed his errors
       by his self-sacrifice in working to pay the debt.

109   _____. "Sir Walter Scott. III. The Novels as We Read Them."
       John O'London's Weekly, 27 (30 July), 629.
       Scott's novels retain the ability to carry the reader
       out of himself and interest him in the characters. The
       descriptions may be skipped, and the characters occasionally
       converse in absurdly stilted dialogue. But Scott "towers
       above his faults" and excels as an entertainer.

1932

110 MACARTNEY, WILLIAM NEWTON. "Scott as a Traveler." The
     S. M. T. Magazine, 8, no. 6 (June), 138–42.
         An account of Scott's journeys in the Border Country, the
     Highlands, England, the western islands, Ireland and France.
     He was an ideal traveler who never complained and always re-
     mained good company. Reprinted: 1932.A29.

111 McDOWALL, ARTHUR. "Scott's Journal and Woodstock," in Scott
     Centenary Articles. London: Oxford University Press,
     pp. 162–73.
         Woodstock was written at the crisis of Scott's life and
     should be read with awareness of the personal history behind
     it. The Journal entries on Woodstock reveal Scott's method
     of composition without plan, "the genius of improvisation."
     Woodstock is strong in its unity of scene but weak in its
     falsely romantic language. First published 27 May, 1926 in
     the Times Literary Supplement.

112 MACK, J. LOGAN. "Romantic Territory. Scott and the Desolate
     Borders." The S. M. T. Magazine, 8, no. 6 (June), 106–108.
         Scott was well acquainted with the areas of the Marches
     where ownership was disputed, and in describing this and
     other areas, he freely mixed actual and invented names.
     Reprinted: 1932.A29.

113 MACKENZIE, AGNES MURE. "The Survival of Scott." London
     Mercury, 25 (January), 270–78.
         Scott's novels are imbued with a love of place and with
     the spirit of the Scottish Renaissance. His fiction covers
     such a broad social range that a passive hero becomes an
     advantage. These heroes are not important in themselves
     but as plot devices which "cause the rest to be." Scott
     should not be condemned for his unwillingness to deal with
     sex.

114 MACKENZIE, COMPTON. "Scott's Appeal to Youth. The Test of
     Time." The S. M. T. Magazine, 8, no. 6 (June), 70–73.
         Contemporary youth displays an alarming lack of interest
     in Scott. Since children tend to skip when they read great
     books, we need a well-illustrated, drastically abridged
     edition of Scott's novels. There is much redundancy that
     could be eliminated. Reprinted: 1932.A29.

115 MACKENZIE, MARGARET. "Scott and Friendship. Sir Walter and
     Willie Laidlaw." Scots Magazine, N.S. 17, no. 6
     (September), 408–14.
         William Laidlaw was the steward of Abbotsford and Scott's
     devoted counselor and friend. He introduced James Hogg to

Scott in 1802, and after Scott's stroke, Laidlaw served as
his amanuensis. Scott's affection for Laidlaw and their
long relationship testify to Sir Walter's genius for
friendship.

116　McLAREN, MORAY. "Scott and Scotland." Listener, 8
　　　(21 September), 412-13.
　　　　　Scott taught the world the romantic view of life and
　　　brought Scotland to the attention of ordinary people
　　　throughout Europe. He was deeply conscious of nationality,
　　　"a Scotsman first and a romantic afterwards." But he is not
　　　responsible for the "sham tartan, Gothic glooms and second-
　　　rate romanticism" which the tourist promoters associate with
　　　Scotland.

117　_____. "Would Scott Be a Nationalist Today?" The S. M. T.
　　　Magazine, 8, no. 6 (June), 84-86.
　　　　　Scott's snobbery, Toryism, and servility to the monarchy
　　　might prevent his being a nationalist today. However on
　　　the other side stand the Malagrowther pamphlets and his
　　　deep interests in the manners, lives and customs of the
　　　Scottish people. Affirms a belief based on faith that
　　　Scott would be a member of the Scottish Nationalist Party.
　　　Reprinted: 1932.A29.

118　M'NEIL, CHARLES. "Sir Walter Scott and Res Medica." Edin-
　　　burgh Medical Journal, 39, no. 8 (August), 486-96.
　　　　　Scott had little interest in science and medicine, de-
　　　spite both his grandfather and uncle being eminent physi-
　　　cians. He disliked using drugs and consulting doctors, and
　　　feared that a physiologist might become calloused to the
　　　value of life. The Journal shows him resigned to an early
　　　death, but he dreaded a lingering illness with loss of
　　　faculties.

119　McNEILL, F. MARIAN. "Old Scottish Hospitality. Feasts in
　　　Fiction and Reality." The S. M. T. Magazine, 8, no. 6
　　　(June), 100-102.
　　　　　Scott was very interested in ancient Scottish cooking
　　　and describes many feasts in the novels and poems. Meg Dods
　　　of St. Ronan's Well inspired The Cook and Housewife's Manual
　　　(Edinburgh: 1826) written by Mrs. Johnson, later the editor
　　　of Tait's Magazine. The introduction to this cookbook,
　　　called "The Institution of the Cleikum Club," may have been
　　　written by Scott himself. Reprinted: 1932.A29.

120　MALCOLM, C. A. "'Mine Own Romantic Town.' Edinburgh as Scott
　　　Knew It." The S. M. T. Magazine, 8, no. 6 (June), 127-31.

1932

A verbal sketch of the milieu and personalities of Edinburgh in 1787, the period of Scott's youth, and forty years later, the period of his greatest fame. Reprinted: 1932.A29.

121   MARTIN, JOHN SMELLIE. "Sir Walter Scott in Clydesdale." Scottish Field, 60 (September), 93.
Scott paid relatively little attention to Clydesdale. In 1799 he visited Bothwell Castle and first saw Craignethan Castle, the original of Tillietudlem in Old Mortality. He also visited Clydesdale in 1801, 1827, and 1829. His last visit was in the course of a trip to Douglasdale to gather material for Castle Dangerous.

122   MILLER, JAMES. "Through a Scottish Layman's Eyes." Queen's Quarterly, 39 (November), 621–32.
Scott's novels stimulate interest in history, because his minor characters and historical personages are all convincing. The real heroes are the characters from humble life. The novels' fascination lies in Scott's artistry in telling a tale and his knowledge of all strata of society.

123   MILLIGAN, JAMES. "The Centenary of Scott." Times Literary Supplement (31 March), p. 229.
Announces the centenary and appeals for funds.

124   MITTON, G. E. "A Hero to His Valet. Highlights on Sir Walter Scott." Scots Magazine, N.S. 16, no. 4 (January), 275–80.
Anecdotal account of the relationship between Scott and William Dalgleish, his butler and valet at Abbotsford. Dalgleish wrote a series of notes about life at Abbotsford from which these stories are taken. After Scott's bankruptcy, Dalgleish refused to leave him and served at reduced wages until forced to retire by illness.

125   MUIR, EDWIN. "Scott and Tradition," in "Sir Walter Scott: A Centenary Commentary by Various Writers." The Modern Scot, 3 (August), 118–20.
Scott possessed the mind of a man of action rather than of a romantic; his sense of mystery was limited to plot complications. His work is characterized by gentility rather than allegiance to truth, and he lowered the standards of the novel from a criticism of life to popular amusement and moral platitudes.

126   _____. "Sir Walter Scott." Spectator, 149 (24 September), 439.
Scott was "a very great writer very greatly watered down." His true genius emerges in the dialect characters,

but his "terror of immediate reality" results in lifeless
heroes and sexless young women. He feared any deeper psychological penetration.

127   MURDOCH, W. G. BLAIKIE. "The Portraiture of Sir Walter
           Scott." The S. M. T. Magazine, 8, no. 6 (June), 109-12.
           Surveys the many likenesses of Scott--miniatures, por-
       traits, silhouettes and busts--made during his lifetime.
       There are about thirty "authentic icons" of Scott, and they
       show him at various stages in his life. Reprinted:
       1932.A29.

128   [NEWMAN, GEORGE]. "More Notes on Sir Walter Scott (1771-1832)
           Part II." Friends Quarterly Examiner, 66 (January), 55-70.
           Scott loved aristocracy and genealogy but was not a
       snob. He wrote by impulse rather than plan and was best
       when improvising. His work teaches Christian morality un-
       obtrusively, and he substituted "humanistic virtue" for the
       strict Calvinism of his parents. Scott revealed the beauty
       and history of Scotland and transfigured the novel. He is
       "the consummate humanist of British Literature."

129   OGILVIE, WILL H. "A Scott Commemoration. How Selkirk Cele-
           brated the Birth Centenary." The S. M. T. Magazine, 9,
           no. 3 (September), 50-52.
           An account of the August, 1871 celebration by the Royal
       Burgh of Selkirk of the centenary of the birth of Scott,
       which took place on the grounds surrounding Newark Tower.

130   ORIANS, G. HARRISON. "The Romance Ferment after Waverley."
           American Literature, 3, no. 4 (January), 408-31.
           Scott's celebration of Scottish nationalism stimulated
       the demand for a native American literature. In The Spy
       (1821) Cooper inaugurated a series of romances on American
       material. The Waverley Novels became the standard of his-
       torical fiction by which American romances were judged.

131   ORRICK, JAMES. "Sir Walter Scott and 'The Trade.'" Publish-
           er's Weekly, 122 (17 September), 1033-35.
           Scott erred in keeping secret his dealings with the Bal-
       lantynes and in not scrutinizing the affairs of the firm.
       In terms of finances, he lived "in a world of his own" and
       did not acknowledge his equivocal position. His secrecy
       resulted from the same vanity which made him conceal the
       authorship of the Waverley Novels and made him unwilling to
       be known as someone who wrote for a living.

1932

132   PARKER, WILLIAM MATHIE. "Scott and the Antiquaries. The
      Surtees Correspondence." Scots Magazine, N.S. 17, no. 6
      (September), 422-30.
         Robert Surtees, the antiquary, deceived Scott on several
      occasions with spurious ballad material which Surtees iden-
      tified as authentic. Although they corresponded from 1806
      to 1829, Surtees never revealed these impostures.

133   _____. "Scott as a Letter Writer. A Study of the Many MSS:
      Some Peculiarities of Handwriting, Spelling, and Punctua-
      tion." John O'London's Weekly, 27 (17 and 24 September),
      863, 866, 920, 922.
         Scott's letters reveal the three facets of his person-
      ality: man of the world, man of business, and imaginative
      creator. Occasional grammatical errors, a minimum of punc-
      tuation, and "inconsistent" spelling result from the ra-
      pidity of his writing. He tended to confuse the names of
      correspondents, and he changed the tone of letters according
      to the recipient.

134   _____. "Where Scott Lived in Edinburgh." The S. M. T.
      Magazine, 9, no. 1 (July), 26-30.
         An account of the several premises Scott either owned or
      occupied in Edinburgh, from his birth in the College Wynd,
      his boyhood in George Square, his triumphant prime at 39
      Castle Street, to the lodgings he occupied after the bank-
      ruptcy and the hotel in St. Andrew Square he slept in on
      his last night in the city.

135   PARSONS, COLEMAN O. "Scott's Experiences in Haunted Chambers."
      Modern Philology, 30, no. 1 (August), 103-105.
         Prints a letter to a Miss Wagner of Liverpool, dated
      8 February, 1828, in which Scott recounts an actual night
      spent in the Haunted Chamber of Dunvegan Castle. He regrets
      that he no longer believes in ghosts. The letter is similar
      to Lovel's adventures in the Green Room at Monkbarns in The
      Antiquary, in which the narrator explains Lovel's super-
      natural vision with a rational cause, thus reflecting
      Scott's own skepticism and spoiling the effectiveness of
      the incident.

136   PERÉS, R. D. "A Spanish Tribute." Translated by R. M.
      Macandrew. Edinburgh Scotsman: Sir Walter Scott Centenary
      Supplement (21 September), p. viii.
         Scott was introduced to Spain in 1823 in a review titled
      El Europo, one of whose editors, López Soler, published in
      1830 a novel which imitated St. Ronan's Well. From 1826 to
      1843, between twenty and thirty editions of Scott appeared

in Barcelona. Unfortunately many of these were translated into Spanish from French rather than from the original.

137 PHILLIPS, LAWRENCE. "Scott and Waverley." Notes and Queries, 163 (12 November), 358.
Reports that Notes and Queries 117:165 said "Waverley" is named after an abbey in Surrey; also that the London Times of 26 June, 1931 quotes Leigh Hunt's Men, Women and Books as claiming Charlotte Smith's Desmond is the source. See 1932.B150.

138 POPE-HENNESSY, UNA. "Scott and the Theatre. Stage Versions of the Waverleys." Scots Magazine, N.S. 17, no. 6 (September), 415–21.
Although Scott read many plays, attended theatre regularly and was a director of the Theatre Royal, Edinburgh, his dramatic judgment was unreliable and he did not supervise the stage adaptations of his works. He became very fond of Daniel Terry but took no serious interest in the melodramas Terry based on the Waverley Novels.

139 _____. "Sir Walter Scott." Quarterly Review, 259, no. 513 (July), 76–94.
Expresses the hope that the Scott centenary will "give Scott a new lease of love in the hearts of the young" by memorializing him as a warm, fallible human being rather than as a remote semi-deity. His portraits reveal both his inner and outer life; he was, with Wellington, "the most painted man of his day." Includes a survey of portraits and busts of Scott.

140 POWER, WILLIAM. "Scott and His Literary Circle." The S. M. T. Magazine, 8, no. 6 (June), 96–99.
Scott had many literary visitors at Abbotsford, which became something of a shrine in his own lifetime. He met and corresponded with an enormous circle of writers. Includes brief accounts of his relationships with Byron, Ferrier, Hogg, Baillie and others. Reprinted: 1932.A29.

141 PRAVIEL, ARMAND. "Walter Scott." Le Correspondant (10 September), pp. 674–91.
Scott's greatest achievement, despite his current unpopularity, was in raising the status of the novel to include its study in programs of education. Includes an account of Scott's life and plot summaries of several works.

142 PRICE, J. ARTHUR. "Wales and Sir Walter Scott." Welsh Outlook, 19 (October), 263–64.

1932

        Although Wales does not appear frequently in his writings, Scott was interested in Welsh history and culture. He alludes to a tale of Owen Glendwr in <u>Marmion,</u> and <u>The Betrothed</u> takes place on the Welsh Border. As a pioneer of the "Celtic awakening," Scott taught that British history is not limited to London.

143   R., F. E. "Scott's Knowledge of Quakers." <u>Notes and Queries</u>, 163 (23 July), 64.
        Queries why in <u>Redgauntlet</u> Joshua Geddes forbids Darsie Latimer to take a sweetcake he had earlier refused.

*144 RAILO, EINO. "Walter Scott ($17\frac{15}{8}71 - 18\frac{21}{9}32$)." <u>Valvoja-Aika</u> (Helsingfors) (September), pp. 433–46.
        Cited in the <u>Annual Bibliography of English Language and Literature</u> (Cambridge: Modern Humanities Research Association, 1933), XIII, 201, item #3241.

145   RAIT, ROBERT S. "Scott as Critic and Judge," in <u>Scott Centenary Articles</u>. London: Oxford University Press, pp. 185–98.
        Scott's contributions to the <u>Edinburgh Review</u> from 1803 to 1806 illustrate his patience and generosity as a critic. His longer connection with the <u>Quarterly</u> (1809–1831) suggests the wide range of his interests. In his review of <u>Old Mortality</u> the censure expresses his awareness of his own faults, while the praise represents what he thought his friends would say. All of his reviews are "the product of an eminently judicial mind."

146   _____. "Scott First Editions." <u>Times Literary Supplement</u> (1 September), p. 607.
        Offers evidence that Scott's <u>Memorials of the Haliburtons</u> was first published in 1819, not 1820 as Cook suggests. <u>See</u> 1932.B38, B46.

147   _____. "Walter Scott and Thomas McCrie," in <u>Sir Walter Scott Today</u>. Edited by H. J. C. Grierson. London: Constable, pp. 3–37.
        McCrie, a Presbyterian minister, attacked the historical validity of Scott's portrayal of the Covenanters in <u>Old Mortality</u>. He believed Scott to have misrepresented details of ritual, the sufferings of the Presbyterians, the characterization of Claverhouse, and the principles and language of the Covenanters. Scott replied (anonymously) in his review of the novel in the <u>Quarterly Review</u> of January, 1817. The "ultra-Covenanters" Scott depicts were not representative Presbyterians, but a fanatical and extreme faction.

148   R.[ENDALL], V.[ERNON]. "Walter Scott: Latin Misprints."
       Notes and Queries, 163 (1 October), 243.
           Discusses two errors in Scott's Latin in his letters to
       Morritt and attributes them to Scott's handwriting or to
       editorial carelessness.

149   ROTH, GEORGES. "Walter Scott et la France de son temps."
       Grande Revue, 36 (December), 189–212.
           Scott's letters written from France shortly after Water-
       loo convey his impression of the French as vain and super-
       ficial. Conversely, the French criticized his Life of
       Napoleon as prejudiced and inaccurate. Many French writers,
       including Hugo, Thierry and Dumas, acknowledged debts to
       Scott, and Balzac and Mérimée wrote consciously "à la Walter
       Scott." Although he received many French visitors at Ab-
       botsford, Scott's last written words on the subject (21
       March, 1831) express the basic incompatibility of French
       and English tastes.

150   ROWNTREE, ARTHUR. "Scott and Waverley." Notes and Queries,
       163 (1 October), 246.
           Queries if "Waverley" comes from the name of a Cistercian
       Abbey. The editors note that Scott wrote that he chose the
       name because it was "uncontaminated." See 1932.B137.

151   S., J. T. "Monks and Ministers in Scott's Novels. Father
       Eustace, the Pastor of Tweedside." British Weekly, 91
       (10 March), 475.
           Scott's revolt from Presbyterianism was total, and his
       sympathies were Anglican. The monk Eustace in The Monastery
       represents his ideal minister, a well-bred gentleman who has
       renounced secular ambition and performs his ministry with
       firmness and compassion.

152   SAROLEA, C. "Scott's Influence in France." Edinburgh Scots-
       man: Sir Walter Scott Centenary Supplement (21 September),
       p. viii.
           The influence of the Waverley Novels in France has been
       extensive and beneficial. Scott changed the course of
       modern French literature by countering the Classical tradi-
       tion. He did not create the French historical novel but
       enormously extended its possibilities. Although Scott is
       no longer read in France, his indirect influence continues
       on serious historical writing.

153   SCHMIDT, ERNST. "Walter Scott: Zum hundertsten Todestage des
       Dichters." Germanisch-romanische Monatsschrift, 20, 445–53.
           Scott sought to achieve for Scotland what Wordsworth and
       Coleridge had done for the Romantic revival of English

1932

poetry. He honored Scottish culture, scenery and history, and his pride in his homeland surpassed his pride in literary achievement. The influence of his works persisted throughout the nineteenth century. Includes a general summary of Scott's life, character, style and literary contributions.

154 SCOTT, ALEXANDER. "Sir Walter Scott and Melrose Abbey." Spectator, 149 (2 December), 790.
A letter to the editor reprints a letter from Scott to Bernard Barton, dated 4 October, 1824, in which Scott admits he has never seen Melrose Abbey by moonlight.

155 SECCOMBE, THOMAS. "The Bride of Lammermoor," in Scott Centenary Articles. London: Oxford University Press, pp. 73-86.
The subject of the novel suggests the ballad tradition, and Scott transfigured the original story of Janet Dalrymple "with the spirit of minstrelsy and great native poetry." The series of auguries adds to the sense of tragedy and avenging fate, while Caleb provides necessary ironic relief. The Bride is "an artistic whole," and the novel is carefully structured along dramatic lines. First published 5 June, 1919 in the Times Literary Supplement.

156 _____. "The Heart of Midlothian," in Scott Centenary Articles. London: Oxford University Press, pp. 56-72.
Because The Heart of Midlothian plunges the reader *in medias res,* Scott pauses several times in the narrative to fill in past details. He finished volume three with "noble simplicity," but the fourth volume is merely padding. The novel is more bourgeois than romantic, and there is relatively little description and scenery. Jeanie represents Scott's ideal, while Davie embodies the spirit of Puritan Scotland. First published 6 June, 1918 in the Times Literary Supplement.

157 _____. "In Honour of Waverley," in Scott Centenary Articles. London: Oxford University Press, pp. 1-17.
Scott's novels had almost no literary models, but were based on the scenes and characters of his own experience; they popularized many distinctive and hitherto unrecognized aspects of Scotland. He showed that history was filled with living people. His work invokes "action and active benevolence" and has no "morbidity or sickliness or flabbiness." First published 9 July, 1914 in the Times Literary Supplement.

158 _____. "Ivanhoe," in Scott Centenary Articles. London: Oxford University Press, pp. 87-93.

Scott did not wish to be called a "mannerist" and so searched for new, non-Scottish material in Ivanhoe. He admitted the historical anachronisms and his artistic mistakes, especially the resurrection of Athelstane as requested by Ballantyne. Some of the anachronisms are justified on the grounds of artistry or intelligibility. Ivanhoe is a romance of chivalry, not of character, and so only Rebecca is highly individualized. First published 18 December, 1919 in the Times Literary Supplement.

159   _____. "Kenilworth and Cumnor," in Scott Centenary Articles. London: Oxford University Press, pp. 116-22.
Scott was motivated to write Kenilworth by his attraction to the character of Queen Elizabeth and by the ballad on Cumnor Hall attributed to Meikle. However, he treated fact and chronology recklessly. Kenilworth is closer to pageant or history chronicle than to either comedy or tragedy. First published 3 February, 1921 in the Times Literary Supplement.

160   _____. "The Monastery and The Abbot," in Scott Centenary Articles. London: Oxford University Press, pp. 106-15.
In The Monastery Scott relied too much on the supernatural. In The Abbot he eliminated the two worst faults of the first novel, the White Lady of Avenel and the Euphuist Sir Piercie. He impartially portrays the favorable aspects of the old Catholicism, and the double plot is well constructed. In spite of the anachronisms, he vividly reveals historical conditions. First published 9 September, 1920 in the Times Literary Supplement.

161   _____. "Old Mortality," in Scott Centenary Articles. London: Oxford University Press, pp. 38-46.
Old Mortality is marked by two characteristic Scott flaws: the use of "prolix, quasi-facetious prolegomena" and his reticent, awkward treatment of love. Although Scott could not portray young ladies of rank, the other female characters are equal to those of Shakespeare and Chaucer. Scott remained ambivalent to "Claverse," and although he mocked the fanaticism of the Covenanters, he did not lampoon the Covenant. First published 11 January, 1917 in the Times Literary Supplement.

162   _____. "A Review of January, 1815: Guy Mannering," in Scott Centenary Articles. London: Oxford University Press, pp. 18-24.
Although the reviews of Guy Mannering originally deemed it inferior to Waverley, modern critics disagree. The plot

1932

derives from several sources in actuality, most notably the famous Annesley case of the lost heir. The <u>Quarterly Review</u> critic who suggested that the novel be translated into English was an "archdullard." First published 21 January, 1915 in the <u>Times Literary Supplement</u>.

163 _____. "<u>Rob Roy</u>," in <u>Scott Centenary Articles</u>. London: Oxford University Press, pp. 47-55.

In <u>Rob Roy</u> Scott returns to the mood and inspiration of <u>Waverley</u>, but the later novel is superior in characterization and humor. Frank Osbaldistone is closer to Scott than any of his other heroes, and the elder Osbaldistone shares Scott's father's devotion to discipline and contempt for literature. Die Vernon is the best of the Waverley heroines. The novel's only two flaws are in the totally villainous nature of Rashleigh and in the contrived happy ending. First published 3 January, 1918 in the <u>Times Literary Supplement</u>.

164 _____. "Scott and the Invader: <u>The Antiquary</u>," in <u>Scott Centenary Articles</u>. London: Oxford University Press, pp. 25-37.

In Monkbarns, Scott projected his own identity as it might be twenty years later. He integrates into the character his own sadness for a lost love and his sense of self-mockery. <u>The Antiquary</u> illustrates contemporary Scots manners, and the background of the invasion threat shows the unanimous spirit of resistance to Napoleon among all classes. First published 28 October, 1915 in the <u>Times Literary Supplement</u>.

165 _____. "The Spoils to the Victors," in <u>Scott Centenary Articles</u>. London: Oxford University Press, pp. 94-105.

In <u>The Antiquary</u> Scott began to fabricate his own chapter mottoes, but when he subscribed "Anon." to an epigraph it was not necessarily his own. As editor-in-chief of the <u>English Minstrelsy</u> he helped several lesser poets to gain acknowledgement for their contributions. He had a special partiality for anonymous authors, and when he borrowed he usually improved the original. First published 29 July, 1920 in the <u>Times Literary Supplement</u>.

166 SETON-ANDERSON, JAMES. "Ward of Scow Hall, Fewston." <u>Notes and Queries</u>, 163 (15 October), 278.

Query asks if Scott ever visited Scow Hall and what is the pedigree of the Ward family?

167 SMITH, M. O. "Scott and His Modern Rivals." <u>Queen's Quarterly</u>, 39 (November), 603-20.

Scott's romances compare favorably to the "dull fidelity"
of the realists, such as Eliot and Hardy. Where Tolstoy
supplies too much particularizing detail, Scott deals in
universal types. He made careful observations, but did not
transfer them directly to his writing; instead, the fruits
of his observations often appeared much later and in unex-
pected places.

168 SPENCE, LEWIS. "Bailie Nicol Jarvie. 'An Inimitable Pen-
Picture.'" The S. M. T. Magazine, 8, no. 4 (April), 53-54.
Scott had a particularly warm regard for his creation of
Bailie Nicol Jarvie and enjoyed the rendition of the character by the actor Charles Mackay at the Edinburgh Theatre in
1819. The contrast between Jarvie, the Lowland merchant,
and the Highlander Rob Roy presents the "everlasting dis-
tinction between the two types of Scotsmen."

169 _____. "Sir Walter Scott as a Student of Tradition," in Sir
Walter Scott Today. Edited by H. J. C. Grierson. London:
Constable, pp. 111-30.
Scott was aware of the need for a more systematic study
of how tales are transmitted through time and across national borders. In the fourth and fifth Letters on Demonology and Witchcraft and the introduction to "Tamlane" in
the Minstrelsy he considers every known example of Scottish
fairy tale.

170 _____. "A Treasure House of Tradition. Scott's Bequest to
Posterity." The S. M. T. Magazine, 8, no. 6 (June), 87-90.
Scott is the father of British folklore. In the Minstrelsy and the notes to the poems and novels he outlined a
methodology and system of classification for the material
of Scottish folklore. Reprinted: 1932.A29.

171 STROUT, ALAN LANG. "Scott and Swift." Times Literary Supplement (21 August), p. 291.
Prints a letter from Scott to C. G. Gavelin, dated 7
March, 1818, in which Scott declines to purchase an unpublished letter of Swift.

172 SWANZY, T. ERSKINE. "The Lay of the Last Minstrel." Times
Literary Supplement (4 August), p. 557.
Queries why, in the British Poets set published by Gall
and Inglis, seventy-seven lines of the Lay describing the
acquisition of Eskdale by the Scotts are omitted. See
1932.B96.

173 THOMPSON, W. J. "Foreword" to the Sir Walter Scott Centenary
Number. The S. M. T. Magazine, 8, no. 6 (June), 32.

1932

Scott brought attention to Scotland as a tourist center
and was "the greatest publicist our country has produced."
His eye for the scenic wonders of Scotland prompted thous-
ands of visitors to view the scenes he described in the
poems and novels. Reprinted: 1932.A29.

174   TORRANCE, JOHN. "Sir Walter Scott's Quaker Ancestors."
      British Weekly, 92 (8 September), 445.
         Scott had Quaker ancestors on the paternal side in Walter
      Scott of Raeburn, who was imprisoned for Quakerism in 1665,
      and on the maternal side in John Swinton, Cromwell's Chan-
      cellor, who also suffered imprisonment and confiscation for
      Quakerism.

175   TREVELYAN, G. M. "Walter Scott: The Novelist As Historian.
      An Estimate of His Influence." London Times (21 September),
      pp. 11-12.
         By showing his characters to be products of their par-
      ticular environments, Scott revolutionized the study of his-
      tory. He influenced Macaulay to focus on the social and
      economic causes of political history. Scott illustrated
      and popularized Burke's protest against the artificial
      unity of mankind. Reprinted: 1949.B6.

176   TRUE, THOMAS. "The Poetry of Sir Walter Scott." The S. M. T.
      Magazine, 8, no. 6 (June), 132-36.
         Carlyle attacked Scott's poetry because it did not con-
      front modern problems, but this was unfair because the
      poetry is essentially spiritual and romantic. Scott in-
      spired the Oxford Movement and the Victorian Arthurian re-
      vival. The greatest strength of the poetry is its natural
      description and its vivid evocation of the past. Reprinted:
      1932.A29.

177   VAN ANTWERP, WILLIAM CLARKSON. "A Forgotten Antiquary."
      Bound with "Sir Walter Scott: 1832-1932" by John Buchan.
      San Francisco: The Book Club of California, pp. 11-27.
         Discusses the friendship between Scott and Joseph Train,
      which began in 1814. Although he has been neglected by
      modern biographers, Train was "a man of ability within
      limitations." He renounced his personal ambitions to de-
      vote his efforts to Scott and asked nothing in return. He
      provided much essential material to Scott, who in turn gave
      his stories form and humanity. Scott and Train were neces-
      sary to each other.

178   WALLACE, M. W. "The Centenary of Sir Walter Scott." Univer-
      sity of Toronto Quarterly, 2, no. 1 (October), 111-32.

Scott's reputation has declined partly due to the modern mood of disillusion and partly due to his conservative temperament. He is primarily interested in his characters, rather than in their historical backgrounds, although he is embarrassed by love relationships. His sense of adventure derives from his belief "in the dramatic values inherent in the simplest events and in the simplest lives."

179 WALPOLE, HUGH. "As a Novelist at Home and Abroad." The
S. M. T. Magazine, 8, no. 6 (June), 57–60.
Scott avoided the absurdities of the Gothic Romance by placing ordinary people in romantic situations. He influenced Goethe, but his most important foreign influence was in France on Hugo, Dumas, Sand, Stendhal and Flaubert. The decline in his influence began when the novel became a self-conscious art, but Scott will be rediscovered as the novel returns to unselfconsciousness and zest. Reprinted: 1932.A29.

180 _____. "A Centenary Estimate." English Review, 54 (April), 350–59.
The younger generation regards Scott's novels as anachronistic, because he was concerned with duty and nobility of conduct. Although Scott is frequently faulty as an artist, and although he neglected the deeper passions of human nature, his supreme strength is as a creator of human character, especially in the Scottish novels.

181 _____. "The Historical Novel in England Since Sir Walter Scott," in Sir Walter Scott Today. Edited by H. J. C. Grierson. London: Constable, pp. 161–88.
Scott was the first English writer to give naturalness and credibility to the historical novel, but after 1932 it became "a battle between realism and romance." After Scott, Thackeray is the greatest historical novelist, but the other Victorians spoilt their historical novels by simple moralizing.

182 _____. "Sir Walter Scott." Bookman, 82, no. 487 (April), 7–9.
Scott's strengths and weaknesses "spring from his absolute masculinity." His reactionary politics were linked with his intense love of the past, and in his financial affairs his heroism balanced his carelessness. His great gift as a novelist was the creation of ordinary people who exist independently of his own personality.

183 _____. "Sir Walter Scott," introduction to The Waverley Pageant. London: Eyre and Spottiswoode, pp. ix–xxxiii.

1932

Scott's life needs to be rescued from both the sentimen-
talists and the cynics. Despite faults of clumsy beginnings,
unnecessary description and melodramatic conversation, he
possessed a magnificent narrative gift and the ability to
create atmosphere. He has declined in popularity due to the
increasing aesthetic self-consciousness of the modern novel
and to the misuse of some of his works as educational exercises. See 1932.A34.

184 WATT, MARGARET H. "Sophia and Anne: the Daughters of Sir
Walter Scott." Cornhill Magazine, N.S. 73 (September),
358-70.
Scott's daughters had a happy childhood. Sophia, who
married Lockhart, belonged to the type of sensible Scots-
woman whom Scott praised in Jeanie Deans. Anne, who provided the model for Alice Lee in Woodstock, was the livelier
of the two sisters and provided comfort for Scott's last
years. Her health declined rapidly after his death, and
she died nine months later, presumably from exhaustion and
nervous breakdown.

185 WEST, REBECCA. "The Dualism of Scott," in "Sir Walter Scott:
A Centenary Commentary by Various Writers." The Modern
Scot, 3 (August), 121-23.
Although the "bookish" have preserved Scott's reputation,
those who read for entertainment now ignore him. He fails
mainly in the pace of his novels and in his unwillingness
to consider deeper human motivations. His dualism arises
from his sense of doom "at the core of life" and his need
to turn away from it to the surface.

186 WHITE, FREDERICK C. "Sir Walter Scott and Dunbar." Notes and
Queries, 163 (30 July), 77.
Scott wrote that his mother's memories helped him to
paint the past. She had known someone who perfectly recol-
lected the battle of Dunbar.

187 WILLIAMSON-ROSS, R. R. "Sir Walter's Parrot. 'Le Perroquet
de Walter-Scott.'" Scots Magazine, N.S. 17, no. 6
(September), 439-42.
Relates the story of the gift of a parrot from Scott to
Amédée Pichot, who wrote the tale named in the subtitle in
1834. Scott's "Pol" had a prodigious memory and recited
snatches of Border lore picked up in listening to Abbotsford conversations. Scott promised Pichot to fill in the
gaps of the parrot's stories but died before he could keep
his pledge.

188   WILSON, W. E. "The Making of the 'Minstrelsy': Scott and
       Shortreed in Liddesdale." <u>Cornhill Magazine</u>, N.S. 73
       (September), 266-83.
          Scott met Robert Shortreed in 1792 and began a friend-
       ship based on mutual antiquarian interests. For seven years
       they made annual trips (or "raids") into Liddesdale to
       gather ballad material. John Shortreed wrote in interview
       form his father's accounts of these trips, and the MS (now
       in the National Library of Scotland) is here reprinted as
       "Conversations with My Father on the Subject of his Tours
       with Sir Walter Scott in Liddesdale, Written in June, 1824."
       Reprinted: 1932.B189.

189   _____. "Robert Shortreed's Account of his Visits to Liddesdale
       with Sir Walter Scott." <u>Transactions of the Hawick Archaeo-
       logical Society</u>, Session 1932, 54-63.
              Reprinted: 1932.B188.

190   WOLFE, CLARA SNELL. "Evidences of Scott's Indebtedness to
       Spanish Literature." <u>Romanic Review</u>, 23, no. 4 (October-
       December), 301-11.
          Scott was extensively influenced by <u>Don Quixote</u>, to which
       he refers over a hundred times in his novels and miscel-
       laneous prose. His acquaintance with Spanish literature
       went significantly beyond Cervantes, and he frequently (and
       often incorrectly) used Spanish words, phrases and proverbs.

191   [WOOD, A.]. "A 'Causerie'--Sir Walter Scott and 'Maga.'"
       <u>Blackwood's Magazine</u>, 232 (July), 1-15.
          Scott was a regular contributor to <u>Blackwood's</u> from its
       founding in 1817 until 1819. In 1821 he cautioned Lockhart
       against indulging his love for personal satire in the Maga-
       zine and thereafter contributed infrequently. Although
       Blackwood declined to print Lockhart's satire of <u>Brambletye
       Hall</u> on the grounds that it might indirectly offend Scott,
       Lockhart himself was angered by Wilson's "Noctes" of Novem-
       ber, 1830 which seemed to mock Scott's love of anecdote
       even while praising him.

192   WOOD, MARGUERITE. "Edinburgh in Sir Walter Scott's Time."
       <u>Scottish Country Life</u>, 21 (September), 266-67.
          During Scott's lifetime the New Town of Edinburgh de-
       veloped as the Old Town gradually deteriorated. The fires
       of 1824, the construction of the bridges, and indiscrimin-
       ate restoration destroyed many old landmarks. Scott has
       written little on the city of his daily life but secured
       several relics from dismantled buildings, including the
       doorway of the Old Tolbooth.

1933

1933 A BOOKS

1   BACHMANN, FREDERICK WILLIAM. <u>Some German Imitators of Walter Scott: An Attempt to Evaluate the Influence of Scott on the Subliterary Novel of the Early Nineteenth Century in Germany</u>. Chicago: University of Chicago Libraries, 111pp.
    Most of Scott's German imitators between 1820 and 1830 read the Waverley Novels in translation, and the imitations usually contain Scott's defects but not his merits. They are weak in description, dialogue, and characterization. They lack knowledge of cultural history, and they do not share Scott's democratic sympathies or religious tolerance.

2   CECIL, DAVID. <u>Sir Walter Scott</u>. The Raven Miscellany. London: Constable, 60pp.
    Slightly revised and re-edited edition in book form of 1932.B32–B34.

*3   DUSTAN, WILLIAM GORDON. "Sir Walter Scott and the Drama." Ph.D. dissertation, University of Edinburgh, 1933.
    No abstract available. Includes a bibliography of dramatic versions of Scott's works.

4   GRIERSON, HERBERT JOHN CLIFFORD, assisted by DAVIDSON COOK, W. M. PARKER, and others. <u>The Letters of Sir Walter Scott, 1815–1817</u>. Volume IV. London: Constable, 544pp.
    Includes letters through 27 October, 1817. <u>See also</u> 1932.A14–A16; 1933.A5; 1934.A2, A3; 1935.A3, A4; 1936.A2, A3; 1937.A1.

5   ____. <u>The Letters of Sir Walter Scott, 1817–1819</u>. Volume V. London: Constable, 511pp.
    Includes letters from 18 October, 1817 through 14 October, 1819. <u>See also</u> 1932.A14–A16; 1933.A4; 1934.A2, A3; 1935.A3, A4; 1936.A2, A3; 1937.A1.

6   JACK, JAMES WILLIAM. <u>Scott's View from the Wicks of Baiglie: The Roads and the Viewpoint</u>. Perth: Milne, Tannahill & Methven, 62pp.
    In chapter I of <u>The Fair Maid of Perth</u> Scott describes a magnificent view of the city and the Tay Valley seen from the Wicks of Baiglie, the summit of a ridge off the road from Kinross. Provides precise directions for the tourist in search of Scott's view, whose beauty he did not exaggerate. Local tradition states that Scott's destination on this journey was Invermay, where Williamina Belsches' grandmother lived.

7 KELLER, WOLFGANG. Walter Scott: Eine Rektoratsrede gehalten
am 5 November 1932. Münster: Aschendorffsche Verlagsbuch-
handlung, 22pp.
In spite of their different attitudes toward tradition
and bourgeois customs, Scott regarded Goethe as his teacher
in romantic prose. However, Scott's kind of romanticism
differed from the German psychic turmoil, revolutionary re-
jection of society and fluctuation between belief and skep-
ticism. As Carlyle pointed out, Scott's romanticism was
more "healthy." Scott resembles Achim von Arnim, who was
also deeply interested in his homeland.

1933 B SHORTER WRITINGS

1 BECK, RICHARD. "Walter Scott: Aldarminning." Lögrjetta, 28,
36-52.
Concerns Scott's influence on Jón Thoroddsen (1818-1868),
"the father of the modern Icelandic novel," and touches on
early Icelandic literary influence on Scott. Includes a
summary of Scott's career and a quotation from Jónas
Sigurdson's translation of The Lay of the Last Minstrel.

2 BENSLY, EDWARD. "A Quotation in Scott." Times Literary Sup-
plement (25 May), p. 364.
The author of the Latin quotation in Count Robert of
Paris appears to be H. Cruserius, who is quoted in Petrarch's
Life of Cimon. The quotation preceding chapter 19 of The
Antiquary is adapted from T. J. Mathias. See 1933.B10.

3 BOATRIGHT, MODY C. "Witchcraft in the Novels of Sir Walter
Scott." University of Texas Studies in English, 13
(8 July), 95-112.
In his treatment of witchcraft, Scott followed traditions
but used them for artistic purposes of comedy, pathos, and
tragedy. His witches are not all evil. Meg Murdockson
represents the criminal as witch, while Meg Merrilies and
Norna of the Fitful Head are half-demented women who be-
lieve themselves to be tools of fate. The Bride of Lammermoor is the only novel in which Scott uses real witchcraft.

4 BRAYBROOKE, PATRICK. "Author's Preface" to Moments with Burns,
Scott, and Stevenson. Stirling, Scotland: Eneas Mackay,
pp. 7-11.
Burns, Scott, and Stevenson shared a love for life, man
and God. They acknowledged human shortcomings but regarded
them as evidence of human potential. Scott was the least
temperamental of the three; neither fortune nor misfortune

1933

deflected his mind from its straightforward channel. These
three writers were literary optimists to whom everything
mattered.

5   CARSWELL, DONALD. "Sir Walter's Secret: a Literary Inquest."
    Scots Magazine, N.S. 20 (December), 192-98.
        Supports Pope-Hennessey's argument that Waverley was not
    Scott's first novel, but only "the first he deemed fit for
    publication." Guy Mannering was a rewritten "'prentice
    work" as were several other novels, refashioned under pres-
    sure of deadlines and financial need. The evidence is
    "purely internal and circumstantial" and most conclusive in
    The Monastery and The Abbot. See 1933.B31 and 1948.A1.

6   CASSON, T. E. "Sir Walter Scott and the Antiquities of Cum-
    berland." Transactions of the Cumberland and Westmoreland
    Antiquarian and Archaeological Society, N.S. 33, 146-62.
        The study of antiquity was Scott's "ruling passion" and
    was not confined to exclusively literary interests. He was
    committed to the preservation of ancient buildings and was
    a member of many antiquarian societies. Reviews his con-
    nection to Cumberland and the Lake District and his refer-
    ences to this area, especially in the Minstrelsy and "Sir
    Tristrem."

7   COBLEY, W. D. "Some Waverley Scots." Papers of the Manchester
    Literary Club, 59, 139-53.
        Scott admired lawyers and the law but acknowledged their
    weaknesses. He valued religion, honor, loyalty, discipline,
    and self-forgetfulness. Although his characters of lower
    rank are the most vivid, his historical personages are as
    much alive as his wholly fictive ones.

8   COLLINS, NORMAN. "Sir Walter Scott," in his Facts of Fiction.
    New York: E. P. Dutton, pp. 132-45.
        Scott's mind was solid and unemotional; he understood
    passion only in the terms of romantic love. His novels are
    notable for their common sense and for their combination of
    "the mists of romance" with "the facts of history." Scott
    lived better than most authors and regarded wealth and rank
    as essentials.

9   COOK, HENRY. "Sir Walter Scott." Baptist Quarterly, N.S. 6
    (January), 204-206.
        We feel our strongest affection for Scott as a man
    rather than as a poet, historian, or novelist. He was a
    devout Christian, and religion was "the mainspring of his
    life." He understood the principles of true religion, and
    his character was "wholesome and balanced and good."

10   DUNBABIN, R. L. "A Quotation in Scott." <u>Times Literary Sup-</u>
      <u>plement</u> (18 May), p. 348.
          Scott quoted Latin from memory and consequently made
      frequent errors. Asks for identification of a Latin quota-
      tion falsely attributed to Ovid in <u>Count Robert of Paris</u>.
      <u>See</u> 1933.B2.

11   EDGAR, PELHAM. "Sir Walter Scott," in his <u>The Art of the</u>
      <u>Novel</u>. New York: Macmillan, pp. 79-92.
          Although Scott's novels lack both "liveliness of attack"
      and "reflective depth," they are valuable as entertainment
      and as reflections of the manners of a period. Scott was
      most successful when he depended on living memory or tradi-
      tion rather than antiquarian studies. Although <u>The Heart</u>
      <u>of Midlothian</u> has a dull opening, its faults are slight
      until the end; Scott should have stopped the novel at its
      natural conclusion when Jeanie brings the pardon from
      London.

12   FOX, ARTHUR W. "In Praise of Sir Walter Scott." <u>Papers of</u>
      <u>the Manchester Literary Club</u>, 59, 1-17.
          Scott teaches the commonplace virtues in a clean, sound,
      and straightforward fashion. His narrative poems approach
      the epics of Homer, and his songs reach "the highest level
      of poetry." In the novels he does not waste time with long
      psychological analyses, but instead he reveals motives and
      feelings through dialogue and suggestion.

13   FYFE, J. G. "Introduction" to <u>Three Stories From Scott</u>.
      London and Glasgow: Blackie and Son, pp. iii-viii.
          Scott wrote few short stories, probably because he ob-
      jected to the confinement of the form. However, "Wandering
      Willie's Tale" is perfect in structure, style, and diction,
      because Scott took great pains in its writing and revision.
      "The Two Drovers" has structural defects but tells an ex-
      cellent story. "The Mirror" is a far slighter work which
      Scott says he wrote as it was related to him.

14   GRIERSON, HERBERT JOHN CLIFFORD. "Sir Walter Scott, 1832-
      1932." <u>Columbia University Quarterly</u>, 25 (March), 9-25.
          Scott's primary contribution to the novel was "the sense
      of the past," created through event, setting, description,
      manners and language. The narrative poems succeeded in
      "the scenic setting and the suggestion of an epoch," while
      the novels' great success lay in their depiction of the true
      life of the Scottish people. Scott's work and character
      created harmony and good will and helped to reconcile Brit-
      ain and the Continent after the Napoleonic wars. Reprinted
      and slightly revised: 1953.B5.

1933

15 GRIEVE, JAMES. "George Meikle Kemp and His Work." <u>Transac-</u>
    <u>tions of the Hawick Archaeological Society</u>, Session 1933,
    15-18.
        A carpenter and cabinet-maker with a love for the Gothic,
    Kemp was a self-taught architect who submitted the winning
    design for the Scott monument under a pseudonym. He closely
    superintended its building, but was accidentally drowned be-
    fore it was finished. A memorial in his honor was erected
    at Redscaurhead, Peebleshire in 1932.

16 GUNN, C. B. "The Passing of Sir Walter Scott: His Last Six
    and a Half Years." <u>Transactions of the Hawick Archaeologi-</u>
    <u>cal Society</u>, Session 1933, 26-29.
        Scott's <u>Journal</u> reveals the parallels between the tragedy
    of his later life and the <u>Book of Job</u>. The <u>Journal</u> served
    as an outlet for his feelings and as his vindication before
    the world.

17 HILSON, OLIVER. "Sir Walter Scott and the Border Reformers."
    <u>Transactions of the Hawick Archaeological Society</u>, Session
    1933, i-iv.
        On 18 May, 1831 Scott faced an angry crowd at Jedburgh,
    where he spoke against Parliamentary Reform. But Lockhart's
    account of the mob's violent reaction is "grossly exagger-
    ated," and Lockhart's example led the historian Archibald
    Allison to slander the Border Reformers in this matter.

18 HOLMES, JOHN HAYNES. "Scott Centenary Publications." <u>Unity</u>,
    110 (20 February), 365.
        Surveys the books published in honor of the centenary of
    Scott's death. This "extensive and important" collection
    refutes the misconception that Scott is now unread.

19 LEGOUIS, ÉMILE. "La Fortune litteraire de Walter Scott en
    France," in "Fêtes du Centenaire de W. Scott." <u>France-</u>
    <u>Grande Bretagne; bulletin des relations franco-britanniques</u>,
    no. 123 (February), pp. 335-48.
        Scott was enormously popular in France. He brought to
    an exhausted French literary generation the novelties of
    the picturesque, local color, history, and the traditions
    of the British novel in dialogue, action, and spectacle.
    He influenced French historians and novelists. Balzac re-
    peatedly acknowledged his debt to Scott, and Lamartine re-
    garded the nineteenth century as the century of Walter
    Scott. But his popularity has not been limited to literary
    people, and his books have been bedside reading in innumer-
    able French homes. Reprinted: 1971.B35.

20 MACHEN, ARTHUR. "Lost Books." <u>Bookman</u>, 76, no. 2 (February),
    134-36.
        The "heroic" Scott who believed in Jacobitism, Catholi-
    cism, and the occult was repressed by his rational intellect
    and "the weight of his time and world." Because his heart
    and reason were divided, Scott could not give his characters
    total liberty with heroic speech.

21 MACKENZIE, COMPTON. <u>Literature in My Time</u>. London: Rich &
    Cowan, 254pp., passim and especially pp. 22-23.
        The author's generation "had outlived Scott" by the
    1890's and could enjoy only his second rate novels of "tin-
    sel romance" like <u>Ivanhoe</u>. Scott remains boring and "will
    never be revived in the future."

22 McKILLOP, ALAN DUGALD. "Sir Walter Scott in the Twentieth
    Century." <u>Rice Institute Pamphlets</u>, 20, no. 2 (April),
    196-215.
        Scott's attitude toward his own work was consistent and
    included good-natured deprecation. Scott's novels move
    through a slow process of trial and error with which the
    modern reader has little patience. His best work unites
    creative imagination and extensive learning, the novel of
    manners and historical fiction.

23 MASSON, ROSALINE ARME. "Why Did Scott and Carlyle Never Meet?"
    in her <u>Poets, Patriots, and Lovers: Sketches and Memories
    of Famous People</u>. London: James Clarke, pp. 9-19.
        In their politics and attitudes toward royalty and ma-
    terialism, Scott and Carlyle were diametrically opposed.
    But they were similar in their love of German literature
    and their "intrinsic greatness." Carlyle was offended when
    Scott did not answer his letter telling of the medals sent
    by Goethe, but Scott probably never received it. Although
    their paths may have crossed in Edinburgh several times,
    Scott and Carlyle never met.

24 PARKER, WILLIAM MATHIE. "How the Waverley Novels Were Pro-
    duced." <u>Scots Magazine</u>, N.S. 18, no. 6 (March), 449-51.
        The printer James Ballantyne punctuated the Waverley
    Novels, and his scrupulous proofreading allowed Scott to
    correct many oversights and inconsistencies. Scott often
    accepted Ballantyne's advice, although sometimes grudgingly.

25 PARSONS, COLEMAN OSCAR. "Association of the White Lady with
    Wells." <u>Folklore</u>, 4 (September), 295-305.
        Scott borrowed the "contradictory traits" of the White
    Lady of Avenel from French, German, and Scottish sources.

1933

He mistakenly linked her with a water well, whereas traditional folklore did not make white ladies the spirits of
fountains or wells, except as a misconstruction of the names
of wells consecrated to the Virgin Mary.

26 _____. "The Death of Catherine in The Monastery." Notes and
Queries, 164 (7 January), 5-6.
   Catherine's battlefield death with her infant in her arms
by the side of Julian Avenel may be taken from the oral tradition of Selkirk. Scott probably found it in the Macfar-
lane MSS in the Advocates' Library.

27 _____. "Demonological Background of 'Donnerhugel's Narrative'
and 'Wandering Willie's Tale.'" Studies in Philology, 30
(October), 604-17.
   In "Donnerhugel's Narrative" in Anne of Geierstein, Scott
combined a medieval succubus legend, an incident from God-
win's St. Leon, and Rosicrucian lore, all enriched by his
own invention. In "Wandering Willie's Tale" in Redgauntlet
Scott makes a similar amalgamation of material from Joseph
Train's Strains of the Mountain Muse and the lives of
Claverhouse, Lagg, and Weir.

28 _____. "Manuscripts of Scott's Letters on Demonology and
Witchcraft." Notes and Queries, 164 (22 April), 276-77.
   The manuscript of the Letters was below Scott's usual
standard in grammar, diction, and clarity. The work gained
logical coherence in the first proof, and the second proof
brought it into its present more satisfactory condition.

29 _____. "Two Notes on Scott." Notes and Queries, 164
(4 February), 75-77.
   Lockhart's changes in "The Shepherd's Tale" were "justifiable editorial revision." "The Tapestried Chamber" belongs to the genre of stories about a "silky," a ghost who
wears rustling silk.

30 _____. "Two Scott Anecdotes." Notes and Queries, 164
(17 June), 421.
   Relates two Scott anecdotes found in Robert Chambers'
notes for a future edition of Traditions of Edinburgh; however neither anecdote appears in the book. One concerns
Constable's description of Scott as a cow who gives much
milk but has to be sold because she eats more than her
share. The other concerns Scott's purchase of a Roman
patera for twenty-five guineas.

31 POPE-HENNESSEY, UNA. "Sir Walter Scott in His Works." Essays
    by Divers Hands, N.S. 12, 79-103.
        Scott's partisans have neglected the artist in favor of
    "Scott the model man." We must revise both the image of
    Scott presented by Lockhart and our idea of the chronology
    of the novels. He wrote much of St. Ronan's Well in 1797;
    thus he began as a realist and only gradually developed the
    technique of the historical novels. Parts of the later
    works were written much earlier than their publication
    dates. Scott's innovative contribution was "man presented
    in his duration in time and his passage through definite
    space." See 1933.B5; 1948.A1; 1971.B57.

32 RAIT, ROBERT. "Boswell and Lockhart." Essays by Divers Hands,
    N.S. 12, 105-27.
        Lockhart followed Boswell's model in refusing to conceal
    the truth. But he did not use Boswell's method of reporting
    conversation, and he was much more careful in sparing
    people's feelings. Unlike Boswell, Lockhart tampered with
    letters, regarding them not as texts but as the biographer's
    raw material. Because he saw his book as a work of art,
    Lockhart did not feel bound to "faithful transcription and
    exact reproduction."

33 RAUBINGER, MELTON. "Aids in Teaching Scott's Novels." English
    Journal, 22, no. 3 (March), 202-208.
        A list of illustrated editions of Ivanhoe, Kenilworth,
    Quentin Durward and The Talisman. Also includes a list of
    films and lantern slides dealing with Scott and his works
    and selected bibliographies of tests and teaching devices,
    of biographical material, and of background material.

34 REDDIE, L. N. "Sir Walter Scott in the Court of Session."
    Notes and Queries, 164 (24 June), 442.
        Queries whether there is any discussion in Scott's works
    of the suggestion advanced by Joseph Hume that Scott em-
    ployed his time in the Court of Session writing novels.
    Scott denied this in a letter to the Lord Advocate.

35 RUFF, WILLIAM. "Scott's Printers." Times Literary Supplement
    (7 September), p. 592.
        Lists novels and editions of Scott that were not printed
    by Ballantyne, although the colophon indicates they were.

36 _____. "Sir Walter Scott and Bishop Percy." Notes and
    Queries, 165 (4 November), 308-309.
        First publication of Scott's first letter to Bishop
    Percy, dated 6 October, 1800. The letter is in effect a
    prospectus for the Minstrelsy of the Scottish Border.

1933

37   SEN, PRIYARANJAN. "In Memory of Scott." <u>Calcutta Review</u>,
      3rd ser. 47 (May), 153-71.
           Scott's poems recall a past when action, rather than
      meditation, seemed the natural mode. His poetry avoids
      "the subtleties of the human mind" and "the mysteries of
      the universe," but he created a distinctively British form
      of Romanticism and drew attention to neglected poets of the
      past. Scott has influenced the Bengali poets Rangalal,
      Rakhaldas Sen, and Nabinchandra.

38   SPINK, GERALD W. "Fontane's Poem: 'Walter Scott in West-
      minster Abtei.'" <u>Modern Language Review</u>, 28, no. 4
      (October), 489-90.
           The poem describes an incident supposed to have taken
      place during the coronation of George IV, in which the pro-
      cession paused to make way for Scott. The incident actually
      took place after the ceremony, and Fontane borrowed Lock-
      hart's description of it.

39   STRUVE, PETER. "Walter Scott and Russia." <u>Slavonic Review</u>,
      11 (January), 397-410.
           As poet, collector of folk-songs, and historical novel-
      ist, Scott profoundly influenced Pushkin. The critic S. P.
      Shevyrev regarded Scott's novels as "the artistic apotheosis
      of history." Other critics disagreed on Scott's merits.
      Where Belinsky compared him to Homer, Senkovsky regarded
      the Waverley Novels as "quackery."

40   SWAEN, A. E. H. "A Letter from Sir Walter Scott to James
      Ballantyne." <u>Neophilologicus</u>, 18 (January), 130-31.
           Prints a letter now in the Royal Library at The Hague.
      It is undated but probably refers to a journey to London to
      be taken in the spring of 1828.

41   VAN ANTWERP, WILLIAM C. "On Collecting Scott." <u>Colophon</u>, 14,
      no pagination, 12pp.
           The disappearance of the MS of <u>The Heart of Midlothian</u>
      is the strangest mystery to Scott collectors. Scott's
      proofsheets are particularly valuable because of the ex-
      changes they contain between Scott and Ballantyne. Author's
      "most interesting" items are a first edition of <u>Guy Manner-
      ing</u> with the correct errata leaf and the first and second
      states of <u>Tales of My Landlord</u>. Collection includes twenty-
      six presentation copies. <u>See</u> 1936.B7.

42   WAGENKNECHT, EDWARD. "For Walter Scott." <u>Virginia Quarterly
      Review</u>, 9, no. 1 (January), 130-38.

A review article which concludes that "For a corpse, Scott seems to be showing signs of uncommon vitality." Reviews Buchan's biography, Grierson's edition of the letters, Holmes's selections from the poetry and the collection of Scott Centenary Articles.

43 WALPOLE, HUGH. "Address to the Thirty-third Annual Dinner of the Edinburgh Sir Walter Scott Club." The Edinburgh Sir Walter Scott Club Annual Report, pp. 18-30.
     Scott's novels demonstrated that poetry and reality could be brought together in fiction. The decline in his popularity accompanied the development of the English novel toward absolute truthfulness and toward a concern with technical form. Scott believed in the moral qualities of his characters, which has also become unfashionable.

1934 A BOOKS

*1 GRADY, SISTER ROSE MARIE. "The Sources of Scott's Eight Long Poems." Ph.D. dissertation, University of Illinois, 1934.
     Cited in MLA American Bibliography for 1935, PMLA, 50 (supplement), 1278.

2 GRIERSON, HERBERT JOHN CLIFFORD, assisted by DAVIDSON COOK, W. M. PARKER, and others. The Letters of Sir Walter Scott, 1819-1821. Volume VI. London: Constable, 512pp.
     Includes letters from 16 October, 1819 to 3 August, 1821. See also 1932.A14-A16; 1933.A4, A5; 1934.A3; 1935.A3, A4; 1936.A2, A3; 1937.A1.

3 _____. The Letters of Sir Walter Scott, 1821-1823. Volume VII. London: Constable, 511pp.
     Includes letters from 7 August, 1821 to 16 May, 1823 and, as an appendix, letters to Thomas Scott and Mrs. Thomas Scott, 1807-1825. Editor's introduction to the appendix (pp. 393-415) traces Scott's relations with his debt-prone brother Tom. Although Scott's use of influence in gaining Tom a post of financial trust may have been ill-advised, he was motivated by family loyalty. He spared neither money, nor time, nor trouble in attempting to help Tom and through it all displayed "unwearied patience and kindness." See also 1932.A14-A16; 1933.A4, A5; 1934.A2; 1935.A3, A4; 1936.A2, A3; 1937.A1.

4 PAUL, ADOLF. Der Einfluss Walter Scotts auf die epische Technik Theodor Fontanes. Sprache und Kultur der germanischen und romanischen Völker, No. 10. Breslau: Priebatsch, 272pp.

1934

Fontane worshipped the works of Scott and shared his interest in history, folklore, and nature. Scott's ballads
influenced Fontane's Historical Songs of Prussian Heroes.
Where Scott's novels concern primarily outward experience,
Fontane was more interested in spiritual drama. Both
writers used the journey motif, loose episodic structure,
and thorough narrative introductions of new characters.

*5   SMOCK, GEORGE E. "Sir Walter Scott's Theory of the Novel."
      Ph.D. dissertation, Cornell University, 1934.
          Cited in MLA American Bibliography for 1937, PMLA, 52
      (supplement), 1269.

6   STUART, DOROTHY MARGARET. Scott: Some Centenary Reflections.
      English Association Pamphlet No. 89. London: Oxford
      University Press, 18pp.
          Scott's three novels of seventeenth century England re-
      quired a greater exercise of imagination than the Scottish
      novels, because Scott was writing of things and people with
      which he had no direct or spiritual contact. In both the
      English and Scottish novels he uses the "stagy" devices of
      recognition scenes, revelatory monologues, and melodramatic
      action. Scott owed much to Walpole but improved upon his
      techniques; both excelled in the simple lyric.

1934 B SHORTER WRITINGS

1   ARMSTRONG, T. P. "Scott Query: 'The Archbishop of Granada's
      Apoplexy.'" Notes and Queries, 167 (15 December), 429.
          References to the Archbishop of Granada are proverbially
      understood as denoting that a writer is publishing some-
      thing "manifestly inferior to what he has already given the
      world." See 1934.B3, B19.

2   BENSLY, EDWARD. "Notes on Scott's Count Robert of Paris."
      Notes and Queries, 167 (15 December), 425.
          Expands 1934.B20 by noting additional editorial careless-
      ness and clarifying the sources of several mottoes. The MS
      of Kenilworth in the British Museum shows Scott quoting cor-
      rectly from The Winter's Tale (II, i, 87-91), but the quoted
      motto has been consistently misprinted.

3   _____. "Scott Query: 'The Archbishop of Granada's Apoplexy.'"
      Notes and Queries, 167 (8 December), 410.
          The Archbishop of Granada is a character in LeSage's Gil
      Blas who asks Gil Blas to tell him when his mental powers
      seem to be declining; but when Gil Blas does so, the Arch-
      bishop discharges him. See 1934.B1, B19.

4   BOATRIGHT, MODY C. "Demonology in the Novels of Sir Walter
     Scott: A Study in Regionalism." University of Texas
     Studies in English, 14 (8 July), 75-88.
          Scott was "the first conscious regionalist in major
     British fiction." When Scott treated demonology as a tra-
     dition with deep human significance he succeeded. When he
     treated it with theatrical sensationalism he failed. His
     success with demonology depends on his closeness to regional
     tradition and on "the cultural inheritance of the characters
     and of the author."

5   CECIL, DAVID. "Introduction" to Short Stories by Sir Walter
     Scott. London: Oxford University Press, pp. vii-xx.
          Scott's short stories are "the most satisfactory things
     he ever wrote," because they emphasize his virtues and give
     limited scope to his faults. They show his inspiration
     without demonstrating his technical incapacity. Although
     each of the other stories is in some ways flawed, "Wandering
     Willie's Tale" and "The Two Drovers" are perfect. In his
     great moments Scott is comparable to Shakespeare. Re-
     printed: 1970.B2.

6   CLARKE, JOHN. "Sir Walter Scott's Gifts to the World Reviewed."
     Border Magazine, 39 (June), 90-92; (August), 115-118; and
     40 (March, 1935), 42-44.
          Scott possesses three claims to immortality. The first
     is the literary heritage of the novels, with their high
     moral outlook and preservation of the Scots tongue. His
     second claim is the "discovery of Scotland" and evocation
     of her natural beauty. His third claim is the development
     of the historical novel.

7   DARGAN, E. PRESTON. "Scott and the French Romantics." Publi-
     cations of the Modern Language Association, 49, no. 2
     (June), 599-629.
          Scott's revival of the past and his feeling for tradition
     appealed to nineteenth century French readers. He speci-
     fically influenced Vigny, Hugo, Mérimée, and especially
     Balzac. Includes some discussion of adaptations of the
     Waverley Novels for the French stage, Delacroix's use of
     subjects from Scott, and Scott's influence on the historian
     Thierry.

8   FREEMAN, DAVID. "Sir Walter Scott's Villains." Dublin Review,
     195 (October), 305-16.
          Scott believed in Providence and inevitably punished his
     villains with a bad end. However, they never repent, al-
     ways die with dignity, and retain their personal heroism.
     They have the vitality missing in his virtuous heroes.

1934

9   GRIERSON, HERBERT JOHN CLIFFORD. <u>Lang, Lockhart and Biography</u>.
      London: Oxford University Press, 38pp.
           In his <u>Life of Lockhart</u> Lang was just in his treatment
      of the Ballantynes, but he did not acknowledge Lockhart's
      "picturesque and dramatic touches" in writing the <u>Life of
      Scott</u>. Lockhart's manipulation of documents went beyond
      the legitimate, and he often relied on imagination rather
      than memory. He diverted attention from Scott's faults by
      attacking Constable and the Ballantynes. The Andrew Lang
      Lecture, delivered at the University of St. Andrews, 6 De-
      cember, 1933.

10 HAWKES, C. P. "Walter Scott," in his <u>Authors-at-Arms: The
      Soldiering of Six Great Writers</u>. London: Macmillan,
      pp. 107-46.
           Relates Scott's experiences from 1799 to 1815 as Quarter-
      master of the Royal Edinburgh Light Dragoons, a regiment of
      volunteer Light Cavalry which he helped to form. In addi-
      tion to being the "chartered comedian" of his troop, Scott
      was an enthusiastic and conscientious soldier. He was a
      good rider, and he used his cavalry experience extensively
      in his writing.

11 KRŻYZANOWSKI, JULIAN. "Scott in Poland." <u>Slavonic Review</u>,
      12 (July), 181-89.
           Scott influenced two of the leading Polish Romantic
      poets, Slowacki and Mickiewicz, and a number of historical
      novels written between 1825 and 1835. The subsequent de-
      velopment of the historical novel "ran along the path dis-
      covered by Scott." In 1897 Sienkiewicz revived the his-
      torical novel in Poland and "gave a new life to the liter-
      ary formula invented by Scott."

*12 McCLELLAND, JOHN. "The Course of Realism in the English
      Novel from Addison and Steele through Sir Walter Scott."
      Ph.D. dissertation, Stanford University, 1934.
           Cited in <u>Comprehensive Dissertation Index</u> (Ann Arbor,
      Michigan: Xerox University Microfilms, 1973), XXX, 468.

13 MEIKLE, HENRY W. "George Grant." <u>Times Literary Supplement</u>
      (23 August), p. 577.
           George Grant's <u>Life of Scott</u> was flagrantly plagiarized
      from the <u>Life of Sir Walter Scott, Bart.</u> by William Weir
      and George Allen (1832-34).

14 NESBITT, GEORGE LYMAN. <u>Benthamite Reviewing: The First
      Twelve Years of the Westminster Review, 1824-1836</u>.
      Columbia University Studies in English and Comparative
      Literature, No. 118. New York: Columbia University Press,
      pp. 105-109.

The Philosophic Radical critics of the <u>Westminster Review</u> departed from the general praise given to Scott's works by the periodical press. The reviewers of <u>Redgauntlet</u> and of <u>Woodstock</u> attacked these works as defective novels and Tory propaganda. Mill's review of the <u>Life of Napoleon</u> criticized Scott's theory of society and his consequently biased understanding of the Revolution. The Utilitarian critics portrayed Scott as "not a novelist or a historian, merely a Tory."

15   PARKER, WILLIAM MATHIE. "A Study of Scott's Topography. Some Puzzling Landmarks." <u>The S. M. T. Magazine</u>, 13, no. 2 (August), 27-32.
    Scott often fused the features of several actual places to provide a composite picture, so many of his original landmarks cannot be precisely identified from descriptions in the novels. Examples are Tully-Veolan in <u>Waverley</u>, the Abbey of St. Ruth in <u>The Antiquary</u>, Tillietudlem in <u>Old Mortality</u>, and Wolf's Crag in <u>The Bride of Lammermoor</u>. Scott often moved his fictitious places from their original sites to imaginary ones to enhance the dramatic effect.

16   PARSONS, COLEMAN OSCAR. "Character Names in the Waverley Novels." <u>Publications of the Modern Language Association</u>, 49, no. 1 (March), 276-94.
    One out of five characters in the Waverley Novels has a self-interpreting name. Some of these names are humorous. Others interpret character or occupation, advance the story, or fill in background. Includes a list of examples organized by novel from <u>Waverley</u> to <u>Castle Dangerous</u>.

17   _____. "The Highland Feasts of Fergus MacIvor and Lord Lovat." <u>Modern Language Notes</u>, 49 (May), 287-90.
    While creating the personality of Fergus MacIvor, especially in the scene of the Highland feast in Chapter 20, Scott was thinking of Simon Fraser, Lord Lovat.

18   _____. "Scott's Translation of Bürger's 'Das Lied von Treue.'" <u>Journal of English and Germanic Philology</u>, 33, no. 2 (April), 240-49.
    Provides location and history of the three known manuscripts of the poem as well as an annotated text of the translation. Scott's choice of subject, the "contrast between the fidelity of dogs and the infidelity of women," was motivated by his unhappy love for Williamina Belsches. Scott's version is a paraphrase of and selection from the original rather than an absolutely faithful translation.

1934

19 PHILLIPS, LAWRENCE. "Scott Query: 'The Archbishop of
Granada's Apoplexy.'" Notes and Queries, 167 (24 November),
368.
What is the meaning of the reference to the Archbishop
of Granada in the Introduction to Peveril of the Peak? See
1934.A1, A3.

20 R[ENDALL], V[ERNON]. "Notes on Scott's Count Robert of Paris."
Notes and Queries, 167 (17 November), 345-47.
Scott's illness led to faulty early texts of Count Robert
of Paris; neither Lockhart nor James Ballantyne paid adequate attention to the proofreading. The many Latin references in the novel testify to Scott's wonderful memory.
Notes errors in the novel listed by chapter. See 1934.B2.

21 RENDALL, VERNON. "Scott and Literary Notches." Times Literary
Supplement (19 July), p. 511.
When gathering material for the Minstrelsy, Scott took
notes by making notches on twigs or pieces of wood. See
1934.B28, B29.

22 RUFF, WILLIAM. "Walter Scott and the Erl-King." Englische
Studien, 69, no. 1, 106-108.
The first appearance in print of "The Erl-King," Scott's
translation from Goethe, was in The Kelso Mail on 1 March,
1798. The poem was signed "Alonzo." Summarizes the four
appearances in print of the poem and includes the text of
the first.

23 ST. VIGEANS, LORD. "Address to the Thirty-fourth Annual Dinner
of the Edinburgh Sir Walter Scott Club." Edinburgh Sir
Walter Scott Club Annual Report, pp. 21-38.
Scott followed the traditional connection between the
Bar and literature in eighteenth century Scotland. His
training as a lawyer deeply influenced him, both in provid-
ing concrete characters and incidents and in acquainting
him with "abstruse doctrines and quaint phraseology."

24 THOMAS, W. "Walter Scott et la littérature allemande."
Mélanges Henry Lichtenberger. Hommage de ses élèves et de
ses amis, Juin 1934. Paris: Librairie Stock, pp. 205-13.
Scott was interested in German literature from the beginning of his writing career. Although his early translations were quickly forgotten, the influence of Bürger's
"Lenore" and Goethe's Götz remain in the Minstrelsy and
Marmion. Scott's reading in German literature left traces
in the novels, especially The Antiquary, Ivanhoe and The

Talisman. Although Scott read German literature enthusias-
tically, he sometimes criticized its overly subtle meta-
physics and prolix descriptions.

25 WALTERS, H. "Similarities of Ideas Between Scott and Dickens."
Dickensian, 30 (Spring), 144-46.
    Although he does not include any Scott characters in his
recollection of childhood reading, Dickens does mention
several Scott novels in a diary entry, and it may be assumed
that he read some if not all of Scott's works. The similarity of incidents and ideas from Pickwick Papers, David Copperfield, A Tale of Two Cities, and Barnaby Rudge to those
in various Scott novels cannot be attributed to mere coincidence.

26 WEST, S. GEORGE. "'Cumnor Hall': The Analogue of Scott's
Kenilworth." Modern Language Review, 29, no. 3 (July),
274-81.
    In Kenilworth Scott unhesitatingly ascribed the author-
ship of the ballad "Cumnor Hall" to William Julius Mickle,
even though Mickle never claimed to have written the poem,
and there is no external evidence to substantiate his authorship. However, internal evidence and the aesthetic
judgment of Southey suggest that Mickle did write the poem
as well as sixteen others in Thomas Evans' collection Old
Ballads With Some of Modern Date (1777).

27 WHITING, B. J. "Scott and Wyntoun." Philological Quarterly,
13, no. 3 (July), 296.
    Scott owes two lines from The Lady of the Lake to
Andrew of Wyntoun's Oryginale Cronykil of Scotland, which
appears in the catalogue of his library and which he mentions in the "Preface" to The Fair Maid of Perth.

28 WILSON, W. E. "George Grant." Times Literary Supplement
(9 August), p. 553.
    Scott's method of note-taking on sticks was recounted by
George Grant in his Life of Scott. Author queries who is
George Grant. In author's copy, dated 1849, Grant sounds
familiar with Edinburgh society. See 1934.B21, B29.

29 _____. "Scott and Literary Notches." Times Literary Supplement (26 July), p. 528.
    The memoranda of Scott's assistant Joseph Shortreed con-
firms Scott's method of taking notes on ballads by making
notches in sticks. See 1934.B21, B28.

1935

1935 A BOOKS

1   GENÉVRIER, P. Walter Scott, historien francais, ou le roman tourangeau de Quentin Durward. Tours: Chez Arrault & Cie., 142pp.
        Scott engaged in extensive research for the setting, events and characters of Quentin Durward. He did not hesitate to rearrange chronology for artistic effect. His anachronistic use of setting and architecture typifies the book's major flaw, the disjunction between the novel as historical narrative and the novel as feudal and supernatural spectacle. However, in spite of its inaccuracies, the novel is redeemed by its evocative quality and the spirited joyousness of Scott's style.

2   GRAY, ELIZABETH JANET. Young Walter Scott. New York: Viking Press, 249pp.
        A fictionalized biography of Scott's childhood and youth, which includes no literary criticism or documentation, except a note which relates certain people mentioned in the book to characters in the novels.

3   GRIERSON, HERBERT JOHN CLIFFORD, assisted by DAVIDSON COOK, W. M. PARKER, and others. The Letters of Sir Walter Scott, 1823-1825. Volume VIII. London: Constable, 512pp.
        Includes letters from 16 May, 1823 to 4 February, 1825. See also 1932.A14-A16; 1933.A4, A5; 1934.A2, A3; 1935.A4; 1936.A2, A3; 1937.A1.

4   _____. The Letters of Sir Walter Scott, 1825-1826. Volume IX. London: Constable, 510pp.
        Includes letters from 14 February, 1825 to 15 April, 1826. See also 1932.A14-A16; 1933.A4, A5; 1934.A2, A3; 1935.A3; 1936.A2, A3; 1937.A1.

*5   LOWE, KENNETH GORDON. The Modern Athens--Sir Walter Scott's Satire on Edina--or, the Lurid Story of the Forgeries of Two Works of the 'Great Unknown,' etc. Dundee, Scotland: Paul and Matthew.
        Cited in the British Museum General Catalogue of Printed Books (1964), v. 217, column 683.

*6   SCHUMACHER, DOUGLAS FREDERICK. "Der Volksaberglaube in den Waverley Novels." Ph.D. dissertation, Göttingen University, 1935.
        Cited in "The Romantic Movement: A Current Selective and Critical Bibliography for 1936," ELH, 4, no. 1 (March, 1937), 18.

*7   STENZAL, ELSA. "Religiöse Charaktertypen der englischen und
       schottischen Kirchengeschichte in den Romanen Walter
       Scotts." Ph.D. dissertation, Breslau University, 1935.
          Cited in "The Romantic Movement: A Current Selective
       and Critical Bibliography for 1936," ELH, 4, no. 1 (March,
       1937), 18.

1935 B SHORTER WRITINGS

1   ANON. "Memorabilia." Notes and Queries, 168 (2 March), 145.
          Goodspeed's Catalogue of Original Autographs, no. 237,
       lists Scott's letter to Ballantyne in which Scott refused
       to restore Oliver Proudfute to life and called the resur-
       rection of Athelstane "a botch." They also have a quatrain
       on Elizabeth, that Scott declared "the worst he ever heard."

2   BAKER, ERNEST A. "Sir Walter Scott," in his The History of
       the English Novel. Volume 6. London: H. F. & G. Witherby,
       122-26.
          Scott realized that the historical novel must also be a
       novel of manners. Although he took over the trite plots
       and heroes of the sentimental novel, his outcasts, fools,
       and beggars show his instinctive understanding of human na-
       ture. Despite his romantic predilections, Scott was a re-
       alist in his picture of society. He was "that anomaly, a
       romancer with a sense of humour."

3   BENSLY, EDWARD. "Queries from Scott's Woodstock." Notes and
       Queries, 169 (19 October), 281.
          "Hog in armour" was a London sign; it is a simile for a
       person accoutred very cumbrously. See 1935.B15.

4   BOATRIGHT, MODY C. "Scott's Theory and Practice Concerning
       the Use of the Supernatural in Prose Fiction in Relation
       to the Chronology of the Waverley Novels." Publications of
       the Modern Language Association, 50, no. 1 (March), 235-61.
          Scott's treatment of the supernatural suggests that The
       Black Dwarf, Guy Mannering, Redgauntlet, and The Monastery
       were written prior to Waverley. Novels closest to Gothic
       traditions or novels in which Scott violates his own rules
       are early compositions which he later revised.

5   CARSWELL, DONALD. "Portrait of Sir Walter." New Statesman
       and Nation, 9 (11 May), 674.
          Relates an unflattering verbal description of Scott,
       given to the German travel writer Johann Georg Kohl, on the
       occasion of his being unable to visit Abbotsford during a
       tour of Scotland in 1842.

1935

*6   CHAVES, CASTELO BRANCO. "Walter Scott: Algumas Notas sobre
       a Introdução de sua Obra em Portugal." Historia, Series A,
       Vol. 2, fascicle 1, 14-26.
          Cited in Corson (1943.A1), #2412.

7   ELWERT, W. THEODOR. "Scott und Guerrazzi," in his Geschicht-
       sauffassung und Erzählungstechnik in den historischen Ro-
       manen F. D. Guerrazzis. Beihefte zur Zeitschrift für Ro-
       manische Philologie, Heft 84. Halle/Salle: Max Niemeyer
       Verlag, pp. 65-78.
          Scott's novels resemble genre pictures; he selects an
       historical epoch and portrays details of daily life. Like
       Hegel he believed that the total cultural expressions of
       man constitute the material of history and that individual
       figures act as the unconscious expression of the spirit of
       an age. On the other hand Guerrazzi does not treat history
       as development and includes almost no descriptions of
       clothes, houses, and manners. What description he does use
       derives from Scott but tends to be parodic and thus unsuc-
       cessful.

8   LINLITHGOW, MARQUESS OF. "Address to the Thirty-fifth Annual
       Dinner of the Edinburgh Sir Walter Scott Club." The Edin-
       burgh Sir Walter Scott Club Annual Report, pp. 20-33.
          Scott's novels taught readers to see and understand Scot-
       land. They healed Scotland's wounded spirit and restored
       her pride. The novels gave vent to his storytelling impulse
       that could not be fully realized in verse. Their charm de-
       rives from their speed and freedom from self-consciousness.

9   M[ABBOT], T. O. "Queries from Scott's Redgauntlet." Notes
       and Queries, 168 (25 May), 375.
          Provides an allusion to Katterfelto from Henry Kirke
       White's The Wonderful Juggler. Reply to 1935.B14.

10   MACBETH, GILBERT. "The Life of Scott," in his John Gibson
       Lockhart: A Critical Study. Illinois Studies in Language
       and Literature, Volume 17, nos. 3-4. Urbana: University
       of Illinois Press, 197-205.
          Lockhart sought to tell the whole truth about Scott and
       to create an accurate portrait of his subject. He empha-
       sizes Scott's admirable qualities but does not overlook his
       failures, especially those flaws of character which led to
       his connection with the Ballantynes. The work as a whole
       exhibits acute observation, sound judgment, and perceptive
       literary criticism; it is Lockhart's most enduring achieve-
       ment.

11 OSGOOD, CHARLES GROSVENOR. "Scott (1771-1832)," in his The
    Voice of England. New York and London: Harper & Brothers,
    pp. 419-26.
        Scott presents a "robust and happy figure" among the
    maladjusted Romantics. The metrical romances matured his
    narrative powers, and the interpolated songs proved his
    eminence as a poet. Although the Waverley Novels contain
    melodrama, superficial heroes and worn plots, they are re-
    deemed by the realism of the Scottish characters and the
    vigor of Scott's imagination.

12 PARKER, WILLIAM MATHIE. "Sir Walter Scott and John Struthers,
    a Glasgow Shoemaker-Poet." Scots Magazine, N.S. 22, no. 6
    (March), 445-50.
        At the urging of Joanna Baillie, Scott facilitated the
    publication by Constable of Struthers' poem "The Poor Man's
    Sabbath." In 1819 Scott contributed to a three volume col-
    lection edited by Struthers called The Harp of Caledonia.
    Scott was always eager to advance the careers of struggling
    writers in whom he perceived literary merit.

13 _____. "William Motherwell: His Correspondence with Sir
    Walter Scott." Scots Magazine, N.S. 24, no. 2 (November),
    144-50.
        A review of Motherwell's life and career, with excerpts
    from his correspondence with Scott (1825-1830), mainly con-
    cerning ballads and Queen Bleareye's Cross.

14 PHILLIPS, LAWRENCE. "Queries from Scott's Redgauntlet."
    Notes and Queries, 168 (13 April), 263.
        Requests clarification of several names, sayings, and
    allusions. See 1935.B9, B22, B24.

15 _____. "Queries from Scott's Woodstock." Notes and Queries,
    169 (5 October), 243.
        Eight queries on word usage and sayings taken mostly
    from the dialogue. See 1935.B3, B23.

16 RANDALL, DAVID A. "Waverley in America." Colophon, N.S. 1,
    no. 1 (Summer), 39-55.
        Scott's novels were "America's first sensational best-
    sellers." Matthew Carey, a Philadelphia printer, unscru-
    pulously secured uncorrected advance sheets of Scott's
    novels from Ballantyne's shop to get them into print ahead
    of his American competitors. Compares errors in the Ameri-
    can editions to cancellations in the original British edi-
    tions of The Pirate, Peveril of the Peak, The Fortunes of
    Nigel, Redgauntlet, Tales of the Crusaders, Woodstock,
    Chronicles of the Canongate, and Tales of My Landlord.

1935

17 RATTIGAN, CLIVE. "The Bayard of Letters." <u>Saturday Review</u>
    (England), 159 (16 February), 208.
        Although Scott's literary genius was subject to certain
    limitations, he earned his greatness as a man in the
    struggle against adversity. He excelled as friend and
    patriot, and after the bankruptcy battled for his honor
    and left his name unstained.

18 R[ENDALL], V[ERNON]. "<u>Quentin Durward</u>: The Astrologer's Ex-
    pedient." <u>Notes and Queries</u>, 169 (14 September), 188.
        Galeotti gains a reprieve from death by predicting he
    will die twenty-four hours before the King. Scott says he
    got this idea from the story of Tiberius in <u>Taciti Annall</u>,
    lib. VI, cap. 22; but he actually confused this story with
    the anecdote which follows it.

19 _____. "Walter Scott and the Southern States of America."
    <u>Notes and Queries</u>, 169 (9 November), 328.
        Defends Scott against Twain's accusations that his novels
    corrupted the South with silly ideas about chivalry.

20 SAUNDERS, W. "Moscheles in Scotland. His Meeting with Sir
    Walter Scott." <u>Scots Magazine</u>, N.S. 23, no. 3 (June),
    199-204.
        Ignaz Moscheles, the Czech pianist and composer, per-
    formed in Edinburgh in 1828, where he was kindly received
    by Scott at Shandwick Place. Scott was impressed with
    Moscheles' music and with the beauty of his wife. Re-
    printed: 1937.B29.

21 SIMMONS, ERNEST J. "Walter Scott and the Russian Romantic
    Movement," in his <u>English Literature and Culture in Russia,</u>
    <u>1553-1840</u>. Harvard Studies in Comparative Literature,
    Volume 12. Cambridge, Massachusetts: Harvard University
    Press, 237-68.
        Although Scott's popularity in Russia was initially
    overshadowed by Byron, his popularity reached its height
    between 1820-1830 and inspired many studies of the Waverley
    Novels. Scott's example persuaded Russian writers to use
    their own national past as subject matter, and he directly
    influenced Zagoskin, Pushkin, and Gogol.

22 STRACHAM, L. R. M. and E. BENSLY. "Queries from Scott's <u>Red-</u>
    <u>gauntlet</u>." <u>Notes and Queries</u>, 168 (27 April), 301-302.
        Katterfelto was a conjuror and empiric. Dolly MacIzzard
    may have been armor-plated "back and breast." "Muisted"
    means powdered, and "seventeen hunder linen" is woven with
    1700 threads in the warp. <u>See</u> 1935.B14.

23 SYERS, EDGAR. "Queries from Scott's Woodstock." Notes and
      Queries, 169 (2 November), 320.
        Clarifies allusion to "cloves" in Woodstock; pomander
      balls were made by inserting cloves closely into the skin
      of an orange. Reply to 1935.B15.

24 TEASDEL, R. H. "Queries from Scott's Redgauntlet." Notes and
      Queries, 168 (11 May), 341.
        Prints one of Gustavus Katterfelto's advertisements from
      the Norwich Mercury alluded to in Redgauntlet. See
      1935.B14.

25 WILLIAMS, A. M. "The Inns of Scott." Chambers' Journal, 8th
      ser. 4 (July), 536-38.
        Although Scottish inns until the late eighteenth century
      offered miserable accommodation, Scott describes inns with
      careful and often affectionate detail in several novels.
      Author's favorite is "the bonny Black Boar" in Kenilworth.

1936 A BOOKS

1 BURR, ALLSTON. Sir Walter Scott: An Index Placing the Short
      Poems in His Novels and in His Long Poems and Dramas. Cam-
      bridge, Massachusetts: Harvard University Press, 136pp.
        The Index is divided into five parts: I. by titles;
      II. by novels--the poems are cited by volume and chapter;
      III. by long poems--the short poems are cited by canto and
      stanza number; IV. by dramas--the poems are cited by act
      and scene numbers; V. index of first lines.

2 GRIERSON, HERBERT JOHN CLIFFORD, assisted by DAVIDSON COOK,
      W. M. PARKER, and others. The Letters of Sir Walter Scott,
      1826-1828. Volume X. London: Constable, 512pp.
        Includes letters from 17 April, 1826 to 4 October, 1828.
      See also 1932.A14-A16; 1933.A4, A5; 1934.A2, A3; 1935.A3,
      A4; 1936.A3; 1937.A1.

3 _____. The Letters of Sir Walter Scott, 1828-1831. Volume XI.
      London: Constable, 496pp.
        Includes letters from 5 October, 1828 to 29 March, 1831.
      See also 1932.A14-A16; 1933.A4, A5; 1934.A2, A3; 1935.A3,
      A4; 1936.A2; 1937.A1.

4 HILLHOUSE, JAMES T. The Waverley Novels and Their Critics.
      Minneapolis: University of Minnesota Press, 360pp.
        Surveys the critical reception of the novels from 1814.
      Despite Scott's enormous popularity in his own time, his

contemporaries were well aware of his defects. Until almost
1900, he was regarded widely as the greatest English novelist. One of the most striking features of Scott criticism
is continual comparison with Shakespeare. The Waverley
Novels have come to be regarded as old-fashioned because of
changes in morality, the development of realism and natural-
ism, the psychological orientation of later fiction, and
experiments in novelistic technique.

*5 MÖLLER, JULIUS. "Die Romantische Landschaft bei Walter Scott."
Ph.D. dissertation, Münster University, 1936.
    Cited in "The Romantic Movement: A Current Selective
and Critical Bibliography for 1937," ELH, 5, no. 1 (March,
1938), 20.

6 MUIR, EDWIN. Scott and Scotland: The Predicament of the
Scottish Writer. London: Routledge & Kegan Paul, 192pp.
    Scottish writers tend to use Scots as the language of
feeling and English as the language of thought. This split
corresponds to the division between emotion and intellect in
Scott's own life and is largely responsible for the disunity
in many of the Waverley Novels. His clumsiness in dealing
with emotion resulted partly from his disastrous love for
Williamina Stuart-Belsches and partly from "the fact that
he lived in an imperfectly integrated society where many
aspects of life were ignored, and sensibility was an im-
ported product."

*7 STEGER, ANNA. "John Banim, ein Nachahmer Walter Scotts (auf
Grund der wichtigsten 'O'Hara Tales')." Ph.D. dissertation,
Erlangen University, 1936.
    Cited in "The Romantic Movement: A Current Selective and
Critical Bibliography for 1936," ELH, 4, no. 1 (March,
1937), 18.

*8 STEVENSON, E. ELIZABETH D. "Sir Walter Scott, a Bibliography
of the Contemporary Editions of the Chief Poems." Dissertation, University of London School of Librarianship and
Archives, 1936.
    Cited in T. H. Howard Hill, Bibliography of British
Literary Bibliographies (Oxford: Clarendon Press, 1969),
item no. 211, p. 15.

9 TAIT, JOHN GUTHRIE. The Missing Tenth of Sir Walter Scott's
Journal. Edinburgh: Oliver and Boyd; London: Gurney and
Jackson, 19pp.
    A comparison of the photostat of the original MS of
Scott's Journal with the 1890 text edited by David Douglas

shows the printed text to be inaccurate. There are numerous
transcription errors; and words, sentences, and whole passages have been omitted. Scott's language has been arbitrarily altered, usually for the worse. Approximately
one-tenth of the original Journal has disappeared in this
edition. Includes examples of each kind of error. This
pamphlet was incorporated into an expanded version. See
1938.A3.

1936 B SHORTER WRITINGS

1   ANDERSON, JAMES R. "Incident in Sir Walter Scott's Journal."
    Notes and Queries, 170 (6 June), 411.
        The suicide victim was Col. Huxley, as identified in a
    letter to Scott's son Charles, 30 November, 1826. See
    1936.B6.

2   ARMSTRONG, T. PERCY. "Queries from Scott's Anne of Geier-
    stein." Notes and Queries, 171 (12 September), 193.
        Scott's insufficient knowledge of history led him to con-
    fuse Boniface III with Boniface IX. In the thirteenth cen-
    tury the Church did cause executions by ordering civil
    authorities to carry them out under pain of excommunication.
    See 1936.B20.

3   BUCHAN, JOHN. "Sir Walter Scott." Proceedings and Transac-
    tions of the Royal Society of Canada. Appendix A, 30,
    xlvii-lviii.
        Scott united the artist and man of action. He enjoyed
    life and was known for his kindness, modesty and courage,
    which made his Journal "one of the most wonderful books in
    the world." His personality was "too normal" and his
    philosophy of life too conventional to give his writing
    very much subtlety. The strength of his work lies in its
    narrative power, its "complete sanity," and its revelation
    of the sublime in ordinary life.

4   BUCK, GERHARD. "In Fortsetzung Bagehots: Waverley-Romane Sir
    Walter Scotts." Britannica: Seminar für englische Sprache
    und Kultur an der Hansischen Universität, 13, 221-45.
        Of Scott's critics, Bagehot has most deeply understood
    the spirit of the Waverley Novels, which lie midway between
    the older novel of universal concerns and the newer novel
    of romantic love. In the world of the Waverley Novels,
    people are bound by social laws which have evolved naturally
    over a long time. Scott's weaknesses include his tendency
    to isolate opposite emotions and over-emphasize cheerfulness.

He substitutes folklore and superstition for the real arousal of horror.

5   COOK, DAVIDSON. "Scott's 1814 Diary." Times Literary Supplement (22 August), p. 680.
      If a new edition of the Journal is forthcoming, it should perhaps include an amended edition of Scott's Diary on Tour to Nova Zembla, which also suffered greatly from Lockhart's editing.

6   CUNLIFFE, WALTER R. "Incident in Sir Walter Scott's Journal." Notes and Queries, 170 (23 May), 372.
      Query concerns the identity of the unnamed person whom Scott says committed suicide in the 28 November, 1825 Journal entry. See 1936.B1.

7   ESDAILE, ARUNDELL. "The National Library of Scotland: The Heart of Midlothian." Library Association Record, 38 (January), 28-30.
      An announcement that the MS of The Heart of Midlothian has been given to the National Library of Scotland by Miss J. G. Topham. Reprints a note from The Times of 17 December, 1935 tracing the history of the MS since it was sold by auction in 1831.

8   GASELEE, STEPHEN. "Queries from Scott's Fair Maid of Perth." Notes and Queries, 171 (19 September), 209.
      Responds to queries about ordeal by battle by quoting Wright's Anglo-Latin Satirical Poets of the Twelfth Century on Hugo Sotovagina and his opinion as a representative of the church.

9   GOWFER. "Walter Scott: Obscure Golf Reference." Notes and Queries, 171 (11 July), 28.
      A description of a golf game in the "Prefatory" chapter to The Surgeon's Daughter indicates that Scott's firsthand knowledge of golf was questionable.

10   GRIERSON, HERBERT JOHN CLIFFORD. "The Problem of the Scottish Poet." Essays and Studies, 21, 105-23.
      Scott revised in his own poetry some of the traditions of Scottish courtly poetry and medieval ballads. He translated these older traditions into contemporary language. Both Burns and Scott rescued the Scots language from its reputation as vulgar; however, neither writer hoped to reestablish it as a language for serious literature or scholarship.

11   . "Scott's Journal." <u>Times Literary Supplement</u>
    (8 August), p. 648.
        Reinforces Tait's recent request for a new and more com-
plete edition of Scott's <u>Journal</u>. Includes samples of
previously omitted passages.

12 HAMMERTON, JOHN. "Burns and Scott in the Hearts of Their
    Countrymen: A Comparison." <u>The S. M. T. Magazine</u>, 16,
    no. 1 (January), 69-71.
        Scott was a good man who was born to comfort and distinc-
tion and earned vast wealth. Unlike Burns he was remote
from the average man. On the contrary, Burns is loved for
his faults, frankness, and closeness to ourselves. He was
a social failure who could not hold onto money. Where
Scott receives admiration, Burns receives sympathy.

13 HEDLEY, A. "Was Sir Walter Scott Musical?" <u>Music and Letters</u>,
    17, no. 2 (April), 151-53.
        Scott knew little of music and could play no instrument.
Despite childhood singing lessons, he could distinguish
melodies only by associating them with words. However, he
appreciated "feeling and expression" in a musician and enjoyed his daughters' music as well as the singing of Thomas
Moore and David MacCulloch.

14 KÜHNE, W. "Alexander Bronikowski und Walter Scott: Ein
    Beitrag zur Geschichte der Romantike." <u>Zeitschrift für
    slavische Philologie</u>, 13, 283-315.
        Although he was influenced by Scott, Bronikowski tried
to create historical fiction which would not be regarded as
a direct imitation. Unlike Scott, he does not use chapter
divisions or prolonged character introductions. He displays
a greater sympathy toward the supernatural than the more
skeptical Scott. As Scott's creative genius is linked to
clan history and Scottish antiquity, so Bronikowski's is
linked to the Polish Szlachta (gentry).

15 MACMILLAN, LORD. "Address to the Thirty-sixth Annual Dinner
    of the Edinburgh Sir Walter Scott Club." <u>The Edinburgh Sir
    Walter Scott Club Annual Report</u>, pp. 20-27.
        Scott owed much to his training in Scots law; his novels
are full of its language, institutions and famous cases.
The centenary celebration at the Sorbonne proves that there
remains "a very living interest" in Scott among the French.
Scott was also highly esteemed in London and was a member
of "The Club" (founded by Johnson and Reynolds) and of the
Athenaeum.

1936

16 MOORE, JOHN ROBERT. "Poe, Scott, and 'The Murders in the Rue
    Morgue.'" <u>American Literature</u>, 8, no. 1 (March), 52-58.
        A defense of Poe's sanity on the grounds that many gro-
    tesque elements in his stories have identifiable literary
    sources. The orang-outang Sylvan in <u>Count Robert of Paris</u>
    bears many resemblances to the one in "The Murders in the
    Rue Morgue" and gave Poe the idea for a mysterious murder
    apparently committed without human agency. <u>See</u> 1938.B22.

17 MUIR, EDWIN. "Walter Scott," in <u>The English Novelists</u>.
    Edited by Derek Verschoyle. London: Chatto and Windus,
    pp. 113-22.
        Despite his prestige in his own time, Scott has exerted
    only a "trivial" influence on the development of the novel.
    He substituted mere clichés for social criticism, and when
    we read him we must give up thinking. The hollowness of
    Scott's imaginary world reflects the "particularly dead
    period of Scottish history in which he lived." His "poetic
    power" is his strong point. It manifests itself in "sudden
    bursts of natural music" from his characters, especially
    those who speak in Lowland Scots.

18 ONSLOW, LORD, E. BENSLY and P. GRIFFITHS. "Queries from
    Scott's <u>Waverley</u>." <u>Notes and Queries</u>, 171 (3 October),
    245-46.
        Tells of an incident in 1727 when the author's ancestor
    demonstrated the same kind of emotion as Waverley throwing
    himself into Fergus MacIvor's arms. Soldiers did indeed
    act that way two hundred years ago.

19 PATTERSON, RICHARD F. "Two Emendations." <u>Times Literary
    Supplement</u> (29 August), p. 700.
        In <u>Ivanhoe</u>, chapter nineteen, Scott probably wrote "I
    can draw a bow as well or better than a crow-keeper" rather
    than "cow-keeper" as it has been printed. The allusion is
    to <u>King Lear</u> (IV, vi, 89).

20 PHILLIPS, LAWRENCE. "Queries from Scott's <u>Anne of Geierstein</u>."
    <u>Notes and Queries</u>, 171, 135-36.
        Queries concern "old Beattie," "belted Knight," "the
    scene of Roman charity," and the "Black priest of St.
    Paul's," all alluded to in <u>Anne of Geierstein</u>. <u>See</u>
    1936.B2.

21 STRESAU, HERMANN. "Der Historische Roman." <u>Neue Rundschau</u>,
    47, 433-48.
        Unlike the epic, the historical novel must present the
    past as plausible and realistic. To avoid the limitation
    of historical facts, Scott concentrated on little people

and on how they are affected by the great figures and
forces in the background. The writers after Scott were
less successful in this strategy, perhaps because they tend
to regard all history as a series of transitions to the
present. Scott also avoided flights into epic untruthful-
ness through his strong bonds to landscape and nation.

22   STROUT, ALAN L. "James Hogg's Familiar Anecdotes of Sir
      Walter Scott." Studies in Philology, 33, 456-74.
          When Lockhart refused to write a biography of Scott under
      Hogg's name, Hogg wrote his own anecdotal biography, which
      Lockhart regarded as a collection of lies. It was first
      published in America in 1834 as Familiar Anecdotes of Sir
      Walter Scott. Since this edition contains few objectionable
      passages, it must have been considerably revised from the
      original version Hogg submitted to the London publisher
      Cochrane. The American publisher bowdlerized Hogg's MS in
      the name of moral purity.

23   WALKER, JAMES F. "Sir Walter Scott as a Popularizer of
      History." Aberdeen University Review, 23, 212-25.
          Scott "allowed himself a rather wide latitude" in the
      historical accuracy of his novels. He preferred contempor-
      ary chroniclers rather than later historians for his
      sources. His greatness as an historical novelist lies not
      in his use of facts but in his recreation of the life and
      ambience of past periods. He was the first to convey
      imaginatively the idea that manners and institutions change
      from generation to generation.

1937 A BOOKS

1   GRIERSON, HERBERT JOHN CLIFFORD, assisted by DAVIDSON COOK,
      W. M. PARKER, and others. The Letters of Sir Walter Scott,
      1831-1832. Volume XII. London: Constable, 520pp.
          Includes letters from 31 March, 1831 to 3 June, 1832
      (misdated by Scott as "3d of May 1834"). Volume XII also
      includes letters to his wife "discovered in 1935 in a se-
      cret drawer in the desk in the study at Abbotsford"; letters
      to George Ellis (1801-1813) taken from the originals rather
      than from Lockhart; letters on literary subjects to Richard
      Heber, Bishop Percy, C. R. Maturin and Mrs. Maturin; mis-
      cellaneous letters 1797-1831; and a complete list of cor-
      respondents with index of letters to them. See also
      1932.A14-A16; 1933.A4, A5; 1934.A2, A3; 1935.A3, A4;
      1936.A2.

1937

2   RATCHFORD, FANNIE E. and WILLIAM H. McCARTHY, JR., eds. The
    Correspondence of Sir Walter Scott and Charles Robert
    Maturin, with a Few Other Allied Letters. Austin: Univer-
    sity of Texas Press, 140pp.
        A series of 73 letters from 18 December, 1812 to 9 April,
    1830; the letters from Scott to Maturin were not included
    in Grierson's Centenary Edition. Although they never met,
    Scott acted as a generous literary patron to Maturin, pro-
    viding him with advice, encouragement and even financial
    assistance. The letters reveal Scott's tact, generosity,
    and "genius for friendship."

1937 B SHORTER WRITINGS

1   A., G. E. P. "Queries from Scott's Antiquary." Notes and
    Queries, 172 (27 February), 158.
        Dr. Orkborne is a character in Mme. d'Arblay's Camilla,
    which is no longer frequently read. See 1937.B24.

2   B., E. and D. COOK. "Walter Scott Detected." Times Literary
    Supplement (7 August), p. 580.
        In the Champion of 14 July, 1814 John Scott gave Walter
    Scott's name as the author of Waverley. See 1937.B4, B8.

3   B., R. S. "A Scott Letter: Meaning of 'Assessed.'" Notes
    and Queries, 173 (11 September), 194.
        "Assessed" meant that the servant did not qualify for an
    exemption and therefore was required to have a game certifi-
    cate. See 1937.B13.

4   COOK, DAVIDSON. "The Waverleys in French: Scott's Authorship
    Revealed in 1822." Times Literary Supplement (17 July),
    p. 532.
        Some of Defauconpret's translations have Scott's name on
    the title pages as early as 1822. Scott wrote to Defaucon-
    pret in 1821 denying authorship of the Waverley Novels. See
    1937.B2, B8.

5   CURLE, JAMES. "Address to the Thirty-seventh Annual Dinner of
    the Edinburgh Sir Walter Scott Club." Edinburgh Sir Walter
    Scott Club Annual Report, pp. 24-47.
        Scott was particularly impressed by his youthful reading
    in Shakespeare, Cervantes, and Ariosto. His daily contacts
    with people in Edinburgh and the country provided other
    sources for his novels. He gave the novel a wider scope
    and sphere of action than it had formerly possessed. His
    characters came from every class, and the life he portrayed
    was "clean and wholesome."

6   CUTHBERTSON, STUART. "Scott's Influence on José Marmol's El
    Cruzado." Hispania, 20, no. 3 (October), 243-49.
        Scott's Talisman influenced the drama El Cruzado (1842)
    by the Argentine José Marmol. Both works deal with the
    crusades. Marmol used Scott for information on Moslem
    habits and beliefs and for some details of characterization.
    Quotes a series of parallel passages.

7   DRUETT, W. W. "Scott at Bentley Priory." Notes and Queries,
    173 (4 December), 406.
        Queries the basis for the belief that Scott corrected the
    proofs of Marmion at Bentley Priory, Middlesex, while visit-
    ing Lord Abercorn in 1806.

8   EVANS, F. D. "Letter to the Editor." Times Literary Supple-
    ment (24 July), p. 548.
        In January, 1820 John Scott, editor of The London Maga-
    zine, voiced his belief that Walter Scott was the editor of
    the Waverley Novels. See 1937.B2, B4.

9   GRIERSON, HERBERT JOHN CLIFFORD. "The Story of Scott's Early
    Love." Blackwood's Magazine, 241 (February), 168-79.
        Scott's love for Williamina Belsches "left an indelible
    mark" on his life. He believed she had failed him, and his
    feelings for his wife never attained the same intensity.
    After marriage Scott became absorbed in literature and "that
    pursuit of profit and outlay" which ended in disaster. He
    could not share his deepest feelings with his family, and
    Lady Scott's interest in "style" did not help to develop
    the spiritual part of his life. She never shared his in-
    terests as Williamina might have done.

10 HARPER, GEORGE McLEAN. "Glorious Sir Walter," in his Literary
    Appreciations. Indianapolis: Bobbs Merrill, pp. 89-102.
        Reprint of 1932.B85.

11 HIBERNICUS. "Scott and Homer." Notes and Queries, 173
    (4 September), 171.
        Allusions in many of the Waverley Novels attest to
    Scott's familiarity with the Odyssey in Pope's version.

12 INSH, G. PRATT. "The Scottish Regalia." The S. M. T. Magazine
    and Scottish Country Life, 18, no. 6 (June), 44-47.
        Scott was "the foremost mover" in obtaining the warrant
    from the Prince Regent which resulted in the discovery of
    the Scottish crown, sceptre, and sword of state in Edinburgh
    Castle in 1818. Scott theorized that the foundation of the
    crown is formed from the crown of Robert Bruce.

1937

13   K., H. G. L. "A Scott Letter: Meaning of 'Assessed.'" <u>Notes</u>
     <u>and Queries</u>, 173 (28 August), 153.
         Questions the meaning of "assessed servant" which Scott
     uses in a letter of 11 August, 1827 to Andrew Lang request-
     ing game certificates. <u>See</u> 1937.B3.

14   KORN, MAX. "Sir Walter Scott und die Geschichte." <u>Anglia</u>,
     61, 416-41.
         Scott's consciousness of history provides the basis for
     his creativity. This sensitivity resulted in both his emo-
     tional participation in the past and his conservatism.
     Scott saw Napoleon's genius undermined by ambition and an
     element of the demonic. The <u>Life of Napoleon</u> reflects
     Scott's distaste for the consequences of the French Revolu-
     tion.

15   LANDIS, PAUL N. "The Waverley Novels, or a Hundred Years
     After." <u>Publications of the Modern Language Association</u>,
     52 (June), 461-73.
         The Waverley Novels have declined in popularity partly
     due to a loss of novelty but primarily due to a change in
     sensibility. Scott as "humanist" illustrated human nature
     manifested in individuals; the century since his death has
     been "humanitarian," more concerned with humanity as an
     abstraction.

16   MacGREGOR, GEDDES. "A Haunt of Scott and Stevenson." <u>Scots</u>
     <u>Magazine</u>, N.S. 28, no. 4 (July), 300-305.
         A history of the Speculative Society of Edinburgh,
     founded in 1764. Scott was admitted in 1790 and read es-
     says "On the Origin of the Feudal System," "On the Authen-
     ticity of Ossian's Poems," and "On the Origin of the Scan-
     dinavian Mythology." Scott began his friendship with
     Jeffrey in the "Spec." Lockhart was admitted in 1815 and
     caricatured the society in <u>Peter's Letters to His Kinsfolk</u>.

17   MARMON, INA. "Vitalizing <u>The Lady of the Lake</u>." <u>English</u>
     <u>Journal</u>, regular edition, 26 (June), 480-82.
         The chief obstacle to the teenage student's comprehension
     of the narrative is the emphasis on description at the ex-
     pense of "the human-activity element." The student may be
     helped to see the dramatic episodes more clearly through
     oral interpretation or dramatization of the poem.

18   MUIR, EDWIN. "Walter Scott," in <u>From Anne to Victoria: Essays</u>
     <u>by Various Hands</u>. Edited by Bonamy Dobrée. New York:
     Scribners; London: Cassell, pp. 528-45.

Scott's life shows a "deep cleft" between the romantic
and the practical. The novels fail to unite the respectable
and fanciful sides of his character, and they are spoilt by
the split between the man of imagination and the man of
"prosaic respect for the establishment."

19 NORVAL. "Old Mortality: A Date in Scottish History." Notes
and Queries, 172 (12 June), 425.
    In Chapter II of Guy Mannering Scott wrote "1648" instead
of the correct date of 1650 for the loss of the estates of
the "resolutioner" Allan Bertram. Since the term refers to
an adherent of Charles II, and since Scott knew that Charles
I was executed in 1649, the mistake probably derived from
the enormous speed at which he wrote the novel. The error
escaped Scott's proofreader and remains in the text.

20 OWEN, WALTER. "Scott in Italian." Times Literary Supplement
(25 September), p. 700.
    There is an Italian edition of A Legend of Montrose pub-
lished in 1822 with Scott's name on the title page.

21 PARKER, WILLIAM MATHIE. "La Donna del Lago." Times Literary
Supplement (16 January), p. 48.
    Describes a recently discovered Italian translation of
The Lady of the Lake, translated by "P," whom author iden-
tifies by means of a letter to Scott, owned by Walpole, as
P. Pallavicini. See 1937.B31.

22 _____. "Lockhart's Life of Scott: a Plea for Revision."
Times Literary Supplement (20 March), p. 210.
    Summarizes the creation and reception of Lockhart's Life
of Scott. The new concept of biography, which includes a
concern for literal accuracy, necessitates a revised and
enlarged edition. See 1938.B26.

23 _____. "Some of Scott's Aberdeen Correspondents." Notes and
Queries, 172 (20 February), 128-30.
    Prints parts of letters sent to Scott in 1831 from cor-
respondents in Aberdeenshire. Mrs. Jourdain wants Scott's
opinion of her poetry; John Murray wishes to send him a
rare book on the Gordon family; Mrs. Maria Isabella Reid
asks about her relationship to the Duke of Gordon.

24 PHILLIPS, LAWRENCE. "Queries from Scott's Antiquary." Notes
and Queries, 172 (13 February), 118-19; (20 February),
136-37; (27 February), 153-54; (6 March), 173.
    A series of queries concerning word usages and allusions
in The Antiquary. See 1937.B1, B26, B27, B33.

1937

25 PRAZ, MARIO. "Walter Scott," in his Studi e Svaghi Inglesi.
    Biblioteca Italiana, Volume 4. Florence: Sansoni,
    pp. 55-63.
        Scott's works are not so much novels as genre pictures
    of Scottish folk traditions, habits, dances, and costumes.
    They repeat the same character types, plots, and situations.
    His novels are like a Gothic castle in moonlight or a folk-
    lore museum, but they are spoilt by dryness.

26 R[ENDALL], V[ERNON] and E. BENSLY. "Queries from Scott's
    Antiquary." Notes and Queries, 172 (6 March), 175-76 and
    (13 March), 194.
        Provides meanings for several colloquial words and
    phrases and sources for the story of Margaret, Almanzor,
    and Johann C. Fischer. See 1937.B24.

27 R[ENDALL], V[ERNON], et al. "Queries from Scott's Antiquary."
    Notes and Queries, 172 (20 March), 211-12.
        Clarifies word usage and allusions for "glass breakers,"
    "Antigonus," "dressing wigs," "Kelso convoy," "remora,"
    "frank to the road," and "St. Wennoc." See 1937.B24.

28 RUFF, WILLIAM. A Bibliography of the Poetical Works of Sir
    Walter Scott, 1796-1832. Transactions of the Edinburgh
    Bibliographical Society, Sessions 1936-1937, 99-239.
        Supplies full descriptive and bibliographical data on
    original editions of the poems and subsequent editions pub-
    lished during Scott's lifetime. Includes facsimiles of se-
    lected title pages, cancels and proof-sheets.

29 SAUNDERS, W. "Moscheles in Scotland." Étude, the Music Maga-
    zine, 55 (June), 371-72.
        Reprint of 1935.B20.

30 VAN PATTEN, NATHAN. "A Newly Discovered Issue of Scott's The
    Vision of Don Roderick." Library, 4th ser. 18, no. 1
    (June), 109-13.
        Lists comparison between the ordinary first edition and
    the new variant. Changes in the text indicate that the
    variant is earlier than the ordinary first edition (July,
    1811), which is the correct text.

31 VINCENT, E. R. "La donna del Lago." Times Literary Supplement
    (23 January), p. 64.
        Pallavicini worked on a periodical, L'Italico, and pub-
    lished in it extracts of his translation in December, 1813
    and February, 1814. See 1937.B21.

32   WEIR, JOHN L. "Thoughts on the <u>Minstrelsy of the Scottish Border</u>." <u>Notes and Queries</u>, 173 (11 September), 183-87.
     Summarizes Scott's early interest in ballads and his methods of research and of editing. This early editorial work must be taken into account in any overall estimation of Scott.

33   WHITE, F. C. "Queries from Scott's <u>Antiquary</u>." <u>Notes and Queries</u>, 172 (29 May), 392.
     After drinking the health of "the King over the water," it was customary to break the glasses. <u>See</u> 1937.B24.

<u>1938 A BOOKS</u>

1   GRIERSON, HERBERT JOHN CLIFFORD. <u>Sir Walter Scott, Bart</u>.
    London: Constable; New York: Columbia University Press, 325pp.
    Attempts to correct the omissions and errors in Lockhart's <u>Life</u>, particularly in reference to Scott's financial affairs. The crash was due to Cadell's lack of capital as well as to "Scott's rash anticipation of funds." Grierson is more candid than Lockhart on several matters, including the limitations of Lady Scott, the decay of Scott's faculties during his last year, and his financial folly. Scott's novels affirm his high principles and sound judgment, but they do not transcend the prejudices and conventions of his age. His heroes and historical characters lack the "intensity and interest" they might have if his mind had been less divided between imagination and his real grasp of social problems. His most powerful characters are "governed by simple, elemental feelings" rather than by the complexities of thought.

*2   HARMAN, ROLAND. "Sir Walter Scott as Editor of John Dryden."
     Ph.D. dissertation, Yale University, 1938.
     Cited in <u>Comprehensive Dissertation Index</u> (Ann Arbor, Michigan: Xerox University Microfilms, 1973), XXX, 468.

3   TAIT, JOHN GUTHRIE. <u>Sir Walter Scott's Journal and Its Editor</u>.
    Edinburgh: Oliver and Boyd, 36pp.
    The 1890 edition of Scott's <u>Journal</u>, edited by David Douglas, was a flawed piece of work which violates both the tone and meaning of the original manuscript. Douglas, who was not trained as a scholar, altered hundreds of passages both intentionally and unintentionally. These errors should be corrected in a new edition. Incorporates earlier pamphlet on the subject and offers a preliminary list of <u>corrigenda</u>. <u>See</u> 1936.A9.

1938

1938 B SHORTER WRITINGS

1   ANON. "Sir Walter Scott and Christmas." <u>Border Magazine</u>, 43
      (January), 6-7.
           Scott antedated Dickens in writing of old English and
      Scottish Christmas customs. In the "Introduction" to Canto
      VI of <u>Marmion</u> he emphasizes the religious as well as the
      celebratory aspects of medieval Christmas observances in
      Scotland.

2   ARMSTRONG, T. PERCY. "The Greatest British General." <u>Notes</u>
      <u>and Queries</u>, 175 (30 July), 86.
           According to Scott, the "greatest British general" was
      the Duke of Wellington. Scott's opinion of Napoleon was
      very harsh as expressed in letters, but he tempered it when
      he wrote the <u>Life of Napoleon</u>. <u>See</u> 1938.B33.

3   BOGNER, HAROLD F. "Sir Walter Scott in New Orleans, 1818-32."
      <u>Louisiana Historical Quarterly</u>, 21, 420-517.
           The enormous vogue for dramatizations of Scott's works
      persisted in New Orleans through the Civil War. Scott's
      popularity on the stage derived mainly from the "melodrama-
      tic elements" of romantic struggle, pageantry, Gothic hor-
      ror, and comic bufoonery. Includes as appendices a Chrono-
      logical List of Plays for Seasons 1820 and 1826 and a
      Chronological Checklist of Scott Dramatizations Performed
      1833-1850.

4   DUNN, M. TRAIN. "A Bookcase and Its Contents: Mementoes of
      Scott, Burns and the Black Douglas." <u>Scots Magazine</u>, N.S.
      29, no. 4 (July), 255-62.
           The bookcase, which belongs to the author, is made from
      the wood of an antique bedstead, belonging to the Earl of
      Douglas, who was assassinated by James II in 1450. It was
      transformed into a bookcase by the antiquary Joseph Train,
      and now contains two letters from Scott to Train (26 May,
      1822 and 21 December, 1816) as well as several relics of
      their friendship.

5   DYER, FLORENCE E. "A Line in Scott." <u>Times Literary Supple-</u>
      <u>ment</u> (17 December), p. 802.
           The last line of the first stanza of the "Dies Irae" in
      <u>The Lay of the Last Minstrel</u> reads differently in Bishop
      Heber's "Hymns . . . for the Church Service," although
      Scott supposedly contributed his translation to this hymnal.

6   F., J. W. "Sir Walter Scott and Mrs. Fawcett." <u>Notes and</u>
      <u>Queries</u>, 175 (23 July), 62.

Queries the identity of Mrs. Fawcett and her literary brother, whom Scott mentions in a letter of 25 April, 1818. See 1938.B36.

7   FORSE, EDWARD J. G. "Queries from Scott's Rob Roy." Notes and Queries, 175 (10 December), 429.
    Tells a personal anecdote to illustrate the restricted meaning of "curate." See 1938.B31.

8   GILL, W. W. "Gaelic Spellings in Scott's Writings." Notes and Queries, 174 (2 April), 248-49.
    The spelling variations in certain Gaelic terms may be explained by the fact that Gaelic spelling is far from rigid; in some cases, such as "Mackrimmon," superfluous letters have been added by English writers before Scott. See 1938.B32.

9   GORDON, ROBERT K. "Shakespeare and Some Scenes in the Waverley Novels." Queens Quarterly, 45, 478-85.
    Scott's imagination often drew on appropriate scenes or analogues from Shakespeare. Frequently the similarity between a scene in a Waverley Novel and a scene in a Shakespeare play is conveyed through a single phrase. However, when Scott's imagination fails and he uses Shakespearean material to supplement his own invention, the implicit comparison is unfavorable to Scott.

10 HOWARTH, R. G. "Scott on Burns." Notes and Queries, 175 (15 October), 279.
    In his praise of Burns's "Ae fond kiss, and then we sever!" in the Quarterly Review of February, 1809, Scott consciously or unconsciously adapted a passage from Tristram Shandy.

11 J., W. H. "Dominie Sampson." Notes and Queries, 174 (5 March), 175-76.
    George Thompson, whose eccentricities kept him from securing a pulpit of his own despite Scott's efforts, was not the only prototype for Dominie Sampson. There was a Dominie Sanson, tutor in Scott's uncle's house, and Scott's discussion in the "Introduction" to Guy Mannering indicates he may have been thinking of a third tutor as part of the Dominie's character.

12 J., W. H. and G. SOUTAR. "Queries from Scott's Heart of Midlothian." Notes and Queries, 174 (5 March), 178.
    Identifies terms from the novel: "arriage, lock, outsight, insight, files, bear, flying stationers, lying dogs,

hagbuts of found, less than the nineteenth part of a
goose's grass, threshie-coat, woodie." See 1938.B28.

13   K[ING], H. G. L. "A Link with Sir Walter Scott." Notes and
       Queries, 174 (8 January), 28.
            Scott's coachman Peter sang evening psalms which Scott
       very much enjoyed. Peter's grandnephew, who remembered
       hearing his granduncle sing those psalms, died recently.

14   KORN, M. A. "Sir Walter Scott's Journal." Anglia Beiblatt,
       49 (May-June), 187-90.
            Scott's Journal, begun in crisis, became a solace to him
       after the bankruptcy and the death of his wife. Although it
       contains many minor details of his daily life, it also re-
       veals the uniqueness of his inner self. Scott discusses
       his family relationships, ties with friends, connections
       within his profession and within the political community.

15   LARSEN, THORLIEF. "The Classical Element in Scott's Poetry."
       Transactions of the Royal Society of Canada, 3rd ser. 32,
       sec. 2, 107-20.
            Unlike the work of the other Romantics, Scott's poetry
       is "objective and impersonal in method, direct and clear-cut
       in expression, manly and heroic in substance." His "essen-
       tial sanity" and "power of acceptance" give his poetry clas-
       sical qualities. His attitude toward the past is realistic,
       not escapist. He is free from Romantic subjectivism and
       glorifies the virtues of loyalty, endurance, and courage.

16   LATHAM, EDWARD. "Dumas et Sir Walter Scott." Mercure de
       France, 281 (1 January), 165-68.
            The first chapter of Scott's The Surgeon's Daughter
       closely resembles the prologue to Dumas' Richard Darlington;
       Dumas may have borrowed from Scott without acknowledgement.

17   MABBOTT, T. O. and EDWARD BENSLY. "Queries from Scott's Heart
       of Midlothian." Notes and Queries, 174 (19 March), 214.
            Identifies "flying stationers" in chapter twelve as chap-
       men or itinerant booksellers. Provides meaning of "files
       the stomach" and "carritch" as allusions to Horace and
       Farquhar. See 1938.B28.

18   M[ABBOTT], T. O. and WILFRED S. JACKSON. "Queries from Scott's
       Bride of Lammermoor." Notes and Queries, 174 (30 April),
       320.
            Identifies a rare coin celebrating the suppression of the
       First Revolt of the Jews, mentioned in The Bride of Lammer-
       moor. Since Barham's "Ingoldsby Legends" were published

some twenty years after the novel, Scott may have been re-
ferring to the original story in Le Nôtre's <u>En Suivant</u>
<u>L'Empereur</u>. <u>See</u> 1938.B27.

19   MACKENZIE, AGNES MURE. "The Scottish Historical Novel:
Successors of Walter Scott," in "Scottish Literature Today."
<u>Times Literary Supplement</u> (30 April), p. viii.
     The historical novel did not flourish in Scotland after
Sir Walter Scott. The efforts of Stevenson, Munroe, and
Crockett were slight beside the Waverley Novels. Many subsequent writers have used parts of the Scott formula, including an imagined character among actual events, a central
character taken from history, biographical romances which
emphasize personality development, and studies of society
in different periods.

20   MENNIE, DUNCAN M. "A MS Variant of Sir Walter Scott's 'Battle
of Sempach.'" <u>Anglia Beiblatt</u>, 49, 57-63.
     Lists variants between the published version of the
translation (<u>Blackwood's</u>, February, 1818) and a MS in the
Abbotsford Collection at the National Library of Scotland.
The printed version shows touches of the traditional Scottish ballad and of Scott's personal style. It is consider-
ably more distant from the original German, even though
Scott claimed in his introduction that it was a literal
translation.

21   _____. "Sir Walter Scott's Unpublished Translations of German
Plays." <u>Modern Language Review</u>, 33, no. 2 (April), 234-39.
     Scott's unpublished translations from the German are of
poor quality, because he mistranslated frequently and tended
to ignore stage directions and difficult sections. Two of
the plays are dramas of chivalry and may have influenced
<u>The Lay of the Last Minstrel</u> and <u>Marmion</u>. However, the
translations offer "antiquarian" rather than "literary" interest, and they are best left unpublished.

22   MOORE, JOHN ROBERT. "Poe's Orang-outang." <u>Times Literary</u>
<u>Supplement</u> (2 April), p. 236.
     Lists details used by Scott in <u>Count Robert of Paris</u> and
by Poe in "Murders in the Rue Morgue" to refute the suggestion of Guy Gardner (<u>TLS</u>, 26 February, 1938) that "Sanford
and Merton" was a more probable source for Poe's story.
<u>See</u> 1936.B16.

23   MUNROE, DAVID. "Sir Walter Scott and the Development of
Historical Study." <u>Queen's Quarterly</u>, 45, 216-17.

1938

Scott was always primarily a "romanticist" and only
secondarily an historian. He shaped history to fit the
purposes of his poems and novels and has many inaccuracies
even when writing "serious history," such as his Life of
Napoleon. However, he stimulated a revival of interest in
history and directly influenced Carlyle and Macaulay.

24   ORIANS, G. HARRISON. "Scott and Hawthorne's Fanshawe." New
England Quarterly, 11, no. 2 (June), 388-94.
Hawthorne's "lifelong romantic tendencies" were nurtured
by his reading of Scott, whose example turned Hawthorne to
Colonial America and local traditions for his subjects. His
anonymously published Fanshawe (1828) reflects Scott's influence in the compressed ending, the neutral hero, the
vaguely beautiful heroine, the retrospective mood, and the
topographical details.

25   OWEN, E. "Critics of The Bride of Lammermoor." Dalhousie
Review (Halifax), 18, no. 3, 365-71.
The Bride of Lammermoor has been controversial since it
was published. The critics have disagreed on the historical
date of the novel as well as on its merits. Perhaps because
Scott wrote it while ill, the novel recalls his love for
Williamina Belsches. In spite of its personal elements, it
is a "masterpiece of form," and critical pronouncements
have not done it justice.

26   PARKER, WILLIAM MATHIE. "Lockhart and Scott." Times Literary
Supplement (1 October), p. 627.
Calls again for a revised Life, as well as collations
and corrections in the works themselves. Like Boswell's
Johnson, Lockhart's Scott requires corrections and supple-
mentation. See 1937.B22.

27   PHILLIPS, LAWRENCE. "Queries from Scott's Bride of Lammermoor."
Notes and Queries, 174 (2 April), 246-47.
Queries concern word usage, sources and allusions in The
Bride of Lammermoor. See 1938.B18, B41.

28   _____. "Queries from Scott's Heart of Midlothian." Notes and
Queries, 174 (19 February), 135; (26 February), 154;
(5 March), 174.
Queries concern meanings of words, sayings, and allusions
in The Heart of Midlothian. See 1938.B12, B17, B44;
1939.B11.

29   _____. "Queries from Scott's Ivanhoe." Notes and Queries,
174 (16 April), 280.

Queries concern the expressions "freedom of the Rules" and "morning vespers" and the authors of several poems used as chapter headings.

30 _____. "Queries from Scott's Old Mortality." Notes and Queries, 174 (18 June), 441-42.
Queries concern some customs of the Covenanters and the meanings of several words and expressions.

31 _____. "Queries from Scott's Rob Roy." Notes and Queries, 175 (26 November), 387-88.
Queries the meaning of eleven words and expressions from Rob Roy. See 1938.B7 and 1939.B10.

32 QUARE. "Gaelic Spelling in Scott's Writings." Notes and Queries, 174 (15 January), 46.
Several phrases in Scott are spelled inconsistently; is this because Gaelic is subject to variations in spelling? See 1938.B8.

33 _____. "Greatest British General." Notes and Queries, 175 (2 July), 10.
In chapter eleven of Kenilworth, Scott refers to Marlborough as "the greatest general (excepting one) whom Britain ever produced." Author queries who was the exception? See 1938.B2.

34 R., O. "Waverley Novels as an Impulse to Fiction." Notes and Queries, 174 (25 June), 457.
In The Literature of the Georgian Era (1894) William Minto states that Waverley stimulated an increase in novels. Author laments this increase and the accompanying decrease in quality.

35 RENDALL, VERNON. "A Scott Error." Times Literary Supplement (30 April), p. 296.
In chapter 26 of Quentin Durward there is an error in the account given to King Louis of the road taken by Quentin to Liège. All editions miss the error except two twentieth century editions designed for examinees. In one of these the annotator erroneously states that the revenue from Scott's books cleared his debt. Lockhart generously donated the profits of his biography for that purpose.

36 R[ENDALL], V[ERNON]. "Sir Walter Scott and Mrs. Fawcett." Notes and Queries, 175 (10 September), 195.
In a letter of 23 December, 1816 from Scott to John Richardson, Mrs. Fawcett's brother is identified as Henry

1938

Weber. Lockhart indicates Weber had been Scott's amanuensis. See 1938.B6.

37 ROSSI, JOSEPH. "Scott and Carducci." Modern Language Notes, 53 (April), 287-90.
Scott's "The Gathering Song of Donald the Black," lines 17-32, may have been a source for Carducci's "Alle Fonti del Clitumno" in Odi Barbare.

38 SENEX. "The Swiss Language: Dickens and Scott." Notes and Queries, 175 (2 July), 7-8.
In chapter seventeen of Anne of Geierstein, Anne speaks to Philipson in "Swiss"; however, there is no such language.

39 SMITH, J. C. "Scott and Shakespeare." Essays and Studies, 24, 114-31.
Shakespeare and Scott were similar in terms of physical appearance, character, methods of composition, love affairs, and socio-economic status. Scott's Toryism was balanced by his sense of kinship with all men, and Shakespeare had a similar respect for the humble virtues. Both were men of the world who were dreamers at heart.

40 STROUT, ALAN LANG. "Walter Scott and Maga." Times Literary Supplement (5 February), p. 92.
Provides a number of corrections to Mrs. Oliphant's William Blackwood and His Sons (1897). In a letter of 21 September, 1817, Scott designates Wilson, not Lockhart, as the friend with whom he wishes to work.

41 SUMMERS, MONTAGUE. "Queries from Scott's Bride of Lammermoor." Notes and Queries, 174 (16 April), 283.
Identifies allusions in the novel to Don Quixote and to "The Black Mousquetaire. A Legend of France," by Thomas Ingoldsby, published in Bentley's Miscellany, 1840. Reply to 1938.B27.

42 TREVELYAN, G. M. "Address to the Thirty-eighth Annual Dinner of the Edinburgh Sir Walter Scott Club." The Edinburgh Sir Walter Scott Club Annual Report.
Scott revolutionized the study of history. He deeply influenced Macaulay, who tried to follow his example by demonstrating the social and economic causes of political events. Because he wrote before Scott, Gibbon failed to understand how people differ in different periods and countries. Reprinted: 1971.A13.

43   WALPOLE, HUGH. "Sir Walter Scott Today," in "Scottish Litera-
        ture Today." Times Literary Supplement (30 April),
        pp. vi-vii.
            Scott's current lack of popularity is due to an entire
        generation of children being forced to read the Waverley
        Novels thirty years ago. Despite his current unread state,
        he was a great humanist with notable gifts of character
        creation and narrative power.

44   WHITE, CHARLES. "Queries from Scott's Heart of Midlothian."
        Notes and Queries, 174 (7 May), 340.
            The "£800 Scots" in The Heart of Midlothian, chapter 43,
        would have been equivalent to about £67 English. See
        1938.B28.

1939 A BOOKS

    1   TAIT, JOHN GUTHRIE, ed. The Journal of Sir Walter Scott,
        1825-26. Text Revised from a Photostat in the National
        Library of Scotland. Edinburgh: Oliver and Boyd, 314pp.
            Tait attempts to correct the errors made by David Douglas
        in the 1890 edition of the Journal. This edition was com-
        pleted by W. M. Parker. See Volume II: 1941.A1 and
        Volume III: 1946.A1. Reprinted: 1950.A3.

  *2   WRIGHT, MARGARET M. "A Comparative Study of the Historical
        Prose Fiction of Sir Walter Scott and Conrad Ferdinand
        Meyer." Ph.D. dissertation, University of Wisconsin, 1939.
            Cited in Comprehensive Dissertation Index (Ann Arbor,
        Michigan: Xerox University Microfilms, 1973), XXX, 468.

1939 B SHORTER WRITINGS

    1   BEITH, JOHN HAY. "Address to the Thirty-ninth Annual Dinner
        of the Edinburgh Sir Walter Scott Club." Edinburgh Sir
        Walter Scott Club Annual Report, pp. 21-34.
            Scott's output was prodigal, and his novels might have
        benefited from some revision and compression. Unlike some
        modern novelists, he always made himself intelligible to
        his readers. Where Burns helps us to endure life, Scott
        helps us to enjoy it.

    2   CORSON, JAMES CLARKSON. "Scott's 'Battle of Killiecrankie.'"
        Modern Language Notes, 54 (March), 235.
            Scott's "Battle of Killiecrankie" had been printed in a
        contemporary edition of Chambers' Edinburgh Journal in

December, 1832. This version has several misreadings and misspellings. See 1939.B31.

3 _____. "Verses on the Death of Scott." Notes and Queries, 177 (2 December), 417-19.

Lists 29 poems on the death of Scott and where they may be found; requests additional information.

4 DODDS, M. H. "Queries from Scott's Rob Roy." Notes and Queries, 176 (7 January), 15.

Clarifies several words and expressions found in the novel: "blood-tit," "Plummet," "I'se e'en lay the head o the sow to the tail of the grise," "cockit," and "mear." See 1938.B31.

5 ERSKINE (OF MARR), RUARAIDH. "Scots History and Sentiment." Times Literary Supplement (4 March), p. 135 and (25 March), p. 175.

Exposes superstitions about Scotland and credits Scott with inventing the "modern" institution of "Clans Tartan." Reply withdraws this credit; Scott was misinformed that the general use of tartan in Scotland dated but from the Union. See 1939.B8, B13.

6 GORDON, ROBERT K. "Dryden and the Waverley Novels." Modern Language Review, 34, no. 2 (April), 201-206.

After Shakespeare, Dryden is the greatest English literary influence on Scott's work. Scott approved of Dryden's politics and his religious conversion. He admired Dryden's revisions of Chaucer and used material from Absalom and Achitophel and The Duke of Guise. Of all Scott's novels, Peveril of the Peak is the most deeply influenced by Dryden.

7 GRIERSON, HERBERT JOHN CLIFFORD. "Scott and the Historical Novel (Abstract)." Proceedings of the Royal Institution of Great Britain, 30, 143-47.

Although Shakespeare did not attempt to reproduce the atmosphere of the past in his history plays, Scott learned much from him. Scott's greatest achievement was making his readers feel the people of the past as real human beings. His best novels deal with seventeenth and eighteenth century Scotland, but his understanding of the Middle Ages was incomplete.

8 HALDANE, M. M. "Clan Tartan." Times Literary Supplement (8 April), p. 204.

The use of tartan goes back at least as far as the sixteenth century, but not as a badge or uniform. Scott was taken in by the forgery "Vestiarium Scoticum." <u>See</u> 1939.B5, B13.

9 J., W. H. "Queries from Scott's <u>Heart of Midlothian</u>: A Campvere Skipper." <u>Notes and Queries</u>, 176 (11 March), 177.

Campvere, now Veer, is northeast of the island Walcheren and faces the island of North Beverland. From 1444 to 1795 it was the site of a Scottish factory.

10 _____. "Queries from Scott's <u>Rob Roy</u>." <u>Notes and Queries</u>, 176 (4 February), 86-87.

Clarifies several words and expressions from the novel: "plummet," "Jack Webster," "jowing-in bell," "bicker," "cocket," "sow playing upon a trumpet," "air," "mear," and "hair in my neck." <u>See</u> 1938.B31.

11 L., G. G. "Queries from Scott's <u>Heart of Midlothian</u>." <u>Notes and Queries</u>, 176 (28 January), 70.

In chapter 32 Scott alludes to Uvedale Price, who argued in favor of natural beauty in his 1794 "Essay on the Picturesque." <u>See</u> 1938.B28.

12 LAMBERT, MILDRED and JAMES T. HILLHOUSE. "The Scott Letters in the Huntington Library." <u>Huntington Library Quarterly</u>, 2, no. 3 (April), 319-52.

The Letters are divided into four groups: A. Letters to Thomas Scott and His Family; B. Letters to Croker Concerning the Regalia Episode; C. Letters to Miscellaneous Correspondents Published by Grierson; and D. Letters to Miscellaneous Correspondents Not Published by Grierson. Thirteen letters do not appear in Grierson's edition, and twenty-four other letters contain variant readings which differ from Grierson's text.

13 LLOYD, T. E. "Scots History and Sentiment." <u>Times Literary Supplement</u> (18 March), p. 163 and (22 April), p. 234.

In a letter of 7 June, 1829 to Sir Thomas Lauder, Scott indicated that he disliked the "affectation" of wearing Clan Tartan. Scott was not taken in by the forgery of the "Vestiarium Scoticum," but he did try to popularize the use of tartan. <u>See</u> 1939.B5, B8.

14 MUNRO, NIALL. "Scott at Gundimore: Literary Associations of a Hampshire Villa." <u>Scots Magazine</u>, N.S. 30, no. 5 (February), 337-40.

In 1807 Scott visited William Rose of Gundimore (in Hampshire), where he worked on Canto III of <u>Marmion</u>. The cottage in which he stayed is still known as "Scott's

House." He modelled Davie Gellatley on William Rose's man-servant David Hines.

15 PARKER, WILLIAM MATHIE. "Burns, Scott, and Turgenev: A Remarkable Linkage." <u>Notes and Queries</u>, 176 (29 April), 291-92.
Scott met Alexander Turgenev (related to Ivan Turgenev, the novelist) at the home of a Mrs. Alexander in London. She was of the same family as Wilhelmina Alexander, whom Burns celebrated in "The Lass o' Ballochmyle."

16 _____. "The Origins of Scott's <u>Nigel</u>." <u>Modern Language Review</u>, 34, no. 4 (October), 535-40.
<u>The Fortunes of Nigel</u> originated in Scott's fictitious "Private Letters of the Seventeenth Century," of which 72 pages were printed. Erskine, Ballantyne, and Lockhart convinced Scott that he was wasting good material which would be better used in novel form. Although Lockhart says Scott did not intend to continue the letters, after the financial crash Scott collaborated with Lady Louisa Stuart on completing the project and had every intention of publishing it.

17 PHILLIPS, LAWRENCE. "Queries from Scott's <u>Abbot</u>." <u>Notes and Queries</u>, 176 (3 June), 388-89.
Queries the meaning of six allusions and three words from the novel. <u>See</u> 1939.B28.

18 _____. "Queries from Scott's <u>Black Dwarf</u>." <u>Notes and Queries</u>, 176 (15 April), 261-62.
Queries the meaning of five verbal expressions and four allusions.

19 _____. "Queries from Scott's <u>Ivanhoe</u>." <u>Notes and Queries</u>, 177 (28 October), 316.
Queries concern meaning of words, dating of events in the plot, and authorship of books mentioned in <u>Ivanhoe</u>. See 1939.B30.

20 _____. "Queries from Scott's <u>Legend of Montrose</u>." <u>Notes and Queries</u>, 176 (8 April), 245.
Queries the meaning of four italicized words used by Dugald Dalgetty.

21 _____. "Queries from Scott's <u>The Monastery</u>." <u>Notes and Queries</u>, 176 (20 May), 352.
Queries the meaning of several words and allusions. In chapter 31, Scott seems to imply that the Church burnt

heretics instead of handing them over to secular authori-
ties; was he likely to have made this error?

22   PHILOSCOTUS. "The Heart of Midlothian: Slips in Quotation."
     Notes and Queries, 176 (22 April), 277.
         Some errors which Grierson identifies as continuing
     through all editions of The Heart of Midlothian have been
     corrected and eliminated from the Centenary Edition (1886).

23   _____. "Johnson and Scott: A Greek Inscription." Notes and
     Queries, 177 (5 August), 96.
         Samuel Johnson put the Greek inscription of Christ's
     words, "the night cometh, when no man can work," on the
     dial-plate of his watch. Perhaps thinking of Johnson,
     Scott wrote these words in his Journal and on his sundial.
     However, he copied the Greek incorrectly on the sundial,
     and Lockhart corrected his mistake in the Life.

24   _____. "A Waverley Original." Notes and Queries, 176
     (17 June), 424-25.
         Crockett did not include in The Scott Originals Scott's
     brother Daniel as a prototype of Conachar in The Fair Maid
     of Perth. Scott clearly states the connection in Lockhart's
     biography.

25   ROZOV, ZOJA. "Denis Davydov and Walter Scott." Year Book of
     the Slavonic and East European Review, 19, 300-302.
         Denis Davydov was a Russian poet, soldier, and war his-
     torian. In defending the Russian Army against writers who
     ascribed Napoleon's defeat merely to winter, he quoted
     Scott's Life of Napoleon as a supporting authority. At
     Scott's request, he offered certain corrections to the
     Napoleon, but his letter did not reach Scott before Scott
     died and was not published until 1840.

26   RUBIN, JOSEPH JAY. "Whitman on Byron, Scott, and Sentiment."
     Notes and Queries (11 March), 171.
         In the Brooklyn Eagle of 10 February, 1847 Whitman edi-
     torialized against the "monkeyism of literature"--people
     doting on Byron, Scott and other English writers. He was
     hotly attacked by the editor of Yankee Doodle.

27   RUSSELL, JAMES ANDERSON. "The Vogue of Scott and Byron," in
     his Dutch Poetry and English: A Story of the Romantic Re-
     vival. Amsterdam: H. J. Paris, pp. 90-104.
         Jacob van Lennep was "the Dutch Scott," but he lacked
     Scott's creative powers and knowledge of the past. Scott's
     other Dutch imitator, Nicholas Beets, began writing in the

1939

Byronic mode but later (1835 and following) followed Scott
in writing narrative poems based on his own country's history. Unlike Scott, both Van Lennep and Beets found themselves at home in contemporary society; they saw no conflict
between it and an emotional attachment to the past.

28   S., W. W. and O. F. BABLER. "Queries from Scott's Abbot."
      Notes and Queries, 176 (24 June), 447.
         A "loaning" is a field track or lane. The "celebrated
      jester" alluded to in chapter fourteen was Till Eulen-
      spiegel. See 1939.B17.

29   SADLEIR, MICHAEL. "Tales of Terror." Times Literary Supple-
      ment (7 January), p. 9.
         In his book, Gothic Quest, Summers confuses Tales of
      Wonder with Tales of Terror. The former was the first book
      printed by Ballantyne and contained ballads by Lewis and
      Scott. Tales of Terror, a parody of Lewis's ballads, was
      printed by John Bell.

30   SETON-ANDERSON, JAMES. "Queries from Scott's Ivanhoe." Notes
      and Queries, 177 (23 December), 467.
         Count Basil and Orra are both tragedies by Joanna
      Baillie. See 1939.B19.

31   STROUT, ALAN LANG. "An Unpublished Ballad Translation by
      Scott, 'The Battle of Killiecrankie.'" Modern Language
      Notes, 54 (January), 13-18.
         Prints the translation and letters referring to it. The
      poem is a translation of Kennedy's Praelium Gilliecrankiense
      and was given to A. G. Hunter in approximately 1805. See
      1939.B2.

1940 A BOOKS

1   FISKE, CHRISTABEL FORSYTHE. Epic Suggestion in the Imagery of
      the Waverley Novels. New Haven, Connecticut: Yale Univer-
      sity Press, 167pp.
         The epic (heroic) element in Scott's temperament is ap-
      parent in his clan-nationalism, his utilitarian attitude
      toward nature, and his interest in the factual material
      underlying his fiction. Concentrates on stylistic analysis
      and recurring motifs in description and figurative language.
      Identifies a series of "epic" (impersonally objective)
      phrases and rhetorical patterns drawn from formal rhetoric.

*2   JONES, DOROTHY WOOTEN. "Indebtedness of the Southern Novel to
     the Waverley Novels." Ph.D. dissertation, Southern Metho-
     dist University, 1940.
         Cited in the Annual Bibliography of English Language and
     Literature (Cambridge: Modern Humanities Research Associa-
     tion, 1950), XXI, 214, item #3987.

1940 B SHORTER WRITINGS

1   B., H. C. "The Story of Mr. Abney." Notes and Queries, 179
    (23 November), 372.
        Requests information on the "calamitous and mysterious
    story" of Mr. Abney told to Scott by Morritt of Rokeby and
    written out by Scott to amuse the Duke of Buccleuch.

2   BAYLEY, A. R. "Queries from Scott's Pirate." Notes and
    Queries, 178 (30 March), 232.
        Provides additional information on the explorer and
    travel writer James Bruce of Kinnaird (1730-94), to whom
    Scott alludes in The Pirate.

3   BRIGHTFIELD, MYRON A. John Wilson Croker. Berkeley: Univer-
    sity of California Press, pp. 216-28.
        Scott met Croker in 1809 when they were engaged in "the
    pleasant conspiracy" of launching the Quarterly Review.
    Croker helped obtain governmental favors for Scott and fa-
    cilitated his communication with the Prince Regent. Their
    relationship deteriorated from 1826 due to disagreement on
    monetary policy. But the breach was healed, and when Scott
    left for Italy in 1831, he and Croker parted with mutual
    goodwill.

4   CROCKETT, W. S. "The Scotts." The S. M. T. Magazine and
    Scottish Country Life, 25, no. 6 (June), 81-83.
        Traces the history of the Lowland Scotts and the House
    of Buccleuch. Sir Walter was descended remotely from the
    "Bold Buccleuch" of The Lay of the Last Minstrel and more
    directly from "Beardie," his great-grandfather who swore
    never to trim his beard until the restoration of the
    Jacobites.

5   CURIOUS. "Poyais Cacique: An Imposter." Notes and Queries,
    178 (15 June), 423.
        Queries the identity of Poyais Cacique, to whom Scott
    refers as an imposter, knave and fool, in a letter of
    November, 1823 to Maria Edgeworth.

1940

6   DOBIE, M. R. "The Development of Scott's <u>Minstrelsy</u>: An At-
     tempt at a Reconstruction." <u>Transactions of the Edinburgh</u>
     <u>Bibliographical Society</u>, 2, part 1, 66-87.
         Traces the development of the <u>Minstrelsy</u> month by month
     from the time Scott met Leyden in the winter of 1799-1800.
     Scott's purposes differed from those of modern ballad edi-
     tors; he was interested not "in what was old, but what was
     alive." When he inserted changes of his own, he was moti-
     vated by standards of poetic excellence and/or a less-than-
     objective memory. "A man with a creative mind does not
     always know that he is creating."

7   GALLAWAY, W. F., JR. "The Conservative Attitude Toward Fic-
     tion: 1770-1830." <u>Publications of the Modern Language</u>
     <u>Association of America</u>, 55, no. 4 (December), 1041-59.
         The widespread objection to fiction in this period de-
     rived from the neo-classic distrust of the imagination.
     Scott's own attitude toward the novel was one of "tolerance
     tinged with snobbery." He regarded it as a money-making
     device, and was a bit ashamed of writing novels. He felt
     more comfortable in his roles of poet, historian, and
     editor.

8   GORDON, ROBERT K. "Le Voyage d'Abbotsford." <u>Transactions of</u>
     <u>the Royal Society of Canada</u>, 34, sec. 2, 71-85.
         Scott received many French visitors, some of whom re-
     corded their impressions in memoirs and travel books. The
     French pilgrims to Abbotsford sought only romantic qualities
     in Scott and Scotland, and some came away inevitably dis-
     appointed.

9   GRANT, WILL. "The Man Who Designed the Scott Monument." <u>The</u>
     <u>S. M. T. Magazine</u> and <u>Scottish Country Life</u>, 26, no. 2
     (August), 22-24.
         Offers a tribute to George Meikle Kemp, on the centenary
     of the laying of the foundation stone of the Scott monument.
     Kemp met Scott twice in incidental encounters, once on a
     roadway and once at Melrose Abbey. Kemp died two and a half
     years before the monument was dedicated.

10   GRIERSON, HERBERT JOHN CLIFFORD. "Scott and Carlyle," in his
     <u>Essays and Addresses</u>. London: Chatto and Windus, pp. 27-54.
         Because the years of Scott's popularity and prosperity
     coincided with the years of Carlyle's poverty and obscurity,
     Carlyle could not write of Scott objectively. He was "the
     tormented man critical of the happy man." Carlyle came from
     the democratic, Presbyterian Scottish tradition, while Scott
     preferred the aristocratic and Episcopalian tradition. Ori-
     ginally published in <u>Essays and Studies</u>, vol. 13 (1928).

11 _____. "Sir Walter Scott: I. The Man and the Poet." <u>Univer-sity of Edinburgh Journal</u>, 11, no. 1 (Autumn), 4-20.
   Scott's narrative poems and novels spring from an inter-action between his poetic imagination and his good sense as a man of the world. The best poems are the ballads and lyrics, but they do not reflect deep personal emotion. To attain "the romance of history and locality" in the narra-tive poems, he includes many proper names and natural de-scriptions which have personal or historical associations. These narrative poems reflect Scott's sense of mutability and melancholy. Reprinted: 1950.B10.

12 H., B. S. "North Country Traders' Illiteracy." <u>Notes and Queries</u>, 179 (31 August), 153.
   In a 1792 letter to William Clerk, Scott told of cattle traders who took business correspondence to the parish clerk, who read and answered the letters. Queries the ac-tuality and extent of this practice.

13 H., C. E. "Elegies on Camp." <u>Notes and Queries</u>, 179 (21 September), 209.
   Scott said he received many elegies for Camp, his beloved dog. Queries whether any of these elegies have survived.

14 HARMAN, ROLAND NELSON. "An Unpublished Letter of Sir Walter Scott." <u>Yale University Library Gazette</u>, 14 (April), 67-68.
   Prints a letter of 25 March, 1808 from Scott to William Miller, a London bookseller, in which Scott acknowledges the assistance he received from various contemporaries on his edition of Dryden. The letter is not included in Grierson's Centenary Edition.

15 J., W. H. "A Prisoner's Escape: Scott and Dumas." <u>Notes and Queries</u>, 179 (6 July), 7-8.
   An incident in chapter 33 of <u>Rob Roy</u> in which a prisoner escapes while crossing a river has a close parallel in chapter 22 of Dumas' <u>The She-Wolves of Machecoul</u>.

16 _____. "Queries from Scott's <u>Pirate</u>." <u>Notes and Queries</u>, 178 (9 March), 177.
   "Bear" is coarse barley. The source of an allusion in chapter 39 of <u>The Pirate</u> is Shakespeare's <u>2 Henry IV</u>, V, iii, 96. <u>See</u> 1940.B32.

17 JONES, W. POWELL. "Three Unpublished Letters from Scott to Dibden." <u>Huntington Library Quarterly</u>, 3, no. 4 (July), 477-84.

1940

Dibden was a bibliographer and book collector who regarded Scott with "elated enthusiasm." The three letters published here for the first time add to our image of Scott as a book collector quite aware of his own "bookomania."

*18 KEHLER, HENNING. "Ivanhoe," in his De Store Romaner. Copenhagen: Gyldendal, pp. 141-58.
Cited in the Annual Bibliography of English Language and Literature (Cambridge: Modern Humanities Research Association, 1950), XXI, 214, item #3990.

19 K[ING], H. G. L. "Scott's Songs Set to Music." Notes and Queries, 178 (23 March), 211.
The bibliography in C. D. Yonge's Life of Scott lists songs that have been put to music. Reply to 1940.B40.

20 _____. "Sir Walter Scott's Niece--Anne Scott." Notes and Queries, 179 (9 November), 335.
His Journal entry for 28 June, 1826 indicates that Scott spent £2 for a gift of paints for his niece. Queries if she had notable artistic talent, and if any of her paintings have been preserved.

21 KNICKERBOCKER, WILLIAM S. "Border and Bar: Revised Interpretations of Sir Walter Scott." Sewanee Review, 48 (October-December), 519-32.
In his own life and in his novels, Scott harmonized the conflicting values of Border ("impulsive exploits of wayward derring-do") and Bar ("the regimen of an ordered social life by the restraints of law"). His ultimate goal was a sympathetic portrayal of Scottish manners which would effect "the cultural consummation of the Union of Scotland and England." The attraction of his novels for today's readers may be found in his prose style and the calm, confident pace of the narrative.

22 L., G. G., V. R., and G. CATALINI. "Queries from Scott's Fortunes of Nigel." Notes and Queries, 179 (3 August), 89.
Identifies allusions to Napier, Axylus of the Iliad, and Burton's Anatomy of Melancholy. Quotes Skeat's definition of "viretot," which is found in "The Miller's Tale" as well as in The Fortunes of Nigel. Reply to 1940.B31.

23 LÜTGEN, K. "Walter Scott und seine Mutter." Der Türmer, 41, 117-19.
Scott's mother exerted a positive influence on his development. She read him Pope, Milton, and Scottish folksongs, and she taught him the art of story-telling. She

inculcated in him the Puritan values of diligence, patriotism, and moral austerity. Although she died shortly before
Scott's financial crisis, her example helped him to bear
his misfortune.

24 M., J. F. "Waverley." Notes and Queries, 179 (12 October),
269.
       Carlisle's Topographical Dictionary of 1808 identifies
Waverley as "extra-parochial" and gives information about
the abbey. See 1940.B25, B34.

25 MORRIS, JOSEPH E. "Waverley." Notes and Queries, 179
(21 September), 211-12.
       Waverley is not the name of a parish or locality, only
of a Cistercian abbey in the parish of Farnham. See
1940.B24, B34.

26 OSBORN, J. M. "Sir Walter Scott," in his John Dryden: Some
Biographical Facts and Problems. New York: Columbia University Press. 2nd ed.; rpt. Gainesville: University of
Florida Press, 1965, pp. 72-87.
       Scott used Dryden's life and works as the foundation for
a critical study of Restoration literature. His Dryden exhibits his ability as a critic, especially in his recon-
struction of the origins and settings of the poems and in
his dramatic criticism. The strength of the Life is Scott's
ability to reconstruct the seventeenth century and to compare Dryden to his contemporaries.

27 PARKER, WILLIAM MATHIE. "Peter's Letters to His Kinsfolk."
Times Literary Supplement (22 June), p. 308.
       Although Peter's Letters to His Kinsfolk has always been
attributed exclusively to Lockhart, a letter of 1818 from
Lockhart to William Blackwood states that John Wilson was
expected to be a collaborator. Two articles on Peter's
Letters which appeared in Blackwood's in February and March,
1819 may have been written by Lockhart himself or by John
Wilson, especially since self-reviewing was a frequent practice in this period. Scott read and enjoyed these articles,
which contained excerpts from the complete work.

28 _____. "Scott's Book Marginalia." Times Literary Supplement
(21 September), p. 488; (28 September), p. 500; (5 October),
p. 512.
       Reproduces a series of Scott's marginal notes, which were
transcribed into a bound folio of extracts by Scott's sons,
his daughter Sophia, and Lockhart. The marginalia repro-
duced here are those which have not been previously

published, either as Scott's own notes to his works or in Lockhart's biography. The folio volume is preserved in the National Library of Scotland. See 1941.B29.

29 _____. "Suggestions for Scott's Muse." Times Literary Supplement (23 March), p. 152.
Several persons suggested to Scott that he use specific figures such as Lord Nelson, Alfred the Great, Wallace, and the Black Prince in his poems. He declined, usually on the grounds that he lacked firsthand knowledge of the subject and that he wished to be accurate when using historical characters.

30 P-G., H., L. R. M. STRACHAN, and J. ARDAGH. "Queries from Scott's Pirate." Notes and Queries, 178 (24 February), 140-41.
Defines several words and allusions from The Pirate. The authors of several poems mentioned are Scott himself, Waller, Crabbe, and Prior. Includes an excerpt from James Bruce's Travels to Discover the Source of the Nile, concerning the massacre of vagrant entertainers. See 1940.B32.

31 PHILLIPS, LAWRENCE. "Queries from Scott's Fortunes of Nigel." Notes and Queries, 179 (20 July), 45-46.
Queries concern meanings of words and allusions, authorship of works mentioned in the novel, and possible errors and misprints. See 1940.B22.

32 _____. "Queries from Scott's Pirate." Notes and Queries, 178 (10 February), 99.
Queries concern meanings of words and allusions, authorship of works mentioned in the novel, and possible errors and misprints. See 1940.B2, B16, B30, B35, and B39.

33 PHILOSCOTUS. "Scott and Jane Porter." Notes and Queries, 178 (8 June), 408.
How accurate is the claim of Jane Porter in her revised edition of The Scottish Chiefs that Scott borrowed an incident from her novel to use in Rokeby (Canto V, stanzas 34-36)?

34 _____. "Waverley." Notes and Queries, 179 (10 August), 99.
According to the Daily Telegraph of 2 November, 1894, the parish of Waverley in Surrey was reluctantly merging with another parish. See 1940.B24, B25.

35 RANKIN, H. "Queries from Scott's Pirate." Notes and Queries, 178 (6 April), 249.

In <u>The Pirate</u>, "bear" (or "bere" as it is called in the Orkney Islands) is not a coarse grain, but similar in form to barley, only smaller and of less yield per acre. <u>See</u> 1940.B32.

36 RHEDECYNIAN. "The Latinity of Scotsmen." <u>Notes and Queries</u>, 179 (28 September), 224.
In a letter of 1812 to James Bailey, Scott implies that Scotsmen are poor Latin scholars. Queries if this was ever a common idea and if the opinion was justified. <u>See</u> 1940.B38.

37 S., S. "The Fly on St. Paul's." <u>Notes and Queries</u>, 179 (9 November), 336.
Queries the meaning of Scott's allusion in an 1816 letter to "the fly on St. Paul's."

38 SETON-ANDERSON, JAMES. "The Latinity of Scotsmen." <u>Notes and Queries</u>, 179 (26 October), 304.
Scotsmen are not necessarily poor Latin scholars. Alexander Seton, for example, was applauded as a Latin composer and orator. <u>See</u> 1940.B36.

39 STRACHAN, L. R. M. "Queries from Scott's <u>Pirate</u>." <u>Notes and Queries</u>, 178 (2 March), 158-59.
In <u>The Pirate</u>, Scott quotes from the Lectures on Moral Philosophy delivered at the Royal Institution in 1804, 1805, and 1806 by "the laughing philosopher," Sydney Smith (1771-1845). <u>See</u> 1940.B32.

40 W., S. "Scott's Songs Set to Music." <u>Notes and Queries</u>, 178 (9 March), 171-72.
Requests information regarding the composers and settings of Scott's songs, especially "Proud Maisie" and "When the glede's in the blue cloud." <u>See</u> 1940.B19.

41 WOOLF, VIRGINIA. "Gas at Abbotsford." <u>New Statesman and Nation</u>, N.S. 19 (27 January), 108-109.
While ostensibly reviewing volume I of Tait's edition of the <u>Journal</u>, Woolf evokes scenes of brilliant hospitality and story-telling at Abbotsford in the heyday of Scott's glory. His novels combine "gas and daylight, ventriloquy and truth"; i.e., the ingeniously false and the perceptively real.

42 YAKUBOVITCH, D. P. "<u>The Captain's Daughter</u> and the Novels of Walter Scott." <u>Vremennik Pushkinskoi Komissii [Pushkin]</u>, 4-5, 165-97.

1941

Pushkin was strongly influenced by Scott. He links the
history of a country with the history of a family in The
Captain's Daughter. Like Scott, he includes prefaces and
titles each chapter. Pushkin shared Scott's concerns with
involuntary disloyalty and the tyranny of the powerful, and
he shared Scott's attitude toward feudalism. Pushkin's use
of analogies to Scott's works may have been an attempt to
avoid censorship.

1941 A BOOKS

1   TAIT, JOHN GUTHRIE, ed. The Journal of Sir Walter Scott,
     1827-28. Text Revised from a Photostat in the National
     Library of Scotland. Edinburgh: Oliver and Boyd, 295pp.
        See Volume I: 1939.A1 and Volume III: 1946.A1. Re-
     printed: 1950.A3.

1941 B SHORTER WRITINGS

1   ANON. "Scott and the Scholars." Times Literary Supplement
     (14 June), p. 287.
        The text of Scott's Journal should be edited for the un-
     derstanding and appreciation of the ordinary reader, not
     primarily for scholars and professional editors.

2   ANON. "Tenbury Discoveries." Times Literary Supplement
     (20 September), p. 476.
        Among the almost 300 letters from famous people found at
     St. Michael's College, Tenbury, Worcestershire, is one from
     Scott to Lady Morton regarding the presentation of a crest
     to the King.

3   C., T. C. "Queries from Scott's Quentin Durward." Notes and
     Queries, 180 (19 April), 286-87.
        Clarifies several allusions; provides meanings for "root
     cellar," "tasker," "sullied," and "Marechaussée." See
     1941.B34.

4   _____. "Walter Scott at Swanage." Notes and Queries, 181
     (9 August), 75-76.
        "Sir Walter Scott" is inscribed on a stone seat on the
     Darleston Road above Swanage. Queries whether he could
     have written it himself? See 1941.B13.

5   CHAPMAN, R. W. "A Problem in Editorial Method." Essays and
     Studies, 27, 41-51.

The Douglas and Tait editions of Scott's Journal present
a case study in the problem of how a later editor should
handle the errors of his predecessor. Tait did well to record Douglas' omissions in his footnotes; "textual particu-
lars" may be enlightening and should not be reserved for a
learned journal.

6   CLUBB, MERREL D. "The Criticism of Gulliver's 'Voyage to the
    Houhynhnms,' 1726-1914," in Stanford Studies in Language
    and Literature. 1941. Fiftieth Anniversary of the Founding
    of Stanford University. Edited by Hardin Craig. Stanford,
    California: The University, pp. 203-32.
        Scott's edition of Swift helped to fix "a conventionally
    orthodox view of the fourth 'Voyage.'" He accepted the
    theory that Swift's misanthropy sprang from mental disease.
    Scott was outraged by what he regarded as a total identifi-
    cation between Yahoos and men.

7   COOK, DAVIDSON. "Additions to Scott's Poems." Times Literary
    Supplement (15 November), p. 572 and (22 November), p. 584.
        Affirms the difficulty of authenticating the originality
    of poetry originally published in the novels, especially
    the mottoes. In his 1841 one volume edition of Scott's
    poems, Lockhart included all the poetry from the novels
    which he did not recognize as having been written by some-
    one else. Some of his errors are here corrected. See
    1941.B28.

8   DICKENS, BRUCE. "The Cleek'um Inn." Times Literary Supplement
    (7 June), p. 275 and (13 December), p. 632.
        J. B. Johnston's Place Names of Berwickshire lists sever-
    al names under the entry "Cleekhimin." Queries if any of
    these names were recorded before the publication in 1824 of
    St. Ronan's Well? Second article confirms that each appear-
    ance of the name on the modern map may be traced to the
    novel. See 1942.B6, B19.

9   DUFFY, CHARLES. "The 'Song of Hybrias the Cretan.'" Notes
    and Queries, 181 (20 September), 167.
        A review of Robert Brand's Collection from the Greek An-
    thology, published in Blackwood's in 1833, prints five
    translations of the song, none of which corresponds to
    Scott's version. This would suggest that, despite his an-
    tipathy to Greek, he may have translated it himself. See
    1941.B17.

10 FORSE, EDWARD J. G. "Queries from Scott's Redgauntlet." Notes
    and Queries, 181 (9 August), 81.

1941

Identifies meanings of "toom whistle," "chapeau bras,"
"borrel man," and "Gustavus Katterfelto." <u>See</u> 1941.B35.

11 _____. "Queries from Scott's 'Two Drovers.'" <u>Notes and
Queries</u>, 181 (16 August), 97.
"St. Mungo" is another name for St. Kentigern, apostle
of the Scottish Border, who died around 600 A.D. <u>See</u>
1941.B32.

12 GRIERSON, HERBERT JOHN CLIFFORD. "Sir William Scott: II.
History and the Novel." <u>University of Edinburgh Journal</u>,
11, no. 2 (Summer), 80-90.
Scott created the historical novel from his combined
knowledge of fiction, archaeology, and history. He never
confused history with historical fiction; he took liberties
with facts in the novels and poems that he would never per-
mit in his histories and biographies. He is most successful
when working with a seventeenth or eighteenth century
setting. His work approaches closer to the "genial humanity" of Fielding than to the spirit of the romantic "terror
and wonder novelists" of the second half of the eighteenth
century. Reprinted: 1950.B10.

13 H., A. J. "Walter Scott at Swanage." <u>Notes and Queries</u>, 181
(6 September), 137.
Scott may easily have visited Swanage while staying at
Mudeford in 1807. <u>See</u> 1941.B4.

14 H., R. "Queries from Scott's <u>Betrothed</u>." <u>Notes and Queries</u>,
181 (16 August), 97.
Confirms the story of the bigamy of the Count of
Gleichens, to which Scott alludes in chapter 22. <u>See</u>
1941.B31.

15 HÉRAUCOURT, W. "<u>Waverley</u> und der mittelalterliche Ritter-
roman." <u>Die Neueren Sprachen</u>, 49, 114-21.
<u>Waverley</u> created a new category of historical novel which
sought to glorify the homeland rather than to inculcate a
specific moral. Scott apprehended events in realistic terms
but endowed them with his characteristic coloring. Scott
idealized a fabricated past to which he compared the present
unfavorably. This negative view of the present sets him
outside the tradition of German romanticism.

16 HIBERNICUS. "Queries from Scott's <u>Talisman</u> and 'Aunt
Margaret's Mirror': 'Mumpsimus.'" <u>Notes and Queries</u>, 181
(13 September), 153.

1941

"Mumpsimus" refers to the post-Communion prayer, and
Henry VIII probably got the tale from Sir Richard Pace.
See 1941.B36.

17   HIPPOCLYDES. "The 'Song of Hybrias the Cretan.'" Notes and
     Queries, 180 (28 June), 462.
          Queries where Scott found the version of "Hybrias" he
     uses in chapter 2 of "The Highland Widow"? See 1941.B9.

18   J., W. H. "The Secret of Scott's Authorship of the Waverley
     Novels." Notes and Queries, 180 (22 February), 140.
          Because Scott used material in the novels that people who
     knew him would recognize, many guessed his secret. In a
     letter of 1820, Croker relates that Londoners flocked to
     see the "great poet and greater novelist" when Scott visited
     the capital. See 1941.B20, B40.

19   K[ING], H. G. L. "The Children of Walter Scott: Their Graves."
     Notes and Queries, 181 (15 November), 272-73.
          Provides the locations of Scott's children's graves and
     the inscriptions on each.

20   _____. "The Secret of Scott's Authorship of the Waverley
     Novels." Notes and Queries, 180 (8 February), 101-102.
          Offers an incomplete list (according to Lockhart) of
     those who knew the secret of Scott's authorship before 1826.
     See 1941.B18, B40.

21   _____. "Sir Walter Scott's Nephew, William Scott." Notes and
     Queries, 181 (23 August), 102-104.
          Scott's treatment of his apparently illegitimate nephew
     William was rather harsh. William Scott went to Canada on
     passage money supplied by Sir Walter. He was found there
     many years later by Alexander Somerville, who endeavored
     unsuccessfully to help him by enlisting sympathy for William
     as Sir Walter's relative.

22   _____. "Walter Scott on the Unseen World." Notes and Queries,
     181 (20 September), 166-67.
          In Letter IV on Demonology and Witchcraft Scott writes
     of Reginald Scot, who believed that good men's souls act as
     guardians. This may have been the source of the confusion
     crediting Scott himself with the belief. See 1941.B39.

23   L., R. E. "Dramatized Versions of Scott's Novels." Notes and
     Queries, 180 (25 January), 63.
          Queries which was the most successful dramatized version?

1941

24   McDAVID, RAVEN I. "<u>Ivanhoe</u> and Simms' <u>Vasconselos</u>." <u>Modern</u>
      <u>Language Notes</u>, 56 (April), 294-97.
            A comparison of the Passage of Arms at Ashby in <u>Ivanhoe</u>
      with the tournament of Havana in <u>Vasconselos</u> (1854) shows
      general similarities such as elaborate description and the
      use of chivalric conventions. More specifically, in both
      works a knight is vanquished by the courtesy of his opponent
      rather than by force. Simms was favorably impressed by
      <u>Ivanhoe</u>, and finding himself working in an alien tradition,
      he may have borrowed some details.

25   MARRIOTT, JOHN. "The Stuart Fiasco: The Waverleys," in his
      <u>English History in English Fiction</u>. New York: E. P.
      Dutton, pp. 196-212.
            As a novelist Scott stimulated historical curiosity and,
      as Trevelyan has argued, demonstrated the complexity of
      history. Historical novels before 1814 prepared the way
      for <u>Waverley</u>, and subsequent historical novels look back to
      Scott "with filial piety." Carlyle's criticisms of his
      superficial characters are not justified. Focuses on
      <u>Waverley</u> and the Battle of Culloden.

26   MOORE, JOHN ROBERT. "Defoe and Scott." <u>Publications of the</u>
      <u>Modern Language Association of America</u>, 56, no. 3
      (September), 710-35.
            Defoe exerted a more important influence on Scott's work
      than did Dryden or Swift. Scott knew not only Defoe's
      novels but also his miscellaneous writings. They shared
      similar ideas regarding the relationship of history and
      fiction, a similar interest in details of daily experience,
      and a fascination with criminals and adventurers. Both
      treated them "with intimate knowledge and without any
      glamorous illusions."

27   ORIANS, G. HARRISON. "Walter Scott, Mark Twain, and the Civil
      War." <u>South Atlantic Quarterly</u>, 40 (October), 342-59.
            Refutes the argument that Scott exerted a profound in-
      fluence on Southern life. Southern militarism antedated
      Scott, and the Southern psychology was created by other in-
      fluences. The average Southerner was neither a slave owner
      nor aristocratic in his political views. Slavery was de-
      fended as an economic, not a feudal institution. Scott may
      have been "a decorative influence on Southern life" but not
      a force for the preservation of the old order.

28   PARKER, WILLIAM MATHIE. "Additions to Scott's Poems." <u>Times</u>
      <u>Literary Supplement</u> (13 December), p. 636.

Scott wrote a mock reply to an eighteenth century ballad formerly ascribed to Swift. Both appear in a MS in Scott's hand, now located in the National Library of Scotland. In a MS written by J. E. Shortreed, there is a copy of another poem by Scott in fourteen verses called "Heads and Tails." See 1941.B7.

29 _____. "More Scott Marginalia." <u>Times Literary Supplement</u> (3 May), p. 220; (10 May), p. 232; (17 May), p. 244.
Prints previously unpublished letters to George Huntly Gordon, Scott's amanuensis from 1818 to 1826. The letters contain instructions on copying, translating, and cataloguing books in Scott's library. Prints additional marginalia from the folio volume transcribed by Lockhart, Sophia, and Scott's son. See 1940.B28.

30 _____. "Scott's Prologue to 'Helga.'" <u>Times Literary Supplement</u> (4 January), p. 12.
Prints Scott's 40-line prologue to his friend Sir George Stewart Mackenzie's play <u>Helga</u>.

31 PHILLIPS, LAWRENCE. "Queries from Scott's <u>Betrothed</u>." <u>Notes and Queries</u>, 181 (2 August), 61.
Questions concern the facts behind three statements in the novel on the Abbot of Glastonbury's jurisdiction, an "extraordinary case" of bigamy, and the effects of a blow from a lance or mace. See 1941.B14.

32 _____. "Queries from Scott's <u>Chronicles of Canongate</u>, 'Highland Widow,' and 'Two Drovers.'" <u>Notes and Queries</u>, 181 (2 August), 61-62.
Requests information on several words, expressions, and customs. See 1941.B11.

33 _____. "Queries from Scott's <u>Fair Maid of Perth</u>." <u>Notes and Queries</u>, 181 (13 December), 332.
Requests identification of "Earish frontier," "Keddie's ring," "St. Fillian's Church," and "St. Barr."

34 _____. "Queries from Scott's <u>Quentin Durward</u>." <u>Notes and Queries</u>, 180 (22 February), 135.
Queries concern the identification of allusions, meanings of words, errors, and authorship of works mentioned in the novel. See 1941.B3, B40.

35 _____. "Queries from Scott's <u>Redgauntlet</u>." <u>Notes and Queries</u>, 181 (26 July), 48-49.
Queries concern a series of meanings, allusions and facts in the novel. See 1941.B10, B37.

1941

36   _____. "Queries from Scott's <u>Talisman</u> and 'Aunt Margaret's
       Mirror.'" <u>Notes and Queries</u>, 181 (23 August), 107.
             Queries concern a faulty quotation from the poet Lovelace
       in <u>The Talisman</u> and the source of a story alluded to in "My
       Aunt Margaret's Mirror." <u>See</u> 1941.B16.

37   PHILOSCOTUS. "Queries from Scott's <u>Redgauntlet</u>." <u>Notes and</u>
       <u>Queries</u>, 181 (20 December), 348.
             Provides meanings for "to chase," "cobbler," "mear,"
       "hosting," "leesome lane," "waste-book," "back spaul," and
       "brent." <u>See</u> 1941.B35.

38   _____. "A Quotation Improved." <u>Notes and Queries</u>, 180
       (19 April), 280.
             In <u>The Antiquary</u>, <u>Rob Roy</u>, and <u>The Monastery</u> Scott used
       various forms of a quotation from Rowe's <u>Fair Penitent</u>,
       Act I, scene i: "At length the morn and cool indifference
       came."

39   _____. "Walter Scott on the Unseen World." <u>Notes and Queries</u>,
       181 (9 August), 74.
             Queries whether Scott ever expressed the belief, as he
       is reported to have done by a German biographer, that the
       souls of good men act as guardian spirits. <u>See</u> 1941.B22.

40   RHEDECYNIAN. "The Secret of Scott's Authorship of the Waverley
       Novels." <u>Notes and Queries</u>, 180 (4 January), 12.
             Requests a list of those who knew of Scott's authorship
       before the disclosure in 1826. <u>See</u> 1941.B18, B20, and B43.

41   RUFF, WILLIAM. "Interleaved Copies of Scott's Poems." <u>Notes</u>
       <u>and Queries</u>, 181 (27 September), 176.
             Queries the location of the interleaved copies of <u>The</u>
       <u>Lay of the Last Minstrel</u> and <u>Marmion</u> used by Lockhart to
       edit the <u>Poetical Works</u> in 1833.

42   TROUBRIDGE, ST. VINCENT. "Queries from Scott's <u>Quentin</u>
       <u>Durward</u>." <u>Notes and Queries</u>, 180 (15 March), 195-96.
             George Wilkins is the author of <u>The Miseries of Forced</u>
       <u>Marriage</u>. The Sultan of Turkey is the Grand Seignior
       alluded to in <u>Quentin Durward</u>. <u>See</u> 1941.B34.

43   _____. "The Secret of Scott's Authorship of the Waverley
       Novels." <u>Notes and Queries</u>, 180 (29 March), 228.
             The comedian Charles Matthews and his wife knew the se-
       cret of Scott's authorship as early as 1815. <u>See</u> 1941.B40.

44 UTLEY, FRANCIS LEE. "The Last of the Miller's Head." <u>Modern
    Language Notes</u>, 56 (November), 534-36.
        Like Chaucer's Miller, David Ritchie, the original of
    Scott's <u>Black Dwarf</u>, was an example of pachycephaly; i.e.,
    he had the ability to run through doors with his hard skull.

<u>1942 A BOOKS</u>

1   WRIGHT, SYDNEY FOWLER. <u>The Siege of Malta; Founded on an Un-
    finished Romance by Sir Walter Scott.</u> London: Frederick
    Muller, 728pp.
        In the last year of his life and in ill health, Scott
    visited Malta to collect material for his book. The MS of
    this projected novel contains the opening scenes, but the
    plot is not developed. The remainder is a straight histori-
    cal account of the Siege of Malta. This continuation is
    built on a slight suggestion in the MS that the Maltese en-
    voy to Don Manuel is not whom he professes to be.

<u>1942 B SHORTER WRITINGS</u>

1   ANON. "Nodier, Scott and 'Trilby.'" <u>Notes and Queries</u>, 183
    (26 September), 197.
        Nodier took the subject of his story "Trilby" from a
    preface or note to a Scott novel; queries where in Scott
    this source is to be found?

2   ANON. "Mordaunt's 'Sound, Sound the Clarion.'" <u>Explicator</u>,
    1, no. 3 (1 December), item 20.
        Although the cited quatrain from <u>Old Mortality</u>, chapter
    34, was not written by Scott, he intended to convey "a
    striking juxtaposition of martial glory and squalor."

3   CORSON, JAMES CLARKSON. "Miscellaneous Letters To and About
    James Hogg." <u>Notes and Queries</u>, 182 (16 May), 268.
        In a letter to Hogg of 23 June, 1834, John M'Crone re-
    fers to M'Crone's projected life of Scott. <u>See</u> 1942.B17.

4   _____. "The Siege of Malta." <u>Notes and Queries</u>, 182
    (21 February), 108.
        There are several inaccurate statements in the article
    on this subject by H. G. L. K. The MS is owned by Gabriel
    Wells of New York; it should be published for the benefit
    of serious students of Scott's life and works. <u>See</u>
    1942.B11.

1942

5   D., A. E. "Scott Quotation." <u>Notes and Queries</u>, 182
    (20 June), 347-48.
        The quotation referred to by Hippoclydes is actually
    from Southey, whom Scott quotes in chapter 12 of <u>The Heart</u>
    <u>of Midlothian</u>. <u>See</u> 1942.B10; 1944.B3, B6.

6   DICKENS, BRUCE. "The Cleek'um Inn." <u>Times Literary Supplement</u>
    (6 June), p. 283.
        Concedes that Scott did not invent the name of the
    Cleek'um Inn, but he gave it wider popularity, especially
    in Scotland. <u>See</u> 1941.B8 and 1942.B19.

7   EWEN, C. L. L'ESTRANGE. "Demonology and Witchcraft." <u>Notes</u>
    <u>and Queries</u>, 182 (18 April), 223.
        According to the Crown Plea Rolls and the Gaol Books,
    there was no triple execution at Chester in 1636. <u>See</u>
    1942.B14.

8   GORDON, ROBERT K. "Shakespeare's <u>Henry IV</u> and the Waverley
    Novels." <u>Modern Language Review</u>, 37, no. 3 (July), 304-16.
        Scott borrows "nobly" from <u>Henry IV</u>, especially for
    characters and situations in the Waverley Novels concerning
    rebellion. Hotspur influenced the characterizations of
    Fergus MacIvor and Redgauntlet, and there are frequent
    verbal echoes of the plays throughout the novels.

9   GRIERSON, HERBERT JOHN CLIFFORD. "Preface" to <u>Songs and</u>
    <u>Lyrics of Sir Walter Scott</u>. Edited by H. J. C. Grierson.
    Published for the Saltire Society. Edinburgh: Oliver and
    Boyd, pp. 5-10.
        Although Scott's earliest poetry expressed his sorrow
    for lost love, most of his inspiration came from wide read-
    ing. He "found himself as a poet" in the imitation of old
    ballads, and his best lyrics are dramatic and impersonal
    rather than subjective. Their tone is both adventurous and
    melancholy. They reflect a sensibility that loved life and
    yet acknowledged its tragic nature.

10 HIPPOCLYDES. "Scott Quotation." <u>Notes and Queries</u>, 182
    (21 February), 108.
        Queries if Scott is quoting Byron in chapter 30 of <u>The</u>
    <u>Antiquary</u>: "Stern to inflict and stubborn to endure, / Who
    smiled in death!" <u>See</u> 1942.B5; 1944.B3, B6.

11 K[ING], H. G. L. "The Siege of Malta." <u>Notes and Queries</u>,
    182 (17 January), 30.
        Summarizes the circumstances surrounding Scott's work
    on <u>The Siege of Malta</u>; queries the possibility (and

advisability) of its publication, now that it is privately
owned. See 1942.B4.

12   NOVIKOV, A. "Denis Davydov and Walter Scott." Russian Litera-
      ture and Art (1 August), p. 4.
           A partisan leader during the war with Napoleon, Davydov
      became a poet and man of letters in peacetime. Scott wrote
      to him, admiring the Russian resistance effort and request-
      ing additional material. After the Napoleon was published,
      Scott asked for Davydov's reaction. He wrote a detailed
      answer in which he differed with Scott's treatment of Mar-
      shal Kutusov, but Scott died before the letter was mailed.
      It was later published with the Russian translation of the
      Life of Napoleon.

13   PARSONS, COLEMAN OSCAR. "Journalistic Anecdotage About Scott."
      Notes and Queries, 183 (5 December), 339-40.
           Summarizes two journalistic anecdotes which have not
      been included in any book-length biography. They suggest
      "Scott's curiosity about the invisible world of spirits--
      a subject which did not particularly excite Lockhart."

14   _____. "Scott's Letters on Demonology and Witchcraft: Outside
      Contributors." Notes and Queries, 182 (21 March), 156-58
      and (28 March), 173-74.
           Summarizes contributions of supplementary materials
      Scott received from at least seventeen outside helpers.
      The popularity of the work and the widely varying reviews
      reflect the conflicting attitudes to the supernatural which
      prevailed in Scott's period. See 1942.B7, B15, B16.

15   SETON-ANDERSON, J. "Demonology and Witchcraft." Notes and
      Queries, 182 (9 May), 264.
           A witch was burned in Spain as late as 1781. See
      1942.B14.

16   SPARKE, ALEXANDER. "Demonology and Witchcraft." Notes and
      Queries, 183 (4 July), 24.
           Provides a list of reference works on the subject. See
      1942.B14.

17   STROUT, ALAN LANG. "Hogg's Domestic Manners." Notes and
      Queries, 183 (26 September), 187-88.
           There is a close connection between M'Crone's and Hogg's
      works on Scott. M'Crone's dispute with Chalmers may explain
      why his own work was not published and also why Cochrane
      did not publish Hogg's work. See 1942.B3.

1942

18   ____. "Lockhart as Gossip: New Letters to J. W. Croker."
        <u>Times Literary Supplement</u> (17 October), p. 516.
            Quotes from letters of Lockhart in the William L. Clements
        Library of the University of Michigan. The letters are
        dated from 1822 to 1843 and concern Scott's later work, his
        attempts to secure a government post for Lockhart, the
        visits of George IV and Crabbe to Edinburgh, and Scott's
        last illness and death. <u>See</u> 1943.B33; 1944.B19; 1945.B16;
        and 1946.B14.

19   THOMSON, GEORGE. "The Cleek'um Inn." <u>Times Literary Supple-</u>
        <u>ment</u> (6 June), p. 283.
            There is a "Cleekimin" in Motherwell that pre-dates <u>St.</u>
        <u>Ronan's Well</u>. <u>See</u> 1941.B8 and 1942.B6.

20   WATT, LAUCHLAN MacLEAN. "Introduction" to <u>Scott's Poetical</u>
        <u>Works</u>. London and Glasgow: Collins, pp. iii-xviii.
            Scott derived his poetic inspiration from Border lore,
        Percy's <u>Reliques</u>, and contact with the Highlands. His
        poems teach the love rather than the fear of Nature, and
        they reflect his fondness for the places memorialized in
        Border legends. Although himself a Borderer, Scott gave to
        Highland song and legend a new beauty. He wrote a poetry
        of action, full of fresh subject matter designed to appeal
        to plain people. His poetry is "life's marching song" which
        reawoke humanity to chivalry and love of nature.

<u>1943 A BOOKS</u>

1   CORSON, JAMES CLARKSON. <u>A Bibliography of Sir Walter Scott.</u>
        <u>A Classified and Annotated List of Books and Articles Re-</u>
        <u>lating to His Life and Works, 1797-1940</u>. Edinburgh:
        Oliver and Boyd, 443pp.
            Listings include only materials which deal exclusively
        with Scott from both learned and popular sources. Contents
        are divided into bibliographies; biographical material ar-
        ranged by chronology as well as by topics; literary criti-
        cism, arranged by genre with a section on literary rela-
        tions; studies which combine literary and biographical
        material, including special subjects such as law, medicine,
        religion, animals and topography; and miscellaneous ma-
        terial.

*2   COWLEY, JOHN P. "Scott in the Dedicatory Epistles to <u>Marmion</u>."
        Ph.D. dissertation, Yale University, 1943.
            Cited in <u>Comprehensive Dissertation Index</u> (Ann Arbor,
        Michigan: Xerox University Microfilms, 1973), XXX, 468.

1943 B SHORTER WRITINGS

1 ANON. "The Anax of Publishers." <u>Times Literary Supplement</u>
   (26 June), p. 308.
       Quotes Scott's favorable impression of John Murray, who
   sought his support for the <u>Quarterly Review</u> after an unfair
   criticism of Scott appeared in the <u>Edinburgh Review</u>. <u>See</u>
   1943.B12.

2 BIRRELL, J. HAMILTON. "Sir Walter Scott's Debt to Burns."
   <u>Burns Chronicle and Club Directory</u>, 2nd ser. 18, 18-25.
       After Burns's death, Scott tried to make amends for de-
   liberately ignoring him during his lifetime. In the <u>Min-
   strelsy</u> he acknowledges Burns's work in ballad preservation,
   and he quotes Burns frequently in the novels and the <u>Journal</u>.
   In his comments on Lockhart's <u>Life of Burns</u>, in his private
   letters, and in his review of Cromek's <u>Reliques of Burns</u>,
   Scott praised Burns's poetry but adversely criticized his
   character.

3 BISSON, LAURENCE ADOLPHUS. <u>Amédée Pichot: A Romantic Prome-
   theus</u>. Oxford: Basil Blackwell, passim.
       Pichot translated Scott into French and shared many of
   his feelings and interests. When he finally met Scott, he
   was disappointed by his commonplace appearance but enchanted
   by his kindness and conversation. He conveyed his "unusual
   understanding" of Scott and Scotland in his <u>Voyage en
   Angleterre et en Écosse</u>.

4 BREWER, WILMON. "Shakespeare in the Career of Sir Walter
   Scott," in his <u>About Poetry and Other Matters</u>. Francestown,
   New Hampshire: Marshall Jones Co., pp. 57-63.
       Scott admired Shakespeare's spontaneity, humor, and com-
   mand of history. In <u>The Lady of the Lake</u> he borrowed from
   <u>Macbeth</u> the device of a prophecy fulfilling itself in the
   hero's death. He borrowed characters and quotations from
   other Shakespearean plays, and he followed both Shakespeare
   and Schiller in linking actual historical events with
   imaginary adventures.

5 BRIGHTFIELD, MYRON F. "Scott, Hazlitt, and Napoleon," in
   <u>Essays and Studies by Members of the Department of English</u>.
   University of California Publications in English, Volume 14.
   Berkeley: University of California Press, pp. 181-98.
       Summarizes the attitudes of four types of literary men
   toward the French Revolution in 1803: the Tories, the
   Whigs, the Lake Poets, and the Radicals. Compares the views
   of Scott, representative of "the unfaltering conservatives,"

1943

and Hazlitt, representative of "the undeterred Radical," on the subjects of patriotism, loyalty in battle, and relations between the people and their government. Both attitudes have deep-rooted defects and clearly apparent merits.

6   CHAPMAN, R. W. "Cancels in Scott's <u>Minstrelsy</u>." <u>Library</u>, 4th ser. 23, no. 4 (March), 198.
        A cancellation in Volume III (Edinburgh, 1803) was made for the sole purpose of changing "so" to "sae." The Scots care deeply for dialectical rectitude.

7   _____. "Scott's <u>Antiquary</u>." <u>Review of English Studies</u>, 19 (July), 295-96.
        Suggests some textual errors in the second edition (1816) of <u>The Antiquary</u>. Most of these are conjectural, as Chapman has not had access to the manuscript.

8   COOPER, LANE. "Wordsworth on Sir Walter Scott," in his <u>Experiments in Education</u>. Cornell Studies in English, No. 33. Ithaca, New York: Cornell University Press, pp. 51-71.
        Wordsworth's criticisms of Scott's poetic method were largely offered in private and show Wordsworth to be a "mature and independent critic" of good judgment. Wordsworth's poetic tributes to Scott ignore the differences in their methods and are "gracious, warm, and fitting." Includes a Supplement of excerpts from various sources quoting Wordsworth on the subject of Scott.

9   CORSON, JAMES CLARKSON. "Goblin's Cave, Mount Benvenue." <u>Notes and Queries</u>, 184 (10 April), 237.
        The Goblin's Cave is now only a deep cleft in the rocks. In editions of <u>The Lady of the Lake</u> subsequent to the second, Scott explains this in a note to Canto III, stanza xxiv. <u>See</u> 1943.B32.

10   D., A. E. "The Polite Letter-Writer." <u>Notes and Queries</u>, 184 (5 June), 342.
        Prints an excerpt from a letter of Bruce of Blackmannon which Scott included in his introduction to the "Proceedings in the court-martial, held upon John, Master of Sinclair," which Scott edited. <u>See</u> 1943.B11, B15.

11   D., A. E. "Shaw (Christina and John)." <u>Notes and Queries</u>, 184 (22 May), 321.
        Christina Shaw was Scott's grandmother. Two Shaw men were murdered by John, Master of Sinclair, in 1708. <u>See</u> Scott's <u>Journal</u>, 21 March, 1828. <u>See</u> 1943.B10, B15.

12   ELWIN, MALCOLM. "The Founder of the Quarterly Review--John
      Murray II." Quarterly Review, 281 (July), 1-15.
          Scott was instrumental in the founding of the Quarterly
      Review. He encouraged Murray, rallied influential support,
      and contributed his own work. When Gifford finally resigned
      the editorship because of ill health, Scott convinced Murray
      to appoint Lockhart in spite of protests from Croker and
      Southey. See 1943.B1.

13   GORDON, ROBERT K. "Scott and Wordsworth's Lyrical Ballads."
      Transactions of the Royal Society of Canada, 3rd ser. 37,
      113-19.
          Most of Scott's quotations from Wordsworth are from the
      Lyrical Ballads, to which he responded emotionally. In the
      Introduction to The Antiquary Scott states that he has at-
      tempted in prose what Wordsworth achieved in the Lyrical
      Ballads. Scott's Edie Ochiltree and Madge Wildfire may
      have been influenced by characters from these poems.

14   GRIEVE, CHRISTOPHER MURRAY. Lucky Poet: A Self-Study in
      Literature and Political Ideas. London: Methuen, 197-205.
          Scott and his modern "eulogists" are responsible for the
      current provincial status of Scotland. Scott's novels cre-
      ated a "paralysing ideology of defeatism in Scotland," and
      he regarded the question of national identity with pessimism
      about Scotland's future. Although his work demonstrates
      that a subject nation must concentrate on its national lan-
      guage and history, the "hireling scribes" of English im-
      perialism have refused to praise him on these grounds. See
      1943.B21.

15   HEWINS, G. S. "Shaw (Christina and John)." Notes and Queries,
      184 (10 April), 227.
          Queries where Scott refers to his ancestress Christina
      Shaw and mentions a murder in her family? See 1943.B10,
      B11.

*16   HUDSON, CHARLES M., JR. "The Roderick Legend in English Ro-
      mantic Literature." Ph.D. dissertation, Yale University,
      1943.
          Cited in Comprehensive Dissertation Index (Ann Arbor,
      Michigan: Xerox University Microfilms), XXX, 468.

17   IGNOTO. "'Like a Tether': Phrase in Scott." Notes and
      Queries, 184 (22 May), 317.
          This phrase is used to describe a long letter Scott
      wrote to Lord Elgin. Queries if the source is Hamlet?

1943

18   J., W. H. "The Dead Hand: Dickens and Scott." <u>Notes and
       Queries</u>, 184 (27 March), 191-92.
            Dickens and Scott both spent valuable time editing worth-
       less material, such as the posthumous poetry of Anna Seward,
       which Scott called "absolutely execrable."

19   _____. "Shakespeare in Modern Dress." <u>Notes and Queries</u>, 184
       (5 June), 329-31.
            Quotes from two letters of Scott on the importance of
       appropriate costumes for actors and actresses, especially
       for tragedy.

20   M[ABBOTT], T. O. "Towns Named After Novels." <u>Notes and
       Queries</u>, 185 (17 July), 56.
            Offers a list of places such as Kenilworth, Illinois,
       Waverley, Iowa, and Ivanhoe, Georgia which have been named
       after places or characters in Scott's novels.

21   MacDIARMID, HUGH. <u>Lucky Poet</u>.
            <u>See</u> 1943.B14.

22   PARKER, WILLIAM MATHIE. "Scott as <u>Amicus Curiae</u>." <u>Juridical
       Review</u>, 55, 55-64.
            Reprints two Scott letters (13 October, 1823 and 5 Novem-
       ber, 1823) to Adam Longmore, a clerk in the King's Remem-
       brancer's office, regarding claimants on the bastard estate
       of Hector Lithgow.

23   PARSONS, COLEMAN OSCAR. "The Bodach Glas in <u>Waverley</u>." <u>Notes
       and Queries</u>, 184 (13 February), 95-97.
            Offers several possible originals for the gray spectre
       that appeared to Fergus MacIvor before his execution at
       Carlisle. The persistence of this kind of warning spirit
       in Scottish legend justified Scott's use of it in <u>Waverley</u>
       as "a vivid detail in the portrayal of bygone manners."

24   _____. "The Dalrymple Legend in <u>The Bride of Lammermoor</u>."
       <u>Review of English Studies</u>, 19 (January), 51-58.
            Summarizes four versions of the witchcraft tale of the
       death of newly married Janet Dalrymple, on which the plot
       of the novel is based. To assimilate these supernatural
       elements into his narrative, Scott employed "two levels of
       consciousness" so that events may be interpreted on the
       realistic-romantic plane or the superstitious plane. This
       "effective duality of mood and action" allows Scott's nar-
       rative to retain the atmosphere of the original family
       legend.

25 _____. "The Interest of Scott's Public in the Supernatural."
Notes and Queries, 185 (14 August), 92-100.
    Surveys the works of Scott's contemporaries on the super-
natural and the critical reception of his Letters on Demonology and Witchcraft. Scott's own attitude toward the
supernatural varied throughout his life; in his youth he
was susceptible to it; in middle age he valued superstition
imaginatively as a reminder of the past; in his last years
his attitude was more logical and critical. He remained
unpredictable throughout his life and works in his relative
evaluation of imaginative and rationalistic modes of judgment.

26 _____. "Minor Spirits and Superstitions in the Waverley Novels." Notes and Queries, 184 (19 June), 358-63 and 185
(3 July), 4-9.
    Describes Scott's library of works on the supernatural,
a collection which was "virtually conterminous with his
life." Summarizes the appearance in the Waverley Novels of
"the less conventional supernatural beings," such as Drows,
Kelpies, and Bogles. Second part summarizes supernatural
animals, wild huntsmen, doppelgängers, and superstitions
used in the novels. Scott enjoyed the color and quaintness
of old beliefs, but was not attempting to encourage credulity. He regarded imaginary creatures and folk-creeds as
one way of understanding past cultures. Includes a bibliography. See 1943.B34.

27 _____. "The Original of the Black Dwarf." Studies in Philology, 40 (October), 567-75.
    The original of the Black Dwarf was David Ritchie, whom
Scott met at least once. Scott also had access to local
information about Ritchie. After the novel was published,
the legend of Ritchie received much "literary embroidery"
that could not have been available to Scott prior to 1816.

28 _____. "Scott's Fellow Demonologists." Modern Language Quarterly, 4, no. 4 (December), 473-94.
    Scott's fellow demonologists ranged from the eccentric
to the sick to the sane. These included the learned John
Leyden, James Hogg who preferred supernatural difficulties
for his characters, the talented but morbid Robert Pearse
Gillies, and Charles Robert Maturin who at times confused
the real and the supernatural. Scott also shared interest
in demonology with Matthew Gregory Lewis, Charles Kirk-
patrick Sharpe, and Robert Surtees. Scott's human values,
wide interests, and self-discipline balanced any tendency
toward morbidity in his own character.

1943

29   ____. "Sir John Sinclair's Raspe and Scott's Dousterswivel." Notes and Queries, 184 (30 January), 62-66.
    Rudolf Raspe's duping of Sir John Sinclair in a mining scheme may have suggested Herman Dousterswivel's cheating Sir Arthur Wardour in The Antiquary.

30   ____. "Walter Scott in Pandemonium." Modern Language Notes, 38, no. 3 (July), 244-49.
    During the summer of 1802 at the house of Lord Minto, Scott participated in a series of ghost story exchanges called "Pandemonium" by the members of the group. The entertainment was reconvened at other times and places until Christmas, 1805. Includes some doggerel verses of mock-serious diablerie, written by Scott probably to Anna Marie, the daughter of Lord Minto.

31 POSTON, M. L. "Addenda to Worthington." Times Literary Supplement (29 May), p. 264.
    As an addition to Worthington's bibliography of the Waverley Novels, the author describes in detail his copies of Tales of My Landlord, Second Series (1818) and The Antiquary (1816).

32 SASSENACH. "Goblin's Cave, Mount Benvenue." Notes and Queries, 184 (27 February), 140.
    Queries if the Goblin's Cave, where Douglas and Ellen take refuge in The Lady of the Lake, really exists. See 1943.B9.

33 STROUT, ALAN LANG. "Some Unpublished Letters of John Gibson Lockhart to John Wilson Croker." Notes and Queries, 185 (9 October), 217-23.
    Adds a few letters referring to Scott which were not published in the Times Literary Supplement article of 17 October, 1942. These relate primarily to the period just before Scott left for Italy and to reminiscences of Scott's relationship with the Prince Regent. See 1942.B18; 1944.B19; 1945.B16; and 1946.B14.

34 SUMMERS, MONTAGUE. "Scott and the Supernatural." Notes and Queries, 185 (11 September), 170-71.
    Adds six works to Parsons' bibliography on the supernatural. See 1943.B26.

*35 SWAEN, A. E. H. "Sir Walter's Tooverstaf." Neophilologus, 28 (April), 212-28.
    Cited in the Annual Bibliography of English Language and Literature (Cambridge: Modern Humanities Research Association, 1956), XXIV, 231, item #4238.

36   TAYLOR, JOHN TINNON. <u>Early Opposition to the English Novel:</u>
     <u>The Popular Reaction from 1760 to 1830</u>. New York: King's
     Crown Press, pp. 97-100.
         Scott "did most to establish the novel on a moral basis
     with the reviewers and with the public." People who had
     previously opposed fiction accepted the Waverley Novels, be-
     cause they were considered either positive moral influences
     or, at worst, not injurious to character.

1944 A BOOKS - NONE

1944 B SHORTER WRITINGS

1   BRIGHTFIELD, MYRON F. "Lockhart's <u>Quarterly</u> Contributors."
     <u>Publications of the Modern Language Association</u>, 59, no. 2
     (June), 491-512.
         Identifies by full name the authors of all literary
     articles appearing in the <u>Quarterly Review</u> during the period
     of Lockhart's editorship (1826-53). Scott is credited with
     ten contributions.

2   C., R. W. "Scott and Jane Austen." <u>Notes and Queries</u>, 186
     (12 February), 91.
         Quotes Mrs. Mary Anne Hughes on Scott's favorable opin-
     ions of Austen's novels.

3   CORSON, JAMES CLARKSON. "A Quotation in <u>The Antiquary</u>."
     <u>Notes and Queries</u>, 187 (18 November), 231-32.
         Henry Wheaton's <u>History of the Northmen</u> (1831) also at-
     tributes to Southey the quotation used in chapter 30 of <u>The</u>
     <u>Antiquary</u>. <u>See</u> 1942.B5, B10; 1944.B6.

4   DIXON, W. MACNEILE. "Our Debt to Scott Today," in his <u>Apology</u>
     <u>for the Arts</u>. London: Edward Arnold, pp. 153-64.
         Reprint of 1932.B49, B50.

5   DODDS, M. H. and E. G. B. "Sir Walter Scott's Quotations."
     <u>Notes and Queries</u>, 186 (17 June), 296-97.
         Identifies sources for quotations Scott used in Suckling's
     "A Ballad Upon a Wedding," Monk Lewis' <u>Journal of a West</u>
     <u>Indian Proprietor</u>, John Farmer's <u>Gaudeamus: Songs for</u>
     <u>Schools and Colleges</u>, and from the children's lore of the
     British Isles.

6   FITZGERALD, MAURICE H. "A Quotation in <u>The Antiquary</u>." <u>Notes</u>
     <u>and Queries</u>, 187 (16 December), 284.

1944

The quotation from chapter 30 of The Antiquary is from
Southey's poetical address to Amos Cottle in Cottle's 1797
volume Icelandic Poetry. See 1942.B5, B10; 1944.B3.

7   FOTHERINGHAM, JOHN A. "Scott's Quotations." Notes and Queries,
     187 (2 December), 257.
         Two quotations from Redgauntlet chapter 22 and Rob Roy
     chapter 8 are probably by Scott himself, although he implies
     that they are not.

8   FREEMANTLE, A. F. "A Plea for the Waverley Novels." Contem-
     porary Review, 165 (May), 284-87.
         The generalization that the Waverley Novels are "diffi-
     cult to get into" is true of some but not most of them.
     Scott's diction evokes the spirit of the past, and his
     lengthy descriptions contribute to the delineation of char-
     acter and atmosphere. Scott honored the most humble people
     and demonstrated their eloquence. Although his heroes and
     heroines are not very interesting, they don't matter as
     much as the other characters.

9   GRAY, A. SPEIR. "Some Blunders of Celebrated Authors." Notes
     and Queries, 186 (26 February), 122-23.
         In Maître Cornelius Balzac criticized Scott for placing
     the castle of Plessis-les-Tours in Quentin Durward upon a
     height. This criticism is not entirely justified, however,
     as Scott describes the ground rising to the castle "by a
     very gentle elevation."

10   K[ING], H. G. L. "Sir Walter Scott: Last Specimen of his
     Handwriting." Notes and Queries, 187 (4 November), 214.
         Queries the location of the inn on the road from Rome to
     the Tyrol where, according to the 1839 edition of Lockhart's
     Life, Scott signed the Book of Guests on his journey home-
     ward in 1832.

11   MOORE, JOHN ROBERT. "Scott and Henry Esmond." Notes and
     Queries, 186 (17 June), 288.
         In both Henry Esmond and St. Ronan's Well the hero gives
     up his claim to legitimate birth, a title, and an estate
     and goes into exile for the sake of the woman he loves.
     Thackeray was influenced by the Scott novel.

12   _____. "Scott's Antiquary and Defoe's History of Apparitions."
     Modern Language Notes, 59 (December), 550-51.
         The episode of the chest of silver bullion in the priory
     in Scott's Antiquary may have been suggested by a tale in
     Defoe's History of Apparitions.

13   PARKER, WILLIAM MATHIE. "Sir Walter Scott's Quotations."
       Notes and Queries, 186 (6 May), 216-17.
            Asks for identification of authors or sources of several
       quotations used by Scott in his letters. See 1944.B16, B22;
       1970.B19; 1972.B40; 1973.B29, B47.

14   PARROTT, T. M. "Mak and Archie Armstrong." Modern Language
       Notes, 59, 297-304.
            The ballad "Archie Armstrong's Aith," written by Marriot
       and edited by Scott for the Minstrelsy of the Scottish Bor-
       der, tells the same story as The Second Shepherd's Play.
       However, it is probably closer to the source, as the Wake-
       field Master adapted the story to fit his own purposes.

15   PRITCHETT, V. S. "Books in General." New Statesman and Na-
       tion, N.S. 27 (10 June), 389-90 and N.S. 28 (1 July), 11-12.
            Scott is a "grown-up" novelist willing to acknowledge the
       limits of the human condition. He does not use the past as
       escape but as a way to "record the common life" of his char-
       acters. His orientation is analytical and psychological,
       and he explores the unconscious through superstitions and
       legends. In The Heart of Midlothian he demonstrates the
       effect of history upon conscience and motive. Reprinted
       slightly revised: 1947.B8.

16   R., H. M. "Sir Walter Scott's Quotations." Notes and Queries,
       187 (12 August), 84.
            Quotes a seventeenth century tobacco song Scott may have
       had in mind in one of his epigrams. See 1944.B13.

17   RENDALL, VERNON. "Lockhart's Life of Scott." Times Literary
       Supplement (8 January), p. 24.
            Identifies instances of Lockhart's carelessness in quot-
       ing and dating from Scott's Journal.

*18   RICARDO, AUGUSTO. Figuras da Literatura Inglesa. Lisbon:
       Editorial Minerva, pp. 27-31.
            Source unknown.

19   STROUT, ALAN LANG. "Some Unpublished Letters of John Gibson
       Lockhart to John Wilson Croker." Notes and Queries, 187
       (9 September), 112-15.
            Includes a letter of 21 February, 1838 which expresses
       Lockhart's relief at having sent off the last proofs for
       the Life of Scott, and his impatience with Fenimore
       Cooper's attack on his account of Scott's visit to Paris.
       See 1942.B18; 1943.B33; 1945.B16; and 1946.B14.

1944

20   STRUVE, GLEB. "Scott Letters Discovered in Russia." <u>Bulletin</u>
     <u>of the John Rylands Library</u>, 28, no. 2, 477-84.
         Prints the text of three Scott letters discovered by
     Dmitry Yakubovich in public libraries of the Soviet Union.
     The letters, which are not included in Grierson's edition,
     are addressed to Lord Bloomfield, British Minister in Stock-
     holm; to Princess Galitzin, who lionized Scott in Paris in
     1826; and to Denis Davydov (in fragmentary form). Re-
     printed: 1945.A1.

21   WARD, WILLIAM SMITH. "Some Aspects of the Conservative Atti-
     tude Toward Poetry in English Criticism, 1798-1820." <u>Pub-</u>
     <u>lications of the Modern Language Association</u>, 60, no. 2
     (June), 386-98.
         Deals with Scott only peripherally. Like Byron, he was
     often censured on the grounds of villainous but sentimental-
     ized heroes.

22   WILLIAMS, HAROLD, E. L., and L. R. M. STRACHAN. "Sir Walter
     Scott's Quotations." <u>Notes and Queries</u>, 186 (3 June),
     273-74.
         Identifies quotations from Swift, Shakespeare, Parnell,
     and other sources. <u>See</u> 1944.B13.

1945 A BOOKS

1   STRUVE, GLEB. <u>Scott Letters Discovered in Russia</u>. Manchester:
     Manchester University Press.
         Reprint of 1944.B20.

1945 B SHORTER WRITINGS

1   A., P. M. "Scott's 'County Guy.'" <u>Explicator</u>, 3, no. 5
     (March), item 13.
         Queries the relationship among poetry, music, and meaning
     in these lines from <u>Quentin Durward</u>. <u>See</u> 1946.B9.

2   ARMS, GEORGE and JOHN P. KIRBY. "Scott's 'Proud Maisie.'"
     <u>Explicator</u>, 4, no. 2 (November), item 14.
         The introduction and punctuation emphasize the fragmen-
     tary nature of the poem in <u>The Heart of Midlothian</u>. The
     introduction states that only parts could be heard, and the
     punctuation includes ellipses between stanzas.

3   B-W., L. "'Is Thy Servant a Dog?'" <u>Notes and Queries</u>, 188
     .(19 May), 212.

The passage, in R. H. Hutton's life of Scott, about the little Blenheim cocker which overcame its shyness to greet Scott, in the streets of Edinburgh, may have inspired the poem of this title by Father J. B. Tabb.

4   CORSON, JAMES CLARKSON. "August and Longevity." Notes and Queries, 189 (29 December), 284.
    Scott attributes delicate health not to birth in August but to premature birth. See 1945.B9.

5   _____. "Scott's Novels: Dramatized Versions." Notes and Queries, 189 (14 July), 17-18.
    Offers a selected list of dramatized versions of Scott's novels in English, written or performed in Great Britain during his lifetime. Reply to 1945.B6.

6   DUNLOP, J. G. "Scott's Novels: Dramatized Versions." Notes and Queries, 188 (2 June), 237.
    Queries who dramatized Scott's novels? See 1945.B5.

7   GORDON, ROBERT K. "Scott and Shakespeare's Tragedies." Transactions of the Royal Society of Canada. 3rd ser. 39, sec. 2 (May), 111-17.
    Scott's habit of using Shakespearean quotations does not always work well in the novels. The dramatic context of the quotations is often more emotionally intense than the scene in the novel, and the juxtaposition makes the Scott character or situation appear relatively superficial. This is "most obvious and least fortunate" in Kenilworth. In St. Ronan's Well and The Bride of Lammermoor, the Shakespearean invocations work more successfully to create a sense of fate or doom.

8   KERN, JOHN D. "An Unidentified Review, Possibly by Scott." Modern Language Quarterly, 6 (September), 327-28.
    A letter from Scott to John Murray, dated 3 December, 1810, suggests that Scott may have written the review of "An Historical and Critical Essay on the Life and Character of Petrarch" which appeared in the Quarterly Review of September, 1812. The author of the essay is not indicated in the review, but it was almost certainly Alexander Fraser Tytler, Lord Woodhouselee.

9   K[ING], H. G. L. "August and Longevity." Notes and Queries, 189 (1 December), 237.
    Queries Scott's justification for the remark in his Journal, under 17 March, 1826, that children born in August are never strong. See 1945.B4.

1945

10 McKEEHAN, IRENE P. "Some Observations on the Vocabulary of
    Landscape Description Among the Early Romanticists," in
    Elizabethan Studies and Other Essays in Honor of George F.
    Reynolds. University of Colorado Studies in the Humanities,
    2, no. 4. Boulder: University of Colorado Press,
    pp. 254-71.
        Scott's descriptions of nature provide accurate details,
    but he uses few adjectival epithets. He does not dis-
    tinguish between "grandeur" and "the sublime."

11 MUIR, EDWIN. "Walter Scott: The Man" and "Walter Scott: The
    Writer." University of Edinburgh Journal, 13, no. 2
    (Autumn), 79-88.
        Scott was both a great and a very bad storyteller. The
    complications of his plots are intended to reflect the com-
    plications of human life, and his narrative power derives
    from scope and variety. His characters appear formulaic
    but are actually complex and, like those of Dostoevsky,
    speak for "whole classes of humanity." Reprinted: 1949.B4
    and 1950.B10. Condensed: 1968.B31.

12 PARSONS, COLEMAN OSCAR. "The Deaths of Glossin and Hatteraick
    in Guy Mannering." Philological Quarterly, 24, no. 2
    (April), 169-74.
        The details of the murder of Glossin and the suicide of
    Hatteraick came from various works of witchcraft literature
    which Scott owned or to which he had access. Some of this
    material appears in the Letters on Demonology and Witch-
    craft.

13 _____. "The Influence of Grillparzer on The Heart of Mid-
    lothian." Notes and Queries, 189 (15 December), 248-49.
        The retributive violence of Grillparzer's Die Ahnfrau
    (1817) may be seen in Staunton's remorse, his son's deprav-
    ity, and his unnatural murder in chapters 49-52 of The
    Heart of Midlothian.

14 _____. "The Supernatural in Scott's Poetry." Notes and
    Queries, 188 (13 January), 2-8; (27 January), 30-33;
    (24 February), 76-77; (10 March), 98-101.
        The almost undisciplined use of the supernatural in
    Scott's very early work gives way later to "restraint, co-
    herence, and appropriateness." He uses haunted places to
    create atmosphere and witchcraft and demonology to enhance
    characterization of villains.

15 POTTLE, FREDERICK A. "The Power of Memory in Boswell and
    Scott," in Essays on the Eighteenth Century Presented to
    David Nichol Smith. Oxford: Clarendon Press, pp. 168-89.

A comparison of journal accounts by Scott and Boswell indicates that although both perceived the world with eighteenth century eyes, Scott had a "double vision" of the world of romance. Boswell's memory combines almost total recall with artistic selectivity and recreates the past on the level of normal experience. Scott's memory is "wildly inaccurate" and colored by imagination. Boswell's disciplined, accurate memory was a product of his time, just as Scott's imaginative recall was characteristic of the Romantic period. Reprinted: 1969.B35.

16   STROUT, ALAN LANG. "Some Unpublished Letters of John Gibson Lockhart to John Wilson Croker." Notes and Queries, 189 (28 July), 34-37.

        A letter of 5 November, 1845 concerns Scott's sundial, and a letter of 28 May, 1847 concerns rings, once used to secure prisoners, which Scott described at Tully-Veolan and which he put on his outer gate at Abbotsford. See 1942.B18; 1943.B33; 1944.B19; and 1946.B14.

1946 A BOOKS

1   TAIT, JOHN GUTHRIE and WILLIAM MATHIE PARKER, eds. The Journal of Sir Walter Scott, 1829-32. Text Revised from a Photostat in the National Library of Scotland. Edinburgh: Oliver and Boyd, 283pp.

        See Volume I: 1939.A1 and Volume II: 1941.A1. Reprinted: 1950.A3.

1946 B SHORTER WRITINGS

1   ANON. (The Librarian, Leeds Library). "Haydon: Annotated Copy of Paul's Letters to His Kinsfolk." Notes and Queries, 190 (23 February), 83.

        Queries the present whereabouts of a volume of Paul's Letters to His Kinsfolk, annotated by Benjamin Robert Haydon, formerly in the Leeds Library's set of Scott's Prose Works.

2   ASPINALL, ARTHUR. "Walter Scott's Baronetcy." Review of English Studies, 22 (October), 319-22.

        Prints three letters between William Adam and Viscount Sidmouth, Secretary of State for Home Affairs, to prove that Scott's baronetcy did not come directly from George IV, as Lockhart affirms. It was not given due consideration until strongly suggested to the government, and even thereafter the Prime Minister, Lord Liverpool, was reluctant to make the recommendation to the King. See 1947.B1.

1946

3   BEATTIE, WILLIAM. "Sir Walter Scott. Miniature Bibliographies:
    Some British Novelists, No. 4." British Book News, 75
    (November), 406-10.
        Scott's work on the Minstrelsy deeply influenced both
    his long narrative poems and his short lyrics. He continued
    developing as a poet even after he stopped writing verse.
    His reading in history also strengthened his creative work,
    the best of which was the fiction on Scottish themes written
    from 1814 to 1824. Includes a selected bibliography of
    editions, biographies, criticism, and studies of Scott's
    influence.

4   BUSHNELL, GEORGE HERBERT. "On the Notices of the Christians
    in Peveril of the Peak." Scots Magazine, N.S. 45, no. 6
    (September), 469-75.
        In the 1831 edition of Peveril, Scott included the "His-
    torical Notices of Edward and William Christian" to clarify
    the true facts concerning his fictional villain. He was
    prompted by Wordsworth to include this material. The pub-
    lication history of the "Notices" and the Wordsworth-Scott
    correspondence indicate that a Mr. Wilks was the author.
    He was probably Colonel Mark Wilks of the Isle of Man, al-
    though he cannot be unquestionably identified.

5   CLARK, ARTHUR MELVILLE. "The Historical Novel," in his Studies
    in Literary Modes. Edinburgh: Oliver and Boyd, pp. 1-30.
        In novels such as Ivanhoe, Scott failed in his attempt
    to recreate earlier speech patterns. However, he captured
    the "spiritual atmosphere" of a period in characters, man-
    ners, and customs. He brought antiquarian accuracy to his
    creation of setting but did not distract his readers with
    arcane details presented solely for verisimilitude. Scott
    saw the differences of the past set off by its likenesses
    to the present, but he always remained detached from the
    past and kept his perspective in the present.

6   CORSON, JAMES CLARKSON. "Scott Prototypes: Wandering Willie."
    Notes and Queries, 190 (29 June), 281-82.
        The blind harper who was the prototype of Wandering
    Willie was a Welsh soldier named William ap Pritchard.
    This information, discovered in a MS letter of Joseph Train
    to Scott written in 1830, was found too late to have the
    name engraved on the stone at Twynholm. See 1946.B10.

7   H., R. M. "Rob Roy: Old Song." Notes and Queries, 190
    (9 March), 103.
        Queries if there is more to the "old song" Sir Hildebrand
    quotes in chapter 7; it is unlikely that Scott made it up
    for the occasion.

8   HOLTHOUSE, E. H. "Scott's First Love." <u>Times Literary Supple-</u>
       <u>ment</u> (25 May), p. 247.
          Offers a correction to Buchan's <u>Sir Walter Scott, Bart</u>.
       Charlotte "pieced" rather than "pierced" his heart.

9   KEISTER, DON A. "Scott's 'County Guy.'" <u>Explicator</u>, 4, no. 7
       (May), item 49.
          In this ballad in <u>Quentin Durward</u> chapter 4, Scott was
       mocking ballad collectors, including himself. He understood
       that words and music must go together. <u>See</u> 1945.B1.

10   K[ING], H. G. L. "Scott Prototypes: Wandering Willie." <u>Notes</u>
       <u>and Queries</u>, 190 (1 June), 237-38.
          In 1871 a monument was erected in Twynholm Kirkyard to
       a blind harper who died in 1816 and was supposedly the pro-
       totype of Wandering Willie. Queries the harper's name and
       if it appears on the tombstone. <u>See</u> 1946.B6.

11   LAMBORN, E. A. GREENING. "Sir Walter's Heraldry." <u>Notes and</u>
       <u>Queries</u>, 190 (18 May), 207-10 and (1 June), 226-28.
          Although Scott refers to heraldry in every novel except
       <u>The Pirate</u>, his knowledge of the subject was both superfi-
       cial and inaccurate. <u>See</u> 1949.B3 and 1951.B13.

12   McCULLOUGH, BRUCE. "The Historical Romance. Sir Walter Scott:
       <u>Old Mortality</u>," in his <u>Representative English Novelists:</u>
       <u>Defoe to Conrad</u>. New York: Harper & Brothers, pp. 113-30.
          Scott saw the historical novel as similar to the novel
       of manners and so considered verisimilitude more important
       than strict factual accuracy. His characters derive from
       observation and are the products of a particular time,
       place, and society. Scott respected the past for its own
       sake and refrained from using it for propaganda. Although
       the intrigue, chivalry, and "pasteboard emotion" of <u>Old</u>
       <u>Mortality</u> may at times strain credulity, it is memorable in
       its picture of the Scottish Puritans.

13   SELLS, A. LYTTON. "The Return of Cleveland: Some Observations
       on <u>The Pirate</u>." <u>Durham University Journal</u>, 38, no. 3
       (June), 69-78.
          <u>The Pirate</u> is "primarily a novel of mystery and romance"
       rather than an historical novel. In the story of Basil
       Mertoun's past, Scott alludes indirectly to Prévost's novel
       <u>Le Philosophe anglais</u>, partly to demonstrate how its ma-
       terial could be transformed into a successful and powerful
       romance. Another element in the popularity of <u>The Pirate</u>
       was the relative novelty of stories on this subject.

1946

14   STROUT, ALAN LANG. "Some Unpublished Letters of John Gibson
        Lockhart to John Wilson Croker." Notes and Queries, 190
        (20 April), 161-64.
            In a letter presumably from 1849, Lockhart discusses
        Scott as an historian and as "the great inspirer & mis-
        leader of our recent history writers French & English."
        See 1942.B18; 1943.B33; 1944.B19; and 1945.B16.

15   WEIR, J. L. "Letter to Archibald Constable." Notes and
        Queries, 191 (24 August), 78.
            Prints a letter to Constable from Alexander Gibson
        Hunter of Blackness, a "worthy man" despite Scott's dislike
        of him.

1947 A BOOKS - NONE

1947 B SHORTER WRITINGS

1   ASPINALL, ARTHUR. "Walter Scott's Baronetcy. Some New
        Letters." Times Literary Supplement (25 October), p. 556.
            Prints letters indicating that William Adam, legal ad-
        visor to King George IV, first made the suggestion that
        Scott should be knighted. The King initially ignored the
        suggestion. See 1946.B2.

*2   FUJII, ICHIGORO. "Backgrounds of Scott's Historical Novels."
        English Study and Teaching (Japan), 9.
            Cited in the Annual Bibliography of English Language and
        Literature (Cambridge: Modern Humanities Research Associa-
        tion, 1956), XXVII, 179, item #3048.

3   GRANT, DOUGLAS. "Introduction" to his edition of Private
        Letters of the Seventeenth Century. Oxford: Clarendon
        Press, pp. 7-54.
            Scott hoped to pass the Private Letters as genuine, and
        his knowledge of Jacobean history, language, and epistolary
        style made him uniquely fitted to do so. He had been con-
        sidering a novel set in this period even before the Private
        Letters or Nigel, and Disraeli's letter of 27 February,
        1821 encouraged him in this direction. In 1827 after the
        bankruptcy he considered finishing the Private Letters in
        collaboration with Lady Louisa Stuart. They possess a "dis-
        tinction and artistry" lacking in Nigel and are inspired by
        the same spirit that vivifies the Scottish novels.

4   KING, H. G. L. "Scott Memorial Tablets." Notes and Queries,
        192 (14 June), 258.

Three tablets mark stages in Scott's last journey home:
one at his lodgings in Rome in 1832, one along the road at
Langlee on Tweedside, and one at the Hamman Baths in London,
which was destroyed in 1941.

5   LAMB, G. F. "Some Anglo-American Literary Contacts." <u>Quarter-
ly Review</u>, 285, 247-58.
        Washington Irving visited Abbotsford in 1817, and he and
Scott mutually delighted in each other's acquaintance.
Three years later Scott helped Irving to convince John
Murray to publish Irving's <u>Sketch Book</u>.

6   McCLYMONT, WILLIAM. "Scott and Lockhart." <u>Times Literary
Supplement</u> (13 December), p. 645.
        Lockhart and Lang should both be excused for errors in
their biographies, since they were working from unreliable
copies of Scott's correspondence.

7   NEFF, EMERY. "The Romantic Garb: Chateaubriand, Scott,
Thierry, Carlyle," in his <u>The Poetry of History: The Contribution of Literature and Literary Scholarship to the
Writing of History Since Voltaire</u>. New York: Columbia
University Press; London: Oxford University Press,
pp. 116-28.
        Scott added patriotism and novelistic form to the writing
of history. His portraits of James I and Louis XI "gave
readers an unwonted intimacy with the mighty."

8   PRITCHETT, V. S. "Scott," in his <u>The Living Novel</u>. New York:
Reynall and Hitchcock, pp. 56-69.
        A revision and condensation of 1944.B15.

9   STEVENSON, PERCY R. "Sir Walter Scott's Diary." <u>Times Literary Supplement</u> (15 November), p. 591.
        A request for the original MS or Davidson Cook's copy of
the diary of Scott's 1814 voyage around Scotland in the
Lighthouse Commission's yacht.

10 WENGER, JARED. "Character-Types of Scott, Balzac, Dickens,
and Zola." <u>Publications of the Modern Language Association</u>,
62 (March), 213-32.
        The typical Scott novel includes a hero, a comic second-
ary hero, a heroine, a second lady, a "heavy emotional"
character, a madman, an old lady, a father figure, and one
important historical figure. These may be classified into
five groups which recur in all the novels: the Man, the
Woman, the Youth, the Animal, and the Villain.

1948

1948 A BOOKS

1   POPE-HENNESSEY, UNA. Sir Walter Scott. English Novelists
     Series. London: Home and Van Thal, 103pp.
          Scott engaged in a long apprenticeship learning to write
     novels. Biographical evidence indicates that the novels
     were not written in the order of publication. They may be
     divided into two groups: "romances that show signs of be-
     ing patched work" such as Redgauntlet, and "romances which
     appear to be woven all of a piece." Related evidence for
     the revised chronology appears in Scott's changing treat-
     ment of Catholicism. Some material in Part II, "The Work,"
     has been revised and expanded from 1933.B31. The argument
     remains the same. See also Carswell, 1933.B5 and Poynton,
     1971.B57.

*2   ROBERTS, PAUL M. "The Influence of Sir Walter Scott on the
     Vocabulary of the Modern English Language." Ph.D. disser-
     tation, University of California at Berkeley, 1948.
          Cited in Comprehensive Dissertation Index (Ann Arbor,
     Michigan: Xerox University Microfilms, 1973), XXX, 468.
     See 1953.B13.

1948 B SHORTER WRITINGS

1   ASPINALL, ARTHUR. "Some New Scott Letters." Times Literary
     Supplement (27 March), p. 184; (10 April), p. 212;
     (24 April), p. 240.
          Letters addressed to the Right Hon. William Adam, from
     MSS at Blair Adam; they concern the building of Abbotsford,
     Scott's Baronetcy, Adam Ferguson's appointment as Keeper of
     the Regalia of Scotland, family matters, Scott's finances,
     and a visit to London.

2   BRIDIE, JAMES [pseud.]. "Address to the Fortieth Annual Dinner
     of the Edinburgh Sir Walter Scott Club."
          See 1948.B7.

3   CHEW, SAMUEL. "Sir Walter Scott," in A Literary History of
     England. Edited by Albert C. Baugh. New York: Appleton-
     Century-Crofts, pp. 1207-1218.
          The Waverley Novels are "historical prose romance(s)"
     which blend the marvelous with elements of real life. How-
     ever, Scott often failed in his use of the supernatural.
     The stories set in the eighteenth century resemble the
     novel of manners. The ones set in more remote times commit
     both historical and moral anachronism. Scott's "supreme

feat was to make the past alive again." The novels are
memorable for great scenes rather than for structure, and
Scott lacked a "profound philosophic conception of life."

4   DAICHES, DAVID. "Introduction" to The Heart of Midlothian.
New York: Holt, Rinehart and Winston, pp. v-xiv.
Scott's novels concern the impact of the past on the
present and how history and character influence each other.
He is interested in "the problem of heroic action in an unheroic civilization." Jeanie Deans' character is a product
of history, and her courage and humility affirm the possi-
bility for heroism. David Deans shows the mellowing of the
old into the new, and Reuben Butler represents the completion of the process. The melodramatic tone of the conclusion emphasizes that heroism may no longer be defined in
terms of physical action.

5   FYNMORE, A. H. W. "John of Skye, Sir Walter Scott's Piper."
Notes and Queries, 193 (7 February), 62.
The death of Scott's piper was reported in the Times of
8 December, 1847.

6   KLANČAR, ANTHONY J. "Scott in Yugoslavia." Slavonic Review,
27 (December), 216-27.
Yugoslavia discovered the genius of Scott rather late;
the first attempt to translate Scott into Serbian did not
come until 1867. He influenced the historical fiction of
Mirko Bogović and Augustus Šenoa, "the first and most pro-
lific writer of historical novels in Yugoslav literature."
The most outstanding imitator of Scott was the Slovene Jos
Jurčič, who designed his Deseti brat as a novel which
would incorporate the history of his country.

7   MAVOR, O. H. "Address to the Fortieth Annual Dinner of the
Edinburgh Sir Walter Scott Club." Edinburgh Sir Walter
Scott Club Annual Report, pp. 15-28.
Scott was intimidated by his critics and defended himself
by arguing that he wrote only for general amusement. His
"hunger for life" made him receptive to everything, and he
transformed all that he absorbed into his novels with enthusiasm and honest escapism. Reprinted: 1971.A13. See
1948.B2.

8   MAYO, ROBERT D. "The Chronology of the Waverley Novels: The
Evidence of the Manuscripts." Publications of the Modern
Language Association, 63 (September), 935-49.
Defends the orthodox view of Waverley chronology, i.e.,
that the novels were written in their order of publication.

1948

The MSS of eleven novels in the Pierpont Morgan Library indicate no revision of Scott's so-called "prentice attempts," and their watermarks support the orthodox chronology. Scott wrote his best work early; his real apprenticeship was his development as a storyteller, which antedates both the poems and the novels.

9   ROBERTS, S. C. "The Fate of a Novelist." University of Edinburgh Journal, 14, no. 3 (Summer), 173-84.
       Despite their authors' similarities in circumstances and temperaments, Trollope's novels enjoyed revived popularity while Scott's are generally neglected. Trollope's novels provide a familiar setting and require no annotation, but Scott's novels discourage the reader with their vast amounts of introductory material. The Journal, however, will escape the revolutions of critical taste as an "imperishable document of a man who faced things as they were." Reprinted: 1950.B10.

10   _____. "The Making of a Novelist." University of Edinburgh Journal, 14, no. 3 (Summer), 160-72.
       Scott was basically of an eighteenth century cast of mind. He most admired natural beauty when it was associated with history or tradition. His religion was primarily ethical and social rather than theological. His shorter poems are his best poems, because they are clear, simple, and unmysterious. Waverley validates the common criticism that Scott's dialogue surpasses his narration and description; its strength lies in "the romantic colour of its characterisation." Reprinted: 1950.B10.

11   ROSA, SISTER M. "Romanticism in Annette von Droste-Hülshoff." Modern Language Journal, 32 (April), 279-87.
       Deals only peripherally with Scott. Droste-Hülshoff admired him and shared with him the portrayal of native scenery, which in her case was Westphalia.

12   SHAND, JOHN. "The Good Natured Genius." Nineteenth Century, 144 (October), 223-30.
       Scott's greatest strength is his humor and knowledge of human nature. His best characters use the Scottish vernacular, which has the imagery and rhythms of poetry. Much of the adverse criticism of Scott from Stevenson to Forster has concentrated on his sloppy craftsmanship. However, in spite of his careless artistry, Scott was a good judge of his own work.

13   TATE, W. E. "Scott and 'Drunken Barnaby.'" Notes and Queries, 193 (10 July), 298.

1949

Scott may have plagiarized part of <u>The Lord of the Isles</u> from Barnaby, Books 2 and 3. The resemblance between Scott and Barnaby in three distinct passages seems too close for mere coincidence.

1949 A BOOKS - NONE

1949 B SHORTER WRITINGS

1   ASPINALL, ARTHUR. <u>Politics and the Press, c. 1780-1850</u>. London: Home and Van Thal; rpt. Brighton, Sussex: Harvester Press, 1973, pp. 267-69.
    Includes a brief discussion of Scott's association with the <u>Beacon</u> in 1821. Scott "had been drawn into the affair rather against his will" and regretted his folly. <u>See</u> 1971.B13.

2   HÄUSERMANN, H. W. "A New Scott Letter." <u>Review of English Studies</u>, 25 (July), 248-49.
    Reprints a letter from Scott to a member of the Bannatyne Club, written between 27 November, 1826 and 30 June, 1827. The letter concerns a poem in Scots verse called "Duncan Laider" in manuscript at Taymouth Castle and the possibility of its being published by the Bannatyne Club.

3   LAMBORN, E. A. GREENING. "The Heraldry of Scott's Poems." <u>Notes and Queries</u>, 194 (20 August), 354-55.
    Discusses errors in Scott's use of heraldry in the narrative poems. <u>See</u> 1946.B11 and 1951.B13.

4   MUIR, EDWIN. "Walter Scott. The Walter Scott Lecture for 1944, Given at the University of Edinburgh," in his <u>Essays on Literature and Society</u>. London: Hogarth Press, pp. 64-82.
    Reprint of 1945.B11.

5   SCOTT, D. F. S. "Sir Walter Scott," in his <u>Some English Correspondents of Goethe</u>. London: Methuen, pp. 33-35.
    Prints the letter of 11 September, 1829 in which Scott thanks Goethe for the two medals sent through Carlyle. Their correspondence was initiated by Goethe in 1827, and both writers refer to the other in terms of deep respect.

6   TREVELYAN, G. M. "Influence of Sir Walter Scott on History," in his <u>An Autobiography and Other Essays</u>. London: Longman's, Green, pp. 200-205.
    Reprint of 1932.B175.

1949

7   WAVELL, EARL. "Address to the Forty-first Annual Dinner of
    the Edinburgh Sir Walter Scott Club." Edinburgh Sir Walter
    Scott Club Annual Report, pp. 13-22.
        Scott is not a great poet, but he is a stirring one,
    addressing himself "to the mortal part of man." Although
    he was primarily a poet of action and adventure, his short
    poems demonstrate that he could deal with deeper matters.
    Scott's poetry offered "a breath of fresh air" and could
    do so again in the difficult post-war period.

1950 A BOOKS

*1 FISCHER, FRANK ELMER. "Social and Political Ideas in Scott's
    Fiction." Ph.D. dissertation, Princeton University, 1950.
        Cited in Comprehensive Dissertation Index (Ann Arbor,
    Michigan: Xerox University Microfilms, 1973), XXX, 468.

.2 NEEDLER, GEORGE H. Goethe and Scott. Toronto: Oxford Uni-
    versity Press, 150pp.
        A chronological account of the relations between Goethe
    and Scott and of German influence on Scott's work from the
    ballads through his translations of "Götz von Berlichingen"
    and German dramas to the Waverley Novels. Goethe's reading
    of Kenilworth in 1821 influenced him to resume work on
    Faust, and he adapted Scott's description of the drunken
    porter's reception of Queen Elizabeth for his account of
    Helena's arrival at Faust's castle.

3   TAIT, JOHN GUTHRIE and WILLIAM MATHIE PARKER. The Journal of
    Sir Walter Scott. Text Revised from a Photostat in the
    National Library of Scotland. Edinburgh: Oliver and Boyd,
    862pp.
        Single volume reprint of 1939.A1; 1941.A1; and 1946.A1.

1950 B SHORTER WRITINGS

1   BOOTH, BRADFORD A. "Trollope on Scott: Some Unpublished
    Notes." Nineteenth Century Fiction, 5, no. 3 (December),
    223-30.
        Although in his Autobiography, Trollope commented posi-
    tively on Scott, his annotations of The Bride of Lammermoor,
    Old Mortality, and Ivanhoe are preponderantly disparaging.
    Trollope criticized Scott's unstructured plots, unconvincing
    characters, and unrealistic dialogue. While Trollope ad-
    mired Scott's ability to tell a story and to vivify history,
    Scott's faulty craftsmanship tried his patience.

2   CECIL, DAVID. "Sir Walter Scott's Vision of Life." <u>Listener</u>
    (9 February), pp. 254-55.
        Like Fielding, Scott saw the novel as an entertaining
    panorama of human life held together in a conventional
    framework. Because he was concerned with "man seen as a
    product of history," he deals with private life only insofar
    as it relates to wider social forces. At his best he
    balances between his consciousness of these historical
    forces and of the uniqueness of each individual.

3   CROWLEY, JOHN. "Sir Walter Scott's 'The Lawyer and the
    Bishop.'" <u>Juridical Review</u>, 62, 129-35.
        Scott's ballad "The Lawyer and the Bishop" was composed
    for a dinner celebrating Lord Melville's acquittal in an
    impeachment trial, a political victory of the Edinburgh
    Tories over the Whigs. Clarifies several allusions in the
    ballad and prints the text with variants.

4   GORDON, GEORGE. "The Chronicles of the Canongate," in his <u>The</u>
    <u>Lives of Authors</u>. London: Chatto and Windus, pp. 139-47.
        Reprint, slightly revised, of 1932.B66.

5   JOHNSTON, GEORGE BURKE. "Scott and Jonson." <u>Notes and Queries</u>,
    195 (25 November), 521-22.
        Cites three hitherto unlabelled references to Ben Jonson
    in <u>Ivanhoe</u>, <u>Kenilworth</u>, and a Scott letter to Daniel Terry.

6   LINCOLN, BISHOP OF. "Address to the Forty-second Annual Dinner
    of the Edinburgh Sir Walter Scott Club." <u>Edinburgh Sir</u>
    <u>Walter Scott Club Annual Report</u>, pp. 13-22.
        Scott provided "the inspiration of insight and faith" to
    a world weary of war. He characteristically worked in con-
    trasts, redeeming honor with courage and demonstrating the
    divine spark in the most humble characters. Unlike much
    modern fiction, the Waverley Novels are not designed to
    illustrate a theory or support a creed. They offer love of
    our fellow men and show some good in all people.

7   LUKÁCS, GEORGE. <u>Studies in European Realism</u>. <u>A Sociological</u>
    <u>Survey of the Writings of Balzac, Stendhal, Zola, Tolstoy,</u>
    <u>Gorki and Others</u>. Translated by Edith Bone. London:
    Hillway, passim.
        Balzac saw Scott and himself working toward the same
    goal, the synthesis of the Enlightenment "literature of
    ideas" with the Romantics' "literature of images" into a
    "literary eclecticism." He admired the way Scott subordin-
    ated great historical characters into secondary figures, and
    he praised Scott's concentration on social milieu rather

1950

than on politics. However, Balzac disliked Scott's use of
dialogue and his tendency to characterize through a few
constantly recurring phrases.

8   McDONALD, T. P. "Sir Walter Scott's Fee Book." Juridical
Review, 62, 288-316.
    Scott's Fee Book covers the period from 28 November,
1792 to 1 September, 1803, eleven of the fourteen years of
his practice as an advocate. His earliest remuneration came
from cases sent to him by his father, but he later developed
a substantial practice, working for some forty solicitors.
The cases covered many branches of the Law of Scotland.

9   MAXWELL, J. C. "Lucy Ashton's Song." Notes and Queries, 195
(13 May), 210.
    Lucy Ashton's song recalls two poems by Thomas Carew,
"Good Counsel to a Young Maid" and "Conquest by Flight."

10 RENWICK, W. L. "Introduction" to Sir Walter Scott Lectures:
1940-1948. Edinburgh: Edinburgh University Press,
pp. vii-x.
    Scott the historian and Scott the novelist were of one
mind; his anachronisms result not from carelessness but
from a deliberate choice of literary symbols. Scott loved
the picturesque past but remained independent of dead
values. He taught the unity of past and present. This
volume includes reprints of 1940.B11; 1941.B12; 1945.B11;
and 1948.B9, B10.

11 SMITH, D. NICHOL. "The Poetry of Sir Walter Scott." University of Edinburgh Journal, 15, no. 2, 63-80.
    Scott excels as a poet in describing movement and action.
In description he concentrates on the physical details of
the object itself rather than on the poet's impression of
it. Although his poetry is neither introspective nor speculative, it does not lack emotion. He deliberately chose not
to write of "the intellectual and moral riddles which life
presents to every thinking man."

12 SMITH, ROLAND M. "Chaucer Allusions in the Letters of Sir
Walter Scott." Modern Language Notes, 65 (November),
488-55.
    The Chaucer allusions in Grierson's edition of Scott's
letters indicate that George Ellis was largely responsible
for keeping alive Scott's interest in Chaucer.

13 STROUDEMIRE, STERLING A. "A Note on Scott in Spain," in Romance Studies Presented to William Morton Dey. Edited by

Urban T. Holmes, Jr., Alfred G. Engstrom, and Sturgis E. Leavitt. Chapel Hill: University of North Carolina Press, pp. 165-68.
Scott's novels were translated into Spanish throughout the nineteenth century. Several of the novels were introduced into Spain through productions of Italian operas.

14   STRUVE, GLEB. "Russian Friends and Correspondents of Sir Walter Scott." Comparative Literature, 2, no. 4 (Fall), 307-26.
The letters from Scott's Russian correspondents and Russian visitors to Abbotsford illustrate Scott's widespread popularity in Russia in the late 1820's and 1830's. The letters of Vladimir Davydov are in English. The others are in French and include letters from Denis Davydov, Alexander Izmailov, Anna Bunina, and Alexander Meyendorff. Scott's friendship with Vladimir Davydov was quite close; he visited Abbotsford frequently during 1825-27, when he was a student at the University of Edinburgh.

15   YOUNG, G. M. "Scott and the Historians. The Sir Walter Scott Memorial Lecture for 1946," in Sir Walter Scott Lectures, 1940-1948. Edited by W. L. Renwick. Edinburgh: Edinburgh University Press, pp. 81-107.
The Border Country and its traditions shaped Scott's sense of the past by giving him a strong sense of locality. This emphasis and his sense of social structure strongly influenced Macaulay's style of writing history. Scott enlarged the scope of history by treating every document as the record of a conversation and by including the lower classes in his scrutiny.

1951 A BOOKS

*1   WALKER, GEORGE W. "The Literary and Personal Relationship of Sir Walter Scott to James Fenimore Cooper." Ph.D. dissertation, University of North Carolina, 1951.
Cited in Comprehensive Dissertation Index (Ann Arbor, Michigan: Xerox University Microfilms, 1973), XXX, 468.

1951 B SHORTER WRITINGS

1   BUCHAN, ALEXANDER M. "Jeffrey, Marmion, and Scott," in Studies in Memory of Frank Martindale Webster. Washington University Studies, N.S. Language and Literature, No. 20. St. Louis, Missouri: Washington University, pp. 34-40.

1951

Scott broke with the Edinburgh Review when he and Jeffrey
became "champions of two totally divergent views of society."
Jeffrey's review of Marmion attacked Scott's attachment to
the past, which was the source both of his Toryism and of
his creativity. Jeffrey also hinted that Scott was writing
for the profit of the booksellers, an ungentlemanly motive.
The review suggested that Scott's romantic dream, rooted in
the past, was a mere fad.

2   DAICHES, DAVID. "Scott's Achievement as a Novelist." Nineteenth Century Fiction, 6 (September), 80-95 and (December),
153-73.
Scott's best novels are anti-romantic and lament the
central paradox of modern life, that civilization must be
paid for by a loss of individual heroism. His best characters accommodate themselves to prudence and progress without
completely sacrificing heroism and tradition. In many of
the Scottish novels, an Englishman or Lowland Scot, func-
tioning as symbolic observer, becomes involved with Highland
passions and then withdraws. The novels reflect the tension
between Scott's love of the past and his belief in the
present. Reprinted: 1956.B4; 1968.B7; and 1969.B11.

3   ELLIOTT, WALTER. "Address to the Forty-third Annual Dinner of
the Edinburgh Sir Walter Scott Club." Edinburgh Sir Walter
Scott Club Annual Report.
Scott was the embodiment of Edinburgh, "a town of an
enormous and over-riding sanity." The humility and magnanimity of his character appear in the erudition of his work.
Study and thought allowed him to understand characters from
whom he was distanced by time or natural sympathy. He created English and Scots characters with equal ease and "made
step-bairns of neither." Reprinted: 1971.A13.

4   GARRATT, J. G. "Daniell (Thomas, William, and Samuel)."
Notes and Queries, 196 (19 November), 502.
Requests the location of a copy of William Daniell's
Voyage Round the Coast of Great Britain, which contained
one or two letters from Scott on interesting views in Scot-
land.

5   GORDON, ROBERT K. "Scott's Prose." Transactions of the Royal
Society of Canada, 3rd ser. 45, sec. 2 (June), 13-18.
The most common fault in Scott's prose style is his use
of high-flown rhetoric and frequent clichés. When he writes
in dialect, however, his prose is economical and clear. He
uses dialect as a contrast to the heroic passages, and it
becomes the "life and soul" of some of the novels. Scott's

good prose is not confined to dialect; it occurs in other parts of the novels and in his letters.

6   GORDON, S. STEWART. "Waverley and the 'Unified Design.'" ELH, 18, no. 2 (June), 107-22.
Waverley is a well-ordered work unified by the actions which result from the character of the protagonist. The early chapters provide the groundwork for all the later action and establish a "vital interdependence between the character of the hero, his actions, and his fortunes." Scott's presentation of scenery, historical incidents, and other characters are all designed to reveal the changes and growth in Edward Waverley. Reprinted: 1968.B19.

7   HOLMAN, C. HUGH. "The Influence of Scott and Cooper on Simms." American Literature, 23 (May), 203-18.
Cooper and Simms wrote in the Scott tradition but modified the pattern in opposite ways to fit their diverse needs. Cooper simplified his plots and placed his major figures outside historical situations. Simms used Scott's basic formula of distantly pictured historical figures, shallowly conceived aristocrats, and believable minor characters. Unlike Scott, however, he failed to create credible relationships among major and minor characters. Because he feared to violate accuracy, he could not present history dramatically.

8   JOYCE, MICHAEL. Edinburgh, The Golden Age, 1769-1832. London: Longman's, Green, 1951, 199pp., passim.
Edinburgh during its "Golden Age" was the site of "an upward surge of intellect" which the historian can describe but not explain. Scott's life and works provide a structural and chronological frame for the author's description of the events and personalities of "the Athens of the North." Includes chapters on Burns, Carlyle, Mackenzie, Lockhart, Jeffrey, Shelley, and Hogg in addition to several on Scott.

9   KETTLE, ARNOLD. "Scott: The Heart of Midlothian," in his Introduction to the English Novel. London: Hutchinson's University Library, pp. 105-22.
Scott's broad range of subject matter and social life gives his novels an epic quality. He substituted a concern for social tensions for the polite tradition of eighteenth century fiction. In The Heart of Midlothian the contrast between the points of view of peasants and city dwellers parallels the relationship between Scotland and England, which pervades the novel. The second half of the novel is

inferior to the first, mainly because Scott changes from
the peasant's point of view to that of Argyle, the paternal-
ist landowner.

10 LANE, LAURIAT, JR. "Dickens and Scott: An Unusual Borrowing."
     Nineteenth Century Fiction, 6, no. 3 (December), 223-24.
        An incident in chapter 45 of Barnaby Rudge, in which a
     character named Stagg drinks a bumper of whiskey and water,
     was written in July, 1841 while Dickens was staying in the
     area of Loch Katrine. The incident may be connected to
     Dickens' recollection of "The stag at eve had drunk his
     fill" from The Lady of the Lake. See 1952.B2 and 1953.B8.

11 MILLER, C. WILLIAM. "Letters from Thomas White of Virginia to
     Scott and Dickens," in English Studies in Honor of James
     Southall Wilson. Edited by Fredson Bowers. University of
     Virginia Studies, Volume 5. Charlottesville: University
     of Virginia Press, 67-71.
        Reprints two letters to Scott from Thomas Willis White,
     an early nineteenth century Richmond printer and publisher.
     The letter of 28 February, 1829 was written to accompany a
     presentation copy of Edge-Hill by James Ewell Heath. The
     letter of 22 July, 1830 requests Scott's help in publicizing
     a poem by Daniel Bryan. Both letters reveal White's patri-
     otic interest in the development of American literature.
     See 1963.B6, B7.

12 MOORE, JOHN ROBERT. "Poe's Reading of Anne of Geierstein."
     American Literature, 22 (January), 493-96.
        Poe drew on a descriptive passage in Anne of Geierstein
     for the characteristics of his ominous bird in "The Raven"
     and on chapters 11 and 21 for the name and some topographi-
     cal details of "The Domain of Arnheim."

13 O'LUNDY, ART. "Sir Walter Scott's Heraldry." Notes and
     Queries, 196 (28 April), 196.
        Geoffrey Plantagenet, Count of Anjou, the son-in-law of
     Henry I, was the first recorded wearer of a coat-of-arms.
     See 1946.B11 and 1949.B3.

14 PARKER, WILLIAM MATHIE. "A Jacobite Refugee Mystery." Notes
     and Queries, 196 (28 April), 182-84.
        Relates Scott's attempt, as requested by the parish
     authorities of Itchingfield, Sussex, to find information
     on John Maclean, an attainted Jacobite who was buried there
     on 28 August, 1724. Scott consulted Mrs. Maclean Clephane
     but was unable to supply the requested information.

15   PEARSALL, ROBERT B. "Scott and Ritson on Allan Ramsay."
      Modern Language Notes, 66 (December), 551-53.
          Scott thought more highly of the gentleman-amateur tra-
      dition than he did of scholarly precision and consequently
      reproved Joseph Ritson for criticizing Allan Ramsay's edit-
      ing of Scottish Songs. However, later Scott also criticized
      Ramsay for many of the same reasons as Ritson had done.

16   R., A. M. L. "Thomas Pringle and Sir Walter Scott." Quarterly
      Bulletin of the South African Public Library, Capetown, 6
      (December), 50-57 and (June), 109-18.
          Prints five letters from Thomas Pringle to Scott, dated
      from 5 February, 1820 to 31 October, 1822. Pringle was a
      poet and leader of a group of South African settlers. He
      later became a librarian and editor of the South African
      Journal. Scott helped the Pringle family to gain free pas-
      sage to South Africa under the Government's emigration plan.

17   RODRIGUES, A. GONÇALVES. "A novelística estrangeira em versão
      portuguesa no período pré-romântico." Boletim da Biblioteca
      da Universidade de Coimbra, 20, 213-94.
          A finding list of foreign novels in Portuguese transla-
      tions, arranged alphabetically by title. Entries provide
      Portuguese title, name of translator, whether translated
      directly into Portuguese or through another language (usu-
      ally French), publisher and place of publication, number of
      pages, and number and size of volumes. There are eleven
      Scott entries.

18   SMITH, ROLAND M. "Sir Walter Scott and the Pictish Question."
      Modern Language Notes, 66 (March), 175-80.
          Scott initially believed with Ellis that the Picts were
      Goths. Ritson's Annals of the Caledonians, Picts, and
      Scots convinced him that they were a Celtic race.

19   THOMAS, L. H. C. "Walladmoor: A Pseudo-Translation of Sir
      Walter Scott." Modern Language Review, 46, no. 2 (April),
      218-31.
          Walladmoor appeared in Germany in 1823-24, claiming to
      be a translation from the English of Sir Walter Scott. But
      volume three was an obvious parody and revealed Walladmoor
      as a hoax. In 1824 DeQuincey reviewed it in the London
      Magazine; he also translated it into English, freely re-
      writing and retouching the original and adding his own
      humorous and parodic elements.

20   TODD, WILLIAM B. "Twin Titles in Scott's Woodstock (1826)."
      Papers of the Bibliographical Society of America, 45, no. 3,
      256.

1952

> The cancel title-page for the first octavo volume of
> Woodstock provides an instance of the setting of a disjunct
> leaf in duplicate to reduce the presswork on the book.

1952 A BOOKS

*1 GORDON, ROBERT CONINGSBY. "The Scottish Novels of Sir Walter
     Scott." Ph.D. dissertation, Harvard University, 1952.
         Cited in Comprehensive Dissertation Index (Ann Arbor,
     Michigan: Xerox University Microfilms, 1973), XXX, 468.

2   MAXWELL-SCOTT, WALTER. Abbotsford. Melrose: privately
     printed, 19pp.
         A guidebook to Abbotsford with a summary of Scott's life,
     an account of the history of Abbotsford, and a description
     of its chief objects of interest. See revised edition,
     1975.A2.

1952 B SHORTER WRITINGS

1   ANON. "The Disinherited Baronet." Times Literary Supplement
     (20 June), p. 404.
         Scott's lack of popularity among academics may be due to
     his "reluctance to fit into any preconceived category." He
     does many things very well, including narration, comedy,
     characteristic speech, and interpretation of Scottish life.

2   FIELDING, K. J. "Dickens and Scott: An 'Unusual Borrowing'
     Queried." Nineteenth Century Fiction, 7 (December), 223-24.
         There is no relationship between Dickens' Stagg in Barna-
     by Rudge and the first line of The Lady of the Lake. The
     character is named much earlier in the novel, considerably
     before Dickens made his visit to Loch Katrine. See
     1951.B10 and 1953.B8.

3   GRAY, ALEXANDER. "Address to the Forty-fourth Annual Dinner
     of the Edinburgh Sir Walter Scott Club." The Edinburgh Sir
     Walter Scott Club Annual Report.
         By 1803 when he completed the Minstrelsy, Scott had
     finished an apprenticeship which provided him with an as-
     toundingly wide variety of information. His later work re-
     flects his start as a balladist. He saw himself as a public
     entertainer rather than as an artist, and he took pride in
     the impromptu quality of his work. He wished to tell
     stories, not to deliver messages to mankind. As an histori-
     an he treated the great clashes of civilization with scrupu-
     lous fairness. Reprinted: 1971.A13.

4   GRIERSON, HERBERT JOHN CLIFFORD. "Introduction" to <u>Kenilworth</u>.
    London: Collins, pp. 9-11.
        Although Scott was familiar with the historical period
    of <u>Kenilworth</u>, he rearranged the facts to highlight Leices-
    ter's conflict between love and ambition. Scott learned
    from Shakespeare how to fuse historical and imaginative
    elements and how to combine scenes of court and battlefield
    with everyday reality.

5   HILLHOUSE, JAMES T. "Sir Walter's Last Long Poem." <u>Huntington
    Library Quarterly</u>, 16, no. 1 (November), 53-73.
        The MS of <u>Harold the Dauntless</u> in the Huntington Library
    illuminates Scott's "well-known habits of rapid, not to say
    slapdash, composition." He began enthusiastically but tired
    of it before the end and finally published the poem anony-
    mously in 1817. The MS was purchased by Frederick Locker
    Lampson, who had the missing leaves copied and autographed
    by a list of nineteenth century literary luminaries includ-
    ing Tennyson, Arnold, Browning, Swinburne, Emerson, Lowell,
    and Longfellow.

6   LOWE, ROBERT LIDDELL. "Scott, Browning, and Kipling." <u>Notes
    and Queries</u>, 197 (1 March), 103-104.
        Browning probably borrowed from <u>Woodstock</u> for his "Cava-
    lier Tunes." Kipling probably borrowed from <u>Ivanhoe</u> for
    his "Recessional."

7   NOYES, ALFRED. "The Poetry of Sir Walter Scott: A Revalua-
    tion." <u>Quarterly Review</u>, 290 (April), 211-25.
        The strength of Scott's poetry, like Shakespeare's, lies
    in its lack of egoism. His "splendid objectivity" offers
    a remedy to a diseased culture suffering from too much mor-
    bid introspection. In the songs of Meg Merrillies and
    Madge Wildfire, Scott achieves the perfection of form and
    the haunting quality of the Border ballads. In the narra-
    tive poems he recaptures the lost romance of history.
    Scott's poetry influenced the early Tennyson and the pre-
    Raphaelites.

8   PARKER, WILLIAM MATHIE. "Scott's Knowledge of Shakespeare."
    <u>Quarterly Review</u>, 290 (July), 341-54.
        Scott's thorough knowledge of Shakespeare is revealed
    throughout the Waverley Novels as well as in his edition of
    Dryden and his 1819 <u>Encyclopaedia Britannica</u> essay on
    "Drama." Scott worked intermittently with Lockhart on an
    edition of Shakespeare for Constable, but the project re-
    mained unfinished. There is one known extant copy--of
    Volume II--located in the National Library of Scotland.

1952

9   PETTET, E. C. "Echoes of <u>The Lay of the Last Minstrel</u> in 'The
    Eve of St. Agnes.'" <u>Review of English Studies</u>, N.S. 3
    (January), 39-48.
        Scott's description of the east oriel window of Melrose
    Abbey is echoed in Keats's description of the window in
    Madeline's chamber. Both poems use the <u>Romeo and Juliet</u>
    motif, and both heroines are associated imagistically with
    flowers and doves. Most of Keats's echoes originate in
    canto II of the <u>Lay</u>, the part most closely parallel to his
    own plot. Keats's subconscious associations "transformed
    the homespun of his reading into the loveliest and richest
    cloth of gold."

10 TREWIN, J. C. "Introduction" to his edition of <u>Selections
    from the Prose of Sir Walter Scott</u>. London: Falcon Press,
    pp. 7-14.
        Scott wrote fast and should be read fast. The passages
    chosen display his particular strengths: battle scenes,
    delineation of Scots character, restoration of Scottish his-
    tory, description, and romantic adventure. Scott's best
    work reflects his nature and his love of pageantry. Despite
    its many flaws, his writing is amply redeemed by its charac-
    terizations.

<u>1953 A BOOKS - NONE</u>

<u>1953 B SHORTER WRITINGS</u>

1   BAUER, JOSEPHINE. <u>The London Magazine, 1820-29</u>. <u>Anglistica</u>,
    1, Copenhagen: Rosenkilde and Bagger, 363pp., passim.
        John Scott, editor of <u>The London Magazine</u>, admired the
    morality and objectivity of the Waverley Novels. After he
    died, however, reviews of the Waverleys in <u>The London Maga-
    zine</u> became progressively less favorable. Under the editor-
    ship of John Taylor, a utilitarian bias replaced the earlier
    admiration for feeling, and Sir Walter Scott's novels came
    to be regarded as merely amusing.

2   BROWN, T. J. "The Detection of Faked Literary MSS." <u>Book
    Collector</u>, 2, no. 2 (Spring), 6-23.
        Faked manuscripts may be distinguished from genuine ones
    through pedigree, contents, and physical appearance. A
    Scott letter forged by Alexander Howland ("Antique") Smith
    may be detected as a fake because its paper is too thick.
    In addition, the handwriting differs from Scott's genuine
    hand, particularly since he hardly ever dotted an "i."

3   COWLEY, JOHN. "Lockhart and the Publication of <u>Marmion</u>." <u>Philological Quarterly</u>, 32, no. 2 (April), 172-83.
       Corrects several inaccuracies in Lockhart's <u>Life</u> related to the publication of <u>Marmion</u>. The introductory epistles were not intended to be published separately; they were composed along with the narrative and intended as part of it. Scott wanted the money from the poem to invest in the printing business, not to help his brother Tom. The letter acknowledging Scott's gift of the poem to the Princess of Wales was written in 1807.

4   FORBES, DUNCAN. "The Rationalism of Sir Walter Scott." <u>Cambridge Journal</u>, 7, no. 1 (October), 20-35.
       Scottish common sense philosophy and the Age of Reason influenced Scott's attitude to religion, concern with morality, anti-clericalism, and rejection of "enthusiasm." Like the eighteenth century rationalist historians, he believed in progress and in the essential uniformity of human nature. Like these early social historians, he emphasized the link between characters and their socioeconomic background. The Waverley Novels are "a triumph of the historical thought of the rationalist Eighteenth Century."

5   GRIERSON, HERBERT JOHN CLIFFORD. "Introduction" to <u>Ivanhoe</u>. London: Collins; New York: Norton, pp. 27-31.
       Scott conveys his period setting through time, place, manners, and diction. Since he had no direct or transmitted experience of the Middle Ages, <u>Ivanhoe</u> was a product of his reading. Although it lacks historical accuracy, it succeeds in its Chaucerian comedy and in the sympathetic portrayal of Rebecca, "probably the finest woman character in the Waverley Novels." This edition also includes a slightly revised version of 1933.B14 here entitled "Grierson on Scott."

6   HEIST, WILLIAM W. "The Collars of Gurth and Wamba." <u>Review of English Studies</u>, N.S. 4 (October), 361-64.
       Scott's source for the collars of Cedric's thralls may have been similar inscribed collars worn by Scottish serfs. Legal serfdom was not abolished in Scotland until 1799, and Scott seems to have known of these inscribed metal collars and regarded them as a heritage from feudalism.

7   KIRK, RUSSELL. "Benthamism and Walter Scott," in his <u>The Conservative Mind: From Burke to Santayana</u>. Chicago: Henry Regnery, pp. 99-108.
       Scott regarded Utilitarianism as inimical to the preservation of the best of the past. He saw it as an enemy of

1953

"nationality, individuality, and all the beauty of the
past," and he objected to the Utilitarians' attempt to re-
form the Scottish judicial system. Like Burke, Scott regarded a slowly evolving law as the safeguard of liberty
and property. The Waverley Novels popularized Burke's
ideas.

8 LANE, LAURIAT, JR. "Dickens and Scott: A Reply to Mr. Fielding." Nineteenth Century Fiction, 8, no. 1 (June), 78.
    The name of Stagg in Barnaby Rudge did not come from
Scott, but it served as a verbal link which suggested the
first line of The Lady of the Lake to Dickens. See
1951.B10 and 1952.B2.

9 LINKLATER, ERIC. "Address to the Forty-fifth Annual Dinner of
the Edinburgh Sir Walter Scott Club." The Edinburgh Sir
Walter Scott Club Annual Report.
    Scott is one of the great storytellers of literature.
His characters reveal themselves while simultaneously advancing the narrative. His study of ballads taught him
both romantic emotion and equanimity, so that he can acknowledge both virtue and folly in a single character, such
as Fergus MacIvor. Scott gave to Scotland a pride in its
past to accompany its growing industrial prosperity. Reprinted: 1971.A13.

*10 LOEWEN, PETER F. "The Historical Novel: A Study in the De-
viations from the Scott Canon." Ph.D. dissertation, University of Denver, 1953.
    Cited in Comprehensive Dissertation Index (Ann Arbor,
Michigan: Xerox University Microfilms, 1973), XXX, 468.

11 NEEDLER, G. H. "Introduction" to Reminiscences of Sir Walter
Scott's Residence in Italy, 1832. By Sir William Gell.
Edited by James Clarkson Corson. Toronto: Burns and Mac-
Eachern; rpt. London: Thomas Nelson & Sons, 1957, pp. xiii-
xxi.
    Sir William Gell, Scott's "constant guide" in Italy from
5 January to 11 May, 1832, wrote the Reminiscences at the
request of Anne Scott. Gell was an archaeologist and antiquary. The Reminiscences were not published in his lifetime, but Lockhart printed them with omissions in the final
volume of his Life of Scott. Gell's manuscript is in
Toronto and is printed here in its entirety. Reprinted in
1957.A1 with 1957.B19.

12 PRICE, LAWRENCE MARSDEN. "Scott and the Historical Novel,"
in his English Literature in Germany. University of

California Publications in Modern Philology, No. 37.
Berkeley: University of California Press, pp. 329-44.
  Scott influenced the development of the German historical
novel from 1820. The earliest novelists to experience this
influence were Tieck, Alexis, and Hauff. Gustav Freytag
regarded Scott as "the father of the modern novel." Scott's
novels hastened the development in Germany of the novel in
which characters "occupy a definite place in the economic
world." Theodor Fontane was the last nineteenth century
German follower of Scott; he integrated many of Scott's
mannerisms into his own carefully planned structures.

13 ROBERTS, PAUL. "Sir Walter Scott's Contribution to the English
    Vocabulary." Publications of the Modern Language Associa-
    tion, 68, no. 1 (March), 189-210.
      Scott contributed about 150 words to English vocabulary,
    most of which were formerly obsolete words which he rein-
    troduced. He resurrected words to give his work local
    color and to satisfy his own antiquarian interests. In
    their effect on English, "the Waverley Novels and the nar-
    rative poems have been a force comparable to Arabic or base-
    ball or World War I." See 1948.A2.

14 SUTHERLAND, JAMES R. "The Sir Walter Scott Lectures for 1952:
    I. The Man and the Artist." University of Edinburgh
    Journal, 16, no. 4 (Summer), 212-23.
      Scott was "the great amateur of letters" who valued life
    more highly than literature. He believed in spontaneous
    composition, and consequently the novels mix "too much
    rubble" with "sound building material." Although he some-
    times did his best work with only a general plan in mind
    (as in Old Mortality), he tended to let characters get out
    of control when they seemed to be developing well. Never-
    theless, his spontaneous composition was balanced by wide
    reading and a retentive memory.

15 _____. "The Sir Walter Scott Lectures for 1952: II. The
    Dialogue of the Waverley Novels." University of Edinburgh
    Journal, 16, no. 4 (Summer), 223-34.
      Scott's worst failures are some of his English-speaking
    characters, especially when the period is pre-seventeenth
    century. He had to make the Scots dialect intelligible
    and also separate it from the prejudices of his contempor-
    aries who regarded it as suitable only for humor. He care-
    fully assigned his characters the dialect appropriate for
    their class.

1953

16   VAN GHENT, DOROTHY. "The Heart of Midlothian," in her The
      English Novel: Form and Function. New York: Harper and
      Row, pp. 113-24.
         The incoherent structure of the novel indicates the
      author's incoherent world view. Scott uses Jeanie's
      Cameronian "conditioning" merely as local color; he fails
      to integrate it into the aesthetic structure of the novel.
      His attitude toward Providential control is paradoxical,
      but he relies on sentimentalism and does not explore the
      problem of self-reliance in a Providentially planned uni-
      verse.

17   VINCENT, ESTHER H. "Scott of Abbotsford." Surgery, Gynecol-
      ogy, and Obstetrics, 96, 629-33.
         Scott suffered from polio as an infant and ulcerative
      colitis as an adolescent. He had an oddly shaped skull,
      perhaps from being kept lying down so long as a child. As
      an adult he was troubled by gallstones, skin rash, depres-
      sion, and rheumatism. He suffered his first stroke in 1830,
      and it was followed by three others before his death in
      1832. Although he bore treatment for all his illnesses
      with good humor, Scott did not think very highly of the
      medical profession.

1954 A BOOKS

1   PEARSON, HESKETH. Walter Scott, His Life and Personality.
      London: Methuen; New York: Harper, 295pp.
         An anecdotal biography which concentrates on the generos-
      ity and openness of Scott's character and overlooks his
      more questionable attributes. Although it includes a mini-
      mum of literary criticism, it gives the romances such as
      Quentin Durward more praise than most critics afford them.

*2   RABEN, JOSEPH. "Proverbs in the Waverley Novels of Sir Walter
      Scott." Ph.D. dissertation, Indiana University, 1954.
         An abstract by the author appears in Dissertation Ab-
      stracts, 14 (1954), 1355.

1954 B SHORTER WRITINGS

1   ALCIATORE, JULES C. "Stendhal et Scott: Le Conte de Nerwinde
      et Sir Piercy Shafton." Symposium, 8, no. 1 (Summer),
      147-50.
         D'Aubigné in Stendhal's Lamiel resembles Sir Piercy
      Shafton in The Monastery. Both affect airs, use pretentious

language, especially when addressing women, and both are
revealed when the occupations of their grandfathers are
discovered.

2   ALLEN, WALTER. "The Nineteenth Century: The First Generation,"
    part 3, in his The English Novel: A Short Critical History.
    London: Phoenix House, pp. 112-119.
        Scott's greatness lies in his portrayal of people as
    they are formed by social and historical processes. He
    roots his characters in material reality and uses external
    detail to imply the nature of their inner lives. Scott
    cannot create plot structures worthy of his characters, and
    he cannot deal adequately with passion or sexual love. Un-
    fortunately his "defects of form and his artistic laziness"
    strongly influenced the next two generations of English
    novelists.

3   CHRISTIE, JOHN TRAILL. "Address to the Forty-sixth Annual
    Dinner of the Edinburgh Sir Walter Scott Club." The Edin-
    burgh Sir Walter Scott Club Annual Report, pp. 11-21.
        Scott treats his royal characters with sympathy and in-
    sight. He is "pre-eminently the novelist of the great pub-
    lic event, the large national issue." He values loyalty
    but is not afraid to reveal the human weaknesses of kings
    and queens.

4   DOWNS, NORTON. "Two Unpublished Letters of Sir Walter Scott."
    Modern Language Notes, 69 (April), 247-49.
        A letter of 25 April, 1802 asks Cadell and Davies to in-
    form Scott on their decision to purchase the copyright to
    the Minstrelsy after the sale of the first edition. The
    second letter, which is undated, concerns the volume ar-
    rangement of Scott's edition of Swift.

5   LECLAIRE, LUCIEN. "Scott, Sir Walter (1771-1832)," in A
    General Analytical Bibliography of the Regional Novelists
    of the British Isles, 1800-1950. Paris: Société d'Édition
    'Les Belles Lettres', pp. 22-30.
        Lists sections on "Scott and Scotland," "Bibliographies,"
    and "Scott and Dialect" in addition to the separate and
    collected editions of the Scottish Waverley Novels with
    brief comments on their physical settings and the real lo-
    cations of Scott's fictive place names.

6   LOCHHEAD, MARION. John Gibson Lockhart. London: John Murray,
    336pp., passim.
        A biography designed to rescue Lockhart from "the still
    persistent tradition that he was detestable." Although he

1954

was guilty of the sin of pride in his youth, Lockhart's relations with Scott and his family prove that he was capable
of deep love and abiding loyalty.

7 MACKENZIE, AGNES MURE. "The Shocking Sir Walter." Saltire
   Review, 1, no. 3 (Winter), 18-21.
      Quotes from two contemporary critics of Scott who at-
   tacked the Waverley Novels on moral, religious, and patriotic grounds. McCrie in The Christian Century of 1817
   argued that the novels are unreadable in England. An 1820
   pamphlet, signed by "Timothy Touchstone," criticized the
   Waverley Novels for inculcating vice and blasphemy, for
   corrupting innocent children, and for advocating treason
   and rebellion.

8 PARKER, WILLIAM MATHIE. "Introduction" to The Antiquary.
   London: J. M. Dent; New York: E. P. Dutton, pp. v-x.
      The Antiquary differs from its predecessors in its con-
   centration on manners. Although the plot is minimal, the
   novel is rich in dialogue, humor, and description. It
   offers a surprisingly democratic view, both in the speeches
   of the elder Mucklebackit and in the courage of all classes
   in facing invasion. Includes a survey of the contemporary
   critical reception.

9 RUFF, WILLIAM. "An Uncollected Preface by Sir Walter Scott."
   Notes and Queries, 199 (November), 484.
      Scott may have written the unsigned preface to the edi-
   tion of Robert Dodsley's The Economy of Human Life (1751),
   reprinted in Kelso by James Ballantyne in 1802.

1955 A BOOKS

*1 POTTER, LEE H. "Walter Scott's Edition of Jonathan Swift's
    Works." Ph.D. dissertation, University of North Carolina,
    1955.
       Cited in Comprehensive Dissertation Index (Ann Arbor,
    Michigan: Xerox University Microfilms, 1973), XXX, 468.

*2 SMYTHE, JAMES ERWIN. "The Religious and Moral Philosophy of
    Sir Walter Scott." Ph.D. dissertation, University of
    Illinois, 1955.
       An abstract by the author appears in Dissertation Ab-
    stracts, 16 (1956), 342.

1955 B SHORTER WRITINGS

1 ALLEN, WALTER. "Sir Walter Scott," in his <u>Six Great Novelists</u>.
   London: Hamish Hamilton, pp. 64-94.
       Scott's use of dialect reveals him as a humorist and a
   shrewd perceiver of the ways people unconsciously reveal
   themselves. He is similar to Chaucer in his democratic acceptance of life. Scott shows people shaped by their role
   in the community and by the time and place in which they
   live. His "feeling for the historic past behind the individual" defines his genius.

2 BERKELEY, DAVID S. "Sir Walter Scott and Restoration 'Pré-
   ciosité.'" <u>Nineteenth Century Fiction</u>, 10, no. 3
   (December), 240-42.
       In <u>Old Mortality</u> Scott mocks the conventions of <u>précios-
   ité</u> in fashionable Restoration society. He parodies the
   high-flown but hackneyed compliments to the ladies, the
   taste for outrageously long French heroic romances, and
   the "soaring ideals and saccharine sentiments."

3 BUCHAN, SUSAN. "Address to the Forty-seventh Annual Dinner
   of the Edinburgh Sir Walter Scott Club." <u>The Edinburgh Sir
   Walter Scott Club Annual Report</u>, pp. 12-25.
       Scott was the central figure in the Scottish renaissance,
   teaching a patriotism which transcended traditional religious and geographic divisions. His women characters lack
   emotional depth. He is given to moralizing and frequently
   wrote beyond the limits of his interest and imagination.
   However, he had an enormous scope and tremendous mental
   discipline. He reserved the best of his talent and genius
   for his vision of the ordinary man and of a unified Scotland.

4 CORSON, JAMES CLARKSON. "Scott Studies--I." <u>University of
   Edinburgh Journal</u>, 18, no. 1 (Autumn), 23-32.
       During Scott's lifetime the general public knew very
   little about his personal life. Contemporary biographies
   usually amalgamated Scott's own autobiographical fragments
   with the errors of other writers. Hogg's <u>Domestic Manners</u>
   shows sincere love of Scott, whereas Lockhart offers more
   accuracy. His frankness offended some readers, and he included some touches of his characteristic sarcasm. However,
   most subsequent biographers have been content to "plunder"
   from Lockhart's <u>Life</u>. <u>See</u> part II: 1956.B3.

5 DUNCAN, JOSEPH E. "The Anti-Romantic in <u>Ivanhoe</u>." <u>Nineteenth
   Century Fiction</u>, 9, no. 4 (March), 293-300.

Ivanhoe is essentially anti-romantic, because it demonstrates that many heroic and romantic elements in both
Norman and Saxon cultures will have to be sacrificed to
form the English nation. Scott shows the danger and futility of adherence to outworn ideals. Like the Scottish
novels, Ivanhoe concerns "the difficult but necessary transition from a romantic, heroic era to a comparatively drab-
ber period of unity, peace, and progress." Reprinted:
1968.B13.

6   FISHER, P. F. "Providence, Fate, and the Historical Imagination in Scott's Heart of Midlothian." Nineteenth Century
Fiction, 10, no. 2 (September), 99-114.
    Scott based his conservatism on a faith in the Provi-
dential order of history, which fits the pattern of individual lives into proven traditions. Divine Providence
guides orderly historical evolution through law and tradition. At its best, civil law compromises between Providence
and Fate, between the moral rigidity of Davie Deans and the
amoral opportunism of Ratcliffe. The Great Man (Argyle) is
formed from the spirit of the people embodied in tradition
and functions as an instrument of the Providential order
behind history. Reprinted: 1968.B15.

7   KER, W. P. "Sir Walter Scott," in On Modern Literature: Lectures and Addresses. Edited by James Sutherland and Terence
Spencer. Oxford: Clarendon Press, pp. 106-12.
    Scott's main defect is the sudden shift "from true ima-
gination to mere literary artifice." His plots often lack
unity, and the endings come too slowly or too abruptly.
His characters are relatively unimportant; as is appropriate
in romance, he diffuses interest among many people and
places.

8   MAJUT, RUDOLF. "Some Literary Affiliations of Georg Büchner
with England." Modern Language Review, 50, no. 1 (January),
30-43.
    There is a "striking resemblance" between Scott's Quentin
Durward and Büchner's Leonce und Lena in the parallel relations between the heroines and their duennas. Both Lena's
governess and Hameline of Croye are "silly old maids" yearn-
ing nostalgically for a lost romanticism. Although there
is no proof that Büchner knew Quentin Durward, "it would be
surprising if he did not."

9   OLIVER, JOHN W. "Scottish Poetry in the Earlier Nineteenth
Century," in Scottish Poetry: A Critical Survey. Edited
by James Kinsley. London: Cassell, pp. 212-235.

The backgrounds of Scott's poetry are folk poetry, German
diablerie, and the genius loci of the Border country. The
narrative poems excel in "the presentation of sheer physical
stir and movement" and in their expression of love of country. Although Scott felt no obligation to deal with moral
or social problems in the narrative poems, they have "a
strong sympathetic perception of the deeper realities of
life." Scott is greatest in his lyrics, which capture "the
emotional essence of a situation" in the appropriate words
and metre.

10   PARKER, WILLIAM MATHIE. "Correcting Scott's Text." Times
     Literary Supplement (9 December), p. 752.
         Scott always had two sets of proofs, one for his correc-
     tions and one for Ballantyne's. Prints a selection of
     proof-sheets showing Ballantyne's notes and Scott's replies,
     often in sharp disagreement.

1956 A BOOKS

 *1   SIEBKE, ROLF. "Sir Walter Scott und das romantische Bewüsst-
      sein." Masters thesis, Hamburg University, 1956.
          Cited in the Annual Bibliography of English Language and
      Literature (Cambridge: Modern Humanities Research Associa-
      tion, 1961), XXXII, 442, item #7813.

1956 B SHORTER WRITINGS

 1   ADAMS, RUTH M. "A Letter by Sir Walter Scott." Modern
     Philology, 54, no. 2 (November), 121-23.
         Prints a letter of 5 May, 1798 from Scott to Cadell and
     Davies proposing a twelve volume edition of translations of
     German plays. The examples Scott gives of translations he
     has already finished are, with one exception, "plays of
     Chivalry" set in the Middle Ages.

 2   CORSON, JAMES CLARKSON. "The Border Antiquities." Biblio-
     theck, 1, 23-26.
         The claim by William Mudford in the Literary Gazette of
     7 November, 1818 to have written nearly half of the Border
     Antiquities is accurate. However, the publishers blundered
     when they stated that the work contained original poetry by
     Scott and placed his name on the title page. See 1957.B24
     and 1960.B3.

1956

3 _____ . "Scott Studies--II." <u>University of Edinburgh Journal</u>,
  18, no. 2 (Summer), 104-13.
  In 1890 the publication of the <u>Journal</u> began a new phase
  in Scott studies; it buried the Ballantyne controversy and
  softened hearts toward Scott. Lockhart has become suspect
  for manipulating facts and giving a false impression of
  Scott. Grierson corrected many of the letters in his Centenary Edition and used the corrections in his own biography
  of Scott, which is the most accurate version. Although
  Pope-Hennessey's theory of the revised Waverley chronology
  is probably wrong, it is "worthy of close examination."
  See part I: 1955.B4.

4 DAICHES, DAVID. "Scott's Achievement as a Novelist," in his
  <u>Literary Essays</u>. Edinburgh and London: Oliver and Boyd,
  pp. 88-121.
  Reprint of 1951.B2.

5 GIRDLER, LEW. "Charlotte Brontë's <u>Shirley</u> and Scott's <u>The
  Black Dwarf</u>." <u>Modern Language Notes</u>, 71, no. 3 (March),
  187.
  The last name of the heroine in <u>Shirley</u> appears in a
  poem by John Leyden in chapter 3 of <u>The Black Dwarf</u>, sup-
  porting the hypothesis that Brontë knew and used <u>The Black
  Dwarf</u>.

6 HENNIG, JOHN. "Goethe's Translation of Scott's Criticism of
  Hoffman." <u>Modern Language Review</u>, 51, no. 3 (July), 369-77.
  Goethe reviewed Scott's essay on Hoffman, written in the
  <u>Foreign Quarterly Review</u> of July, 1827. Goethe translated
  much of Scott's essay into German and modified Scott's view
  that Hoffman's works are of primarily psychological, not
  literary interest. Goethe's version is "clearer" and "more
  agreeable" than Scott's original essay.

7 HUMPHRIES, WALTER R. "Blinkhoolie: A Mosaic." <u>Aberdeen University Review</u>, 36, 386-95.
  Blinkhoolie was a fictitious sixteenth-century monk
  loyal to Queen Mary. Scott used him as Abbot Boniface in
  <u>The Monastery</u> and as Goodman Blinkhoolie in <u>The Abbot</u>. His
  characterization is "one of the minor triumphs of Scott's
  art." Although <u>The Monastery</u> is a seriously flawed novel,
  it successfully captures the atmosphere of the period immediately preceding the Scottish Reformation.

8 JOHNSON, EDGAR. "Introduction" to <u>Rob Roy</u>. Boston: Houghton
  Mifflin, pp. v-xvi.

Rob Roy has obvious flaws in technique and structure: the autobiographical memoir form lacks credibility; the character of Rashleigh fails to develop; the happy ending is contrived. However, the novel is redeemed by the pace and movement of the narrative. Scott delineates characters through direct action rather than through psychological analysis. Frank Osbaldistone and Diana Vernon are superior to the sometimes flat heroes and heroines of the other novels. Revised and enlarged in 1970.A5.

9   LEWIS, C. S. "Address to the Forty-eighth Annual Dinner of the Edinburgh Sir Walter Scott Club." The Edinburgh Sir Walter Scott Club Annual Report.
    Scott's Journal reveals both sincerity and self-knowledge. Its passages of pessimism and anxiety do not necessarily invalidate the more fully realized version of life in the novels. The Journal contains Scott's two characteristic styles: the inferior public style, and the living, concrete style he uses for dialogue in the novels. The dual strengths of the Waverley Novels are their historical sense and their "essential rectitude," or proportion. Reprinted: 1962.B9; 1969.B23; and 1971.A13.

10 MAYHEAD, ROBIN. "The Heart of Midlothian: Scott as Artist." Essays in Criticism, 6, no. 3 (July), 266-77.
    The first half of The Heart of Midlothian, concerned with defining the nature of human justice, is "a piece of concentrated and sustained art" unequalled elsewhere in the Waverley Novels. However, Scott's serious interest ends after the trial of Effie Deans, and the second half of the novel "partakes of the usual qualities of the Scott adventure story." See replies: 1957.B22 and 1958.B5. Reprinted: 1968.B29. Partially reprinted: 1973.A3.

11 MONTGOMERIE, WILLIAM. "Sir Walter Scott as a Ballad Editor." Review of English Studies, N.S. 7 (April), 158-63.
    Scott has been given too much credit as a ballad collector in direct touch with oral tradition. The evidence indicates that Scott edited rather than collected and that his sources were primarily manuscript ballads. He assumed that the music was superadded to the ballad itself.

12 PARKER, WILLIAM MATHIE. "Preface" to The Heart of Midlothian. London: J. M. Dent; New York: E. P. Dutton, pp. v-xiv.
    Although the novel's characters are very memorable and even Shakespearean at times, the plot construction is weak; many critics have strongly objected to the last chapters. As a "national epic," The Heart of Midlothian has frequently

1956

been compared to Shakespeare's history plays and has been
highly praised by Saintsbury, Croce, and Hazlitt. Includes
a summary of dramatic adaptations, contemporary critical
reception, and a brief history of the manuscript.

13   _____. "Preface" to The Talisman. London: J. M. Dent;
New York: E. P. Dutton, pp. v-xi.
In The Talisman Scott committed "an occasional anachronism" but remained faithful to the spirit of the twelfth
century. He relied on his reading and on the first hand
information of travel writer John Carne for topographical
details. However, his creation of atmosphere and oriental
character was a "triumph of imagination." Includes a brief
history of the manuscript.

14   PRAZ, MARIO. "Sir Walter Scott," in his The Hero in Eclipse
in Victorian Fiction. Translated by Angus Davidson.
London: Oxford University Press, pp. 54-64.
Scott's scenes of Scottish manners and customs parallel
the paintings of Sir David Wilkie. His detailed descriptions of clothes and furnishings are another characteristic
of genre painting. Scott made romantic subjects acceptable
to bourgeois readers, because he treated the mysterious
with humor and the supernatural with rationality. His
heroines are bourgeois madonnas, and his humor deflates
upper class pretensions to superiority.

1957 A BOOKS

1   CORSON, JAMES C., ed. Reminiscences of Sir Walter Scott's
Residence in Italy, 1832. By Sir William Gell. London:
Thomas Nelson and Sons, 76pp.
The text of the original Canadian edition has been re-
vised, using the manuscript at Abbotsford; includes notes.
Includes 1953.B11 and 1957.B19.

*2   MENON, K. R. A Guide to Sir Walter Scott's The Lady of the
Lake. Singapore: India Publishing House, 144pp.
Cited in the British Museum General Catalogue of Printed
Books, Ten Year Supplement 1956-1965, XLI, column 691.

*3   MERRILL, HERBERT JAMES. "A Reappraisal of Sir Walter Scott:
His Commercial Motivation and His Reliance upon Formula
Fiction for Popular Markets." Ph.D. dissertation, Indiana
University, 1957.
An abstract by the author appears in Dissertation Ab-
stracts, 18 (1958), 222-23.

1957 B SHORTER WRITINGS

1 ALTICK, RICHARD. The English Common Reader: A Social History
of the Mass Reading Public, 1800-1900. Chicago: University
of Chicago Press, 439pp., passim.
The enormous popularity of Scott's poems and novels led
to the growth of the reading public, an upsurge of book
prices, and the consequent rapid growth of the circulating
libraries. Includes statistics on the sales and prices of
Scott's works.

2 BAYLEY, JOHN. The Romantic Survival: A Study in Poetic Evolution. London: Constable, pp. 28-30.
Scott adapted to his own purposes the conflict between
two ideals which is the basis of Shakespeare's history
plays. In Waverley Scott treated his subject matter with
the dramatic neutrality and intuitive sympathy of Shakespeare.

3 BENJAMIN, EDWIN B. "A Borrowing from the Faerie Queene in
Old Mortality." Notes and Queries, 202 (December), 515.
The description of Habbakuk Mucklewrath in Old Mortality,
chapter 22, may have been suggested by the description of
Despair in the Faerie Queene (I, ix, 35-36).

4 BRANSON, C. "Abbot of Walthamstow." Notes and Queries, 202
(July), 316.
Queries if the Abbot of Walthamstow from Scott's Halidon
Hill ever really existed, and if there are other details
known about him.

5 CAHOON, HERBERT. "A Scott Facsimile." Book Collector, 6,
no. 1 (Spring), 74.
Requests the origin of the facsimile or the location of
other copies of Scott's letter to Charles Tilt, Bookseller,
postmarked 14 May, 1830, and printed in Grierson's edition,
vol. 12, p. 471.

6 CRUTTWELL, PATRICK. "Walter Scott," in From Blake to Byron.
Edited by Boris Ford. The Pelican Guide to English Literature, Volume 5. Baltimore: Penguin Books, 104-11.
Although Scott was a leader of Romanticism, his mind was
primarily Augustan, humorous, and sane. The tales he heard
as a child combined with his orthodox eighteenth century
education and the intellectual milieu of Edinburgh to form
his creative power. The Waverley Novels are best when set
in Scotland. They decline in quality when Scott uses remote settings and "heavy English."

1957

*7 DAVIS, NELSON V. "Five English Romantics and Napoleon Bona-
parte." Ph.D. dissertation, Princeton University, 1957.
An abstract by the author appears in Dissertation Abstracts, 18 (1958), 586-87.

8 GOLDSTONE, HERBERT. "The Question of Scott." English Journal,
46, no. 4 (April), 187-95.
Scott uses complicated plots and presents history realis-
tically. Although his villains and heroes are often stereotyped, he can bring ordinary people to life. The Lady of
the Lake is dull and artificial with wooden characters,
little action, and monotonous language. Ivanhoe has a more
skillful plot and livelier characters, but the hero and
heroine are "boring," and it lacks thematic unity. Its
language is strained, and the novel is only partially "a
serious work of fiction."

9 GORDAN, JOHN D. "Sir Walter Scott. Autograph Manuscript of
Bizarro. A Calabrian Tale of Recent Date." Bulletin of
the New York Public Library, 61, no. 7 (July), 359.
Description of a 1955 purchase of two manuscript note-
books of "Scott's final effort to continue to earn money by
his pen." There is apparently a third notebook, but it is
missing. The tale was begun in Naples and based on the
history of a local bandit; it was never finished.

10 GORDON, ROBERT C. "The Bride of Lammermoor: A Novel of Tory
Pessimism." Nineteenth Century Fiction, 12, no. 2
(September), 110-24.
In contrast to the other Scottish novels, The Bride of
Lammermoor represents "an extreme reaction against modern-
ism." Edgar Ravenswood and Caleb Balderstone stand for the
ancient virtues of the past in an alien world; they embody
the disinherited condition of Scotland after 1707 where
"injustice thrives on social change and brings good men to
destruction." Ravenswood encounters an inevitably tragic
end in a world of corrupt justice and political factionalism, shown in microcosm in the greedy villagers of Wolf's-
hope. See reply by Hook, 1967.B15, and exchange, 1969.B14.
Reprinted: 1968.B17.

11 _____. "A Victorian Anticipation of Recent Scott Criticism."
Philological Quarterly, 36, no. 2 (April), 272-75.
Julia Wedgwood's article, "Sir Walter Scott and the
Romantic Reaction," Contemporary Review, 33 (1878), 514-39,
subverts Carlyle's famous attack and anticipates modern
Scott criticism. It focuses on Scott's ambivalence toward
Western European history and on the conflict in his attitude
toward the past.

12   GREEN, F. C. "Scott's French Correspondence." Modern Language
      Review, 52, no. 1 (January), 35-49.
         The Walpole and Abbotsford Collections in the National
      Library of Scotland contain some fifty letters in French
      addressed to Scott. His only literary correspondents were
      Charles Nodier and Amédée Pichot. Prints letters concerning
      the Defauconpret and Pichot translations of Scott's works
      and some correspondence from the French publisher Gosselin.

13   GUTHKE, KARL. "Die erste Nachwirkung von Herders Volkslieden
      in England." Archiv, 193, no. 4, 274-84.
         Reprints a series of letters written 1799-1800 from
      Matthew Gregory Lewis to Scott, concerning the selection
      and translation of ballads for Lewis' Tales of Wonder
      (1801). This collection contains the first English trans-
      lations of ballads from Herder's Volkslieden.

14   HANFORD, JAMES HOLLY. "The Manuscript of Scott's The Pirate."
      Princeton University Library Chronicle, 18, no. 4 (Summer),
      215-22.
         Like several other Waverley manuscripts, part of the
      manuscript of The Pirate was given to Constable by Scott
      and sold at auction after the bankruptcy. It was purchased
      by Robert Cadell, who had received the rest of the manu-
      script from Scott in April, 1831. The manuscript demon-
      strates Scott's unwillingness to revise or delete and his
      habit of using the verso of the preceding page for second
      thoughts or amplifications.

15   HILLHOUSE, JAMES T. "Sir Walter Scott," in The English Roman-
      tic Poets and Essayists: A Review of Research and Criti-
      cism. Edited by Lawrence Huston Houtchens and Carolyn
      Washburn Houtchens. New York: Modern Language Association
      of America, pp. 114-157.
         A survey in essay form of I. Bibliographies; II. Edi-
      tions; III. Biographies; IV. Criticism. Section IV is
      subdivided into 1) Poems; 2) Novels; 3) Superstition and
      the Supernatural; 4) Influence; 5) Political and Religious
      Views; 6) Miscellaneous Writing and Editing. This edition
      has been expanded and updated through 1964 in the revised
      edition, 1966.B8.

16   KASER, DAVID. "Waverley in America." Papers of the Bibliog-
      raphical Society of America, 51, no. 2, 163-67.
         The publishing firm of Carey and Lea of Philadelphia has
      been suspected of purloining Waverley proof-sheets to issue
      the first American reprints of the novels. New documents
      indicate that Carey and Lea were not at fault; they

1957

obtained the sheets from Philadelphia bookseller Thomas
Wardle, who purchased them from Hurst, Robinson and Company,
Constable's London agents.

17   KILMUIR, VISCOUNT. "Address to the Forty-ninth Annual Dinner
of the Edinburgh Sir Walter Scott Club." The Edinburgh Sir
Walter Scott Club Annual Report, pp. 11-25.
        Scott honored both traditions of eighteenth century Scot-
land: the Calvinistic and "theocratic-democratic" ideology
of the Civil War, and the Cavalier values which led to the
Jacobite uprisings. The eighteenth century imbued the
Scottish character with the qualities of loyalty and the
willingness to risk all; these qualities manifest themselves
in Waverley, Rob Roy, Redgauntlet, The Antiquary, and The
Bride of Lammermoor.

18   MEIKLEJOHN, M. F. M. "Sir Walter Scott and Alessandro Manzoni."
Italian Studies, 12, 91-98.
        Italian writers on Manzoni and Scott have exaggerated the
influence of Ivanhoe and overlooked the resemblances between
I Promessi Sposi and The Heart of Midlothian. Both deal
with towns well known to their authors and contrast city and
country. Both novels attempt to "make virtue attractive"
and to convey "the spirit of resignation to Divine Providence." Manzoni probably read The Heart of Midlothian in
Defauconpret's French translation before beginning his own
novel.

19   NORMAND, LORD. "Preface" to Reminiscences of Sir Walter
Scott's Residence in Italy, 1832. By Sir William Gell.
Edited by James Clarkson Corson. London: Thomas Nelson &
Sons, pp. ix-xi.
        Scott's last journey in search of health was sadly un-
successful, but he continued to show courage and kindness
to his companions. Gell especially commemorated the devotion of Scott's daughter Anne. Unanswered questions have
arisen concerning Lockhart's possibly unauthorized use of
the Reminiscences. See 1953.B11 and 1957.A1.

20   PARKER, WILLIAM MATHIE. "Introduction," to The Life of Sir
Walter Scott. By J. G. Lockhart. London: J. M. Dent;
New York: E. P. Dutton, pp. v-xvi.
        Although Lockhart had been authorized by Scott to write
the Life, several other erstwhile biographers, including
Hogg, tried to publish theirs first. Lockhart's Life was
published in seven volumes from March, 1837 through February, 1838. Most of the early reviews praised it. The first
abridged edition appeared in 1848; the 1871 reprint of the

156

1853 edition, with a prefatory letter by James R. Hope-Scott, has become the standard abridgement. Lockhart's Life shows Scott's many-sidedness and lovingly celebrates his genius. Despite the many inaccuracies, Lockhart is to be commended for his self-effacement.

21   ____. "Preface" to Guy Mannering. London: J. M. Dent; New York: E. P. Dutton, pp. v-xiii.
      Scott used many sources for the raw material of Guy Mannering, especially the legal battle between James Annesley and Richard, Earl of Anglesey for possession of the Anglesey estate and title. Dandie Dinmont is a composite portrait of several Border farmers, and Dominie Sampson is based partly on George Thompson, the tutor of Scott's sons. The gypsy Jean Gordon provided the model for Meg Merrilies. Includes a summary of stage versions of the novel and a brief history of the manuscript.

22   PITTOCK, JOAN H. "The Heart of Midlothian: Scott as Artist?" Essays in Criticism, 7, no. 4 (October), 477-79.
      The first half of The Heart of Midlothian is not a unified artistic design; it presents "Scott's usual bundle of conflicting interests and attitudes." The excellence of the novel lies not in its unified theme but in its crystalization of "Scott's own national, antiquarian, and legal interests." See 1956.B10 and 1958.B5.

23   RUFF, WILLIAM. "Cancels in Sir Walter Scott's Life of Napoleon." Transactions of the Edinburgh Bibliographical Society, 3, 138-51.
      There are 125 cancels in the first edition and 28 in the second edition, both published in 1827. The unavailability of some materials and the financial and physical pressure under which he was writing caused Scott to make many mistakes. Lists the cancelled leaves and the bindings for the nine volumes of the first edition. The second edition was a reprint of volumes I and II and signatures A-E of volume III of the first edition. Signatures F-Y of volume III and volumes IV-IX are new printings but contain no cancels.

24   TODD, WILLIAM B. "The Early Editions and Issues of Scott's Border Antiquities." Studies in Bibliography, 9, 244-51.
      Attempts to identify the first true edition in book form of the Border Antiquities of England and Scotland and to distinguish it from several reprints and piracies. Scott was involved with the work from the seventh number to its termination. See 1956.B2 and 1960.B3.

1958

1958 A BOOKS

1 ANON. "Introduction" to <u>Valter Skott: Bibliografichesky ukazatel'k 125-letiyu so dnya smerti</u> [Walter Scott: Bio-bibliographical Index to the 125 Years Since His Death]. Writers of Foreign Countries. Moscow: State Library of Foreign Literature, pp. 3-18.

Cataclysmic social change turned the attention of the early nineteenth century to the past. In his historical novels, Scott combined deep knowledge of the past with creative fantasy. He managed to see beyond his own conservatism, to understand that bourgeois progress implies the necessary destruction of the old order. He demonstrated the organic connection between the personal destinies of his characters and the logic of history. Directory lists Scott's works published in England and Russia, selected criticism, and an appendix of forgeries published under his name but not written by him.

*2 FRENCH, RICHARD AUBREY. "Sir Walter Scott: An Amateur." Ph.D. dissertation, University of Texas, 1958.

An abstract by the author appears in <u>Dissertation Abstracts</u>, 19 (1958), 1071.

3 JACK, IAN. <u>Sir Walter Scott</u>. Writers and Their Work. London: Longman's, Green, 40pp.

<u>Waverley</u> and the Scottish novels were intended to convey Scott's romantic excitement about Scotland's past. When he turned away from Scotland, "he ceased to be a major writer." Scott was candid about his shortcomings and uninterested in technique; most of his work is "ramshackle wholes with magnificent parts." He had a visual imagination and often described scenes and characters with consciously pictorial techniques.

1958 B SHORTER WRITINGS

1 ANON. "<u>Christabel</u> and Coleridge's 'Recipe' for Romance Poems." <u>Notes and Queries</u>, 203 (November), 475.

Coleridge ridiculed Scott's <u>Lady of the Lake</u> and developed a mocking "recipe for poems of this sort" which he seems to have followed himself in <u>Christabel</u>.

2 BRAMLEY, J. A. "The Genius of Walter Scott." <u>Contemporary Review</u>, 193 (March), 149-53.

Scott is misunderstood by modern critics, who argue that he is unrealistic and irrelevant. His great discovery was

"that we are moulded both as a nation as well as individuals
by our past history." He warned against fanaticism and advocated the old patriarchal loyalties. The Journal reveals
a convincing picture of heroism and greatness, particularly
in misfortune.

3   BUTLER, R. F.   "Maria Edgeworth and Sir Walter Scott: Unpub-
    lished Letters, 1823."   Review of English Studies, N.S. 9
    (February), 23-40.
       Includes letters from Maria Edgeworth to members of her
    family expressing her pleasure in a visit to Edinburgh in
    June, 1823 and a fortnight's stay at Abbotsford in August.
    Edgeworth was deeply impressed by Scott's kindness, "prodi-
    gious memory," and "original genius."

4   CLARK, ARTHUR MELVILLE.   "Address to the Fiftieth Annual Dinner
    of the Edinburgh Sir Walter Scott Club."   The Edinburgh Sir
    Walter Scott Club Annual Report.
       Scott and Shakespeare both exhibited a "fine disregard of
    niceties" which sprung from a plenitude of inspiration.
    They both wrote to amuse, and their works combine gravity
    with humor.   Although Shakespeare's characters are more pro-
    found, Scott's are more relevant because they "are involved
    in time, place, and circumstance."   Unlike Shakespeare, how-
    ever, Scott never condescends to middle class and working
    class people.   Reprinted: 1971.A13.

5   CRAIG, DAVID.   "The Heart of Midlothian: Its Religious Basis."
    Essays in Criticism, 8, no. 2 (April), 217-25.
       Although the novel includes much "dead wood," Scott's
    subject in his most forceful chapters is "the moral and re-
    ligious ethos produced by Presbyterianism."   Scott presents
    "the total weight of circumstances" felt by Jeanie as a re-
    sult of her intensely Presbyterian upbringing.   See
    1956.B10 and 1957.B22.

6   DAICHES, DAVID.   "Scott's Redgauntlet," in From Jane Austen to
    Joseph Conrad.   Essays Collected in Memory of James T. Hill-
    house.   Edited by R. C. Rathburn and Martin Steinmann, Jr.
    Minneapolis: University of Minnesota Press, pp. 46-59.
       Scott's best novels concern the conflict between pic-
    turesque tradition and sober modernity and end with the
    "reluctant" victory of prudent realism over exciting roman-
    ticism.   Redgauntlet is "the story of two worlds"--modern
    legal Edinburgh and the wildly anachronistic Stuart cause,
    linked with Scottish nationalism.   The plot juxtaposes
    "historical emotion" to "present fact" and demonstrates the
    decay of sentimental Jacobitism.   Peter Peebles' obsession

with a lost cause parallels Redgauntlet's, and "Wandering Willie's Tale" offers a thematic counterpart of the main action. Reprinted: 1968.B8.

7 GETTMAN, ROYAL A. "Colburn-Bentley and the March of Intellect." Studies in Bibliography, 9, 197-213.
Constable inaugurated the cheap series with Scott's Life of Napoleon, which was to become part of Constable's Miscellany. It was thwarted by the financial crash of 1826, but later John Murray published in a cheap series the Napoleon as revised by Lockhart.

8 MAXWELL, J. C. "An Uncollected Scott Letter." Review of English Studies, N.S. 9 (November), 410-11.
Prints a letter of 15 May, 1808, not included in Grierson's edition, from Scott to the actor Charles Mayne Young, regarding legal details of the leasing of a theatre.

9 PARKER, WILLIAM MATHIE. "Introduction" to Kenilworth. London: J. M. Dent; New York: E. P. Dutton, pp. v-xiii.
The rich pageantry of the novel compensates for Scott's liberties with history and chronology. Scott provides a romantic rendering of Elizabethan speech and manners and treats the Queen herself with admiration and psychological subtlety. Includes a brief history of the manuscript.

10 _____. "Preface" to Old Mortality. London: J. M. Dent; New York: E. P. Dutton, pp. v-xvii.
Scott's treatment of the Covenanters has aroused controversy. He portrayed them as extremists but admired their courage. In his defense against Thomas McCrie's rebuke that he had caricatured them, Scott distinguished between moderates and extremists and argued that fanaticism destroys both freedom and social cohesion. He tried to present an impartial view and to teach that intolerance breeds more intolerance. Includes a summary of the contemporary reception and a brief history of the manuscript.

11 _____. "Preface" to Redgauntlet. London: J. M. Dent; New York: E. P. Dutton, pp. v-xiii.
More than any other novel, Redgauntlet reveals Scott himself and his memories of his father and of early love and friendship. The novel as a whole is "the prose threnody of a lost cause," and its conclusion is touched with sadness. Includes a summary of its contemporary critical reception and a brief history of the manuscript.

12 TILLYARD, E. M. W. "Scott," in his <u>The Epic Strain in the</u>
    <u>English Novel</u>. London: Chatto and Windus, pp. 59-116.
       Scott's novels are epic in their attempt to express gen-
    eral sentiments held by a large group of people. However,
    they are deficient in organization and conscious art. Their
    basic ethical principle is the need to reconcile individual
    or cultural aspiration with the pressure of existing circum-
    stances. Like Burke, Scott respects the adjustments that
    have evolved from a long period of historical trial and
    error.

13 _____. "Scott's Linguistic Vagaries." <u>Études Anglaises</u>, 11,
    112-18.
       The Waverley Novels are "strange in the disorder of their
    linguistic elements." In the Scottish novels Scott used
    contemporary English for narration and description and Low-
    land Scots for humble dialect. The archaic "tushery" of
    <u>Ivanhoe</u> was derived from many sources. The "linguistic con-
    fusion" of <u>The Monastery</u> mixed English, Scots, "tushery"
    and the archaism of the neo-Gothic romance. In the later
    novels Scott used "the historico-heroic norm" for the pa-
    geantry his reader demanded. Reprinted: 1962.B23.

14 WITTIG, KURT. "Walter Scott," in his <u>The Scottish Tradition</u>
    <u>in Literature</u>. Edinburgh: Oliver and Boyd, pp. 221-238.
       Scott was interested in the clash of traditions and in
    human nature in the context of history. The Scottish novels
    reveal the formative power of history, whereas the ones
    with English or Continental settings are mere "pageant."
    Scott's emphasis on the importance of the common people
    links him with Scottish literary tradition. He writes best
    in Scots dialogue and is "greatest when most Scottish."

1959 A BOOKS - NONE

1959 B SHORTER WRITINGS

1 BUTLER, R. A. "Address to the Fifty-first Annual Dinner of
    the Edinburgh Sir Walter Scott Club." <u>The Edinburgh Sir</u>
    <u>Walter Scott Club Annual Report</u>, pp. 11-18.
       Scott's works exemplify the value of loyalty--to clan,
    cause, family, and principles. This theme is most evident
    in <u>A Legend of Montrose</u> and <u>The Fair Maid of Perth</u>, which
    show loyalty as the most important virtue essential to the
    well-being of a nation.

1959

2   CARLTON, WILLIAM J. "Sir Walter Scott and the Pilgrim Penman."
     Notes and Queries, 204 (April), 127-29.
         Quotes excerpts from a letter of 24 May, 1826 from the
     teacher of penmanship, James Henry Lewis, to his family.
     Lewis describes meeting with Scott in Scott's rented flat
     in St. David's Street. Lewis later dedicated to Scott his
     Portraits of the Art of Writing and of the Teachers of that
     Art.

3   DREW, FRASER. "The Loving Shepherdess of Jeffers and Scott."
     Trace, 31 (April-May), 13-16.
         Jeffers' Clare Walker, heroine of The Loving Shepherdess,
     is based on one of Scott's notes in The Heart of Midlothian,
     which tells the story of Feckless Fanny, who always travel-
     led with a flock of twelve or thirteen deeply devoted sheep.

*4   DROP, WILLEM. "De Oudste Nederlandse Vertalingen van Scott's
     Romans" [The Oldest Dutch Translations of Scott's Novels].
     De Nieuwe Taalgids, 52, 213-27.
         Cited in the Annual Bibliography for 1959, PMLA, 75,
     no. 2, 392, item #12298.

5   INGLIS-JONES, ELISABETH. "Chapter Twelve: 1823," in The Great
     Maria: A Portrait of Maria Edgeworth. London: Faber and
     Faber, pp. 192-207.
         Maria Edgeworth visited Edinburgh and Abbotsford in the
     summer of 1823. She and Scott found that they shared "a
     spiritual kinship" and a similar philosophy of life, which
     valued humility and discipline. Both were also interested
     in a wide variety of activities besides literary work.

6   McDONALD, W. U., JR. "Scott's Conception of Don Quixote."
     Midwest Review, 1 (March), 37-42.
         Scott's critical attitude toward Don Quixote was midway
     between those who regarded it as pure farce and those who
     regarded it as basically tragic. He saw Don Quixote as "a
     comprehensive work of art with an unmistakable foundation
     in reality," especially in its depiction of period manners
     and sentiments. Scott did not necessarily regard "romance"
     as a demeaning term and believed the satire in Don Quixote
     was directed against the later degradations of romance.

7   MAXWELL, J. C. "J. S. Le Fanu's The Cock and Anchor." Notes
     and Queries, 204 (December), 460.
         In Redgauntlet Scott wrote "Nanty likes the turning up
     of his little finger unco weel." The expression means
     "drinking heavily" and is much earlier than other quotations
     in the E.D.D.

8   MENEN, AUBREY. "The Myth of English Literature." Holiday,
     26, no. 1 (July), 8, 11, and 12-14.
          Scott's later novels "cheat the public," and the best
     that can be said for his work is that it set a fashion in
     fiction.

9   METZDORF, ROBERT F., ed. The Tinker Library: A Bibliographi-
     cal Catalogue of the Books and Manuscripts Collected by
     Chauncey Brewster Tinker. New Haven, Connecticut: Yale
     University Library, pp. 376-80.
          Lists two letters written by Scott (to Sir Samuel Eger-
     ton Brydges, 20 February, 1808 and to Miss Wagner of Liver-
     pool, 7 February, 1828) plus eighteen printed works, mainly
     narrative poems, with bibliographical data for each.

10   PARKER, WILLIAM MATHIE. "Preface" to Ivanhoe. London: J. M.
     Dent; New York: E. P. Dutton, pp. v-xv.
          Scott chose the name "Ivanhoe" from an old rhyme because
     it suggested the Middle Ages without indicating a particular
     story. Rebecca may have been based on Rebecca Gratz of
     Philadelphia, whose story Scott heard from Washington
     Irving. Includes a summary of the contemporary critical
     reception and a brief history of the manuscript.

11   SHANNON, EDGAR F., JR. "'Locksley Hall' and Ivanhoe." Notes
     and Queries, 204 (June), 216-17.
          Tennyson's "Locksley Hall" was partially inspired by
     Ivanhoe. Scott's Locksley (Robin Hood) and Tennyson's per-
     sona are both refugees from materialism. The opening coup-
     let of the poem mentions a bugle-horn, an important object
     in Ivanhoe. Both writers compare a woman to a dog.

12   STROUT, ALAN LANG. A Bibliography of Articles in "Blackwood's
     Magazine" Volumes I through XVIII, 1817-1825. Library
     Bulletin No. 5, Texas Technological College. Lubbock:
     Texas Tech Press, 208pp.
          Lists seventeen articles by Scott, including "Alarming
     Increase of Depravity Among Animals" (October, 1817) and a
     series of articles on Scottish Gypsies.

1960 A BOOKS

*1   OCHOJSKI, PAUL M. "Walter Scott and Germany: A Study in
     Literary Cross Currents." Ph.D. dissertation, Columbia
     University, 1960.
          An abstract by the author appears in Dissertation Ab-
     stracts, 21 (1961), 2704-2705.

1960

*2   WILKINSON, ROBERT GEORGE. "Ideals and Idealism in the Waverley
      Novels." Ph.D. dissertation, University of California,
      Claremont, 1960.
          An abstract by the author appears in <u>Dissertation Ab-
      stracts</u>, 21 (1961), 2280.

1960 B SHORTER WRITINGS

1   BRAMLEY, J. A. "Walter Scott Today." <u>John O'London's</u>
     (30 June), p. 785.
         Many modern critics misunderstand Scott because they
     fail to appreciate the historical and social settings of
     his novels. He was a realistic writer whose best books
     deal with eighteenth century Scotland and whose best charac-
     ters are drawn from life.

2   CHANCELLOR, PAUL. "British Bards and Continental Composers."
     <u>Musical Quarterly</u>, 46, no. 1 (January), 1-11.
         Scott appealed to composers because of his use of Celtic
     folksong and myth and his Romantic medievalism. Schubert
     set eight of Scott's songs to music. Berlioz, who composed
     overtures to <u>Waverley</u> and <u>Rob Roy</u>, was deeply moved by the
     wilder elements of English Romanticism. The "British Ro-
     mantic bards" provided the inspiration for some of the most
     memorable music of the nineteenth century.

3   CORSON, JAMES CLARKSON. "A Supplementary Note on <u>The Border
     Antiquities</u>." <u>Bibliotheck</u>, 3, 15-23.
         John Grieg was the actual editor of the work, and Scott
     provided only suggestions and notes to help him. Corrects
     several errors made by William B. Todd regarding the publi-
     cation problems of <u>The Border Antiquities</u> as it was issued
     in seventeen parts. There were seven editions, not five as
     Todd states. <u>See</u> 1956.B2 and 1957.B24.

4   DAICHES, DAVID. "Scottish Literature to Scott," in his <u>A
     Critical History of English Literature</u>. Volume II.
     New York: The Ronald Press, 831-53.
         Scott's work reflects "a deep sense of Scottish history
     and nationhood" and is formed by "a peculiarly Scottish ex-
     perience." His ambivalence toward tradition and progress
     makes him almost anti-romantic and gives his novels their
     uniqueness. As his subject matter approaches closer to his
     own time, he becomes a more complex and mature novelist.
     The "Scotch Novels" are informed by a tragic sense of the
     inevitability of progress and of the impotence of tradition-
     al heroism. In characterization he is concerned with the

impact of past and present on individuals. Includes individual analyses of the Scottish novels.

5 DYSON, GILLIAN. "The Manuscripts and Proof Sheets of Scott's Waverley Novels." <u>Transactions of the Edinburgh Bibliographical Society</u>, 4, no. 1, 15-42.
To preserve Scott's anonymity, the manuscripts and corrections on the proof-sheets were transcribed, so that the printers would not see Scott's handwriting. The manuscripts were first sold in 1831, and their prices rose through the nineteenth century. The manuscripts and proof-sheets reveal mistakes and corrections in the texts and are useful for determining at what stage a correction was made and by whom. Lists details of the sales history and present locations of surviving manuscripts and proof-sheets.

6 ENKVIST, NILS ERIK. "Sir Walter Scott, Lord Bloomfield, and Bernadotte." <u>Studia Neophilologica</u>, 32 (June), 18-29.
Reprints correspondence between Scott and Benjamin Bloomfield, British Ambassador to Stockholm. The bulk of the letters concern a packet of papers sent by the Swedish King Charles XIV, formerly Count Bernadotte, to Scott to aid in Scott's research on Napoleonic history.

7 FIEDLER, LESLIE. <u>Love and Death in the American Novel</u>. New York: Criterion Books, pp. 151-70.
The historical romance is not serious; it is "the tribute that philistinism pays to the instinctive." Scott's outsiders are tame and anti-demonic; his heroes are defined as the ones who receive the rewards. His essentially bourgeois vision rejected the Faustian and the Gothic. Scott achieved his greatness not as an artist but as a "maker of legends" who transformed the past of Scotland into a European myth. Includes an analysis of <u>Rob Roy</u> as "the classic formulation of Scott's white Romantic myth."

8 GETTMAN, ROYAL A. <u>A Victorian Publisher: A Study of the Bentley Papers</u>. Cambridge: Cambridge University Press, passim.
Scott offers a good illustration of the influence of nineteenth century publishers on authors. Archibald Constable claimed to be "all but the author" of the Waverley Novels, and Scott acknowledged the importance of his suggestions. Ballantyne extensively edited Scott's proof-sheets for stylistic awkwardness and unconscious repetitions of characters and ideas. Scott profited from his editing but was less gracious when William Gifford, as literary advisor to John Murray, offered suggestions for rewriting <u>The Black Dwarf</u>.

1960

9 KROEBER, KARL. "The Narrative Pattern of Scott," in his <u>Roman-</u>
   <u>tic Narrative Art</u>. Madison: University of Wisconsin Press,
   pp. 168-87.
       Because Scott saw history as process and organic evolu-
   tion, the sequential order of the story becomes more important than the causal order of the plot. The progress
   from ballads to narrative poems to novels parallels Scott's
   developing vision of encompassing historical unity. Scott
   was the most committed of the Romantics to the narrative
   mode and was thus incapable of any technique which complicated the direct telling of the story. The deficiencies in
   the poems reveal his inherent novelistic bias.

10 LYNSKEY, WINIFRED. "The Drama of the Elect and the Reprobate
    in Scott's <u>Heart of Midlothian</u>." <u>Boston University Studies</u>
    <u>in English</u>, 4, no. 1 (Spring), 39-48.
        The last ten chapters are based on strict Calvinist doc-
    trines. Staunton, the reprobate, is predestined to evil
    and incapable of repentance. Jeanie is of the elect and
    incapable of worldly evil. Their fates demonstrate God's
    inexorable judgment and the helplessness of the individual
    to change his sphere. The Calvinistic doctrines of predes-
    tination, the grace of God, the omnipresence of the devil,
    and the depravity of fallen man are pronounced throughout
    the novel. However, Scott modified the harsh precepts of
    the Calvinistic struggle, particularly in the characteriza-
    tion of Jeanie and Davie Deans.

11 OGILVIE, R. M. "Sir Walter Scott and Livy." <u>Listener</u>, 64
    (3 November), 792 and 795.
        Livy and Scott share several characteristics as histori-
    cal novelists: the combination of contemporary setting
    with archaic language; a wide stylistic range; high moral
    seriousness; little interest in women; and "a refreshingly
    amateur enthusiasm."

12 PARKER, WILLIAM MATHIE. "Preface" to <u>Quentin Durward</u>.
    London: J. M. Dent; New York: E. P. Dutton, pp. v-xi.
        Topographical rather than historical details gave Scott
    most trouble while writing <u>Quentin Durward</u>. It was his
    first attempt to use foreign material, and it achieved
    great popularity abroad. The novel has a well constructed
    plot, graphic description, and dialogue suited to the sev-
    eral speakers. Scott compensated for his historical errors
    with vital characterization, especially of Louis XI. In-
    cludes a brief history of the manuscript.

13 PEARSON, HESKETH. "Address to the Fifty-second Annual Dinner of the Edinburgh Sir Walter Scott Club." The Edinburgh Sir Walter Scott Club Annual Report.
Scott's letters and Journal reflect his intelligence, common sense, and unimpeachable character. He had a mind both sound and profound, but he delighted in simple people and things. Despite being pestered by a succession of boors, he remained unfailingly courteous to guests. His only vice was modesty and the tendency to depreciate his own work. His artistic greatness matched his human fortitude. Reprinted: 1971.A13.

14 RINSLER, NORMA. "Gérard de Nerval and Sir Walter Scott's Antiquary." Revue de Littérature Comparée, 34, no. 3, 448-51.
Nerval may have found the legend of the "main de gloire" in Dousterswivel's explanation of its preparation and magical powers in The Antiquary. Nerval incorporated the legend into his own story, "La Main Enchantée." He may also have been led to investigate the inscription of "Aelia Laelia" by an incidental conversation early in the novel between Oldbuck and Lovel.

15 ROMERO MENDOZA, PEDRO. "Walter Scott," in his Siete Ensayos Sobre el Romanticismo Español, Vol. II. Cáceres: Servicios Culturales de la Excma, 261-73.
Scott used the favorite props of German romanticism—legends, mysteries, superstitions, and ruins. However, he also created his characters as real people and knew their habits, attitudes, and manners. They become individualized representatives of the collective soul of their country. Although later writers became more aesthetically scrupulous, Scott has not been surpassed by his followers.

16 ROSENBERG, EDGAR. "The Jew as Clown and the Jew's Daughter: Scott," in his From Shylock to Svengali: Jewish Stereotypes in English Fiction. Stanford, California: Stanford University Press, pp. 73-115.
Scott was the first to give the Jews prominence in English fiction. In Ivanhoe they function as "touchstones of social integrity," a measurement of the moral worth of the other characters. Although Isaac of York is the fictional heir of Shylock, Scott absolves Isaac by explaining the social and historical forces behind his vices. Rebecca is "the Jewish paragon in word and deed." In The Surgeon's Daughter, Zilia is another type of the high-minded, beautiful, and defenseless "Noble Jewess."

1960

17 SMITH, JANET A. "The End of the Old Dominion." <u>New Statesman</u>
    <u>and Nation</u>, 59 (14 May), 718-19.
        There are similarities between Allen Tate's <u>The Fathers</u>
    and <u>Waverley</u>. Both Tate and Scott wrote of events earlier
    than their own times but still within the memories of some
    living people. Both novelists wrote of the last days of an
    order which has become unrealistic but whose style and
    values they admired. Both gave their finest speeches to
    doomed men. However, whereas Scott wrote <u>Waverley</u> with
    "artless gusto," Tate wrote "with conscious art and skill."

<u>1961 A BOOKS</u>

1 DAVIE, DONALD. <u>The Heyday of Sir Walter Scott</u>. London:
    Routledge & Kegan Paul, 168pp.
        Scott's strength lies in his perception of society and
    manners and of the composition and interactions of communi-
    ties. This concern with the tensions of history as they
    form unique social structures constitutes his most important
    influence on such diverse writers as Pushkin, Mickiewicz,
    William Carlton, Charles Lever, Joseph Sheridan LeFanu, and
    Cooper. Implicit in all Scott's work is this "fact of com-
    munity considered as a state of being or a state of feel-
    ing." Waverley's values of reasonableness, public spirit,
    and justice embody this feeling for community, making him
    "the man of feeling" who replaces the heroic figure in the
    new Scottish culture. Extracts reprinted: 1968.B9, B10.

*2 McEWEN, FRED BATES. "Techniques of Description in Eight Se-
    lected Novels of Sir Walter Scott." Ph.D. dissertation,
    University of Pittsburgh, 1961.
        An abstract by the author appears in <u>Dissertation Ab-</u>
    <u>stracts</u>, 22 (1962), 3648-49.

<u>1961 B SHORTER WRITINGS</u>

1 BIGGINS, D. "<u>Measure for Measure</u> and <u>The Heart of Midlothian</u>."
    <u>Études Anglaises</u>, 14 (July), 193-205.
        Effie's offense in <u>The Heart of Midlothian</u>, like
    Claudio's in <u>Measure for Measure</u>, is sexual in nature and
    caused by the revival of an old statute. Both works depend
    on the tension between moral conviction and ties of blood.
    Scott deliberately emphasizes the likeness between Jeanie
    and Isabella and implies that in both cases laws that may
    be sound legal abstractions may be applied inhumanely. The
    treatment of law and justice in <u>Measure for Measure</u> may
    also have influenced <u>The Surgeon's Daughter</u>.

2   BLUNDEN, EDMUND. "On Regency Fiction: A Fragment." Essays
    and Studies, N.S. 14, 52-65.
        Scott was read and worshipped by the multitudes in his
    own time and in the early Victorian period. He was "not a
    provincial nor a national but a European author" whose
    strength in detail and in the picturesque compensated for
    his lack of philosophic distance.

3   CECCHI, EMILIO. "Miss Austen e Walter Scott," in his I grandi
    romantici inglesi. Florence: G. C. Sansoni, pp. 169-182.
        Scott created colorful and intoxicating scenes and nar-
    cotized his readers with dreams. His romanticism consisted
    of medieval pictures of monasticism, pretty ladies, and
    moonlight. Scott did not understand the new political and
    economic forces developing in England. He lamented the de-
    cline of aristocracy and failed to perceive it as part of
    a universal trend toward democracy.

4   CRAIG, DAVID. "The Age of Scott," in his Scottish Literature
    and the Scottish People, 1680-1830. London: Chatto &
    Windus, pp. 139-165.
        Scottish fiction of this period is unconcerned with con-
    temporary urban life. Scott's portraits of "varied human-
    ity" of the lower classes remain peripheral to the main
    action of his plots. He was interested in manners only
    when they were distanced in time and space, and he was pre-
    occupied with the picturesque elements of history. In his
    own life, Scott recoiled from the present. His "irresponsi-
    bility of romance-writing" derived from his insufficient
    awareness of the society around him.

5   DAVIE, DONALD. "The Poetry of Sir Walter Scott." Proceedings
    of the British Academy, 47, 61-75.
        The most obvious stylistic feature of Scott's poetry is
    "elegant variation," or saying one thing several ways. His
    "copiousness of invention" is his greatest quality, but too
    often it is uncontrolled by structure. Scott is insensitive
    to metre. After The Lady of the Lake, Scott's imaginative
    resources were being saved for the novels.

6   GREEN, DAVID BONNELL. "New Letters of Sir Walter Scott:
    1813-1831." Notes and Queries, 206 (January), 16-19;
    (February), 67-70 and 72; (March), 92-96.
        Prints previously unpublished letters to and from a wide
    range of correspondents, most of whom do not appear in
    Grierson's list of recipients of Scott's letters. Corre-
    spondents include Mrs. Harriet Falconer Walker, who sought
    Scott's patronage for her poet-son, the genre-painter

1961

Edward Bird, and the artist William Stewart Watson. Notes
identify correspondents and provide locations for the
letters.

7   HART, FRANCIS RUSSELL. "Proofreading Lockhart's Scott: The
    Dynamics of Biographical Reticence." Studies in Bibliog-
    raphy, 14, 3-22.
        Lockhart's proof-sheets together with certain letters re-
    veal his manipulation of documents and anecdotes. He as-
    sumed the biographer had the right to edit and to adapt raw
    materials. He amalgamated passages from several separate
    letters and Journal entries, and he touched up conversa-
    tions. Scott's friends and associates, especially Cadell,
    Laidlaw, Croker, and Lady Louisa Stuart, pressured Lockhart
    to restrain his candor. Morritt of Rokeby urged reticence
    in dealing with Scott's last days.

8   KOŻUCHOWSKA, STANISLAWA. "O Ludowości Waltera Scotta i George
    Sand" [On the Folk Art of Walter Scott and George Sand].
    Kwartalnik Neofilologiczny, 8, no. 2, 171-84.
        Scott influenced George Sand's conception of popular art
    and of the role of folklore in fiction. There are resem-
    blances in their attitudes toward the supernatural in
    Scott's Letters on Demonology and Witchcraft and Sand's
    Visions de la nuit dans les campagnes. However, Sand felt
    more strongly than did Scott the conflict between thought
    and intuition, reality and fantasy. Sand's gift for as-
    similation and her thorough knowledge of Scott's works in-
    fluenced her gradual development of the rural novel.

9   LASCELLES, MARY. "The Sir Walter Scott Lectures for 1960: I.
    Scott and Shakespeare." University of Edinburgh Journal,
    20, no. 1, 23-33.
        Through deep familiarity with Shakespeare's plays, Scott
    discovered the romantic novel as an alternative to "the
    hitherto pent-up forces of romantic drama." Shakespeare
    taught Scott to link history and romance and to think his-
    torically about the relations between past and present.
    They were similar in temperament and in their attitudes to
    compromise and extremism. Both could command dialect as
    well as formal language. Scott is at his best when he
    finds the counterparts of Shakespeare's characters within
    his own experience. Revised: 1972.B23.

10 _____. "The Sir Walter Scott Lectures for 1960: II. Scott
    and the Sense of Time." University of Edinburgh Journal,
    20, no. 1, 33-45.

1961

Scott placed more emphasis on "change regarded as loss"
than on "change regarded as renewal." He dwelt on the sense
of loss within ourselves which may be stimulated by a relic
of the past. He feared the changes that overcome civilizations, such as the depopulation of the Highlands. Although
the novels often deal with family renewal over a period of
time, they reflect little sense of seasonal pattern. They
gain narrative distance through the reader's sense of lapsed
time between the events and the narration. Revised:
1972.B25.

11   McDONALD, W. U., JR. "A Letter of Sir Walter Scott to William
      Scott on the Jeffrey-Swift Controversy." Review of English
      Studies, N.S. 12 (November), 404-408.
      Prints a letter to William Scott, author of an article
      in the Edinburgh Monthly Review of July, 1820 which at-
      tempted to refute Jeffrey's attack on the character of
      Swift. Jeffrey had reacted to what he regarded as Sir
      Walter Scott's falsely favorable version of Swift's charac-
      ter. The letter thanks William Scott for his defense of
      Swift and deplores the "worst spirit of party" which moti-
      vated Jeffrey.

12   MARSHALL, WILLIAM H. "Point of View and Structure in The
      Heart of Midlothian." Nineteenth Century Fiction, 16,
      no. 3 (December), 257-62.
      Jeanie's morality provides the novel's controlling point
      of view. The historical situation dramatizes it, and the
      religious background provides plausible motivation for her
      actions. She views life allegorically and tends to see all
      events as symbolic affirmations of God's justice. The
      resolution of the plot substantiates her belief that jus-
      tice prevails and that her strict but simple morality is
      right. This view of earthly justice gives the novel unity;
      the weak points of the novel occur when Jeanie's point of
      view is not present.

13   NICOLSON, HAROLD. "The Romantic Revolt." Horizon, 3, no. 5
      (May), 58-87.
      Deals with Scott only peripherally. The Waverley Novels
      created "a virtual cult of Scotland" stressing its remote-
      ness and twilight atmosphere.

14   RAMSEY, ARTHUR MICHAEL. "Address to the Fifty-third Annual
      Dinner of the Edinburgh Sir Walter Scott Club." The Edin-
      burgh Sir Walter Scott Club Annual Report, pp. 11-18.
      Scott's genius manifests itself in the drawing of con-
      trasts between two worlds. His sympathy lies not with a

particular cause but with those human qualities "which heal the wounds of history." In the Waverley Novels tragedy passes and common sense survives.

15   RONALD, MARGARET LOFTUS and RALPH ARTHUR RONALD. "Shelley's Magus Zoroaster and the Image of the Doppelgänger." <u>Modern Language Notes</u>, 76, no. 1 (January), 7-12.
          In the dialogue between the Earth and Prometheus in <u>Prometheus Unbound</u>, Act I, Shelley may have been using the superstition of the doppelgänger as a presage of death. His interest in this phenomenon may have been stimulated by Scott's references to it in note ten to <u>Rob Roy</u> and note nine to <u>A Legend of Montrose</u>. The latter novel was published while Shelley was writing <u>Prometheus Unbound</u>.

16   SIMEONE, WILLIAM E. "The Robin Hood of <u>Ivanhoe</u>." <u>Journal of American Folklore</u>, 74 (July-September), 230-34.
          Scott gives his Robin Hood the great mission of delivering the country from evil misrule. Robin Hood's power derives from the common people whose grievances he articulates, and his moral perfection glorifies the people as well as himself. The feast at the end of the novel symbolizes the unity of King and people and "the renewed oneness of the dominions of the King of England and the king of outlaws."

17   WELSH, ALEXANDER. "Sir Walter Scott and Eisenhower." <u>New Republic</u> (23 January), pp. 16-18.
          In many ways President Eisenhower resembles a Waverley hero. The heroes are good and upright, dedicated to the sanctity of private property but unwilling to pursue it actively, and they remain passive until they are absolutely forced to act. Their total respect for law and authority prevents them from becoming actual leaders. Like Eisenhower, the Waverley hero "represents the morality of restraint" and has little personality of his own.

1962 A BOOKS

*1   HOUSE, JACK. <u>The Scott Country. Around the Borders</u>. Seeing Scotland, no. 1. Edinburgh: Oliver and Boyd.
          Cited in the <u>British Museum General Catalogue of Printed Books, Ten Year Supplement 1956-1965</u>, XLI, column 696.

*2   KREISSMAN, BERNARD. "The Great Unknown: A Descriptive and Critical Survey of the Miscellaneous Prose Writings of Sir Walter Scott." Ph.D. dissertation, University of Nebraska, 1962.

1962

An abstract by the author appears in <u>Dissertation Abstracts</u>, 23 (1962), 235-36.

*3   PETERSON, CLELL THOMPSON. "Romance and Realism in the Waverley Novels." Ph.D. dissertation, University of Minnesota, 1962. An abstract by the author appears in <u>Dissertation Abstracts</u>, 23 (1963), 3900-3901.

1962 B SHORTER WRITINGS

1   BOYDEN, BARTLETT W. "Foreword" to <u>The Lady of the Lake and Other Poems</u>. New York: New American Library, pp. ix-xvi. Scott brought together the burgeoning forces of Romanticism and the popular novel. His poems were "popular rather than artistically admirable" and do not require sophisticated criticism. Scott makes the reader understand "the essential nobility of human life." Includes a summary of Scott's life and of the historical backgrounds of the poems.

2   CLYDE, LORD. "Address to the Fifty-fourth Annual Dinner of the Edinburgh Sir Walter Scott Club." <u>The Edinburgh Sir Walter Scott Club Annual Report</u>, pp. 11-18. Scott as lawyer stands behind all his writings as "the lifeblood and inspiration of all the rest." Includes a review of Scott's legal career, which he pursued with a conscientious attention to duty.

3   CORSON, JAMES C. "Scott's Boyhood Collection of Chapbooks." <u>Bibliotheck</u>, 3, no. 6, 202-18. The Library at Abbotsford includes over a hundred chapbooks collected by Scott in his early years. Itemizes the collection in six volumes which Scott said he accumulated before he was ten years old. They are all printed works and, contrary to Lockhart's account, contain no ballads or MSS. Scott's statement that he collected them before he was ten may be inaccurate, as the chapbooks are dated from 1776 to 1786.

4   FERGUSON, DELANCEY. "Foreword" to <u>Ivanhoe</u>. New York: Collier Books, pp. 7-12. <u>Ivanhoe</u> employed old conventions and established new ones, such as the rival heroines. Its action bears only a coincidental relation to historic fact, and many of its characters have literary origins. The novel lacks "salty characters" to deflate the pompous rhetoric of its dialogue, and it is full of both factual and moral anachronism. However, the strength of <u>Ivanhoe</u> lies in Scott's ability to tell a story and in his use of timetested ingredients.

1962

5   GRANT, DOUGLAS. "Sir Walter Scott and Nathaniel Hawthorne."
      University of Leeds Review, 8 (June), 35-41.
         Both Hawthorne's early novel Fanshawe and his mature
      writings are indebted to Scott. Hawthorne wished to use
      history to identify a special American consciousness, as he
      believed Scott had done for Scotland. Scott's use of Gothic
      material and the Puritan character in Peveril of the Peak
      foreshadows Hawthorne's work. In plot and in the use of
      prefatory material, The Heart of Midlothian influenced The
      Scarlet Letter.

6   GUGGISBERG, HANS RUDOLF. "Walter Scott in Amerika." Schweizer
      Monatshefte, 42, 303-13.
         Scott was widely respected by nineteenth century American
      historians and deeply influenced Washington Irving. In the
      North he received praise for his awakening of the past, his-
      torical accuracy, balance of style, and general good sense.
      Southern readers, living in a feudal tradition, identified
      with his knightly heroes and romantic dedication to the
      past. Although greatly exaggerated, Twain's belief that
      Scott formed the pre-war Southern character and thus caused
      the Civil War accurately conveys the Southern propensity to
      live in the past.

7   HARTVEIT, LARS. "Scott's The Bride of Lammermoor: An Assess-
      ment of Attitude." Arbok For Universitetet I Bergen
      (Norway), Humanistisk Serie No. 1, pp. 3-42.
         Scott regards Ravenswood's inheritance as an obstacle to
      his happiness, and he repeatedly expresses the superiority
      of his own times to those of the past. Scott does not en-
      dow the Jacobite past of the Ravenswoods with its usual
      "romantic halo," and he emphasizes its uselessness.

8   KIES, PAUL P. "An Unpublished Letter of Scott." Research
      Studies (Washington University), 30, no. 1 (March), 1-8.
         Prints a letter of 17 January, 1803 from Scott to a Mr.
      Slade, one of the trustees for the marriage contract of
      Scott and Charlotte Carpenter. The letter refers to Scott's
      purchase of the cottage at Lasswade and reveals that he had
      already realized the incompetence in business of his
      brother Thomas. The MS is in possession of the author.

9   LEWIS, C. S. "Sir Walter Scott," in his They Asked For a
      Paper. London: Geoffrey Bles, pp. 93-104.
         Reprint of 1956.B9.

10   LUKÁCS, GEORG. "Sir Walter Scott," in his The Historical
      Novel. Translated by Hannah and Stanley Mitchell. London:
      Merlin Press, pp. 30-63.

Scott portrays the great transformations of history as transformations of popular life. He shows the human greatness, liberated by historical crisis, in apparently average, simple people. Scott's "authenticity of local colour" embodies historical trends in human terms and conveys the relationship between the spontaneous reactions of the masses and the historical awareness of the leaders. He shows historical necessity emerging from the social and economic basis of life. As Scott portrays the necessary decline of the past and acknowledges its splendor, he reveals it as the pre-history of the present. Reprinted: 1969.B25.

11   McALEER, JOHN J. "Captain Cox: Paragon of Black-Letter Antiquaries." Drama Critique, 5, no. 1 (February), 34-38.
      A Coventry mason and collector of ballads and romances, Captain Cox was present during Queen Elizabeth's visit to Leicester at Kenilworth Castle in July, 1575. He is mentioned in Robert Laneham's letter describing the events of her stay. Captain Cox owned an extensive library of ballads and appears in Jonson's The Masque of Owls (1626) as well as in Scott's Kenilworth.

12   McDONALD, W. U., JR. "Scottish Phrenologists and Scott's Novels." Notes and Queries, 207 (November), 415-17.
      Between 1823 and 1829, essays and notes on Scott's novels in the Phrenological Journal and Miscellany attempted to apply the principles of phrenology to Scott's characterizations. They often paid tribute to Scott's accurate portrayals.

13   MACKENZIE, COMPTON. "Afterword" to Ivanhoe. New York: New American Library, pp. 491-97.
      Although Scott designed Ivanhoe to captivate English readers, it also achieved great popularity on the Continent and in America. In his introduction he admitted the possibility of anachronisms, but he assumed they would not disturb most readers. Although Ivanhoe is "a glorious fairy-story," Scott refrained from marrying Wilfrid to Rebecca because of both historical and moral reservations.

14   McVEIGH, HUGH. "When Sir Walter Came to Ireland." Irish Digest, 75, no. 2 (August), 35-37.
      An account of Scott's visit to Ireland in the summer of 1825, derived from Lockhart and from Scott's letters. Scott was shocked at the widespread poverty, but he was delighted by the enthusiastic affection with which he was greeted everywhere.

1962

15   MASSEY, IRVING. "Mary Shelley, Walter Scott, and 'Maga.'"
     Notes and Queries, 207 (November), 420-21.
          Scott thought Frankenstein was by Shelley himself and
     reviewed it favorably in Blackwood's. Mary Shelley informed
     him of his error in a letter of 14 June, 1818, printed here.
     In a letter of 21 March, 1831 (also included), she offered
     to contribute an article to Blackwood's, but she was appar-
     ently rebuffed.

16   MAXWELL, J. C. "Touch." Notes and Queries, 207 (May), 167.
          Scott's use of the word "touch" in a letter to John Bal-
     lantyne of 29 April, 1816 does not include the use of a
     qualifier, as the Oxford English Dictionary suggests is
     necessary.

17   MEDCALF, J. E. "Lukács on Scott." Notes and Queries, 207
     (November), 402.
          In the original edition of The Historical Novel, Lukács
     made two factual errors concerning Scott: (1) Rob Roy is
     said to take place "several decades later" than Waverley;
     (2) Jeanie Deans is called "the daughter of a radical
     soldier of Cromwell's army." Lukács unfortunately chose
     not to correct these errors when the work was translated
     into English.

18   PARKER, WILLIAM MATHIE. "Lady Davy in Her Letters." Quarterly
     Review, 300 (January), 79-89.
          Includes correspondence between Scott and his cousin,
     Lady Jane Davy, wife of Sir Humphrey Davy. At her request,
     Scott reviewed Davy's Salmonia in the Quarterly of October,
     1828.

19   _____. "Preface" to Rob Roy. London: J. M. Dent; New York:
     E. P. Dutton, pp. v-xvi.
          The novel's rich background and characterization redeem
     a clumsy plot and contrived ending. Bailie Jarvie is a
     "human microcosm" of the commercial spirit of Glasgow;
     Andrew Fairservice is another of Scott's "quaint Henchmen";
     and Rob Roy himself emerges as a man of integrity and hu-
     manity. Despite her stilted speech, Diana Vernon remains
     attractive. Includes a brief history of the novel's con-
     temporary critical reception and of the manuscript.

20   PARSONS, COLEMAN OSCAR. "Scott's Prior Version of 'The Tapes-
     tried Chamber.'" Notes and Queries, 207 (November), 417-20.
          Scott may have written the "Story of an Apparition,"
     which appeared in Blackwood's for April, 1818 over "the
     suspicious initials 'A.B.'" He first heard the tale from
     Miss Seward of Lichfield in 1807. Verbal and material

similarities to Scott's acknowledged work "The Tapestried
Chamber" indicate that he wrote them both. This conjecture
is reinforced by Scott's habit of contributing anonymously
or pseudonymously to the early Edinburgh Monthly Magazine
or Blackwood's.

21 PECKHAM, MORSE. Beyond the Tragic Vision: The Quest for
    Identity in the Nineteenth Century. New York: George
    Braziller, pp. 191-193.
        Scott historicized the nineteenth century mind. He
    sought a new vision of human nature in detachment from the
    confusing, conflicting forces of the present. To construct
    an analogy between the finite and thus controllable past
    and the infinite present, he created the novel as social
    history and set it in an unchanging geography. This inno-
    vation led to Balzac's technique of selecting and control-
    ling every detail of his characters' environments.

22 THORSLEV, PETER L. The Byronic Hero: Types and Prototypes.
    Minneapolis: University of Minnesota Press, pp. 77-83.
        In Marmion and Rokeby, Scott developed the Noble Outlaw
    figure of German Sturm und Drang to its fullest extent be-
    fore Byron. Marmion has the physical appearance, secret
    sin, and servants' loyalty of this type, but his crime of
    forgery is particularly "unknightly," and he is less than
    courteous to women. Rokeby has two Noble Outlaws, Mortham
    and Bertram. Byron replaced Scott's Gothic medievalism
    with Eastern exoticism and deepened the mystery and passions
    of the characters.

23 TILLYARD, E. M. W. "Scott's Linguistic Vagaries," in his
    Essays Literary and Educational. London: Chatto & Windus,
    pp. 99-107.
        Reprint of 1958.B13.

24 VORTRIEDE, WERNER. "Achim von Arnims Kronenwächter." Neue
    Rundschau, 73, no. 1, 136-45.
        Although Von Arnim's Kronenwächter appeared at the same
    time Scott was becoming known in Germany, it should not be
    regarded as an historical novel in the same sense as the
    Waverley Novels. Compared to them, it is unrealistic and
    overly elaborate. Although Arnim read widely in historical
    tales and chronicles, he did not strive for historical
    truth. He was more interested in filling in the gaps of
    history with fictive creations.

1963

1963 A BOOKS

*1 CAMERON, JOHN ARTHUR. "Dramatic and Symbolic: The Problem of
    Meaning in The Heart of Midlothian." Dissertation, Yale
    University, 1963.
        Cited in the Annual Bibliography of English Language and
    Literature (Cambridge: Modern Humanities Research Associa-
    tion, 1966), XXXIX, 346, item #6338.

2 WELSH, ALEXANDER. The Hero of the Waverley Novels. Yale
    Studies in English, No. 154. New Haven, Connecticut: Yale
    University Press, 287pp.
        The nominal Waverley heroes are passive and ideal members
    of society. They accept the public morality of rational
    self-restraint and support the values of prudence, law, and
    civil society. They are prey to anxiety, since they fear
    being misunderstood or being implicated in the romantic and
    extra-legal events of the novels. The "dark heroes" by con-
    trast represent passion, lawlessness, and individualism.
    At the end, the dark hero dies, while the passive hero gets
    the blonde heroine and inherits money and/or property. Ex-
    tracts reprinted: 1968.B41.

1963 B SHORTER WRITINGS

1 BOSTROM, IRENE. "The Novel and Catholic Emancipation."
    Studies in Romanticism, 2, no. 3 (Spring), 155-76.
        Scott believed only halfheartedly in Catholic Emancipa-
    tion. In The Monastery and The Abbot his characters present
    opposing views on Catholicism, but they retain their human-
    ity and do not become mere mouthpieces for propaganda.
    Scott presents sympathetic pictures of monks in decline,
    and his medievalism made him "an unconscious collaborator
    with Newman."

2 BROGAN, D. W. "Afterword" to Quentin Durward. New York:
    New American Library, pp. 525-32.
        Although inferior to the Scottish novels, Quentin Dur-
    ward spread Scott's fame through Europe. He used the con-
    flict between Louis XI and Charles the Bold to epitomize
    the waning days of chivalry. Despite his liberties with
    historical facts, Scott displayed great political awareness
    in his delineation of this conflict. Like other Waverley
    heroes, Quentin is brave, honorable, and dull. The novel
    conveys "a great deal of the spirit of the decadent fif-
    teenth century."

3 BUSHNELL, NELSON S. "Walter Scott's Advent as Novelist of
   Manners." Studies in Scottish Literature, 1, no. 1 (July),
   15-34.
      For Scott the term "manners" refers to attributes of a
   particular economic, political, and social organization in
   a particular time, place, and culture. His concern with
   manners is apparent in the "Introduction" to the Minstrelsy
   and in the narrative poems. Although Waverley did not realize the full potential of the novel of manners, it committed Scott to further work of this kind. See 1965.B3.

4 CARLTON, WILLIAM J. "George Hogarth--A Link with Scott and
   Dickens." Dickensian, 59, no. 2 (May), 78-89.
      George Hogarth, the father-in-law of Dickens, was a
   friend of Scott's and a distinguished musical critic. He
   became financial advisor to both Scott and Ballantyne, introduced Lockhart to Scott, and set to music a song from
   The Pirate. No adequate biography exists.

5 COGSWELL, FRED. "Scott-Byron." Studies in Scottish Literature, 1, no. 2, 131-32.
      Reprints an incomplete sketch of Scott and Byron by John
   Galt, which mentions a brief meeting between Scott and Galt
   just before Scott left for Italy. The manuscript is owned
   by the Dominion National Archives, Ottawa.

6 CORSON, JAMES CLARKSON. "A Correction." Bibliotheck, 4,
   no. 5, 210.
      The "correction" refers the reader to 1951.B11 for the
   accurate authorship and circumstances of presentation of
   Scott's copy of Edge-Hill. See 1963.B7.

7 _____. "Some American Books at Abbotsford." Bibliotheck, 4,
   no. 2, 44-65.
      The library at Abbotsford includes about 200 works re-
   lating to America, quite a substantial collection for
   Scott's day. Henry Brevoort first aroused Scott's interest
   in American literature and sent him Irving's History of New
   York. George Ticknor helped to keep Scott informed on
   American writing and presented him with at least seven
   works. See 1951.B11 and 1963.B6.

8 DEVLIN, D. D. "Scott and Redgauntlet." Review of English
   Literature, 4, no. 1 (January), 91-103.
      In Redgauntlet Scott is concerned with the social and
   economic changes after Culloden and the ways in which a
   love of the past can be adapted to successful adjustment to
   the present. He defines his attitude to Redgauntlet through

1963

the comic characters. Peter Peebles is a comic parallel to
Redgauntlet, because both have been ruined by the law and
fail to live in the present. The novel demonstrates that
Scotland will be henceforth controlled by the representatives of Law (Fairford) and Commerce (Geddes), and that
honor and courage must be redefined.

9   FEUCHTWANGER, LION. "The Serious Historical Novel: Walter
    Scott," in his The House of Desdemona, or The Laurels and
    Limitations of Historical Fiction. Translated by Harold A.
    Basilius. Detroit: Wayne State University Press,
    pp. 44-80.
        Scott's combination of a dense historical milieu and the
    characterization of average people resulted in "a radically
    new kind of historical fiction." Scott was strongly in-
    fluenced by the nationalistic nature of Goethe's Götz von
    Berlichingen, which he translated in 1799. He wrote his-
    torical fiction in a period which had become aware that
    history is the fate of the masses and the experience of
    nations. Although his novels accept the uniformity of hu-
    man nature, they demonstrate how human action may be condi-
    tioned by a particular epoch. Includes extended discussion
    of The Fortunes of Nigel and of Scott's influence on
    Manzoni.

10 FISHER, JOHN. Eighteen Fifteen: An End and a Beginning.
    London: Cassell, 295pp., passim.
        Anecdotal and historical account of this pivotal year
    concludes with the story of a football match between Selkirk
    and Yarrow on 4 December, 1815. The event included pipers,
    quasi-military ceremonies, refreshments, and an evening
    dance. As Sheriff of Selkirkshire Scott was in attendance
    and, along with James Hogg, wrote a poem for the occasion.

11 GRIERSON, HERBERT JOHN CLIFFORD. "Introduction" to The Heart
    of Midlothian. London: Collins, pp. 8-10.
        The Heart of Midlothian takes place in a period whose
    spirit lingered into Scott's own day and which he under-
    stood well. Scott was "perfectly at home" with the charac-
    ter and dialect of the common people. In Jeanie Deans he
    created a character dramatically real and true to the
    period. She and Davy Deans convey an accurate picture of
    the morality of Scottish Presbyterianism.

12 HART, FRANCIS RUSSELL. "The Fair Maid, Manzoni's Betrothed,
    and the Grounds of Waverley Criticism." Nineteenth Century
    Fiction, 18, no. 2 (September), 103-18.

1963

The Fair Maid of Perth provides "a significantly coherent fictive structure" with a consistent metaphoric pattern in the symbol of the hand. In comparison, the structure of Manzoni's I Promessi Spozi is loose and faulty. Scott regarded various heroic periods in the past not as contrasts but as analogues to the present, designed to be scrutinized with detachment. He offers a "tragicomic vision" of the perennial anachronism of the rigidly heroic temperament. Reprinted: 1968.B20.

13 HARWOOD, BARONESS ELLIOT. "Address to the Fifty-fifth Annual Dinner of the Edinburgh Sir Walter Scott Club." The Edinburgh Sir Walter Scott Club Annual Report, pp. 9-16.
    Scott drew his inspiration from the Border Country. He was a man of courage who refused to allow fear to interrupt his activities.

14 JACK, IAN. "The Waverley Romances," in English Literature, 1815-1832. Oxford History of English Literature. Volume X. London: Oxford University Press, 185-212.
    Scott's best novels have a "common form," in which a young man's adventures provide the framework for "a series of scenes describing the life of a given place and period." Scott was careless in characterization and plot construction and had a "cavalier attitude to prose fiction." In delineating historical conflicts, he was guilty of oversimplification. He had a conventional view of the novel as a form. Many of his descriptions conform to Gilpin's standards of the picturesque. Scott regarded the dramatic use of dialogue as his most important innovation.

15 JAMES, LOUIS. Fiction for the Working Man, 1830-1850: A Study of the Literature Produced for the Working Classes in Early Victorian Urban England. London: Oxford University Press; rpt. Harmondsworth, Middlesex: Penguin Books, 1974, pp. 102-104.
    Because Scott's novels were expensive when they appeared, their main impact on the lower classes came through popular dramatizations. Although lower class interest in the Waverley Novels declined in the 1930's, Ivanhoe dominated the field of historical fiction until Ainsworth. It exerted an "omnipresent influence" on dramatists, plagiarists, and writers of penny-issue novels, who concentrated on the Isaac and Rebecca figures.

16 JOHNSON, EDGAR. "Sceptered Kings and Laureled Conquerors: Scott in London and Paris, 1815." Nineteenth Century Fiction, 17, no. 4 (March), 299-319.

181

1963

In the spring of 1815, Scott and his family visited London where he was entertained by the Prince Regent and generally lionized. He met Byron, with whom he "agreed on everything except politics and religion." He went home on June 11 and left for the Continent on August 3. He travelled through the Low Countries to Brussels and Waterloo and then on to Paris, "a conquered city," where Scott was warmly entertained and met the Duke of Wellington. He sailed from Dieppe for home in early September. Reprinted slightly revised: 1970.A5.

17 KREISSMAN, BERNARD. "Introduction" to The Life of John Dryden, by Sir Walter Scott. Lincoln: University of Nebraska Press, pp. vii-xiii.
    Despite its omissions and inaccuracies, Scott's Dryden remains worthy of study as "an artful blend of literary history and criticism, social history, and personal biography." Scott's extensive knowledge of the period allows him to place Dryden's personality in its historical setting. It is also a rich source for Scott's own general critical theory. The biography reveals facets of Scott's personality, such as his attitudes to class and religion and his sense of fair play.

18 LAUBER, JOHN. "Scott on the Art of Fiction." Studies in English Literature, 3, no. 4 (Autumn), 543-54.
    Scott regarded the novel as a minor form of literature and was indifferent toward its artistic qualities. His criticism of fiction is neoclassically oriented with a respect for genre and rules and frequent references to "nature." He is a pragmatic critic who regards the reader's pleasure as of primary importance. His main concern is for subject matter, not for technique. Scott's criticism is basically conservative, "the last expression of the neoclassic position by a major writer."

19 LOCHHEAD, MARION. "Victorian Abbotsford." Quarterly Review, 301 (January), 57-66.
    After Scott's death, Abbotsford passed into the hands of Charlotte Lockhart and her husband John Hope. They took the name Hope-Scott and converted to Catholicism. "Abbotsford became the centre of a little Catholic world on the Borders." Newman visited there in the winter of 1852-53, and Queen Victoria visited in 1867. The Hope-Scott's daughter, Mary Monica, married Joseph Constable Maxwell and took the name Maxwell-Scott.

1963

20   MOLDENHAUER, GERARDO. "Estudio filológico de una tradducción
      española de 'The Wild Huntsman' de Sir Walter Scott."
      Instituto de Filología Moderna, Universidad National del
      Litoral, 2, 1-16.
          Scott's ballad "The Wild Huntsman" was an imitation of
      Bürger's "Der wilde Jaeger" (1796). The legend of the
      ghostly hunter who cries on windy nights has existed in
      written form since the twelfth century. The Spanish manu-
      script translation, now in the Biblioteca Nacional of
      Buenos Aires, was written by an unknown translator either
      in Spain or Argentina. It is in prose and is less interest-
      ing, less precise, and simpler than Scott's version. Al-
      though it retains the emotional tone, it falls short
      stylistically.

21   MONTGOMERIE, WILLIAM. "William Macmath and the Scott Ballad
      Manuscripts." Studies in Scottish Literature, 1, no. 2
      (October), 93-98.
          William Macmath materially assisted Francis James Child
      by making three trips to Abbotsford in 1890, 1891, and 1892
      to examine the manuscripts of Scott's ballad collection.

22   NUÑEZ DE ARENAS, MANUEL. "Simples Notas Acerca de Walter
      Scott en España," in L'Espagne: des Luminères au Roman-
      tisme. Edited by Robert Marrast. Paris: Centre de Ré-
      cherches de l'Institut d'Études Hispaniques, pp. 363-68.
          Lists thirteen Spanish translations of Scott with accom-
      panying notes. The list is derived from the work of Church-
      man and Peers (Revue Hispanique, v. 127), a documented
      study of the influence of Scott in Spain with a bibliography
      of translations. Churchman and Peers have demonstrated
      that Scott's influence in Spain was well received and
      widely acknowledged.

23   RALEIGH, JOHN HENRY. "What Scott Meant to the Victorians."
      Victorian Studies, 7 (September), 7-34.
          The Victorians admired the Waverley Novels for their
      realism, large scope, and wealth of information. They be-
      came a sort of national epic, testifying of freedom and of
      the improvement of the human condition. Scott and Words-
      worth embodied the Victorians' reverence for what is per-
      manent in human nature. Summarizes a number of nineteenth
      century commentators on Scott, such as Nassau Senior,
      Walter Bagehot, David Masson, and Leslie Stephen.

24   RUSSELL, NORMA H. "New Letters of Sir Walter Scott." Review
      of English Studies, N.S. 14 (February), 61-65.

1963

> Prints two unpublished letters from Scott to Dr. Thomas
> Somerville, written in 1801, dealing with a ballad called
> "The Flowers of the Forest," which Scott was interested in
> for the Minstrelsy. Scott acknowledges his lack of the
> true antiquarian spirit in his inability to feel regret at
> the ballad's modern date. The third letter, to Dr. William
> Somerville, expresses Scott's sympathy on the death of his
> brother Samuel.

*25 SANDY, STEPHEN MERRILL. "Studies in the Form of the Romantic
      Novel, Otranto to Waverley." Ph.D. dissertation, Harvard
      University, 1963.
          Cited in the Annual Bibliography of English Language and
      Literature (Cambridge: Modern Humanities Research Associa-
      tion, 1966), XXXIX, 346, item #6351.

*26 THOMAS, GEORGE STEPHEN. "Wordsworth, Scott, Coleridge,
      Southey, and DeQuincey on Catholic Emancipation, 1800-1829:
      The Conservative Reaction." Ph.D. dissertation, New York
      University, 1963.
          An abstract by the author appears in Dissertation Ab-
      stracts, 25 (1964), 487-88.

 27 WEBER, ALFRED. "Hugh Henry Brackenridges Epistel an Sir
      Walter Scott." Jahrbuch für Amerikastudien, 8, 269-79.
          In his Epistle Brackenridge acknowledges the inferiority
      of his literary gift and laments the absence of an American
      environment and tradition to inspire him as Scotland in-
      spired Scott. Despite his patriotism, Brackenridge became
      enthusiastically interested in his Scottish background and
      compared it unfavorably to American society, which, he be-
      lieved, offered no favorable conditions for the development
      of a noteworthy body of literature.

 28 WRIGHT, A. DICKSON. "Sir Walter Scott's Laudanum?" Annals of
      the Royal College of Surgeons of England, 32, 194-95.
          The Day Book of Edinburgh chemist Charles Bayley indi-
      cates that the Scott household ordered enormous quantities
      of laudanum between 1823 and 1825. Scott took large amounts
      of laudanum for colic until 1819, but probably did not con-
      tinue with it thereafter. Possibly Lady Scott used it to
      treat her chronic asthma.

*29 WYATT, SYBIL WHITE. "The Nineteenth Century English Novel and
      Austrian Censorship." Ph.D. dissertation, Rice University,
      1963.
          An abstract by the author appears in Dissertation Ab-
      stracts, 25 (1964), 3587. See 1967.B25.

1964 A BOOKS

1 ANON. Scott and His Circle. Edinburgh: Scottish National
    Portrait Gallery, 70pp.
       A collection of black and white reproductions from the
    Scottish National Portrait Gallery of pictures of Scott,
    his friends, and his contemporaries. Each is accompanied
    with a page of biographical information.

*2 HOLLINGSWORTH, MARIAN EVERETT. "Narrative Structures in the
    Novels of Sir Walter Scott." Ph.D. dissertation, University
    of North Carolina, 1964.
       An abstract by the author appears in Dissertation Ab-
    stracts, 25 (1965), 6627. See 1969.A5.

3 KEITH, CHRISTINA. The Author of Waverley: A Study in the
    Personality of Sir Walter Scott. New York: Roy Publishers,
    189pp.
       Scott's personality is enigmatic and "quizzical." Be-
    cause his mind's pictorial faculty was developed at the ex-
    pense of the others, the appeal of his work is primarily
    visual. His novels are prudish regarding sex but amoral
    regarding violence; he revels in bloody scenes. Scott's
    delight in the secular made Christianity seem irrelevant
    in his work.

4 PARSONS, COLEMAN OSCAR. Witchcraft and Demonology in Scott's
    Fiction: With Chapters on the Supernatural in Scottish
    Literature. Edinburgh and London: Oliver and Boyd;
    New York: Clarke, Irwin, 373pp.
       Scott's imagination enjoyed the unknown, but his reason
    sought explanations. His attitude toward the supernatural
    combined "temporary belief and objective scrutiny." He
    used weird phenomena most frequently to give a sense of the
    past. When the supernatural elements are intrinsic to the
    novel, they help to define the setting, advance the plot,
    interpret character, and emphasize the forces of history.
    However, Scott's eighteenth century rationalism undercut
    his own use of the supernatural.

1964 B SHORTER WRITINGS

1 BRAEKMAN, W. "Letters by Robert Southey to Sir John Taylor
    Coleridge." Studia Germanica Gandensia, 6, 103-230.
       Includes some comments by Southey on Scott and Lockhart
    in reference to the editorship of the Quarterly Review.

1964

2   COLVIN, CHRISTINA. "A Visit to Abbotsford." <u>Review of English
    Literature</u>, 5, no. 1 (January), 56-65.
        Prints two letters from Harriet Edgeworth to her sister
    Lucy and stepsister Honora describing her visit to Abbots-
    ford in August, 1823. Maria Edgeworth accompanied her
    sister Harriet on this visit.

3   DAICHES, DAVID. <u>The Paradox of Scottish Culture: The Eigh-
    teenth Century Experience</u>. London: Oxford University
    Press, 104pp., passim.
        Scott illuminates the central paradox of Scottish culture
    in his enchantment with the heroic past combined with his
    sense of the most prudent course for his country's self-
    interest. The paradox springs from the Union of 1707, which
    led to the transformation of Jacobite sentiment into Scot-
    tish national feeling. Only after the Stuarts were exiled
    did they become identified with lost Scottish independence,
    and the Church and the Law became the symbols of Scottish
    individuality. However, the Edinburgh literati, believing
    in progress and common sense, regarded themselves as
    British.

4   FRENCH, RICHARD. "The Religion of Sir Walter Scott." <u>Studies
    in Scottish Literature</u>, 2, no. 1 (July), 32-44.
        Scott rebelled early against Calvinist theology and
    strict Presbyterian discipline. His selection of the Epis-
    copal Church may have been influenced by his devotion to
    the Union. Although almost every one of his novels exhibits
    Scott's negative feelings toward Catholicism, he believed
    that "his works taught the practical lessons of morality
    and Christianity."

5   _____. "Sir Walter Scott, Gentleman Soldier." <u>Midwest
    Quarterly</u>, 5, no. 4 (September), 333-43.
        Scott had a lifelong affection for the military. He
    helped to organize the Edinburgh Light Horse in 1797 and
    devoted much of his time to the regiment. <u>The Vision of
    Don Roderick</u> and <u>The Field of Waterloo</u> have contemporary
    military backgrounds. Scott maintained an active interest
    in his son's military career.

6   ISER, WOLFGANG. "Möglichkeiten der Illusion im historischen
    Roman (Sir Walter Scott's Waverley)," in <u>Nachahmung und
    Illusion</u>. Edited by Hans R. Jauss. Munich: Eidos,
    pp. 135-56 and 228-36.
        Scott views historical reality as the interactions be-
    tween a set of circumstances and the human responses to it.
    History guarantees its own verisimilitude, and events must

186

take precedence over character. The passivity and imper-
fection of the Waverley hero allow him effectively to com-
municate the imaginative reality of history to the reader.
His personality remains subordinate to events, and so
Scott glosses over Waverley's circumstances at the end,
because the hero's self-fulfillment is not his primary interest. The multiplicity of viewpoints through which history is presented in the novel gives credibility to the
past. Scott imposes a fictitious consistency on history
to make it comprehensible to the imagination. <u>See</u> translation and revision: 1974.B16.

7   JOHNSON, EDGAR. "Afterword" to <u>Waverley</u>. New York: New
    American Library, pp. 561-74.
        <u>Waverley</u> is "an ironic model of a young man's education,"
    and Scott emphasizes the irony with frequent touches of
    comedy. The plot begins with intentional slowness and in-
    creases in pace and intensity, culminating in the trial and
    death of Fergus. However, Scott's detached narrative tone
    places the emphasis on reality and normal human life as a
    balance to the eccentric or the genuinely heroic. <u>Waverley</u>
    demonstrates that Scott is basically a realistic novelist
    rather than an historical romancer. Revised and expanded
    in 1970.A5.

8   JOHNSTON, ARTHUR. "Walter Scott," in his <u>Enchanted Ground:</u>
    <u>The Study of Medieval Romance in the Eighteenth Century</u>.
    London: Athlone Press, pp. 177-194.
        Scott's edition of <u>Sir Tristrem</u> (1802) was "the first
    adequate edition of a single romance." His patriotism
    motivated his belief in the Celtic origin of <u>Tristrem</u>, and
    he "invented" a school of thirteenth century Lowland Scots
    romance writers. His notes to his own poems and novels
    demonstrate his interest in other medieval romances. He
    used the freedom from strict rules, typical of the medieval
    romance, to liberate his own narrative poetry from rigid
    adherence to critical doctrine.

9   KARL, FREDERICK. "Sir Walter Scott: The Moral Dilemma," in
    his <u>An Age of Fiction: The Nineteenth Century British</u>
    <u>Novel</u>. New York: Farrar, Straus and Giroux, pp. 63-75.
        Scott's novels are almost totally lacking in literary
    merit. They do not deal with important ideas or emotions,
    and his characters are meaningless outside their romantic
    context. Scott wrote "too much and too fast." His Toryism
    and his dislike of the complexities of the present left him
    unable to find a middle way between realism and romanticism.
    The novels are structurally disorganized and present a

1964

simplistic view of human nature. Scott shrinks from the
ambiguity of the moral issues he raises.

10   LEVIN, JU. "V. K. Kjuxel'beker o Poèzi Val'tera Skotta"
[W. K. Küchelbecker on the Poetry of Walter Scott].
Russkaja Literatura, 7, no. 2, 95–101.
Wilhelm Küchelbecker was a Russian poet jailed after the
Decembrist rebellion in 1825. His prison diary, now in the
Institute of Russian Literature (Pushkin's House, Lenin-
grad), contains his comments on Scott's poems. He regarded
The Lady of the Lake as the best of the narratives and the
songs in Rokeby superior to Scott's other poetry. He ad-
mired the poetry and details of The Lay of the Last Minstrel
but deplored its lack of plot. His criticisms of Marmion
and The Lord of the Isles were generally unfavorable.

11   MAHONEY, JOHN L. "Some Antiquarian and Literary Influences of
Percy's Reliques." College Languages Association Journal,
7 (March), 240–46.
In the Minstrelsy of the Scottish Border Scott followed
Percy's example by unifying the separate entries into a
complete work. The Reliques influenced both Wordsworth
and Coleridge and exerted a "persuasive" influence on
Scott.

12   MARQUARDT, HERTHA and KURT SCHREINERT, eds. Henry Crabb
Robinson und seine deutschen Freunde: Brücke zwischen England und Deutschland im Zeitalter der Romantik. Palaestra,
237 and 249 (1967). Göttingen: Vandenhoeck, 976pp.,
passim.
Robinson concurs with Goethe's judgment of Scott as "the
best narrator of the age." He compares Scott's skill in
connecting fictive and historical events to the clumsiness
of Henrik Steffens in Malcolm: A Norwegian Short Novel.
He praises Tieck's portrayal of religious enthusiasm in his
Rebellion in the Cevennes by comparing it to Old Mortality.

13   MUGGERIDGE, MALCOLM. "Address to the Fifty-sixth Annual Dinner of the Edinburgh Sir Walter Scott Club." The Edinburgh
Sir Walter Scott Club Annual Report, pp. 9–19.
Scott's love of romantic adventure and of the heroic
came as a refreshing change after the rationalist eighteenth
century. His popularity has declined in our own time because we have had too much adventure, and we have reacted
against it. Scott's characters have become unfashionable
in the age of the anti-hero. Contemporary snobbishness
rejects his veneration of humble characters.

14   OGDEN, JAMES. "Isaac D'Israeli and Scott." <u>Notes and Queries</u>,
      209 (May), 179-80.
            Isaac D'Israeli dreamed of being a poet and was very
      flattered when, at their first meeting, Scott recited a
      poem D'Israeli wrote in his early youth. According to Ben-
      jamin Disraeli's memoir of his father, Scott included the
      poem in his English <u>Minstrelsy</u> (1810). <u>See</u> 1965.B16.

15   OSTROWSKI, WITOLD. "Walter Scott in Poland: I. Warsaw and
      Vilno." <u>Studies in Scottish Literature</u>, 2, no. 2 (October),
      87-95.
            Scott's greatest influence in Poland extended from 1820
      to 1860. He and Byron influenced the literature of the
      Great Emigration after 1830, in which poets were endowed
      with quasi-religious significance as guides of the nation.
      Scott particularly influenced the Polish writers Mickiewicz
      and Malewski. <u>See</u> Part II: 1965.B17.

16   SIMPSON, W. DOUGLAS. "Craignethan Castle." <u>Transactions of
      the Glasgow Archaeological Society</u>, N.S. 15, no. 2, 33-45.
            Craignethan Castle is the "Tillietudlem" of <u>Old Mortal-
      ity</u>. Traces the actual rather than the fictive history of
      the castle and of its architectural peculiarities. In-
      cludes pictures and diagrams.

17   SMITH, JANET ADAM. "The Sir Walter Scott Lectures for 1963:
      Scott and the Idea of Scotland, Part I." <u>University of
      Edinburgh Journal</u>, 21, no. 3, 198-209.
            In his depiction of Scotland, Scott hoped to preserve
      old customs and to promote the Union. In <u>Waverley</u> he ex-
      amines the Forty-five as "the last serious attempt to under-
      mine the Union settlement," and his view of the Highlanders
      is unromantic and unflattering. However, he shows sympathy
      for both sides and regards them above all as Scots. <u>Red-
      gauntlet</u> displays a similar view of the necessity of the
      lost cause and the dignity of its representatives. <u>The
      Antiquary</u> demonstrates British patriotism in all classes.

18   _____. "The Sir Walter Scott Lectures for 1963: Scott and
      the Idea of Scotland, Part II." <u>University of Edinburgh
      Journal</u>, 21, no. 4, 290-98.
            Scott's foreign readers saw the "tartan-wrapped" Scotland
      that he invented. It appealed to both French and American
      readers as "a place of romance and picturesque survivals."
      The Scottish patriotism stimulated by the Waverley Novels
      was exemplified by the Celtified visit of George IV to
      Edinburgh. By this time Scott had become caught up in his
      own creation and chose to ignore or forget the truth about
      the greediness of Highland chiefs who evicted their tenants.

1964

19   SUTCLIFFE, EMERSON GRANT. "Scott in Emerson's Poems," in
      Essays and Studies in Language and Literature. Edited by
      Herbert H. Petit. Duquesne Studies Philological Series,
      No. 5. Pittsburgh: Duquesne University Press, pp. 158-75.
         Much of the thought, incident, and phrasing in Emerson's
      poems are derived from Scott's work. Emerson held Scott in
      high esteem and knew his work closely. Scott sometimes
      provided Emerson with the central idea of a poem or, more
      frequently, a way of elaborating it.

20   TUTTLETON, JAMES W. "The Devil and John Barleycorn: Comic
      Diablerie in Scott and Burns." Studies in Scottish Litera-
      ture, 1, no. 4 (April), 259-64.
         There are several similarities between Scott's "Wandering
      Willie's Tale" and Burns's "Tam O'Shanter." Steenie Steen-
      son and Tam O'Shanter play similar roles, and both must
      confront the Devil. Both works are narrated by a Scots
      peasant who grows increasingly excited as he comments on
      the action. Both tales relate a similar comic moral re-
      garding the effects of whiskey.

21   WOOD, GEORGE A. M. "Letters Between Sir Walter Scott and the
      Marquis of Lothian." Notes and Queries, 209 (October),
      376-79; (November), 410-11; (December), 469-77.
         The letters are dated from 11 June, 1802 to 17 January,
      1826. The Scott letters are transcribed from the originals
      in the Newbattle Abbey papers, now in the Register House,
      Edinburgh. The letters demonstrate Scott's acquaintance
      with the Lothian family, his concern for Roxburghshire af-
      fairs, and the "friendship between Scott, landowner and
      acknowledged antiquarian, and the ruling interest of the
      county."

1965 A BOOKS

1   CRAWFORD, THOMAS. Scott. Writers and Critics Series. Edin-
      burgh: Oliver and Boyd, 119pp.
         The Minstrelsy of the Scottish Border reflects "a ten-
      sion between reality and romance" that reappears in the
      novels. The longer poems, like the novels, grew out of
      ballad imitations and excel in description and dialogue.
      The Scottish novels present Scotland as a fundamental unity
      transcending conflicts, but Scott's own attitude toward his
      country deteriorated from "the pessimistic antiquarian" to
      the quaint apologist. Includes a separate chapter on The
      Heart of Midlothian and a selected bibliography. First and
      last chapters reprinted 1969.B10.

*2   JORDAN, FRANK, JR. "'The Convenient Tribe': A Study of
      Scott's Narrators." Ph.D. dissertation, Duke University,
      1965.
            An abstract by the author appears in <u>Dissertation Ab-
      stracts</u>, 26 (1966), 4661-62.

3   REIZOV, B. G. <u>Tvorchestvo Val'tera Skotta</u> [Works of Walter
      Scott]. Moscow and Leningrad: Izdatelstvo, 496pp.
            Scott's approach in literary history coincided with the
      new historical epoch after the French Revolution. Although
      his traditionalism led him to oppose the Revolution and its
      doctrines of state interest, rationalism, and historical
      planning, he also opposed the extreme reactions against it.
      In his own theory of history, Scott saw humanity constantly
      struggling for justice against all forms of violence. He
      regarded historical collisions as dramas of conscience
      wherein catharsis emerges from apparent tragedy. He did
      not idealize his characters, and his fiction is based on
      historical truth. <u>See</u> 1967.B9.

1965 B SHORTER WRITINGS

1   BARRON, RODERICK. "Some Words Used by Sir Walter Scott in His
      Writings." <u>Transactions of the Gaelic Society of Inverness</u>,
      42, 121-34.
            Scott acquired his considerable knowledge of Gaelic from
      books, visits to Perthshire, and correspondence. His poems
      and novels set in the Highlands are rich in words derived
      from Gaelic such as "slogan," "henchman," "cateran,"
      "coronach," "linn," and "brae." He popularized many of
      these words and gave them a place in the English dictionary.

2   BRAMLEY, J. A. "The Journal of Sir Walter Scott." <u>Contempor-
      ary Review</u>, 206 (March), 159-61.
            Scott's true greatness as a man becomes apparent in his
      <u>Journal</u>, as it reveals his concern for human frailty and
      his consciousness of mortality. The <u>Journal</u> is free of
      self-pity and shows consistent compassion. Scott held "in
      the last resort . . . a Christian interpretation of life."

3   BUSHNELL, NELSON. "Scott's Mature Achievement as Novelist of
      Manners." <u>Studies in Scottish Literature</u>, 3, no. 1 (July),
      3-29.
            Scott is as much a novelist of manners as an historical
      novelist. His own experiences, sense of comedy, and anti-
      quarian interest helped to shape his treatment of manners.
      He uses the conflict between two systems of manners as an

analogue of his theory of historical evolution. Manners
help to explain characters to the reader and to stimulate
action. Scott regards the machinery of manners as the sign
of a stable culture. See 1963.B3.

4   CHANDLER, ALICE. "Sir Walter Scott and the Medieval Revival."
    Nineteenth Century Fiction, 19, no. 4 (March), 315-32.
        Just as Scott's work provided an impetus to nineteenth
    century medievalism, so the eighteenth century interest in
    "the scholarly, the Gothic, and the primitive" strongly in-
    fluenced him. Scott's medievalism links Burke's conserva-
    tism with the "new feudalism" of the Victorians. His
    pictures of medieval communities with "paternalistic lords
    and contented commons" impressed Ruskin, Carlyle, and Dis-
    raeli. Scott's "fundamental social aim . . . was to recon-
    cile liberty and security." Revised and expanded: 1970.B3.

5   CORRIGAN, EILEEN M. "Charlotte Brontë and Scotland." Brontë
    Society Transactions, 14, no. 5, 31-34.
        Charlotte Brontë visited Edinburgh in July, 1850. She
    was deeply impressed by the city and by Melrose and Abbots-
    ford. Her interest in Scotland may have come originally
    from Scott's Tales of a Grandfather, which she read when
    she was twelve.

6   DAICHES, DAVID. "Address to the Fifty-seventh Annual Dinner
    of the Edinburgh Sir Walter Scott Club." The Edinburgh Sir
    Walter Scott Club Annual Report.
        Scott had no illusions about the sometimes brutal nature
    of past heroism; even while he loved traditions, he knew
    that they must give way to "an age of merchants and lawyers
    and respectable citizens." He acknowledges that although
    civilization needs the picturesque, it is ultimately in-
    sufficient. Although he yearned to be a feudal laird, he
    showed the limitations of this ideal in Redgauntlet. His
    greatest novels concern "the development of the past
    through the present into the future." Reprinted: 1971.A13.

7   EVANS, BERGEN. "Introduction" to Waverley. Greenwich,
    Connecticut: Fawcett Publications, pp. v-viii.
        Waverley initiated a new kind of fiction which combined
    romantic background with real people and recognizable
    events. Scott keeps history at a distance and emphasizes
    character interacting with circumstance. He parallels the
    historical contrasts between new and old with physical and
    social contrasts.

8   GREENE, MILITSA. "Pushkin and Sir Walter Scott." Forum for
    Modern Language Studies, 1, no. 3 (July), 207-15.
        Pushkin admired Scott's sense of humor, use of local
    color, and historical objectivity. In his Tales of Belkin
    he parodied Scott's anonymity and elaborate introductions.
    In The Captain's Daughter he adopted Scott's methods by
    combining historical events with a family chronicle,
    choosing an average man as hero, and using dialogue to
    give a sense of locality. Despite additional parallels in
    plot and character relationships, Pushkin's novel differs
    from his Waverley models in moving straightforwardly and
    swiftly.

9   HENRY, NATHANIEL H. "Wordsworth's 'Thorn' an Analogue in
    Scott's Heart of Midlothian." English Language Notes, 3
    (December), 118-20.
        Scott seems to acknowledge the similarity between the
    story of Effie's seduction and trial for child murder and
    the kernel of the plot in Wordsworth's poem. As a lawyer,
    Scott may have been looking for a literary precedent to
    help him plead the case for Effie.

10 JACK, IAN. "Two Biographers: Lockhart and Boswell," in
    Johnson, Boswell, and Their Circle: Essays Presented to
    Lawrence Fitzroy Powell. Oxford: Oxford University Press,
    Clarendon Press, pp. 268-85.
        Lockhart approached the Life of Scott as an imposed task;
    he lacked the "inquisitive veneration" for Scott that Bos-
    well felt for Johnson. Lockhart had considerably more
    material at his disposal, but Boswell enjoyed less inter-
    ference from his subject's friends and family. Boswell
    also demonstrated more initiative and enthusiasm in as-
    sembling his material. Where Boswell had a passion for
    accuracy, Lockhart mingled truth and fiction. Boswell's
    "reverence for life" makes his work finally superior to
    Lockhart's.

11 JOHNSON, EDGAR. "Scott and Dickens: Realist and Romantic."
    Victorian Newsletter, 27 (Spring), 9-11.
        Dickens and Scott were "fundamentally unlike in every
    major way." Scott was a Tory, profoundly aware of the past
    and respectful of tradition and custom. Dickens was im-
    patient with tradition and deeply distrusted established
    institutions. Scott provided rationalistic explanations
    for the supernatural, but Dickens never explained away his
    ghosts and relied heavily on coincidence. Whereas Dickens,
    basically a romantic, wished to change society, Scott,
    basically a realist, wished to portray it clearly.

1965

12 KINNEY, ARTHUR F. "Two Unique Copies of Stephen Gosson's 'Schoole of Abuse' (1579): Criteria for Judging Nineteenth Century Editing." <u>Papers of the Bibliographical Society of America</u>, 59, no. 4, 425-29.
   Scott probably used the Huntington copy of "The Schoole of Abuse" for his edition in volume III of the <u>Somers Tracts</u> (1810). Apparently Scott did not collate his text, probably borrowed from Heber's private library, with any other texts. He modernized the spellings inconsistently, made several visual errors, and added indiscriminate paragraphing. The other nineteenth century edition by Edwin Arber followed Scott's practice in also failing to collate texts.

13 KRAUSE, SYDNEY J. "Twain and Scott: Experience Versus Adventures." <u>Modern Philology</u>, 42, no. 3 (February), 227-36.
   In <u>Huckleberry Finn</u> Twain includes a group of "critical analogies" to question Scott's representation of history as adventure for its own sake and to distinguish fictional realism from romance. Twain linked Scott with the attitudes toward class and caste of the Southern aristocracy. His steamboat "Walter Scott" is "a symbol of romance that loses its fight for life in the cold, fast-running waters of experience." This incident and similarities between <u>Huckleberry Finn</u> and <u>Ivanhoe</u> create a "symbolic comment on romantic fiction" that runs throughout the novel.

14 LINK, FREDERICK M. "Editor's Introduction" to <u>The Fortunes of Nigel</u>. Lincoln: University of Nebraska Press, pp. vi-xvii.
   The structure of <u>Nigel</u> juxtaposes contrasts of character and varied points of view to present an immediate picture of an historical era. James embodies the paradoxes of his age and "suggests the eventual absorption of the old order into the new." Nigel is the passive observer in the Waverly pattern whose anti-heroism demonstrates what belongs to the future. Includes a summary of contemporary critical reception.

15 McCLARY, BEN HARRIS. "Washington Irving to Walter Scott: Two Unpublished Letters." <u>Studies in Scottish Literature</u>, 3, no. 2 (October), 114-18.
   The letters, dated 3 November, 1819 and 15 August, 1820, concern details of Irving's publishing arrangements with John Murray, which Scott had helped to advance. Irving indirectly thanks Scott for his influence on Lockhart, who had written a favorable review of Irving's work in <u>Blackwood's</u> of June, 1820.

16 OGDEN, JAMES. "Isaac D'Israeli and Scott." <u>Notes and Queries</u>,
    210 (November), 417-18.
    D'Israeli and Scott met occasionally at the home of John
    Murray. D'Israeli admired Scott's work and his balance of
    Romanticism and eighteenth century sympathies. He sent
    Scott a summary of his <u>Inquiry Into the Literary and Politi-</u>
    <u>cal Character of James the First</u>, but Scott used little of
    it in <u>The Fortunes of Nigel</u> and in a footnote to the intro-
    duction of the 1831 edition refuted D'Israeli's vindication
    of James. <u>See</u> 1964.B14.

17 OSTROWSKI, WITOLD. "Walter Scott in Poland: II. Adam
    Mickiewicz and Scott." <u>Studies in Scottish Literature</u>, 3,
    no. 2 (October), 71-95.
    Adam Mickiewicz was known as "the Lithuanian Walter
    Scott," and there are many parallels between the two writ-
    ers' family situations, national backgrounds, and reactions
    to Napoleon. Both were patriots interested in history, and
    their writing developed in the direction of increasing re-
    alism. Surveys Mickiewicz's attitude toward and ultimate
    repudiation of Scott and the similarities and differences
    between <u>Waverley</u> and <u>Pan Tadeusz</u>. <u>See</u> Part I: 1964.B15.

18 PATERSON, J. H. "The Novelist and His Region: Scotland
    through the Eyes of Sir Walter Scott." <u>Scottish Geographi-</u>
    <u>cal Magazine</u>, 81, no. 3 (December), 146-52.
    Although he is a national rather than a strictly regional
    novelist, Scott has the regional novelist's ability to
    evoke an imaginative dimension from the landscape. His
    descriptions blend people, scenery, and ruins but fail to
    connect the environment to the livelihood of the population.
    His urban descriptions are livelier than his romantic moun-
    tain scenes. The success of both depends on Scott's "capa-
    city for glimpsing and presenting the significant feature."

19 RAO, BALAKRISHNA. "Scott's Proposed Edition of Shakespeare."
    <u>Indian Journal of English Studies</u>, 6, 117-19.
    In 1818 Scott began to think about editing an edition of
    Shakespeare. He and Constable planned an "entertaining and
    popular edition" in 12 or 14 volumes. Scott began the
    project but stopped working on it after the 1826 bankruptcy,
    and only three volumes were printed. He had planned an
    edition for the common reader with a minimum of scholarly
    and critical apparatus.

20 TODD, WILLIAM B. "Scott's <u>Vision of Don Roderick</u>, 1811."
    <u>Book Collector</u>, 14 (Winter), 544.

1965

> Writer possesses the only known copy of the second edition of the poem and compares registers, press-figures, and watermarks of the first and second editions.

21   WELSH, ALEXANDER. "A Freudian Slip in The Bride of Lammermoor." Études Anglaises, 18 (April), 134-36.
     In Chapter 22 Scott deliberately has Sir William Ashton introduce his daughter Lucy as "his wife, Lady Ashton." The conversational slip betrays an habitual Oedipal relationship between the father and daughter. Ashton's partly conscious, partly unconscious replacement of his wife with his daughter is both sexually and politically motivated. The dearth of ordinary mothers in Waverley Novels and Romance in general may exist because a mother suggests the corporeal and mortal nature of the hero or heroine.

22   YOUNG, DOUGLAS. Edinburgh in the Age of Sir Walter Scott. Centers of Civilization Series, No. 17. Norman: University of Oklahoma Press, 183pp., passim.
     Provides the historical, religious, and economic background of Edinburgh in Scott's time and includes colorful details on daily living, entertaining, worshipping, and drinking. The chapters on "Sciences and Arts" and "Literature and Journalism" acknowledges the element of Scottish nationalism in Edinburgh intellectual activity but focus on expository prose in English. The genius of the Scottish Enlightenment developed from "the habit of kindly intercourse among different income groups" and from the relative informality of Edinburgh social life.

1966 A BOOKS

*1   BRADLEY, PHILIP. "An Index of the Supernatural, Witchcraft and Allied Subjects in the Novels, Poems, and Principal Works of Sir Walter Scott." Thesis, 830pp.
     A thesis submitted for Fellowship of the Library Association; available in microfilm, National Library of Scotland.

*2   HARRELL, ROBERT BRUCE. "Scott and the Jacobites: A Study of Four Novels." Ph.D. dissertation, University of Texas, 1966.
     An abstract by the author appears in Dissertation Abstracts, 27 (1967), 2498A.

3   HART, FRANCIS R. Scott's Novels: The Plotting of Historical Survival. Charlottesville: University of Virginia Press, 385pp.

The Waverley Novels confront the problem of the simultaneous preservation of individual humanity and cultural
continuity. Scott presents history as a process of individual ordeal; survival involves an escape from historical
fatality, in a victory of the future over the past which
preserves what is most valuable from the past. Scott's
highest value is the triumph of humanity and personal loyalty over ideology and opposing fanaticisms. Consequently
the characters he most admires, such as Geddes, Jarvie,
and Ochiltree, combine the qualities of fidelity and
prudence.

4 LAUBER, JOHN. Sir Walter Scott. English Authors Series,
   No. 39. New York: Twayne Publishers, 166pp.
       A general introduction to Scott which includes chapters
   on his life, poetry, literary theory, major Scottish novels,
   and critical reputation and influence. Although Scott was
   "a great innovator," he is now a "purely historical figure"
   whose work is "no longer part of the living novel." Includes a selected bibliography.

1966 B SHORTER WRITINGS

1 ALCIATORE, JULES C. "Quelques remarques sur Stendhal et les
   héroines de Walter Scott." Stendhal Club, 8 (July), 339-45.
       Scott's work, especially The Bride of Lammermoor, in-
   fluenced Stendhal. The simplicity and courage of heroines
   like Flora MacIvor and Minna Troil possibly helped him in
   the characterization of Mathilde de La Mole. In general,
   however, Stendhal believed that Scott was incapable of
   writing about love and that his heroines lacked real passion and depth.

2 ANDERSON, JAMES. "Sir Walter Scott as Historical Novelist:
   I. Scott's Opinions on Historical Fiction." Studies in
   Scottish Literature, 4, no. 1 (July), 29-41.
       Scott preferred to use historical events and persons
   familiar but not too well known to the public. He de-
   pended on his own extensive knowledge to add period detail,
   verisimilitude, and the "passions" common to all people.
   He claimed creative freedom in manipulation of fact and
   chronology and used "plausibility" as his guideline. He
   also limited his own freedom as a novelist according to
   "the claims of individual and party sensibility." See
   Part II, 1966.B3; Parts III, IV, V, 1967.B1-B3; Part VI,
   1968.B1.

1966

3   _____. "Sir Walter Scott as Historical Novelist: II.
      Scott's Practice in Historical Fiction." Studies in
      Scottish Literature, 4, no. 2 (October), 63-78.
          In writing Waverley and The Antiquary, Scott drew on a
      rich variety of historical materials as well as his exten-
      sive literary background and personal experience. His his-
      torical sources were extensive, "the records of several
      nations over many centuries," and he freely transposed their
      details to fictional contexts. See Part I, 1966.B2; Parts
      III, IV, and V, 1967.B1-B3; Part VI, 1968.B1.

4   CAMERON, LORD. "Address to the Fifty-eighth Annual Dinner of
      the Edinburgh Sir Walter Scott Club." The Edinburgh Sir
      Walter Scott Club Annual Report, pp. 11-22.
          Scott felt deep affection for Edinburgh and saw its past
      and present fused in both history and daily life. He was
      intimately involved with the life of the city in his day,
      and his work "catches the living likeness of his Edinburgh
      folk." Edinburgh owes much to him, because "his genius
      floodlit her past" and brought it alive into the present.
      Reprinted: 1971.A13.

5   DAICHES, DAVID. "Introduction" to Kenilworth. New York:
      Heritage Press, pp. v-xiii.
          Kenilworth creates a "peculiarly Elizabethan" atmosphere
      and uses the actual historical and psychological situation
      of the period to enhance the elaborate plot. The "tushery"
      dialogue is relatively unobtrusive and helps to convey a
      sense of Elizabethan eloquence. Although the historical
      inaccuracies are intentional, they tend to spoil the read-
      er's sense of illusion and hence make the novel less cred-
      ible. Kenilworth demonstrates Scott's ability to transform
      historical crisis into action.

6   DONOVAN, ROBERT ALAN. "Redgauntlet, Henry Esmond, and the
      Modes of Historical Fiction," in his The Shaping Vision:
      Imagination in the English Novel from Defoe to Dickens.
      Ithaca: Cornell University Press, pp. 173-205.
          Scott connects his fictive characters to actual time and
      space to smooth the transition between the fictitious world
      and the "real" world of historical significance. He forms
      the readers' judgment of public events by using private ac-
      tions to comment on them. Darsie Latimer, for example, is
      not important in the development of the plot, but he pro-
      vides a perspective on the actions of others. Henry Esmond,
      on the other hand, fails to integrate history and fiction.
      Its best qualities owe nothing to its narrative structure
      or historical context.

7   GOZENPUD, A. A. "Val'ter Skott: romantičeskie komedii A. A.
    Schahovskoy" [Walter Scott and the Romantic Comedies of
    A. A. Schahovskoy], in Russko-evropeĭskie literaturnye
    sujazi: Sbornik statej k 70-letiju so dnja roždenija
    akademika Alekseev [Russian-European Literary Connections:
    A Volume of Articles Dedicated to the 70th Birthday of
    Academician M. P. Alekseev]. Moscow: Nauka, pp. 38-48.
        Russia owes its first acquaintance with Scott to the ro-
    mantic comedies of A. A. Schahovskoy. His plays were ideal-
    ized dramatic versions of Scott's novels, presented from
    1821 through 1824. Schahovskoy sometimes incorporated ele-
    ments from several novels into one extremely long play; he
    helped to transform Russian audiences of Scott into Russian
    readers of Scott. The manuscripts, located in the State
    Theatrical Library, Leningrad, have never been published.

8   HILLHOUSE, JAMES T. and ALEXANDER WELSH. "Sir Walter Scott,"
    in The English Romantic Poets and Essayists. Edited by
    Carolyn Washburn Houtchens and Lawrence Huston Houtchens.
    Revised edition. New York: New York University Press,
    pp. 115-54.
        A survey in essay form of I. Bibliographies; II. Edi-
    tions; III. Biographies; IV. Criticism. Section IV is
    subdivided into 1) Poems; 2) The Novels; 3) Special Prob-
    lems; 4) Influence; 5) Political and Religious Views; 6)
    Miscellaneous Writing and Editing. This edition is a re-
    vised version of 1957.B15 and has been expanded and updated
    through 1964.

*9 HOLCOMB, ADELE MANSFIELD. "J. M. W. Turner's Illustrations
    to the Poets." Ph.D. dissertation, Columbia University,
    1966.
        An abstract by the author appears in Dissertation Ab-
    stracts, 28 (1967), 164A.

10 LAWSON, LEWIS A. "Poe's Conception of the Grotesque." Mis-
    sissippi Quarterly, 14, no. 4 (Fall), 200-205.
        By 1839 Poe had almost certainly read Scott's essay "On
    the Supernatural in Fictitious Composition" (1827). Many
    of the elements in Scott's description of Hoffman's Das
    Majorat appear in "The Fall of the House of Usher." In the
    Preface to his Tales of the Grotesque and Arabesque, Poe
    apparently assumed his audience's familiarity with Scott's
    essay and so did not define his terms. He regarded the
    grotesque positively as a form of the ideal, "the known
    stretched to the point of originality."

1966

11 McCULLEN, J. T., JR. "Scott's The Fortunes of Nigel, Chapter
    II, Paragraph 1." Explicator, 24, no. 8 (April), item 72.
    The oath "by the bones of the immortal Napier" alludes
    to John Napier (1550-1617), inventor of logarithms.

12 MACINTYRE, D. G. "Scott and the Waverley Novels." Review of
    English Literature, 7, no. 3 (July), 9-19.
    The characteristic Scott novel fuses picaresque form
    with a theatrical plot derived from eighteenth century comic
    drama. The heroes function merely to bring the reader into
    the action and are not intended to have psychological com-
    plexity. Scott is tolerant of all religions and treats
    English, Lowlanders, and Highlanders with equal sympathy.
    Scott accepted public taste as his standard. He wrote in
    the ethical tradition of Fielding and regarded the novel-
    ist's function as entertainment and moral improvement.

13 MACRAE-GIBSON, O. D. "Walter Scott, the Auchinleck MS, and
    MS. Douce 124." Neophilologus, 50, no. 4 (October), 449-54.
    MS. Douce 124 in the Bodleian Library is a copy of part
    of the Auchinleck text of the Middle English romance,
    "Arthour and Merlin." The MS was copied by Robert Leydon
    and Scott to aid George Ellis in his work on the Specimens
    of Early English Metrical Romances. After completion of
    this work, Ellis passed the transcript on to Francis Douce.

14 MADDEN, WILLIAM A. "The Search for Forgiveness in Some Nine-
    teenth Century English Novels." Comparative Literature
    Studies, 3, no. 2, 139-53.
    In The Heart of Midlothian, Scott combines the theme of
    Christian forgiveness with realistic technique. The first
    half of the novel demonstrates the conflict between ancient
    Biblical law and new secular law, equally operative in the
    Queen's compassionate pardon of Effie and the King's prag-
    matic pardon of Porteous. In the second half of the novel
    Jeanie has no place in the modern, urban world, so Scott
    sends her to "an unreal pastoral world that is the literary
    product of debased romanticism."

15 NUNNALLY, CLAY. "The Death of Alasco." Studies in Scottish
    Literature, 3, no. 3 (January), 174-76.
    The source for the death of the alchemist in Kenilworth
    is located in John Beckmann's History of Inventions and
    Discoveries, in which he relates the ironic death of the
    prisoner Godin de Sainte Croix.

16 OCHOJSKI, PAUL M. "Sir Walter Scott's Continuous Interest in
    Germany." Studies in Scottish Literature, 3, no. 3
    (January), 164-73.

Scott's interest in things German continued well after
1800. He continued to use his knowledge of German language
and literature in his novels, miscellaneous writings, correspondence and even in the names of his animals. He owned
over 300 German books.

17 PARKER, WILLIAM MATHIE. "Preface" to The Bride of Lammermoor.
London: J. M. Dent; New York: E. P. Dutton, pp. v-viii.
Tragedy dominates The Bride of Lammermoor, the novel
which most clearly reveals Scott's similarity to Shakespeare. The plot is unusually well constructed for Scott.
His skillful use of supernatural elements and of dialect
gives the novel the tone of a Border ballad. It is "the
most dramatic of the Scott romances." Includes a brief
summary of its mixed critical reception.

18 PARSONS, COLEMAN OSCAR. "Chapbook Versions of the Waverley
Novels." Studies in Scottish Literature, 3, no. 4 (April),
189-220.
Chapbooks were intended "to simplify, cheapen, and dif-
fuse works among the poor and less literate readers."
Waverley chapbooks covered most of the novels written between 1814 and 1823, with The Heart of Midlothian, Ivanhoe,
and Kenilworth the most popular. The peak period for these
pamphlet epitomes was 1820-1823. Most of the "epitomizers"
took their work seriously and greatly extended Scott's impact on the masses.

19 PIGGOTT, STUART. "The Roman Camp and Three Authors." Review
of English Literature, 7, no. 3 (July), 21-28.
The Roman Camp episode in The Antiquary may have been
influenced by Scott's conscious or unconscious recollection
of a similar incident in Robert Bage's Hermsprong, or Man
As He Is Not (1796). Peacock also has a similar episode in
Crotchet Castle (1831). See 1972.B11.

20 PIKE, B. A. "Scott as Pessimist: A View of St. Ronan's Well."
Review of English Literature, 7, no. 3 (July), 29-38.
Scott's changes in St. Ronan's Well deepen its pessimism.
When Clara and Francis are freed from sexual guilt, they
become figures "of primal innocence at the mercy of evil."
Scott uses clothes symbolism to emphasize Clara's isolation
and the discrepancy between appearance and reality. The
extreme rigor of Tyrrel's sense of honor puts him out of
place in the world, and thus reinforces Scott's pessimism.
Reprinted: 1968.B32.

1966

21   RALEIGH, JOHN HENRY. "Introduction" to The Heart of Midlothi-
     an. Boston: Houghton Mifflin, pp. v-xxviii.
          The Heart of Midlothian displays "an anatomy of a na-
     tion" and dramatizes an immense social range as well as
     Scott's theory of history. Its moral crux is the conflict
     between general principles and individual conscience, il-
     lustrated by the ambiguities inherent in law and justice.
     The narrative frame reflects Scott's ideal of rough but
     strong simplicity being molded by a more complicated and
     self-conscious culture. The characters, who embody trends
     in Scottish history, live in a world where mental horizons
     are limited, but where the imagination can animate the en-
     vironment with irrational force.

22   _____. "Waverley and The Fair Maid of Perth," in Some British
     Romantics: A Collection of Essays. Edited by James V.
     Logan, John E. Jordan, and Northrop Frye. Columbus: Ohio
     State University Press, pp. 235-66.
          The Fair Maid of Perth modifies or reverses character
     types, social and political conventions, and attitudes to-
     ward history begun in Waverley and developed in subsequent
     novels. The Fair Maid is unique among the Waverley Novels
     for its grimness, and the characterizations of Conachar and
     Henry Smith reverse Scott's customary conventions of High-
     lander and hero. By arranging the characters almost alle-
     gorically, the novel suggests "a dream of what might have
     happened in Scottish history." Smith links Highland bravery
     with Lowland common sense and marries Catherine, the "soul"
     or anima of Scotland.

23   REED, JOSEPH W., JR. "Lockhart's Scott," in his English Biog-
     raphy in the Early Nineteenth Century, 1801-1838. Yale
     Studies in English, No. 160. New Haven, Connecticut: Yale
     University Press, pp. 127-153.
          Lockhart rejected the idealizing tendency of contemporary
     biography, believing that Scott's genius and dignity would
     speak for themselves. Lockhart's approach is novelistic,
     and he does not assume an active presence in the book. He
     combines seeming objectivity with occasional reminders of
     his relationship to Scott in order to reinforce his author-
     ity. His manipulations and concealments were designed to
     serve an aesthetic end rather than to deceive.

24   REIZOV, B. G. "V. A. Zukovskij, perevodčik Val'tera Skotta"
     [V. A. Zschukovsky, Translator of Walter Scott], in Russko-
     evropeĭskie literaturnye sujazi: Sbornik statej k 70-letiju
     so dnja rŏzdenija akademika Alekseev [Russian-European
     ·Literary Connections: A Volume of Articles Dedicated to

the 70th Birthday of Academician M. P. Alekseev]. Moscow: Nauka, pp. 439-46.

Zschukovsky's 1822 translation of Scott's "The Eve of St. John" bears a spiritual if not a literal correspondence to the original. It is a Russian literary ballad which retains the style of the genuine Scottish folk ballad. Zschukovsky wished to retain the ballad's medieval tone while adjusting it for Russian readers. He changed some traditional names and archaic expressions and slightly modified the plot. However, he kept the ballad rhythm and achieved an artistic and emotional impression of genuine Scottish flavor.

25 SERDYUKOV, A. "Obshchestvenno-istoricheskie uzglyady Val'tera Skotta" [The Socio-historical Views of Walter Scott]. <u>Azerbaidzhanskii Gosudarstvennyi Universitet, Baku</u>. Seriia Istoricheskikh I Filisofskikh, 7, 92-97.

Scott's novels demonstrate his belief that economic factors and class antagonisms underlie all social changes. He believed that economic pressures caused both the Saxon-Norman struggle and the religious wars of the seventeenth century. Novels such as <u>Quentin Durward</u> and <u>Old Mortality</u> concern the class war between the bourgeoisie and the feudal aristocracy. Scott was aware that people's rebellions often benefited only the leaders.

26 WELSH, ALEXANDER. "Introduction" to <u>Old Mortality</u>. Boston: Houghton Mifflin, pp. vii-xviii.

<u>Old Mortality</u> raises questions about the moral implications of political revolution. Although Scott demonstrates that tyranny and deceit are parts of this revolution, he believes in its historical necessity and reluctantly allows his hero to join the cause. While Morton perceives the inability of revolution to fulfill its goals and keep pace with history, the lower-class characters manage either to accommodate themselves to events or to escape from them. Scott connects the love story to the theme of revolution by showing the close relationship of both to decisions of life and death.

<u>1967 A BOOKS</u>

*1 GLICKFIELD, CHARLOTTE WOODS. "Some Underlying Themes in the Waverley Novels." Ph.D. dissertation, University of Tennessee, 1967.

An abstract by the author appears in <u>Dissertation Abstracts</u>, 28 (1968), 4127A.

1967

2   SCHULTZ, PEARLE HENRIKSEN. <u>Sir Walter Scott: Wizard of the</u>
    <u>North</u>. New York: Vanguard Press, 212pp.
        A dramatized biography told through dialogue and inci-
    dent. Includes a glossary and a table relating dates in
    Scott's life to "Interesting Events Elsewhere in the World."

<u>1967 B SHORTER WRITINGS</u>

1   ANDERSON, JAMES. "Sir Walter Scott as Historical Novelist,
    Part III." <u>Studies in Scottish Literature</u>, 4, no. 3
    (January), 155-78.
        Scott drew most of the historical framework and details
    of <u>Old Mortality</u> from Covenanting annals. He imitated their
    characteristic scriptural style and grounded most of his
    fictitious episodes in verifiable historical record. Al-
    though <u>Rob Roy</u> has no actual historical foundation, the
    economic details grant it credibility. For <u>The Heart of</u>
    <u>Midlothian</u> Scott took much material from Cameronian writers.
    <u>See</u> Parts I and II, 1966.B2, B3; Parts IV and V, 1967.B2,
    B3; Part VI, 1968.B1.

2   _____ . "Sir Walter Scott as Historical Novelist, Part IV."
    <u>Studies in Scottish Literature</u>, 5, no. 1 (July), 14-27.
        In <u>A Legend of Montrose</u> Scott used materials from clan
    and family histories. <u>The Bride of Lammermoor</u> is based on
    a family tragedy of the seventeenth century, but it is also
    linked to the Gowrie Conspiracy of 1600. The "backward-
    looking tendency" in <u>Redgauntlet</u> comes from Scott's use of
    a sixteenth century family story and seventeenth century
    tradition and superstition. He also used materials from
    the annals of 1715 for his novel of 1765. <u>See</u> Parts I and
    II, 1966.B2, B3; Parts III and V, 1967.B1, B3; Part VI,
    1968.B1.

3   _____ . "Sir Walter Scott as Historical Novelist, Part V."
    <u>Studies in Scottish Literature</u>, 5, no. 2 (October), 83-97.
        In the "sub-Scottish" novels, <u>The Monastery</u>, <u>The Abbot</u>,
    and <u>The Fair Maid of Perth</u>, Scott does not use Scots dialect
    because he deemed it unsuitable for the periods of these
    novels. In the English novels, <u>Kenilworth</u>, <u>The Fortunes of</u>
    <u>Nigel</u>, <u>Woodstock</u>, and <u>Peveril of the Peak</u>, he concentrates
    on period authenticity and handles factual detail freely.
    In the novels on the Crusades, <u>Ivanhoe</u>, <u>The Betrothed</u>, and
    <u>The Talisman</u>, he manipulates details of geography as freely
    as those of history. <u>See</u> Parts I and II, 1966.B2, B3;
    Parts III and IV, 1967.B1, B2; Part VI, 1968.B1.

4   BERTACCHINI, RENATO. "Lo Svolgimento del romanzo storico nel
     primo Ottocento." Cultura e Scuola, 6, no. 24 (October-
     December), 13-26.
         After the translation of Kenilworth into Italian in 1821,
     the popularity of Scott's novels spread rapidly. He was
     imitated by the Italian writers Lancetti, Bazzoni, Varese,
     and the Grossis. Scott's interest in local color and so-
     cial conflict inspired several Italian composers to model
     operas upon his plots. Manzoni admired Ivanhoe for its
     balance of fictionalized history with accurate details of
     costume and manners, and he adapted this formula in his
     Fermo e Lucia.

5   BURWICK, FREDERICK. "Associationist Rhetoric and Scottish
     Prose Style." Speech Monographs, 34, no. 1 (March), 21-34.
         Uninfluenced by the Scottish rhetoricians, Scott "writes
     prose in the grand old Ciceronian manner," with careful
     balances and rotund periods. His periodic sentences sus-
     tain suspense by withholding the crucial point until the
     end, a technique the Scottish rhetoricians regarded as dis-
     ruptive of the process of association.

6   CHRISTIE, JOHN TRAILL. "Scott's Chronicles of the Canongate."
     Essays and Studies, N.S. 20, 64-75.
         In the Introduction to Chronicles of the Canongate, pub-
     lished shortly before he gave up his anonymity, Scott speaks
     in his most personal voice. Although "The Surgeon's Daugh-
     ter" and "The Highland Widow" are inferior to most of
     Scott's other work, "The Two Drovers" is "among the best
     dozen English short stories of the century." The Fair Maid
     of Perth does not rank among the best of Scott's writing,
     but it needs to be reappraised.

7   COLBY, ROBERT. "Edward Waverley and the Fair Romance Reader,"
     in his Fiction With a Purpose: Major and Minor Nineteenth
     Century Novels. Bloomington: Indiana University Press,
     pp. 28-65.
         Scott attempted to broaden his audience beyond the tra-
     ditional one of immature young ladies; he "masculinized"
     the novel and returned it to the vigor of Fielding and
     Smollett. Like many other imitations of Don Quixote,
     Waverley follows "the romantic youth maturing into the re-
     alistic adult." The life of action cures Waverley's roman-
     tic delusions, and his marriage to Rose represents his
     reconciliation to realism and the civilized nineteenth cen-
     tury. Scott's emphasis on visual effects and tangible data
     brought the novel "into the realm of the actual." Includes
     a list of "Characteristic Fiction Contemporaneous with
     Waverley (1814)."

1967

8   DEKKER, GEORGE. "An American Scott: Imitation of Exploration
     and Criticism," in his James Fenimore Cooper the Novelist.
     London: Routledge and Kegan Paul, pp. 20-42.
         Cooper admired Scott's politics, nationalism, and breadth
     of literary culture. Although he disliked being called the
     American Scott, Cooper owed him a major debt. The Waverley
     Novels written by 1819 exerted the decisive influence on
     Cooper. Although The Spy is written in direct imitation of
     Scott, its emphasis on the moral implications of "Neutral
     Ground" implicitly criticizes Scott's simple morality.
     Lionel Lincoln incorporates the techniques of both Scott
     and Edgeworth, but the faulty ending destroys the novel.
     Both works demonstrate how well Cooper could apply Scott's
     methods to American material. American edition: James
     Fenimore Cooper: The American Scott. New York: Barnes
     and Noble.

9   ELISTRATOVA, A. "Val'ter Skott--nash sovremennik?" [Walter
     Scott--Our Contemporary?]. Voprosy Literatury, 2, 220-25.
         Reizov has attempted to conceal Scott's political short-
     sightedness, prejudices, and limitations. He distorts his-
     torical truth by presenting Scott only as a good-humored,
     socially-minded Christian, who did not really glamorize the
     Middle Ages. Although Scott is close to us in the best as-
     pects of his work--his vision of social dialectics, and his
     concepts of fairness and justice--in other ways he is
     limited by his time and social class. See 1965.A3.

10   EWING, DOUGLAS C. "The Three Volume Novel." Papers of the
     Bibliographical Society of America, 61, no. 3, 201-207.
         Scott was the first professional author of prose fiction,
     and the three-decker novel began with Kenilworth in 1821.
     Constable sold it for half a guinea per volume. The high
     price of this and subsequent three-deckers stimulated the
     growth of lending libraries and resulted in handsome profits
     for both publishers and authors.

11   FALLE, GEORGE. "Sir Walter Scott as Editor of Dryden and
     Swift." University of Toronto Quarterly, 36, no. 2
     (January), 161-80.
         Scott was a scrupulous historian, biographer, and inter-
     pretive critic, but he was remiss in his attention to the
     text. His "temperamental affinities with Dryden and his
     age" make the work on Dryden superior to the work on Swift.
     Because Scott was unable to sympathize with Swift's complex
     kind of irony, he sometimes undervalued him and even over-
     looked Dryden's subtler ironies. Scott lacked "an awareness
     of the ironies that inhere in life itself."

12 FRENCH, RICHARD. "Sir Walter Scott as Historian." <u>Dalhousie</u>
    <u>Review</u>, 47, no. 2, 159-72.
        Scott studied history throughout his life, regarding it
    as essential for both his legal and literary professions.
    Most of the historical inaccuracies in the novel are inten-
    tional, such as the introduction of Shakespeare into <u>Kenil-</u>
    <u>worth</u>. Scott often cited his sources either in notes or
    in the body of the novel. His non-fictional histories
    demonstrate the same inaccuracy and variety as the novels.
    Scott's "greatest merit" comes from his conjunction of the
    historian and the creative artist.

13 HARKNESS, BRUCE. "Faulkner and Scott." <u>Mississippi Quarterly</u>,
    20, no. 3 (Summer), 164.
        In <u>The Hamlet</u> Faulkner borrows from <u>The Talisman</u> a de-
    scription of a sword severing a veil. <u>See</u> 1969.B40.

14 HOME, ALEC DOUGLAS. "Address to the Fifty-ninth Annual Dinner
    of the Edinburgh Sir Walter Scott Club." <u>The Edinburgh Sir</u>
    <u>Walter Scott Club Annual Report</u>, pp. 11-18.
        Through his writings about the Highlands and the Borders,
    Scott created a picture of Scotland "heroic, primitive, un-
    tamed, wild and beautiful." He also understood the natural
    beauty and tranquility of the countryside.

15 HOOK, ANDREW D. "<u>The Bride of Lammermoor</u>: A Reexamination."
    <u>Nineteenth Century Fiction</u>, 22, no. 2 (September), 111-26.
        <u>The Bride of Lammermoor</u> shows Scott balancing "the ro-
    mance and realism of old world and new." The conflict be-
    tween the civilized, moderate present and the heroic,
    romantic past lies at the heart of the novel's form and
    subject matter. Scott uses "indirect narration, tentative
    statement, and rationalized romanticism" to balance the
    novel's more wildly romantic elements. He views Ravens-
    wood's values very equivocally and qualifies his admiration
    for the feudal ideal. Scott characterizes Ravenswood more
    as an "eighteenth-century gentleman of sense and moderation"
    than as a traditional hero of romance. Reply to Gordon,
    1957.B10; <u>see</u> exchange, 1969.B14.

16 MacINTYRE, D. G. "Ambivalence in Scott's Novels." <u>Review of</u>
    <u>English Literature</u>, 8, no. 4 (October), 63-73.
        As "an emotional Jacobite," Scott preferred a romantic
    attitude to the past that ignored its unpleasant physical
    realities. The novels exhibit a tension between Scott's
    rational respect for reality and his emotional attraction
    to romance. A similar ambivalence characterizes his treat-
    ment of supernatural and melodramatic elements in the novels.

The basic quality of Scott's writing is this "dichotomy between intellect and emotion."

17   NUNNALLY, CLAY. "The Manna of Saint Nicholas." English Language Notes, 5 (December), 106-108.
In Kenilworth Wayland Smith diagnoses the illness of the Earl of Sussex as caused by "the manna of St. Nicholas." The phrase derives from the legend of Tophania, who sold poison of this name to wives who wanted to kill their husbands. Scott read of this in his copy of Beckman's History of Inventions and Discoveries (1817).

18   PARKER, WILLIAM MATHIE. "Scott and Russian Literature." Quarterly Review, 305 (April), 172-78.
Scott enjoyed great popularity among Russian literary figures. The reception of his novels surpassed even the high praise accorded to his poetry; they were popular not only in the salons, but also in "humbler family circles." Russian imitators of Scott include Zagoskin, Pushkin, Bulgarin, and Gogol. Summarizes the literary debate on Scott's merits in the 1830's and the 1840's between O. I. Senkovsky and V. G. Belinsky.

19   PARSONS, COLEMAN OSCAR. "Scott's Sixpenny Public." Columbia Library Columns, 16 (February), 13-21.
The Waverley chapbooks, pamphlet condensations published in Scott's own day, are now extremely rare. They were priced from one penny to one shilling and designed for children and working class adults. The pamphlet makers extended Scott's influence to the masses during his own lifetime.

20   PETERSON, CLELL T. "The Writing of Waverley." American Book Collector, 18, no. 3 (November), 12-16.
The writing of Waverley was "the deliberate consequence" of Scott's ideas on the novel as a literary form. The brief fragment of 1805 was begun as a romance, and the longer part of 1813-14 was finished as a novel. The contradictions between Chapter I, written in 1805, and the "Postscript," written in 1814, demonstrate Scott's changing conception of the novel. In the early chapters he regards Waverley with amusement; from Chapter VIII on, the reader sees through Waverley's eyes. The failure of Strutt's Queenhoo Hall shifted Scott's interest away from prose romance and toward the novel as a description of manners.

21   RUFF, WILLIAM and WARD HELLSTROM. "Some Uncollected Poems of Sir Walter Scott--a Census." Notes and Queries, 212 (August), 292-94.

Provides titles, first lines, number of lines, and
printed sources for poems and fragments by Sir Walter Scott
found since the 1904 J. L. Robertson standard edition.

22 WELSH, ALEXANDER. "Waverley, Pickwick, and Don Quixote."
    Nineteenth Century Fiction, 22, no. 1 (June), 19-30.
        As Don Quixote satirizes the heroes of chivalric romance,
    so Mr. Pickwick satirizes and parodies the Waverley hero.
    Where a Scott hero seriously fears embarrassment, Mr. Pick-
    wick's parallel ineptness is treated comically. He is the
    comic inversion of Scott's passive hero, and he parodies
    the Waverley hero's concern for law and justice and his
    unquestioning adherence to principle.

23 WOLFF, ERWIN. "Zwei Versionen des historischen Romans: Scotts
    Waverley und Thackerays Henry Esmond," in Lebende Antike:
    Symposium für Rudolf Sühnel. Edited by Horst Miller and
    Hans-Joachim Zimmerman. Berlin: Erich Schmidt, pp. 348-69.
        Influenced by historians and antiquarians, Scott re-
    garded the novel as an appropriate form for serious histori-
    cal scholarship. These influences show in Waverley in the
    romantic dreamer Edward and the theoretical antiquarian
    Bradwardine. Although both Thackeray and Scott fuse the
    factual outline of history with fictional anecdote,
    Thackeray demythifies history through ironic distance and
    parody. His journey into the past becomes a reacquaintance
    with the present and a demonstration of the uniformity of
    human nature.

24 WOOD, GEORGE A. M. "The Date of a Scott Letter." Notes and
    Queries, 212 (January), 12-13.
        A letter from Scott to Anna Seward, for which Grierson
    has supplied a conjectural date of September, 1806, can be
    more precisely dated as 26 August, 1806. Anna Seward dis-
    cusses Scott's letter in her own letter of 31 August to
    Mrs. Penelope Sophia (Weston) Pennington.

25 WYATT, SIBYL WHITE. The English Romantic Novel and Austrian
    Reaction: A Study in Hapsburg-Metternich Censorship.
    New York: Exposition Press, 176pp., passim.
        Metternich used literary censorship to help maintain the
    security of his absolutist government. He feared the in-
    fluence of Scott's novels, because they questioned the
    values of the Old Order and the Roman Church. The censors
    also disapproved of fiction which advocated rebellion
    against authority, promoted democracy, or implied disre-
    spect for the nobility. Includes discussion of Anne of
    Geierstein, The Fair Maid of Perth, The Fortunes of Nigel,

1968

Ivanhoe, A Legend of Montrose, The Pirate, Quentin Durward, Waverley, and Woodstock. See 1963.B29.

1968 A BOOKS

*1 HENDRICKSON, RICHARD HENRY. "The Prose Style of Sir Walter Scott's Waverley Novels." Ph.D. dissertation, University of Connecticut, 1968.
   An abstract by the author appears in Dissertation Abstracts, 29 (1969), 2674A.

2 JOHNSON, EDGAR. Sir Walter Scott in the Fales Library. Bibliographical Series, No. 4. New York: New York University Libraries, 44pp.
   Traces Scott's writing career and concurrently describes the Fales holding(s) of each work. The Library also holds a great many translations of Scott, numerous association items, many first editions of works by Scott's associates, and all the important biographies. The Library owns 235 autograph letters which span Scott's entire literary career. One group, dated from February, 1815 to July, 1824, comprises the correspondence between Scott and Sir Thomas Dick Lauder on the proposed editing of the papers of Lord Fountainhall, a seventeenth century Scottish lawyer.

*3 KOSKENLINNA, HAZEL MARIAN. "Sir Walter Scott and Nathaniel Hawthorne: Parallels and Divergencies." Ph.D. dissertation, University of Wisconsin, 1968.
   An abstract by the author appears in Dissertation Abstracts, 28 (1968), 5059A.

4 LOCHHEAD, MARION. Portrait of the Scott Country. Portrait Books. London: Robert Hale, 187pp.
   The Border country helped to form Scott's spirit, and he in turn helped to make it famous. It is a region of intense local pride and still-living tradition. Includes chapters on the history, legends, topography, country houses, weather, animals, and occupations of the Scott country. Also includes illustrations, a map, and a bibliography of books about the Borders.

5 MAYHEAD, ROBIN. Walter Scott. Profiles in Literature Series. London: Routledge and Kegan Paul, 124pp.
   A collection of extracts from the novels illustrating Scott's techniques of characterization, treatment of the heroic, attitudes toward tensions in a changing society and toward political and religious issues, and use of the vernacular. See 1968.B30.

6   Moscow, Idaho. University Library. The Earl Larrison Collec-
    tion of Sir Walter Scott. Moscow: University of Idaho
    Library Publications, No. 1, 50pp.
        A descriptive shelflist catalogue of the collection
    which was presented to the University of Idaho in 1962.
    Includes the donor's description of his collection, re-
    printed from Bookmark, 15, no. 1 (September, 1962), 5. The
    collection consists of over 350 volumes by and about Scott.

7   QUAYLE, ERIC. The Ruin of Sir Walter Scott. London: Hart
    and Davis, 290pp.
        Lockhart created a mythic Scott of saintly goodness and
    exaggerated the responsibility of the Ballantynes in Scott's
    financial downfall. Scott's own status-seeking land hunger,
    snobbishness toward business, and reactionary attitudes to-
    ward social change caused his ruin. Cadell, the only per-
    son to gain lasting profit from Scott's writing, died a
    rich man. See replies: 1969.B17, B26, B37.

*8 ZUG, CHARLES G., III. "The Last Minstrel: Folklore and the
    Poetry of Sir Walter Scott." Ph.D. dissertation, University
    of Pennsylvania, 1968.
        An abstract by the author appears in Dissertation Ab-
    stracts, 29 (1969), 3546A.

1968 B SHORTER WRITINGS

1   ANDERSON, JAMES. "Sir Walter Scott as Historical Novelist,
    Part VI." Studies in Scottish Literature, 5, no. 3
    (January), 143-66.
        Scott's attitude to the past was on the whole unfavor-
    able; he regarded it as barbarous and lawless although some-
    times picturesque. He hated the fanaticism of his own
    ancestors, and he shared the eighteenth century admiration
    for compromise. In the novels he sees the Highlands as a
    sympathetic visitor would, but he does not sentimentalize
    Highland characters and conditions. Although the novels
    reflect Scottish patriotism and Scott's sympathy for the
    weaker party, they are never anti-English or blindly na-
    tionalistic. See Parts I and II, 1966.B2, B3; Parts III,
    IV, and V, 1967.B1-B3.

2   ANKENBRANDT, KATHERINE WARE. "Charlotte Brontë's Shirley and
    John Leyden's 'The Cout of Keeldar.'" Victorian Newsletter,
    34 (Fall), 33-34.
        Leyden's poem "The Cout of Keeldar" appears in Part III
    of the Minstrelsy of the Scottish Border, and Scott also

refers to it in his notes to The Lady of the Lake. The Brontës probably knew Leyden's poem in both contexts. Shirley Keeldar's surname suggests her heroic character and courage.

3 BEN-ISRAEL, HEDVA. English Historians on the French Revolution. Cambridge: Cambridge University Press, 324pp., passim.

Scott's novels, rather than his history, influenced the Romantic historians Carlyle and Macaulay. Scott's Life of Napoleon was "reflective" rather than "Romantic" history; because he lacked admiration for Napoleon, he could not write a romantic portrayal of a great hero. Nevertheless, he overcame his own political bias to write a largely unprejudiced account.

4 BROWN, RAYMOND LAMONT. "Introduction" to Letters on Demonology and Witchcraft by Sir Walter Scott, Bart. Facsimile rpt. of 1884 edition. East Ardsley, Yorkshire: S. R. Publishers, pp. i-ii.

Scott conducted his research on the Letters with lawyer-like diligence enriched by the enthusiasm for legends and folklore he acquired from his mother and from his Border childhood. He was "in love with the supernatural," but his realistic and rational outlook controlled his treatment of it.

5 CADBURY, WILLIAM. "The Two Structures of Rob Roy." Modern Language Quarterly, 29, no. 1 (March), 42-60.

Rob Roy fits both the pregeneric form of romance and the generic form of the novel. Frank Osbaldistone's adventures are characteristic of romance, but the reader sees through them to limitations of knowledge and values, a response characteristic of the novel audience. Frank and the reader both learn that what is most humane in the Highlands must be internalized and that it cannot be contingent on place.

6 CAMERON, DONALD. "History, Religion, and the Supernatural: The Failure of The Monastery." Studies in Scottish Literature, 6, no. 2 (October), 76-90.

The Monastery suffers from vagueness of tone and the disproportionate roles given to the White Lady and Sir Piercie Shafton. Scott's bias against the Catholics prevented him from presenting the central religious conflict with evenhanded sympathy. To compensate, he offers the supernatural phenomena as literal truth rather than psychological or symbolic reality, and they assume more importance than he originally intended.

7   DAICHES, DAVID. "Scott's Achievement as a Novelist," in <u>Walter
     Scott: Modern Judgments</u>. Edited by D. D. Devlin. London:
     Macmillan, pp. 33-62.
         Reprint of 1951.B2.

8   _____. "Scott's <u>Redgauntlet</u>," in <u>Walter Scott: Modern Judg-
     ments</u>. Edited by D. D. Devlin. London: Macmillan,
     pp. 148-62.
         Reprint of 1958.B6.

9   DAVIE, DONALD. "<u>Rob Roy</u>," in <u>Walter Scott: Modern Judgments</u>.
     Edited by D. D. Devlin. London: Macmillan, pp. 122-29.
         Partial reprint of 1961.A1.

10   _____. "<u>Waverley</u>," in <u>Walter Scott: Modern Judgments</u>. Edited
     by D. D. Devlin. London: Macmillan, pp. 84-97.
         Partial reprint of 1961.A1.

11   DEVLIN, D. D. "Character and Narrative in Scott: <u>A Legend of
     Montrose</u> and <u>Rob Roy</u>." <u>Essays in Criticism</u>, 18, no. 2
     (April), 136-51.
         <u>A Legend of Montrose</u> illustrates the clash of different
     cultures in the conflict between feudal honor and Dalgetty's
     modern sense of prudence. Scott unites the hero and chief
     comic character in the same person, which adds force to Dal-
     getty's view of the inadequacies of the older way of life.
     By contrast, <u>Rob Roy</u> offers no single focus for Scott's
     contrast of old and new orders. The comic characters are
     largely extraneous to the narrative, and the marriage of
     Frank Osbaldistone and Diana Vernon is an artistic and
     historical mistake.

12   _____. "Introduction" to <u>Walter Scott: Modern Judgments</u>.
     London: Macmillan, pp. 11-23.
         Scott criticism in this century has shown "a pattern of
     complaint," partly due to Scott's denigration of his own
     work and to Lockhart's descriptions of Scott's methods of
     composition. The revaluation began in the 1950's, and the
     modern critic owes Scott "something of the critical atten-
     tion and intelligence that has been lavished on other novel-
     ists in the past thirty years." Includes a general survey
     of Scott criticism since 1932.

13   DUNCAN, JOSEPH. "The Anti-Romantic in <u>Ivanhoe</u>," in <u>Walter
     Scott: Modern Judgments</u>. Edited by D. D. Devlin. London:
     Macmillan, pp. 142-147.
         Reprint of 1955.B5.

1968

14 ELWIN, MALCOLM. "Preface" to Ivanhoe. London: Heron Books,
pp. ix-xiii.
Ivanhoe has declined in popularity because of changing
attitudes toward war and because it contains less "thought"
than the Scottish novels. Nevertheless, Scott had a shrewd
sense of his market and understood that the English have
always valued pageantry above thought and art. Ivanhoe is
a masterpiece of action and melodrama which exhibits Scott's
skill in the art of storytelling.

15 FISHER, P. F. "Providence, Fate, and the Historical Imagination in Scott's The Heart of Midlothian," in Walter Scott:
Modern Judgments. Edited by D. D. Devlin. London: Macmillan, pp. 98-111.
Reprint of 1955.B6.

16 FRENCH, RICHARD. "Sir Walter Scott and His Literary Contemporaries." College Language Association Journal, 11, 248-54.
Scott was familiar with the works of most of his contemporaries, but except for Maria Edgeworth, they did not influence him. He disliked Coleridge as a man and as a poet,
and he valued Wordsworth's friendship more than his poetry.
He sincerely admired Byron's work, but was oblivious to
Keats and Shelley. Scott liked Southey but objected to his
opposition to Lockhart's appointment as editor of the Quarterly Review in 1825. In general Scott overrated the works
of his contemporaries but "ignored the trends others were
taking and set patterns himself."

17 GORDON, ROBERT C. "The Bride of Lammermoor: A Novel of Tory
Pessimism," in Walter Scott: Modern Judgments. Edited by
D. D. Devlin. London: Macmillan, pp. 130-141.
Reprint of 1957.B10.

18 _____. "In Defence of Rob Roy." Essays in Criticism, 18,
no. 4 (October), 470-75.
Rob Roy is "Scott's version of the Prodigal Son." Frank
Osbaldistone flirts with a romantic style of life but
learns that he cannot accept the violence which accompanies
it. The novel progresses through a series of devoted
filial relationships which contrast to Frank's initial dis-
obedience. William Osbaldistone emerges as the mediator
between heraldic and mercantile values.

19 GORDON, S. STEWART. "Waverley and the 'Unified Design,'" in
Walter Scott: Modern Judgments. Edited by D. D. Devlin.
London: Macmillan, pp. 71-83.
Reprint of 1951.B6.

20 HART, FRANCIS R. "The Fair Maid, Manzoni's Betrothed, and the
Grounds of Waverley Criticism," in Walter Scott: Modern
Judgments. Edited by D. D. Devlin. London: Macmillan,
pp. 171-184.
Reprint of 1963.B12.

21 HAYDEN, JOHN O. "The Satanic School, Sir Walter Scott," in
his The Romantic Reviewers, 1802-1824. Chicago: University
of Chicago Press; London: Routledge and Kegan Paul,
pp. 125-34.
Scott is included in "The Satanic School" because his
vicious heroes raised a moral controversy. Like Byron and
Shelley, he was also attacked on stylistic grounds. Although The Lay of the Last Minstrel and The Lady of the
Lake received generally favorable notices, Marmion, The
Vision of Don Roderick, and The Lord of the Isles provoked
reviewers' hostility. Rokeby received some praise, but it
was largely attributable to Scott's enormous popularity.
Many of his critics rightly regarded his narrative poems
as "a corrupting influence on the language and literature
of England."

22 HAYTER, ALETHEA. Opium and the Romantic Imagination. London:
Faber and Faber; Berkeley: University of California Press
(1970), 388pp., passim.
Scott took opium only occasionally. The Bride of Lammermoor was written during a painful illness, for which Scott
took large doses of opium. When the novel was published,
Scott did not recognize it as his own work and feared what
he might find in it. The difference between Jeanie Deans
and Lucy Ashton corresponds to "the difference between
Scott's imagination in its natural and in its opium-
influenced condition."

23 JORDAN, FRANK, JR. "Walter Scott as a Dramatic Novelist."
Studies in Scottish Literature, 5, no. 4 (April), 238-45.
The dramatic quality of Scott's novels stems from his
generous use of dialogue. In Old Mortality, his most
dramatic novel, he uses dialogue regularly for both exposition and characterization. His own review of Old Mortality
in the Quarterly Review of January, 1817 indicates the high
value Scott placed on "what the dramatis personae say to
each other." In the Preface to The Bride of Lammermoor,
Scott questions the appropriateness of the dramatic method
but affirms its usefulness to him.

24 LASCELLES, MARY. "Scott and the Art of Revision," in Imagined
Worlds: Essays on Some English Novels and Novelists in

1968

Honour of John Butt. Edited by Maynard Mack and Ian
Gregor. London: Methuen; New York: Barnes and Noble,
pp. 139-56.

Scott's frequent carelessness results sometimes from mere
negligence and sometimes from writing too quickly in order
to capture his imaginative vision. Close examination of
the revisions of "Wandering Willie's Tale" from Redgauntlet
shows Scott reposing much trust in both his transcriber and
in Ballantyne. However, his revisions at their best were
deliberate attempts to advance his artistic purpose and to
attain an equilibrium between natural and supernatural interpretations of the tale. Revised: 1972.B24.

25   LIGHTFOOT, MARTIN. "Scott's Self-Reviewal: Manuscript and
Other Evidence." Nineteenth Century Fiction, 23, no. 2
(September), 150-60.

Uses manuscript and stylistic evidence to determine which
parts of the review of Tales of My Landlord (Quarterly Review, January, 1817) were written by Gifford, Erskine, and
Scott. Most of the high praise may be ascribed to Gifford,
while the technical discussion at the beginning is "the
novelist's own commentary on his art."

26   McCLARY, BEN HARRIS. "Ichabod Crane's Scottish Origin." Notes
and Queries, 213 (January), 29.

In a letter to Scott of 3 November, 1819, Washington
Irving refers to a figure introduced to him by Scott who
may have provided the prototype for Ichabod Crane.

27   MACIEJEWSKI, MARIAN. "Zagadka i Tajemnica: Z Zagadnien
Swiadomosci Literackiej W Okresie Przelomu Romantycznego"
[Puzzle and Mystery: On the Problem of Literary Conscious-
ness in the Period of the Romantic Breakthrough].
Rocziniki Humanistyczne, 16, no. 1, 5-28.

Classical critics attacked Romantic poetry for its obscurity and lack of clarity. However Romantic criticism,
particularly of the works of Scott and N. L. Artaud, found
positive aesthetic value in obscurity and replaced it with
the word "mysteriousness." Romantic poetry and the poetic
novel are characterized structurally by "the impossibility
of verbalization" and by a resistance to rhetoric.

28   MARCHOU, GASTON. "Chez Walter Scott." Revue de Paris, 75
(August-September), 76-83.

A meditation upon Abbotsford. Like Montesquieu, Scott
thought of himself first as a social man and second as a
literary man. They shared the same attitudes toward nobility and toward the law. However, Scott honestly acknowledged that without his novels he would never have gained

his baronetcy. As Abbotsford provided him with a position
in society, so the novels provide him with a secure place
in history.

29 MAYHEAD, ROBIN. "The Heart of Midlothian: Scott as Artist,"
    in Walter Scott: Modern Judgments. Edited by D. D. Devlin.
    London: Macmillan, pp. 112-121.
        Reprint of 1956.B10.

30 _____. "Walter Scott--His Life and Works," in his Walter
    Scott. Profiles in Literature Series. London: Routledge
    and Kegan Paul, pp. 1-9.
        Scott shares the Romantic taste for wild landscapes and
    the supernatural. His work was also influenced by the
    Gothic "thriller" and Scottish oral tradition. However,
    Scott's best work is fundamentally anti-Romantic. His
    feeling for landscape comes from its human associations,
    and he does not participate in the cult of Romantic indi-
    vidualism. In his demonstration of the tensions of a
    changing society, he is a "kind of northern Thomas Hardy."
    See 1968.A5.

31 MUIR, EDWIN. "Walter Scott: The Writer," in Walter Scott:
    Modern Judgments. Edited by D. D. Devlin. London: Mac-
    millan, pp. 27-32.
        Reprint of second part only of 1945.B11.

32 PIKE, B. A. "Scott as Pessimist: A View of St. Ronan's Well,"
    in Walter Scott: Modern Judgments. Edited by D. D. Devlin.
    London: Macmillan, pp. 162-70.
        Reprint of 1966.B20.

33 POLWARTH, LORD. "Address to the Sixtieth Annual Dinner of the
    Edinburgh Sir Walter Scott Club." The Edinburgh Sir Walter
    Scott Club Annual Report, pp. 10-18.
        Scott was not a snob; he felt at home with both the no-
    bility and the common country people of the Borders. His
    devotion to Chief and Sovereign was actually a devotion to
    stability, law, and order. Scotland, rather than a politi-
    cal party or a dogma, drew his primary loyalty.

34 ROMAGNOLI, SERGIO. "Narratori e prosatori del romanticismo,"
    in Storia della letteratura italiana, vol. 8. Edited by
    Emilio Cecchi and Natalino Sapegno. Milan: Garzanti,
    pp. 7-9.
        The Italian translations of the Waverley Novels popular-
    ized a taste for historical documentation, folk legends,
    and songs. Ivanhoe especially appealed to the current

1968

interest in the origin of the modern nation. Its optimis-
tic demonstration of the dialectic of history contrasts to
Manzoni's pessimistic picture of the dispersion of the
Italian nation in Adelchi.

35 RUFF, WILLIAM and WARD HELLSTROM. "Scott's Authorship of the
Songs in Daniel Terry's Plays." Studies in Scottish Litera-
ture, 5, no. 4 (April), 205-15.
Scott probably collaborated anonymously with Terry from
1816 to 1820 on the dramatized versions of the Waverley
Novels and wrote the songs contained in these plays.

36 SCHULZ, MAX F. "Pop, Op, and Black Humor: The Aesthetics of
Anxiety." College English, 30, no. 3 (December), 230-41.
Scott's passive Waverley heroes were the first modern
protagonists to experience the anxiety of trying to conform
to a society whose rules they did not understand. They are
analogous to the Black Humor heroes of Heller, Pynchon,
Friedman, Donleavy, Barth, and Nabokov, who cannot act in
"the ecumenical anonymity of American culture," which
stresses conformity and reduces individual personality to
a ratio.

37 SERDYUKOV, A. "Val'ter Skott i Nemetskii Roman" [Walter Scott
and the German Novel]. Azerbaidzhanskii Gosudarstvennyi
Universitet (Baku), 6, 80-85.
Unlike Scott, the German Romantics sought universality
manifested through the individual genius of an historical
figure. They could not present a person in relation to the
life of his times but were concerned instead with the highest moments in his life in the context of world history.
However, Scott did influence the "Heimatkunst" tendency in
German novels written in dialect about peasant life.

*38 SHIMAMURA, AKIRA. "Scott no Shosetsu--Redgauntlet ni truite"
[Scott's Novels, Especially Redgauntlet]. Oberon (Tokyo),
30, 2-9.
Cited in the 1970 MLA International Bibliography (New
York: Modern Language Association, 1972), I, 78, item
#4688.

39 SIMMONS, JAMES C. "Of Kettledrums and Trumpets: The Early
Victorian Followers of Scott." Studies in Scottish Literature, 6, no. 1 (July), 47-59.
The success of the Waverley Novels stimulated many imitations and resulted in "a sharp artistic depreciation" of
the genre of the historical romance. Many of the early
Victorian historical romances were escapist literature

designed for light amusement. Scott's imitators arbitrarily inserted historical personages and events into their plots and sprinkled their novels with details of local color. The formula became "intrigue, costume, and history mixed together with little imagination and less art." Reprinted: 1973.B48.

40   STUBBS, JOHN C. "A Note on the Source of Hawthorne's Heraldic Device in The Scarlet Letter." Notes and Queries, 213 (May), 175-76.

In the opening chapter of Waverley, Scott uses the heraldic colors sable and gules "to differentiate between the passions of his contemporaries and the passions of their ancestors." This passage may have provided the source for Hawthorne's symbolic device on the tombstone of Hester Prynne and Arthur Dimmesdale, "On field, sable, the letter A, gules."

41   WELSH, ALEXANDER. "Scott's Heroes," in Walter Scott: Modern Judgments. Edited by D. D. Devlin. London: Macmillan, pp. 63-70.

Partial reprint of 1963.A2.

42   WILDI, MAX. "'Proud Maisie' und die Lyrik von Sir Walter Scott," in Versdichtung der englischen Romantik: Interpretationen. Edited by Teut Andreas Riese and Dieter Riesner. Berlin: Erich Schmidt, pp. 244-50.

Scott wrote two kinds of lyrics: the major key poems of hunting, drinking, and fighting, which are unreflective and primitive; and plaintive, reserved lamentations, which resemble a motif in a minor key. In "Proud Maisie," among the best in the second group, Scott combines the objectivity, concrete imagery, and tragic irony of the ballad with the musical and emotional qualities of elegiac verse.

43   WILLIAMS, IOAN M. "Introduction" to Sir Walter Scott on Novelists and Fiction. London: Routledge and Kegan Paul; New York: Barnes and Noble, pp. 1-12.

Scott was a practical rather than a theoretical critic. His devotion to the eighteenth century English novel may have led to his defense of the novel on moral grounds and his lack of seriousness toward form or design in fiction. He disliked prescribed rules and insisted that the critic must work according to his own principles of construction. Thus he could apply the standard of realism only where appropriate and deal justly with the romance as well as the novel.

1968

44   ZENTAI, ÉVA. "Confrontando Manzoni e W. Scott," in Il Roman-
      ticismo: Atti del sesto congresso dell'associazione inter-
      nazionale per gli studi di lingua e letteratura italiana.
      Edited by Vittore Branca and Tibor Kardos. Budapest:
      Akadémiai Kiado, pp. 437-39.
           Both Scott and Manzoni deal with the struggle between
      established power and opposing forces. Scott regards the
      ensuing compromise as a validation of the rights of the
      ruling class. He seeks to neutralize rebellion and pre-
      serve the status quo. By contrast, Manzoni wishes to edu-
      cate the masses to greater awareness of social and economic
      injustice and eventually to bring about the unification of
      Italy.

1969 A BOOKS

1   CALDER, ANGUS and JENNIE CALDER. Scott. Literature in Per-
      spective. London: Evans Brothers; New York: Arco (1971),
      160pp.
           A general introductory study which places Scott's life
      in the contexts of contemporary Edinburgh and British his-
      tory. In his novels Scott presented a new view of histori-
      cal process and a new interest in the past, although he was
      "perhaps unconscious of what he was doing." His strengths
      lie in his use of history, creation of character and atmos-
      phere, and recording of social detail.

2   CLARK, ARTHUR MELVILLE. Sir Walter Scott: The Formative
      Years. London: Blackwood; New York: Barnes and Noble,
      338pp.
           Scott was formed by the social, cultural, and intellec-
      tual milieu of late eighteenth century Edinburgh. His
      formal education was of only secondary importance to his
      development. More significant were his wide reading, es-
      pecially in English and German, his hunger for anecdotes
      and scraps of folk legends, and his membership in several
      social, literary, and debating societies. Introductory
      chapter argues that Scott was born in 1770. See 1932.B36
      and 1970.A2.

3   COCKSHUT, A. O. J. The Achievement of Sir Walter Scott.
      London: Collins; New York: New York University Press,
      216pp.
           Scott's achievement as an historical novelist was to
      reconcile the conflicts between the "social" and "prophetic"
      voices. Despite flaws in structure and narration, the best
      novels achieve this "double focus." His grasp of the

220

importance of social influences and moral standards of a
given culture made Scott an historical relativist who also
acknowledged the importance of the irrational in human affairs. His novels fall into two categories: the "logical
narrative of history" and the "fantastic romance." See
1971.B82.

4   CORNETTI, ALBERT E. Scott's Lady of the Lake. Athens,
    Georgia: William Murray, 46pp.
        A prose version of the poem divided into six cantos.
    Includes a summary of Scott's life and a "Preface" in which
    the author defends a prose version on the grounds that the
    long poetic form is now outmoded.

5   CUSAC, MARIAN H. Narrative Structure in the Novels of Sir
    Walter Scott. The Hague: Mouton, 128pp.
        Scott's novels have two kinds of structures: the causal-
    ly linked "romances," and the episodically linked "chron-
    icles." In the comic romances, the hero is active; he
    makes a decisive choice and gains a happy ending as reward.
    In the tragic romances, the protagonist is passive; he
    fails to respond at a crucial moment and must suffer from
    an unhappy ending. In the chronicles the hero is passive
    but attains a happy ending simply by not threatening the
    status quo. See 1964.A2.

6   GORDON, ROBERT C. Under Which King? A Study of the Scottish
    Waverley Novels. Edinburgh: Oliver and Boyd; New York:
    Barnes and Noble, 186pp.
        Scott's structural sloppiness resulted from his dim view
    of the novel as an art form, but his "impure" techniques
    enlarge the context of the action. Several novels place
    two characters, who are reciprocally indebted to each other,
    on opposite sides in a conflict. Scott sees spontaneous
    charity possible only in a world of custom and tradition,
    and he repeatedly demonstrates the impossibility of de-
    termining truth amid violence and factional strife. Never-
    theless, he sees historical process, and thus historical
    conflict, as inexorable. Includes chapters on the Scottish
    novels plus Quentin Durward and The Fortunes of Nigel.

7   MacNALTY, ARTHUR SALUSBURY. Sir Walter Scott: The Wounded
    Falcon. Medical Viewpoint Series. London: Johnson,
    189pp.
        A brief biography which incorporates Scott's medical
    history, this is "less a biography than a eulogy." General-
    ly accepts Lockhart's more sentimentalized accounts,

1969

> particularly of the journey home from Italy. Scott's lame-
> ness originated from polio at 18 months. He suffered as an
> adolescent from intestinal hemorrhage but later regained
> robust health. The attacks of gallstone lasted from late
> 1816 until the summer of 1819. Scott had an hereditary
> tendency to high blood pressure and arteriosclerosis and
> eventually died of it. Incorporates parts of 1932.A22.

*8   RUBENSTEIN, JILL. "Scott's Historical Poetry." Ph.D. disser-
tation, Johns Hopkins University, 1969.
>An abstract by the author appears in <u>Dissertation Ab-
stracts International</u>, 30 (1969), 2497-98A.

*9   SHAFER, MICHAEL R. "Distance in Scott's Fiction: The <u>Tales
of My Landlord</u>." Ph.D. dissertation, University of California at San Diego, 1969.
>An abstract by the author appears in <u>Dissertation Ab-
stracts International</u>, 30 (1969), 1994-95A.

1969 B SHORTER WRITINGS

*1   ADAMS, THOMAS FREDERICK. "The Castle Builders: The Medieval-
ist Imagination in the Age of Scott." Ph.D. dissertation,
University of Washington, 1969.
>An abstract by the author appears in <u>Dissertation Ab-
stracts International</u>, 31 (1970), 750A.

2   BRUMM, URSULA. "Thoughts on History and the Novel." <u>Compara-
tive Literature Studies</u>, 6, no. 3 (September), 317-30.
>Disagrees with Lukács. Scott does not celebrate the
progress emerging from revolutions and upheavals. He describes lost ways of life with nostalgia, and sees historical turmoil in terms of personal dispossession. The
historical novel works through a tension between the auth-
or's imaginative involvement in the story and his necessary
submission to the historical frame of given realities. The
three main motifs in Scott's fiction are treason, illegiti-
macy, and property; his treatment of them is primarily
mythical rather than historical. His relation to history
is "prerealistic," as he deals with "the skirmishes between
retreating myth and advancing historicity."

3   CAMERON, DONALD. "The Web of Destiny: The Structure of <u>The
Bride of Lammermoor</u>," in <u>Scott's Mind and Art</u>. Edited by
A. Norman Jeffares. Edinburgh: Oliver and Boyd, pp. 185-
205.

1969

Scott uses the supernatural "to suggest certain qualities of the historical context, to express the secret desires of the characters, and to control the pace of the narrative." He creates tension between the supernatural predictions of disaster and the individual's historically determined psychology which makes him go on despite the warnings. Scott uses the psychological effects of these supernatural prophecies to explain action and experience not adequately accounted for by rational symbolism. They realize themselves in Ravenswood's search for self-destruction and his "subconscious desire for a tragic death."

4   CLARK, ARTHUR MELVILLE. "Introduction" to The Fair Maid of Perth. London: J. M. Dent; New York: E. P. Dutton, pp. v-xi.
     The two central historical events of the novel--the Battle of the Clans and the murder of Rothsay--are shrouded in mystery, which gave Scott freedom to invent his own details and manipulate historical sequence. Nevertheless, the novel presents a true impression of the reign of Robert III and creates a convincing medieval context through the accumulation of many tangible details of daily life. Scott presented Conachar's failure of nerve sympathetically in expiation of his own harshness to his disgraced brother Daniel.

5   _____. "Preface" to The Abbot. London: J. M. Dent; New York: E. P. Dutton, pp. v-ix.
     Although The Abbot is a sequel to The Monastery, it was not merely an afterthought. By eliminating the White Lady and Sir Piercie Shafton and adding a more prominent historical situation, Scott made it superior "in invention, variety, and vigour." Instead of impersonal religious ideologies, he substituted allegiance or hostility to Mary Stuart as the dividing line between his main characters. The plot links the historical background with a love story and with one of Scott's favorite themes, the just restoration of an ancient house through the discovery of its lost heir.

6   _____. "Preface" to The Monastery. London: J. M. Dent; New York: E. P. Dutton, pp. v-x.
     The setting of the novel resembles Melrose Abbey and Scott's immediate surroundings. Their connection to folklore led Scott to make the supernatural integral to the plot. Although he places the novel in a turbulent period of Border history in the 1550's and 1560's, it includes no actual historical incident, and the historical figures play

223

1969

only minor roles. Scott parallels the religious conflict
in the contrast between Halbert and Edward Glendinning and
in the opposition between Henry Wellwood and Eustace. He
was interested in the theological dispute only in the ways
it affected his characters.

7   CORSON, JAMES C. "Introduction" to Woodstock. London: J. M.
     Dent; New York: E. P. Dutton, pp. v-xi.
        Although Scott wrote Woodstock in the midst of personal
     disasters, the novel does not reflect these adverse circum-
     stances. The last of his novels set in England, it is a
     work of pure fiction based only loosely on "scraps of his-
     tory." The plot is flawed by clumsy use of the supernatural,
     but it is strong in unity of time and place and in its
     rapid pacing.

8   _____. "Preface" to The Fortunes of Nigel. London: J. M.
     Dent; New York: E. P. Dutton, pp. vii-xiii.
        Nigel is a period novel in which Scott blends actual and
     fictive characters in a fictitious setting with no real his-
     torical events. His Private Letters of the Seventeenth
     Century bear little resemblance to the novel and did not
     provide its inspiration. Although he lacks the "goodiness"
     of previous Waverley heroes, Nigel's passivity makes him
     difficult to admire. However, the characterization of King
     James places this novel among Scott's greatest works. In
     his comic role, James resembles the officious Bailie Jarvie
     of Rob Roy, but at the same time he retains the respect due
     to his high office.

9   _____. "Preface" to Waverley. London: J. M. Dent; New York:
     E. P. Dutton, pp. v-xi.
        Although he set his stories in the past, Scott is primar-
     ily a period rather than an historical novelist. The his-
     torical and fictional characters mingle naturally together,
     and the private lives of the latter group draw most of the
     readers' attention. The strengths of Waverley lie in char-
     acterization and description of manners, but the novel has
     a weakly constructed plot. Many of its faults arise from
     the character of the hero and his position in the forefront
     of the action.

10   CRAWFORD, THOMAS. "Scott's Life and Works," in Scott's Mind
     and Art. Edited by A. Norman Jeffares. Edinburgh: Oliver
     and Boyd, pp. 1-20.
        Excerpted from 1965.A1.

11 DAICHES, DAVID. "Scott's Achievement as a Novelist," in
    <u>Scott's Mind and Art</u>. Edited by A. Norman Jeffares. Edin-
    burgh: Oliver and Boyd, pp. 21-52.
        Reprint of 1951.B2.

12 DEVLIN, D. D. "Scott and History," in <u>Scott's Mind and Art</u>.
    Edited by A. Norman Jeffares. Edinburgh: Oliver and Boyd,
    pp. 72-92.
        Scott's concept of history and of human nature takes a
    middle way between the Enlightenment view of fixed human
    nature and the historicist view of the past as constant
    change. Scott's historicism rests on compromise; he sees
    history as process and dynamic movement, but his characters
    are recurring human types who "supply the continuous thread
    in history." His comic characters emerge as his true he-
    roes, because they recognize the need for adaptation to
    change.

13 ELWIN, MALCOLM. "Introduction" to <u>The Fair Maid of Perth</u>.
    London: Heron Books, pp. ix-xii.
        <u>The Fair Maid of Perth</u> has been undeservedly ignored by
    critics. Scott conveys Catherine Glover's thoughts and
    feelings vividly, and Henry Smith is superior to the usual
    Waverley hero. Conachar is based on Scott's attempt to ex-
    piate his repudiation of his cowardly brother Robert. The
    novel brilliantly reflects the civic life of medieval Perth,
    and its comic element is equal to Scott's best work.

14 GORDON, ROBERT C. and ANDREW D. HOOK. "<u>The Bride of Lammermoor</u>
    Again: An Exchange." <u>Nineteenth Century Fiction</u>, 23, no. 4
    (March), 493-99.
        Letters to the editor defending each author's previously
    stated interpretation of the novel and elaborating on their
    points of disagreement. <u>See</u> 1957.B10 and 1967.B15.

15 HARRIS, RONALD WALTER. "Romanticism and History: Sir Walter
    Scott," in his <u>Romanticism and the Social Order, 1780-1830</u>.
    London: Blandford Press; New York: Barnes and Noble,
    pp. 233-62.
        Scott intended the Waverley Novels to provide "an accu-
    rate historical picture of social conditions . . . in the
    process of passing away." The purposes of fiction were
    secondary to those of historical reconstruction. History,
    sociology, and class structures are Scott's main interests
    in <u>Waverley</u> and <u>The Heart of Midlothian</u>. Although he never
    advocated a particular creed in the novels, Scott demon-
    strated in them that "men's loyalties were stronger than
    their reason," a condition of which he approved.

1969

16 HAYNE, BARRIE. "'Ossian,' Scott, and Cooper's Indians."
   Journal of American Studies, 3, no. 1 (July), 73-87.
   Cooper absorbed the "elegiac quality" of the Ossian
   poems and the Waverley Novels; they offered him a model of
   the past enshrined as a demonstration of national greatness.
   Like Scott, he united epic sublimity and a timeless, mythic
   past with a concern for domestic realism. Cooper shares
   with both Scott and Macpherson a "pervasive melancholy,"
   a romantic treatment of nature, and deep sympathy for a
   dying race.

17 HOOD, F. C. "Scott and His Printers." Times Literary Supplement (3 April), p. 369.
   For material on Scott's business affairs, Grierson relied on James Glen, W. S., an accountant who had studied
   Scott's life for many years. Queries whether Quayle in The
   Ruin of Sir Walter Scott has really added significantly to
   our understanding of Scott's bankruptcy. See 1968.A7;
   1969.B26, B37.

18 JEFFARES, A. NORMAN. "Introduction" to his Scott's Mind and
   Art. Edinburgh: Oliver and Boyd, pp. ix-xii.
   The obstacles to Scott's popularity today include the
   magnitude and inclusiveness of his work, the need to understand his purposes within the context of Scottish history,
   and "a modern fashion for the purely contemporary." Although his is a "particularly Scottish form of narrative
   art," he is nevertheless "a continental writer, not an in-
   sular one." This collection of essays by several writers
   includes a selected bibliography.

19 JEFFERSON, D. W. "The Virtuosity of Scott," in Scott's Mind
   and Art. Edited by A. Norman Jeffares. Edinburgh: Oliver
   and Boyd, pp. 53-71.
   "Scott was the master of a number of styles." He used
   fiction and colloquial detail to embody encompassing social
   and historical ideas; in his novels, the factual and the
   fictitious coexist harmoniously. His command of the differ-
   ing idioms appropriate to so many milieux gives his work a
   sense of enormous human richness. His narratives excel in
   "contrasts of coloring, milieu and language, enhanced by
   surprising transitions and felicitious timing."

20 KENNEDY, LUDOVIC. "Address to the Sixty-first Annual Dinner
   of the Edinburgh Sir Walter Scott Club." The Edinburgh Sir
   Walter Scott Club Annual Report.
   Scott lived with great zest, and both his life and works
   reflect a pervasive sense of humor. In his role as Scotland's great reconciler, he offers an important message to

our own time, which is beset by the double problems of en-
croaching uniformity and resurgent individualism and nationalism. Reprinted: 1971.A13.

21 LAMBERTSON, C. L. "Speaking of Byron." Malahat Review, 12
(October), 18-42 and 13 (January, 1970), 24-46.
Prints sixteen letters from Joanna Baillie to Scott,
written from 8 February, 1814 to 7 January, 1819. The letters concern, among other subjects, Lord and Lady Byron,
whom Baillie knew personally.

22 LEEMING, GLENDA. "Introduction" to Ivanhoe. London: Penguin
Books, pp. 7-11.
Scott's best works show the past in the course of change
and the pattern of historical progress. In Ivanhoe he
abandoned the Scottish material of the first nine novels,
because he feared his readers might tire of it. He substituted the Saxon-Norman conflict to embody his favorite
theme of the clash between civilizations. Rebecca and the
humanitarian ideals she represents have no place in an England of Norman chivalry and Saxon simplicity.

23 LEWIS, C. S. "Sir Walter Scott," in his Selected Literary
Essays. Edited by Walter Hooper. London: Cambridge Uni-
versity Press, pp. 206-18.
Reprint of 1956.B9.

24 LOW, DONALD A. "Scott's Criticism of 'The Jolly Beggars.'"
Bibliotheck, 5, 207-209.
Part of Scott's commendation of Burns's "The Jolly Beggars," which he reviewed in 1809 in the Quarterly, came
originally from an advertising "puff" written for Burns's
publishers in 1801, presumably by Thomas Stewart. Scott
neglected to use quotation marks, and critics for the last
hundred and fifty years have been quoting the praise as
Scott's own.

25 LUKÁCS, GEORG. "Scott and the Classical Form of the Historical
Novel," in Scott's Mind and Art. Edited by A. Norman
Jeffares. Edinburgh: Oliver and Boyd, pp. 93-131.
Reprint of 1962.B10.

26 McLAREN, MORAY. "Scott and His Printers." Times Literary
Supplement (14 April), p. 440.
Scott was not responsible for ruining the Ballantynes;
on the contrary, they acknowledged that they could not exist
without his patronage. James never told Scott about the
precarious system of "accommodation bills," and John was

1969

dishonest and apparently embezzled from the firm. <u>See</u>
1968.A7; 1969.B17, B37.

27   MAXWELL, J. C. "A Deletion in Scott's 'Private Letters of the
      Seventeenth Century.'" <u>Notes and Queries</u>, 214 (February),
      57.
          A sentence Scott deleted from the 1832 edition was in-
      tended to be the first sentence of a footnote by the editor.

28   MAYHEAD, ROBIN. "Scott and the Idea of Justice," in <u>Scott's</u>
      <u>Mind and Art</u>. Edited by A. Norman Jeffares. Edinburgh:
      Oliver and Boyd, pp. 167-84.
          In <u>The Heart of Midlothian</u> the theme of justice is cen-
      tral, and in other novels Scott turns an "alarmed scrutiny"
      on the law. In <u>Guy Mannering</u> and <u>Redgauntlet</u> he is con-
      cerned with the nature of both legal and less rational
      "human" justice in differing circumstances, and he asks to
      what extent justice actually exists within the law. <u>Red-</u>
      <u>gauntlet</u> contrasts the totally lawless world of the Jacob-
      ites with the pedantry of legal Edinburgh and demonstrates
      overwhelming evidence of the breakdown of law and order.
      Partially reprinted: 1973.A3.

29   MORGAN, PETER F. "Scott as Critic." <u>Studies in Scottish</u>
      <u>Literature</u>, 7, nos. 1-2 (July-October), 90-101.
          Scott views the author as "man of feeling, as conscious
      artist, and as responsive and responsible citizen." His
      critical vocabulary derives from this emphasis on feeling
      and leads to ambivalence in his view of satire. He regards
      the proper subject of art as "nature and human nature" and
      believes that the writer exists in a symbolic relationship
      to his society and that his function is to entertain his
      audience.

30   MURISON, DAVID. "The Two Languages of Scott," in <u>Scott's Mind</u>
      <u>and Art</u>. Edited by A. Norman Jeffares. Edinburgh: Oliver
      and Boyd, pp. 206-29.
          In the Scottish Waverley Novels, Scott uses English for
      narration and description and Scots for the dialogue of the
      native, mostly lower-class characters. Although he was
      "fully bilingual," Scots was the "language of his natural
      expression of action and emotion," while English remained
      essentially a foreign language learned from books. He added
      some 200 words to the language by reviving them from obscure
      sources. His use of Scots dialect as well as the alterna-
      tion between Scots and English can produce a wide range of
      nuances in different characters and contexts.

31 NEWLIN, PAUL A. "Scott's Influence on Poe's Grotesque and
    Arabesque Tales." <u>American Transcendental Quarterly</u>, 2,
    9-12.
        Poe found the source for his title, <u>Tales of the Gro-</u>
    <u>tesque and Arabesque</u>, in Scott's essay "On the Supernatural
    in Fictitious Composition; and particularly on the Works of
    Ernest Theodore Hoffman." Scott's ideas on exaggeration of
    the supernatural for grotesque effect, the supernatural ro-
    mance satire, and the fantastic supernatural tale influenced
    Poe's professed literary theories.

32 PARKER, WILLIAM MATHIE. "Scott's Continental Tour in 1815."
    <u>Blackwood's Magazine</u>, 305 (May), 396-403.
        Prints a previously unpublished Scott manuscript, his
    diary of a "Tour on the Continent August 1815." The main
    object of the trip was to visit the field of Waterloo. The
    diary presents many of the virtues of Scott's fiction in
    its narrative pace, curiosity about military matters, en-
    joyment of country scenes and the fine arts, and Scott's
    "sympathetic response to human character."

33 _____. "Sir Walter Scott--Coin Collector." <u>Coin Monthly</u>
    (November), 113-15.
        Scott was seriously interested in coin collecting.
    Quotes two letters on the subject to Charles Kerr of Abbot-
    rule, dated 30 June, 1794 and 9 May, 1795.

34 POTTER, LEE H. "The Text of Scott's Edition of Swift."
    <u>Studies in Bibliography</u>, 22, 240-55.
        The text of Scott's edition of Swift is untrustworthy.
    It is primarily a reprint of John Nichols' third edition of
    Swift's works, published in 1808. Although Scott took some
    material directly from manuscripts, his carelessness and
    haste diminish its value.

35 POTTLE, F. A. "The Power of Memory in Boswell and Scott," in
    <u>Scott's Mind and Art</u>. Edited by A. Norman Jeffares. Edin-
    burgh: Oliver and Boyd, pp. 230-53.
        Reprint of 1945.B15.

36 PUNZO, FRANCA RUGGIERI. "Henry Mackenzie: Lettere degli
    ultimi anni del 'Man of Feeling' a Sir Walter Scott."
    <u>English Miscellany</u>, 20, 183-227.
        In spite of his authorship of <u>The Man of Feeling</u>, Mac-
    kenzie was not a sentimental personality. Scott recalled
    him as a man of the world and a sharp businessman who re-
    garded literature as a secondary activity. Prints thirteen
    previously unpublished letters, dated from 1803 to 1826,

1969

which complete the circle of the twelve letters from Scott to Mackenzie published by Grierson.

37 QUAYLE, ERIC. "Scott and His Printers." <u>Times Literary Supplement</u> (17 April), p. 414.
Affirms that in <u>The Ruin of Sir Walter Scott</u> he presents new evidence from previously unpublished material and original sources to substantiate his exoneration of the Ballantynes. Reiterates charge that Lockhart was "a liar who deliberately suppressed facts, distorted the truth, and manufactured evidence." <u>See</u> 1968.A7; 1969.B17, B26.

38 RICHARDSON, JOANNA. "George IV: Patron of Literature." <u>Essays by Divers Hands</u>, N.S. 35, 128-46.
Although Scott declined the laureateship in 1813, he was the writer on closest terms with George IV. The Regent's conversation with Byron concerning Scott in 1812 helped to heal the breach between the two poets. A frequent Royal guest in London, Scott used the favor of George IV to obtain permission to search for the Scottish regalia. He did not hesitate to use his influence with the King and confided to Lockhart that "my interest lies Windsor ways."

39 SERDYUKOV, A. I. "Literaturnaya sreda Val'tera Skotta" [The Literary Milieu of Walter Scott]. <u>Azerbaidzhanskii Gosuderstbennyi Universitet</u> (Baku), 1-2, 131-36.
Scott was influenced by Gothic writers, the late eighteenth century interest in history, and Scottish customs and folk songs. The Jacobite rebellion created a national renaissance and a European-wide interest in Scotland. Smollett, Burns, and Scott created a uniquely Scottish school of literature. Scott amalgamated the influences of his literary predecessors while emphasizing the strong links between the individual and his socio-historical milieu.

40 SHOWETT, H. K. "Faulkner and Scott: Addendum." <u>Mississippi Quarterly</u>, 22, no. 2 (Spring), 152-53.
Scott and Faulkner share the same basic theme: "the confrontation, clash, or amalgamation of cultures." However, Faulkner may have taken the description of the sword rending the veil from a speech by Lucius Q. C. Lamar to the State Convention in Jackson, Mississippi on 3 August, 1875. <u>See</u> 1967.B13.

41 SILLERY, V. "Scott's <u>Minstrelsy</u> and Other Reprints." <u>Notes and Queries</u>, 214 (February), 42.
An announcement that the standard edition of Scott's <u>Minstrelsy</u>, edited by T. F. Henderson, was reprinted in 1968 by Singing Tree Press.

42 WALKER, WARREN S. "A 'Scottish Cooper' for an 'American Scott.'" American Literature, 40, no. 4 (January), 536-37.
    In an 1826 pamphlet entitled "The Life of Paul Jones the Pirate one of the Principal Characters in the Celebrated Novel The Pilot by Sir Walter Scott, Bart.," the anonymous pamphleteer substituted Scott for Cooper as the author of The Pilot and gave Cooper's hero John Paul Jones the worst qualities of Scott's villain-hero Cleveland.

43 WOOD, G. A. M. "Sir Walter Scott and Sir Ralph Sadler: A Chapter in Literary History, Part I." Studies in Scottish Literature, 7, nos. 1-2 (July-October), 11-20.
    Scott wrote the Introduction and Notes and completed the editorial work on The State Papers of Sir Ralph Sadler (1809). He welcomed the editing task as a rest from creative composition. Reprints correspondence primarily between Scott and Robert Surtees of Mainsforth regarding the availability of certain sources. The letters reflect the "looseness" of Scott's standards of editorial commentary. See Parts II and III, 1970.B24, B25 and Part IV, 1971.B87.

1970 A BOOKS

1 ANON. "Lord Crawford in Quentin Durward." Dundee: Rathalpin Press, 15pp.
    Dedicated "To David Erll of Craufuird, Wise and Wicht" and dated 20 November, 1970. Reprints a passage dealing with Lord Crawford from chapter 7 of Quentin Durward. The dedication is from "Squire Meldrum" by David Lindesay, the poet Scott describes in Marmion. Privately printed in a limited edition of 35 copies.

2 CLARK, ARTHUR MELVILLE. "The Date of Sir Walter Scott's Birth." Edinburgh: William Blackwood, 6pp.
    Provides additional arguments to support the case that Scott was born in 1770. This evidence includes the testimony of John Irving, Scott's boyhood friend born in 1770, that Scott was three months his senior; Scott's admission to the Bar in July, 1792; and also includes a facsimile of a manuscript "remit" signed by Henry Erskine and dated 14 June, 1791, certifying Scott to be examined in Civil Law on condition he provide proof of being twenty years of age. For earlier statements of this theory see 1932.B36 and 1969.A2. See replies 1970.B5 and 1974.B10.

*3 CROWL, SAMUEL RENNINGER. "The Waverley Pattern: Imagination and Experience in Four Scott Novels, Waverley, Old Mortality,

1970

Rob Roy, and The Heart of Midlothian." Ph.D. dissertation, Indiana University, 1970.
    An abstract by the author appears in Dissertation Abstracts International, 31 (1971), 4708A.

4   HAYDEN, JOHN O., ed. Scott: The Critical Heritage. London: Routledge and Kegan Paul; New York: Barnes and Noble, 568pp.
    Contains seventy items divided into two parts: criticism (formal reviews) and commentary (letters, diary entries, conversations) on individual works from The Lay of the Last Minstrel through Woodstock; and a chronological series of comments on assorted subjects (Scott's character, morality, religion, use of history, influence, etc.) from 1827 to 1883. An appendix lists reviews of Scott's novels. See 1970.B9.

5   JOHNSON, EDGAR. Sir Walter Scott: The Great Unknown. 2 volumes. New York: Macmillan; London: Hamish Hamilton, 1423pp.
    A definitive critical biography which posits Scott as "the noblest and wisest" of nineteenth century British writers. Attempts to recreate Scott's milieu, both physical and intellectual, and includes copious details of history and local color. The biographical chapters rely heavily on Scott's own autobiographical documents and correspondence and on the journals and memoirs of his associates. The critical chapters follow the main line of Scott criticism, emphasizing the realism of the novels and Scott's own rationalistic, eighteenth century, and worldly orientation. Includes revisions of 1956.B8; 1963.B16; and 1964.B7. See also 1970.B8; 1971.B47, B82.

*6 LAFFERTY, MARY LOU. "The Landscape Art of Sir Walter Scott: Scenic Description in Selected Waverley Novels." Ph.D. dissertation, University of Wisconsin, 1970.
    An abstract by the author appears in Dissertation Abstracts International, 31 (1971), 6015A.

7   McLAREN, MORAY. Sir Walter Scott: The Man and the Patriot. London: Heinemann, 255pp.
    A biography with some critical commentary. The unique character of late eighteenth century Edinburgh was instrumental in developing Scott's "dual personality." Considers Scott's wide influence in Scotland and his influence in popularizing his native land abroad, particularly in America.

1970 B SHORTER WRITINGS

*1   BOTTONI, LUCIANO. "Scott e Manzoni 1821: tecniche descrittive
     e funzoni epistemologiche." Lingua e Stile, 5, 409-34.
         Cited in the 1971 MLA International Bibliography (New
     York, Modern Language Association, 1973), I, 92, item #5614.

2   CECIL, DAVID. "Introduction" to Short Stories by Sir Walter
     Scott. St. Clair Shores, Michigan: Scholarly Press,
     pp. vii-xx.
         Reprint of 1934.B5.

3   CHANDLER, ALICE. "Origins of Medievalism: Scott," in A Dream
     of Order: The Medieval Ideal in Nineteenth Century English
     Literature. Lincoln: University of Nebraska Press,
     pp. 12-51.
         A revised and expanded version of 1965.B4. This chapter
     adds a history of scholarship on the Middle Ages through
     the eighteenth century, by which time medievalism shared
     with romanticism the concerns with time, nature, liberty,
     and primitivism. Also adds a consideration of the influence
     of Goethe on Scott and expands discussions of Ivanhoe,
     Quentin Durward, and Anne of Geierstein. Scott's attitudes
     to contemporary politics were closely related to his ideali-
     zation of feudal relationships and of the social order of
     the Middle Ages.

4   CLAY, EDITH. "Rhodes: Sir William to Sir Walter. Notes to
     Save Sir Walter Scott the Trouble of Looking Out Information
     about Rhodes. W. Gell, 1832." Journal of the Warburg and
     Courtauld Institutes, 33, 336-43.
         Sir William Gell, the classical archaeologist and topog-
     rapher, accompanied Scott in Naples in 1832. Gell's Notes
     on Rhodes were based on diaries kept during a trip in 1812.
     He collected them when Scott expressed interest in writing
     a poem on the Rhodian legend of the slaying of the dragon
     by the Chevalier Donnédieu de Gozon. Reproduces Gell's
     sketches as well as the Notes.

5   CORSON, JAMES C. "Birth of the Last Minstrel: Vital Year in
     Debate." Edinburgh Scotsman (26 December), supplement
     pp. 1-2.
         Arthur Melville Clark has not produced any documentary
     evidence to support his thesis that Scott was born in 1770,
     and the evidence he offers is based on false inferences
     from previously known information. Additional arguments
     provide evidence that Scott was born in 1771. These in-
     clude his childhood visit to Bath, his statement of his

1970

    birthdate in the family Bible, other solemn declarations of his age on various instances, and the record of births to Scott's mother. Reply to 1970.A2. <u>See also</u> 1974.B10.

6   CRAWFORD, THOMAS. "Political and Protest Songs in Eighteenth Century Scotland. I. Jacobite and Anti-Jacobite." <u>Scottish Studies</u>, 14, no. 1, 1-33.
    After 1750, Jacobite songs depicted the Chevalier as a romantic figure in a tone of nostalgic love-melancholy. This development of "sentimental Jacobitism" was counterbalanced by the anti-Jacobite satires of the archetypal Highlander. Eventually Jacobite and anti-Jacobite sentiment coalesced into a loyalty to Scotland as part of Great Britain. This "uneasy synthesis" informs "the ambivalent vision of the Author of Waverley."

7   FAULKNER, PETER. "Scott as Editor of Bage." <u>Notes and Queries</u>, 215 (October), 376-78.
    In his "Prefatory Memoir" to the selections by Robert Bage included in Ballantyne's <u>Novelist's Library</u>, Scott claims that Bage's "indelicacy of expression" has been "in some degree chastened in the present edition." Despite this claim, Scott was actually a remarkably restrained editor who made only minimal changes, primarily in spelling and punctuation.

8   HART, FRANCIS RUSSELL. "The Romance of Apollo's Venal Son: Edgar Johnson's <u>Scott</u>." <u>Virginia Quarterly Review</u>, 46, no. 4 (Autumn), 680-88.
    Johnson's <u>Scott</u> is a "critical assimilation" of Lockhart, in which Johnson has chosen to accept some anecdotes and to correct others. However, Johnson's assessment of Scott is more flattering and less balanced than Lockhart's. Where Lockhart showed Scott as unstable and contradictory, Johnson sees him as triumphantly rational. <u>See</u> 1970.A5.

9   HAYDEN, JOHN O. "Introduction" to his <u>Scott: The Critical Heritage</u>. London: Routledge and Kegan Paul; New York: Barnes and Noble, pp. 1-23.
    Scott's contemporary reviewers confronted for the first time the phenomenon of the best seller. They tolerated his flaws and appreciated his virtues. The Victorian critics were primarily concerned with his mixture of history and fiction, his craftsmanship, and his characterization. Their assessments are usually "vigorous, pertinent, and thoughtful." Most twentieth century critics of Scott have been academics, and, although interest in him has not died, it does not compare to the degree of interest in the other romantics. <u>See</u> 1970.A4.

10   KANBAR, MAXINE. "Walter Scott." La Revue des Lettres Mo-
     dernes, vols. 234-37, 63-79.
          Barbey D'Aurevilly borrowed and improved upon Scott's
     ideas and developed Scott's characters, settings, and inci-
     dents for his own plots. Although one cannot speak of
     "sources" in the strict sense, there are definite similari-
     ties between L'Ensorcelée and Guy Mannering, between Un
     Prêtre marié and Kenilworth, and between Un Histoire sans
     nom and The Heart of Midlothian.

11   KILBRANDON, LORD. "Address to the Sixty-second Annual Dinner
     of the Edinburgh Sir Walter Scott Club." The Edinburgh Sir
     Walter Scott Club Annual Report, pp. 10-18.
          The intense political hatreds of his time hardly touched
     Scott, and he remained on good terms with his Whig friends.
     Quotes from the Reminiscences of Sir Walter Scott, by Mr.
     Stevenson, chief of the 1814 voyage to inspect the northern
     lighthouses, on which Scott was a guest: "Sir Walter had
     the happy talent of being on easy terms with all around
     him."

12   KLEIN, H. M. "'Sangrado'--Byron Before Scott." Notes and
     Queries, 215 (May), 174.
          The Oxford English Dictionary credits Scott in an 1820
     letter with the first usage of "Sangrado" as an English
     word denoting an ignorant pretender to medical knowledge.
     However, Byron used it in an 1812 speech to the House of
     Lords.

*13 MADDOX, JAMES HUNT, JR. "The Survival of Gothic Romance in
     the Nineteenth-Century Novel: A Study of Scott, Charlotte
     Brontë, and Dickens." Ph.D. dissertation, Yale University,
     1970.
          An abstract by the author appears in Dissertation Ab-
     stracts International, 32 (1971), 442A.

14   POLLIN, B. R. "Poe's Use of the Name Ermengarde in 'Eleonora.'"
     Notes and Queries, 215 (September), 332-33.
          In both "Ligeia" and "Eleonora," the Saxon names of the
     second mate of the narrator are derived from Scott's novels.
     The names suggest a contrast with the more exotic and mys-
     terious first women in the narrators' lives. In Scott's
     Betrothed, Ermengarde is the name of the ancient Saxon Lady
     of Baldringham. Although the situation and description of
     Poe's Eleonora may have been suggested by parallels in
     Scott's Lady Eveline, Poe gave his character the "more
     characteristically Saxon name" of Eveline's great-aunt
     Ermengarde.

1970

15   RALEIGH, JOHN HENRY. "Waverley as History: or 'Tis One
       Hundred and Fifty-Six Years Since.'" Novel, 4, no. 1
       (Fall), 14-29.
         Waverley is "realistic and satirical rather than roman-
       tic." Like Macaulay, Scott believed that history works
       toward "collective progress," but he also knew that certain
       kinds of human uniqueness can disappear in its passage. He
       wrote Waverley as the memorial of a way of life now extinct.
       Waverley himself is one of the first "modern" heroes who
       transforms reality through imagination. He suffers isola-
       tion and alienation as he progresses from a consciousness
       of history as dream to history as tragic myth to history as
       unambiguous present. This transformation exemplifies Scott
       as "a classic apostle of progress."

16   ROBB, KENNETH A. "Scott's The Two Drovers: The Judge's
       Charge." Studies in Scottish Literature, 7, no. 4 (April),
       255-64.
         The Judge's charge to the jury near the end of the story
       does not in itself reveal its "deeper significance," as
       Lord David Cecil has argued. It drives the reader to a re-
       valuation of the character of Robin, who is trapped by fate
       and "given a tragic nobility and dignity."

*17   RONALD, MARGARET A. "Functions of Setting in the Novel: From
       Mrs. Radcliffe to Charles Dickens." Ph.D. dissertation,
       Northwestern University, 1970.
         An abstract by the author appears in Dissertation Ab-
       stracts International, 31 (1971), 5373A.

18   SERDYUKOV, A. I. "Poèmy Val'tera Skotta" [The Poems of Walter
       Scott]. Azerbaidzhanskii Gosuderstbennyi Universitet
       (Baku), 5-6, 83-89.
         Although critics traditionally link The Lay of the Last
       Minstrel and Marmion with Gothic novels, the narrative poems
       were also influenced by folk songs, ballads, and history.
       In The Lady of the Lake Scott used an historical situation
       and character types which he would later transfer to the
       novels. Rokeby also has a real historical background, which
       Scott developed in Woodstock.

19   SHIPPS, ANTHONY W. "Sir Walter Scott's Quotations." Notes and
       Queries, 215 (October), 385.
         Identifies quotations used by Scott from Thomson's The
       Seasons, Jonson's Eastward Ho, and George Colman the Young-
       er's The Maid of the Moor. Reply to 1944.B13.

20 SPINK, GERALD W. "Walter Scott's Musical Acquaintances."
Music and Letters, 51, no. 1 (January), 61-65.
Scott preferred the emotional and nationalistic qualities
in music. He encouraged collections of national songs by
George Thomson and Alexander Campbell, and he gave the composition rights of his songs to John Clarke-Whitfield and
several other Englishmen. Among Continental musicians,
Scott was most closely acquainted with Moscheles, who
visited him in Edinburgh and later dedicated his "Fantaisie
sur des Airs des Bardes Écossais" to Scott.

21 TREVOR-ROPER, HUGH. "Great Scott." Spectator, 224 (17 January), 78-79.
At his best, Scott viewed the past with a mixture of sympathy and reason. He simultaneously appreciated different
societies and admired British progress in the eighteenth
century. Scott balanced his romanticism with Augustan common sense. He should be judged by his best novels, those
written between 1814 and 1820. Although the later novels
are "poor stuff," the Journal reveals his "reserved and
complex personality."

22 VALKAMA, LEEVI. "Kuusi ja seitsemän veljestä" [Six and Seven
Brothers]. Sananjalka, 12, 133-47.
The Finnish novelist Aleksis Kivi learned from Scott to
represent life through the language and humor of ordinary
people and to give the narration dramatic and concrete
qualities. A comparison of Kivi's The Seven Brothers to
Scott's Rob Roy shows that whereas Scott's picture of the
six brothers remains static, Kivi uses the developing tensions within his group to define both the private situation
of the characters and the shape of the novel.

*23 WADDEN, ANTHONY T. "The Novel as Psychic Drama: Studies of
Scott, Dickens, Eliot, and James." Ph.D. dissertation,
University of Iowa, 1970.
An abstract by the author appears in Dissertation Ab-
stracts International, 31 (1971), 4737A.

24 WOOD, G. A. M. "Sir Walter Scott and Sir Ralph Sadler: A
Chapter in Literary History, Part II." Studies in Scottish
Literature, 7, no. 3 (January), 147-58.
Prints nine letters between Scott and William Hayley,
dated from June, 1808 to May, 1810, relating primarily to
Richard Vernon Sadleir, a friend of Hayley and a lineal
descendant of Sir Ralph Sadler. See Part I, 1969.B43;
Part III, 1970.B25; and Part IV, 1971.B87.

1970

25   _____. "Sir Walter Scott and Sir Ralph Sadler: A Chapter in
Literary History, Part III." Studies in Scottish Literature, 7, no. 4 (April), 229-37.
        Prints a letter from Scott to Thomas Sadleir, dated 14
August, 1808. Also includes three letters between Scott
and Arthur Clifford, the titular editor of the Sadler
papers. The relationship between them was "strangely formal," and Scott never again collaborated with Clifford.
See Part I, 1969.B43; Part II, 1970.B24; and Part IV,
1971.B87.

26   WOODRING, CARL. Politics in English Romantic Poetry. Cambridge, Massachusetts: Harvard University Press, pp. 71-73
and passim.
        Scott's novels are politically ambiguous, as may be de-
monstrated by the contradictory interpretations of Mark
Twain and Georg Lukács. In general, however, Scott accepted
"the conservative implications of his taste and ethics."
In the narrative poems, Scott plays the role of National
Bard, but he was "ensnared by patriotism and romantic nostalgia."

27   WROBEL, ARTHUR. "'Romantic Realism': Nathaniel Beverley
Tucker." American Literature, 42, no. 3 (November), 325-35.
        Tucker (1784-1851) and his contemporaries wrote for "a
public whose literary standards had been trained by Sir
Walter Scott and the moralistic Scottish reviewers." The
Scottish critics demanded realism in the delineation of
manners but also emphasized neoclassical decorum in content, form, and language. They attacked pessimism, skepti-
cism, and what they considered to be immorality. In trying
to conform to these guidelines, Tucker's characters became
stereotyped, and he failed to attain the verisimilitude of
manners and speech of the Waverley Novels.

28   ZUG, CHARLES G., III. "Sir Walter Scott and the Ballad Forgery." Studies in Scottish Literature, 8, no. 1 (July),
52-64.
        It is unfair to call Scott a ballad forger according to
the modern definition. His editorial liberties with the
Minstrelsy material were consistent with the taste of his
readers, who wanted intelligible and artistically polished
texts. He readily acknowledged his ballad imitations as
his own work.

1971 A BOOKS

1   ANDERSON, W. E. K. "Scott and the Scottish Virtues." Edin-
     burgh: Society of Friends of the Kirk of the Greyfriars,
     8pp.
          The Address at the Service of Commemoration, Greyfriars,
     Sunday, 15 August, 1971. The neighborhood around Greyfriars
     is "the Edinburgh of the Waverley Novels." Scott's father
     and the great men of his time lie buried in the churchyard.
     A great man as well as a great writer, Scott possessed
     "those qualities which as Scotsmen we traditionally value."
     He was a man of integrity and of perseverance in work. He
     loved his country and was simultaneously a nationalist and
     a citizen of the world.

2   ANON. "The Last Minstrel: A Monograph on the Occasion of the
     Bicentenary of the Birth of Sir Walter Scott, Born 15th
     August 1771." Glenrothes, Fife: Tullis Russell, 33pp.
          Scott's lameness forced him to become a writer, although
     he would have preferred a more active life. The only seri-
     ous flaws in his character were his "delusions of grandeur"
     and his desire to establish his family in feudal splendor.
     He wanted anonymity because he did not regard authorship of
     the novels as consistent with his position as laird and
     sheriff.

3   ANON. "Scott and His Scotland: A Catalogue to Mark the Bi-
     centenary of the Birth of Sir Walter Scott." Pitlochry:
     K. D. Duval.
          Descriptive sale catalogue which includes Scott and his
     contemporaries.

4   ANON. "A Sir Walter Scott Tour of Edinburgh." Edinburgh and
     Glasgow: Pillans and Wilson, 6pp.
          A walking tour with map and descriptions of places in
     Edinburgh associated with Scott. Includes his birthplace
     (now demolished), the High School, his boyhood home at 25
     George Square, Greyfriars Church, Parliament House, and his
     home at 39 Castle Street in the New Town.

5   BLISS, DOUGLAS PERCY. "Sir Walter Scott and the Visual Arts."
     Glasgow: Foulis Archive Press, 31pp.
          Scott lacked taste in art and believed that a picture
     should tell a story. However, he was the master architect
     and landscape gardener of Abbotsford, and his descriptions
     stimulated a Scott vogue in English art that lasted through-
     out the nineteenth century. The Scottish school of histori-
     cal and landscape painting also used many subjects from his

poems and novels. Presented in the David Cargill Lecture for 1970.

6   Buffalo, New York. Lockwood Memorial Library of the State
     University of New York at Buffalo. "Scott and His Scotland:
     The Catalogue of an Exhibition in Lockwood Memorial Library,
     Together with A Catalogue of Scott's Works in the Rare Book
     Room." Buffalo: State University of New York, 54pp.
         Includes selected bibliographies on Scott's Edinburgh,
     the cultural and political milieu, the publishing and artis-
     tic life of the time, Scott's friends, and his literary
     background in balladry and historical studies. The cata-
     logue of Scott's works in the Rare Book Collection is di-
     vided into 1) Collections, 2) Letters, speeches, etc., 3)
     Single Works, 4) Works edited by Scott, and 5) Works trans-
     lated by Scott.

*7   COONEY, SEAMUS. "Narrative Voice, Personae, and Frame Stories
     in Scott's Fiction." Ph.D. dissertation, University of
     California at Berkeley, 1971.
         Cited in Comprehensive Dissertation Index (Ann Arbor,
     Michigan: Xerox University Microfilms, 1973), XXX, 467.

8   CORSON, JAMES CLARKSON, et al. Sir Walter Scott Bicentenary
     Supplement. Berwick: Tweedale Press, 23pp.
         Special commemorative supplement includes articles on
     Abbotsford by James C. Corson, on the Scott Bicentenary
     Outlook by John McMurtrie, on Chiefswood (home of the Lock-
     harts) by Hugh Trevor-Roper, on the Scotts of Raeburn by
     Sir Tresham Lever, and others.

9   DAICHES, DAVID. Sir Walter Scott and His World. London:
     Thames and Hudson; New York: Viking, 143pp.
         An illustrated biography which recreates Scott's person-
     ality and the social-cultural milieu from which it developed
     and in which it flourished. He was a product of both the
     Romantic Revival and the Scottish Enlightenment who had an
     intuitive grasp of past and present but lacked a feeling
     for the future.

10   DEVLIN, D. D. The Author of Waverley: A Critical Study of
     Walter Scott. London: Macmillan; Lewisburg, Pennsylvania:
     Bucknell University Press, 142pp.
         Scott regards the novelist's main job as the celebration
     of human life. His comments on fiction emphasize character
     and a unity which does not depend on plot, and he assumes a
     basic uniformity in human nature. He adopts a middle way
     between the Enlightenment view of human nature as an eternal

constant and the opposite view of historical relativism.
Includes separate chapters on <u>Waverley</u>, <u>A Legend of Montrose</u>
and <u>Rob Roy</u>, <u>The Bride of Lammermoor</u>, and <u>Redgauntlet</u>.

11 Dubuque, Iowa. Wahlert Memorial Library of Loras College.
"Sir Walter Scott, 1771-1971: A Bicentenary Exhibition."
Dubuque: Wahlert Memorial Library, Cultural Series No. 3,
44pp.
Exhibition catalogue dividing the works into 1) the
Poems, 2) the Edited Works, 3) the Novels, and 4) Miscel-
laneous. Catalogue includes a bibliography of Scott's works
with dates of first publication.

12 Edinburgh. National Library of Scotland. "Sir Walter Scott,
1771-1971: A Bicentenary Exhibition." Edinburgh: Her
Majesty's Stationery Office, 62pp.
A Catalogue of the exhibition organized by the Court of
Session, the Faculty of Advocates, and the National Library
of Scotland, displayed in Parliament House, Edinburgh, 15
August to 11 September, 1971. Includes descriptions and
some illustrations of the paintings, manuscripts, editions,
models, and relics assembled for the bicentenary celebration. Also includes a chronology of Scott's life and a
brief reading list.

13 FRAZER, ALLAN, ed. <u>Sir Walter Scott 1771-1832: An Edinburgh</u>
<u>Keepsake</u>. Edinburgh: Edinburgh University Press, 191pp.
Contains "a selection of the speeches delivered by the
Presidents of the Edinburgh Sir Walter Scott Club at Annual
Dinners." The selections were chosen by the Edinburgh University Press. Includes reprints of 1938.B42; 1948.B7;
1951.B3; 1952.B3; 1953.B9; 1956.B9; 1958.B4; 1960.B13;
1965.B6; 1966.B4; 1969.B20; and 1971.B78.

14 HOWARTH, ROBERT GUY. "The Poetry of Sir Walter Scott." Cape
Town, South Africa: University of Cape Town, 30pp.
Scott's alterations of original ballads were not mere
tinkering but artistic re-creations. His work on the <u>Min-</u>
<u>strelsy</u> helped him to acquire "a masculine, impetuous style."
Scott's poetry is strong in action but deficient in emotion.
Although his style in the narrative poems is often careless,
he attains true greatness in the lyrics, especially those
in the elegiac mode.

15 Lisbon. Instituto Britânico em Portugal. "Exposîcão comemo-
rativa do il centenário de Walter Scott, Lisboa, 16-26 de
Fevereiro de 1971."
A catalogue for a commemorative exposition divided into
1) Portuguese translations of Scott's poetry; 2) Portuguese

1971

translations of Scott's novels; 3) Portuguese imitations
and adaptations (mostly dramatic) of Scott's works; 4) Portuguese dissertations on Scott; and 5) Portuguese critical
studies of Scott.

16   London. The British Council. "Walter Scott, 1771-1832: A
      Book Exhibit Arranged by the British Council." London:
      Westerham Press, 4pp.
         An exhibition of books by and about Scott by British
      publishers.

17   OLIVER, JANE. The Blue Heaven Bends Over All. New York:
      Putnam's; London: Collins, 384pp.
         A biography for general readers told through narrative
      and fictionalized dialogue. Includes no critical or edi-
      torial material.

18   SPINA, GIORGIO. Il romanzo storico inglese (Walter Scott).
      Genoa: Fratelli Bozzi, 149pp.
         Scott was an artist rather than an historian; he invented
      situations, characters, incidents, and costumes and often
      violated actual chronology. He regarded history as per-
      formance, involving many actors and highly dramatic moments.
      Includes three appendices, which classify the novels accord-
      ing to genre, subject matter, narrative methods, themes,
      activity or passivity of characters, contrast of cultures
      and economic systems.

*19   SROKA, KENNETH M. "Reality and Imagination in the Waverley
      Novels: The Experience of Fiction as Literary Theory."
      Ph.D. dissertation, University of Wisconsin, 1971.
         An abstract by the author appears in Dissertation Ab-
      stracts International, 32 (1972), 4025-26A.

20   THOMSON, WALTER. "Sir Walter Scott's Courtroom, Town Hall,
      Market Place, Selkirk." Selkirk: Royal Borough of Selkirk,
      3pp.
         A descriptive pamphlet for visitors. Scott was Sheriff
      of Selkirk from 1799 until his death. The present Courtroom
      contains his bench and chair. One of his judgments there
      went against James Hogg, the Ettrick Shepherd. The Court-
      room contains a portrait of Scott and a Chantrey bust.

21   TIPPKOTTER, HORST. Walter Scott: Geschichte als Unterhaltung.
      Eine Rezeptionsanalyze der Waverley Novels. Frankfurt:
      Vittorio Klostermann, 260pp.
         A study of the critical reception and subsequent reputa-
      tion of the Waverley Novels. Part I covers the criticism

during Scott's lifetime and includes excerpts from reviews
as well as statistics on sales and Scott's reading public.
Part II documents the fate of the novels from the time of
Scott's death with emphasis on critical comments regarding
the picturesque. Part III analyzes "The Picturesque in
Action" as a principle of composition, particularly in <u>Old
Mortality</u> and <u>Quentin Durward</u>.

22   WRIGHT, S. FOWLER. <u>The Life of Sir Walter Scott</u>. New York:
     Haskell House, 739pp.
         Reprint of 1932.A35.

1971 B SHORTER WRITINGS

1   ANDERSON, W. E. K. "A Saga of Courage." Edinburgh <u>Scotsman</u>
    (14 August), supplement p. 5.
         Scott's <u>Journal</u> relates a sad story of struggle, loss,
    and illness; but it is also an inspiring "saga of courage"
    and perseverance. Throughout his period of hardship, Scott
    retained his generosity and hospitality. The <u>Journal</u> also
    gives a glimpse of Scott's daily routine, modes of travel,
    and life in Edinburgh's New Town.

2   ANON. "Scott Exhibitions." <u>Times Literary Supplement</u>
    (27 August), p. 1036.
         Reviews bicentenary exhibitions in Scotland and expresses
    disappointment at their commercialism, faulty organization
    of material, lack of foreign items, and treatment of Abbots-
    ford and of the Royal Visit of 1822. Praises John Pater-
    son's Waverley Market exhibition.

3   BEATY, FREDERICK L. "Marital Love. The Idealization of
    Marriage: Coleridge and Scott," in his <u>Light From Heaven:
    Love in British Romantic Literature</u>. DeKalb: Northern
    Illinois University Press, pp. 97-106.
         Scott's narratives argue the value of emotional stability
    and love guided by rational judgment. He avoided rapturous
    love in his works because "he lacked sympathy for characters
    overwhelmed by passion." In <u>The Lady of the Lake</u> true love
    conventionally triumphs over conflicting loyalties. <u>The
    Heart of Midlothian</u> demonstrates the shortcomings of both
    polarities of rational affection and destructive passion.
    The fates of Effie and Staunton, however, reinforce Scott's
    "grave mistrust of any love unbridled by reason." In <u>The
    Bride of Lammermoor</u> sentimental love which cannot culminate
    in marriage leads to inevitable tragedy.

1971

4 BELL, A. S. "The Walter Scott Manuscripts in the National
   Library of Scotland." <u>Times Literary Supplement</u> (9 July),
   pp. 813-14.
      Describes the National Library's Scott holdings, es-
   pecially five new additions: the Ashestiel Manuscript, 120
   letters to Constable and Ballantyne, 130 letters to Cadell,
   Cadell's letters, journal, and diary, and letters between
   Constable and Ballantyne.

5 BELL, ALAN. "Scott and His Wine Merchant." <u>Blackwood's Maga-</u>
   <u>zine</u>, 310 (August), 167-75.
      Although Scott drank only moderately, the claims of hos-
   pitality required him to keep a well stocked cellar at Abbotsford. His butler William Dalgleish attests to Scott as
   a generous and considerate master. Scott's wine merchant,
   Robert Cockburn, dealt with many other distinguished cus-
   tomers, including the Duke of Buccleuch. Includes one
   folio of Scott's wine account for 1821-23 with a total bill
   of £467 5/ 6d.

6 BÉREAUD, JACQUES G. A. "La Traduction en France à l'époque
   romantique." <u>Comparative Literature Studies</u>, 8, no. 3
   (September), 224-44.
      The change in aesthetic sensibility at the beginning of
   the nineteenth century led to a change in the theory and
   practice of translation around 1830. In his 1817 translation of <u>Old Mortality</u>, Defauconpret took many liberties with
   the original text. In the 1835 translation he remained as
   faithful to the original as possible, according to the new
   Romantic theories of translations which accepted foreign
   tastes. In France Scott's English novels have been more
   successful than the Scottish novels, because Defauconpret
   did a better translating job on the novels dealing with
   English subjects, such as <u>Ivanhoe</u>.

7 BRAMLEY, J. A. "Sir Walter Scott's Journal." <u>Ariel: An In-</u>
   <u>ternational Review of English Literature</u>, 2, no. 3, 95-104.
      A summary of Scott's last years taken from the <u>Journal</u>
   and Lockhart. Scott's <u>Journal</u> reveals "his quiet and unob-
   trusive heroism" and "the natural simplicity and dignity of
   his character."

8 BREWSTER, ELIZABETH. "Two Friends: George Crabbe and Sir
   Walter Scott." <u>Queen's Quarterly</u>, 78, no. 4 (Winter),
   602-13.
      The friendship between Scott and Crabbe was rooted in
   their shared interest in narrative poetry and in tradition,
   and in their similar senses of humor. They corresponded

intermittently from 1812 to 1822 and first met during the
visit to London in 1820 when Scott received his baronetcy.
Crabbe's visit to Edinburgh in the summer of 1822 coincided
with the visit of George IV.

9   BROOKS, DOUGLAS. "Feast and Structure in The Bride of Lammer-
     moor." Ariel: An International Review of English Litera-
     ture, 2, no. 3, 66-76.
         Eating has symbolic significance in The Bride of Lammer-
     moor. Whereas Edgar is linked with ancient hospitality,
     the ostentatious entertainments of the Ashtons demonstrate
     their inadequacy as Masters of Ravenswood. The representa-
     tives of the new Scotland cannot feast in pleasure and or-
     der, and Scott alludes to interrupted banquets in "The Rime
     of the Ancient Mariner" and Macbeth to reinforce the theme
     of disordered ritual.

10   BUCHAN, DAVID D. "Nicol, Scott, and the Ballad Collectors."
     Ariel: An International Review of English Literature, 2,
     no. 3, 88-94.
         James Nicol was the source of most of the ballads in
     Scott's Abbotsford MSS. The relative harmony and coopera-
     tion among early nineteenth century ballad collectors may
     have come from their common purpose: to preserve a distinc-
     tively Scottish culture and to further the search for a
     national identity.

11   BUNIN, P. "Val'ter Skott." Komsomolskaya Pravda (15 August),
     p. 2.
         One of the best writers of his time, Scott was imitated
     in France, Russia, and America. He has been admired for
     simplicity of style, sincerity, and realism. Although he
     loved his own country deeply, Scott never insulted other
     nations.

12   BURT, DAVID. "The Heart of Midlothian: Madge Wildfire's Ra-
     tional Irrationality." Studies in Scottish Literature, 8,
     no. 3 (January), 184-89.
         Scott uses Madge's wild ravings to comment upon the re-
     ality perceived by the sane characters, to contrast charac-
     ters or to establish parallels in their situations, to
     anticipate subsequent events, and to reinforce patterns of
     theme and imagery. Madge occasionally manifests a "twilight
     sort of rationality" which contributes substantially to the
     novel's structure and themes.

13   CLINE, C. L. "The Fate of Cassandra: The Newspaper War of
     1821-22." Texas Quarterly, 14, no. 4 (Winter), 6-60.

1971

Because of his Tory partisanship, "the weak link in the
armor of his character," Scott became involved in the political conflicts of opposing Edinburgh newspapers. These
conflicts eventually led to a duel in 1822 in which Alexander Boswell was killed by James Stewart. See 1949.B1.

14   COLVIN, CHRISTINA EDGEWORTH. "Maria Edgeworth's Tours in Ireland. II. Killarney." Studia Neophilologica, 43, no. 1,
252-56.
Prints a letter of 19 August, 1825 from Maria Edgeworth
to Joanna Baillie describing a visit to Killarney in the
company of Scott and his family. They were in Ireland
visiting Scott's elder son, who was stationed there with
his regiment. Edgeworth includes much praise for Scott's
charm, kindness, and retentive memory.

15   CRAWFORD, THOMAS. "Scott as a Poet." Études Anglaises, 34,
no. 4 (October-December), 478-91.
Scott was indebted to both folk narrative and the tradition of spontaneity and free variation. The narrative
structure of the longer poems incorporates these elements,
and their true originality lies in the interplay of narrative with sight, sound, and verse. The novels, especially
The Bride of Lammermoor, also fuse sight, sound, description, and dialogue in a new way. In prose Scott can attain
wider symbolic effects than in the octo-syllabic lines of
the narrative poems.

16   CURRY, KENNETH. "Sir Walter Scott--Sources." Notes and
Queries, 216 (November), 422.
Requests identification of four quotations used by Scott
about 1810.

17   DAICHES, DAVID. "Sir Walter Scott and History." Études Anglaises, 24, no. 4 (October-December), 458-77.
Scott drew his inspiration from both nostalgic and progressive movements in Scottish political and cultural life;
he modified Enlightenment insights with traditionalist sym-
pathies. His novels focused on how history influenced the
lives and feelings of ordinary people. He avoided "historical villains" who were bad because they supported a particular side in a conflict, and he admired mediating figures
who connected past and present. His "double vision" of
glorious heroism and unheroic prosperity is clearest in
Redgauntlet.

18   DEL LITTO, V. "Stendhal et Walter Scott." Études Anglaises,
24, no. 4 (October-December), 501-508.

In his attack on Scott in "Walter Scott et La Princesse de Clèves" Stendhal attempted to separate himself from Scott's imitators and to establish his own theories of fiction. Scott caused Stendhal to reflect on the novel as a genre and to realize that novels need not be purely fictive.

19   EASTON, CHARLES C. "Sir Walter Scott--A Bi-Centenary Assessment." Burns Chronicle and Club Directory, 3rd ser. 20, 48-71.
      Scott's career exhibited a mixture of tragedy and success. Like Burns, he "was unfortunate in some of his biographers." In his legal profession, his love life, his descendants, and his financial affairs, Scott experienced a "quivering balance" of success and sorrow.

20   FERGUSSON, JAMES. "The Black Dwarf: A Peebleshire Legend." Scottish Studies, 15, 146-49.
      Scott met David Ritchie, the original of the Black Dwarf, in 1797. After the novel was published in 1816, the legend was extended by William Chambers and by Robert Chambers in his Illustrations of the Author of Waverley (1822). Later accounts include those by Dr. John Browne in 1864 and by Professor John Veitch in an essay, "The Vale of Manor and the Black Dwarf."

21   FLEISHMAN, AVROM. "Scott," in his The English Historical Novel: Walter Scott to Virginia Woolf. Baltimore and London: Johns Hopkins University Press, pp. 37-101.
      Scott's view of the world emerges from the principles of historical evolution developed by the Scottish speculative philosophers. His vision emphasizes growth, development, and progress, and is "guardedly optimistic" that the present can recall the virtues of the past to meet the new social order. The Waverley Novels chronicle the growth and decline of Western European aristocracy. The superiority of the Scottish novels rests in their greater sociological specificity. They demonstrate "the gradual emergence of a natural aristocracy in the life of modern Scotland." Includes a lengthy study of The Heart of Midlothian.

22   FOGLE, RICHARD H. "Hawthorne and Coleridge on Credibility." Criticism, 13, no. 3 (Summer), 234-41.
      Deals with Scott peripherally. Coleridge praised the psychological validity of the supernatural and superstitious in Waverley as a reflection of the realm of the mind between known and unknown. This parallels Coleridge's account in Biographia Literaria of his own share in the Lyrical Ballads.

1971

23 FRASER, GEORGE S. "Scott: Ballad Novelist?" <u>Ariel: An In-</u>
   <u>ternational Review of English Literature</u>, 2, no. 3, 77-87.
       Refutes Leavis' criticisms of Scott in <u>The Great Tradi-</u>
   <u>tion</u>. Scott used a prose-style suited to the storyteller.
   His leisurely openings and footnotes root the plot in tradition and in social and historical reality. The ballad
   elements in Scott's novels (use of token characters and
   functional use of scenery and objects) succeed because they
   are embedded in a realistic context and "have the truth of
   tribal memory."

24 GARDINER, LESLIE. "The Reluctant Traveller." Edinburgh
   <u>Scotsman</u> (14 August), supplement p. 9.
       Scenes abroad stirred Scott's interest only to the extent
   that they evoked memories of Scotland.

25 GIBAULT, HENRI. "Renouveau des Études sur Scott." <u>Études</u>
   <u>Anglaises</u>, 24, no. 4 (October-December), 509-17.
       A survey of recent Scott criticism, especially since the
   Bicentenary Conference. Lukács and Daiches deserve much of
   the credit for renewed interest in Scott. Includes a short
   bibliography of principal works on Scott published or reprinted since 1951.

*26 GICZKOWSKI, WILLIAM. "Cooper and Hawthorne: American Innova-
   tors in the Tradition of Sir Walter Scott." Ph.D. dissertation, Stanford University, 1971.
       An abstract by the author appears in <u>Dissertation Ab-</u>
   <u>stracts International</u>, 32 (1972), 5737A.

27 GORDON, CATHERINE. "The Illustrations of Sir Walter Scott:
   Nineteenth Century Enthusiasm and Adaptation." <u>Journal of</u>
   <u>the Warburg and Courtauld Institutes</u>, 34, 297-317.
       Scott's popularity inspired hundreds of artists. From
   1830 to 1850, Scott remained a consistent inspiration for
   painters of serious subjects. However, the pre-Raphaelites
   generally ignored him, and after 1870 the number of paintings of Scott subjects began to dwindle.

28 GRABAR, TERRY H. "The English Dialogue of <u>Waverley</u>." <u>Journal</u>
   <u>of Narrative Technique</u>, 1, 30-42.
       In <u>Waverley</u>, as in the other Scotch novels, Scott's Eng-
   lish dialogue at its best is as effective as the Scots dialogue in differentiating and enlivening the characters.
   Waverley's own speech moderates from the inflated diction
   of a romantic youth to "a relatively plain and serviceable
   prose." Scott's spelling and minimization of inflectional
   and syntactical differences sometimes make it difficult to

determine if a character speaks Scottish--accented English, modified Scots, or broad Scots.

29   GUSEINOV, GASAN. "Na Rodine Velikogo Romantika" [In the Native Land of the Great Romantic]. Literaturnaia Azerbaidzhan (Baku), 8, 133-34.
      A visit to Abbotsford invokes the spirit of Scott and reminds one of scenes from his novels. Books such as Rob Roy and A Legend of Montrose may serve as tourist guides to the traveler in Scotland.

30   HART, FRANCIS R. "The Making of the Life of Scott," in his Lockhart as Romantic Biographer. Edinburgh: Edinburgh University Press, pp. 163-252.
      The informing ideals of Lockhart's biographical theory and practice include an ambivalence toward the value of imaginative vision, an epistemology based on the sympathetic imagination, a sense of organic narrative form, and a deep admiration for Wordsworth and Coleridge. By applying the manipulative freedom of fiction to factual material, he resolved the central paradox between the biographer's roles as objective compiler and sympathetic personality. His Life of Scott combines intense sympathy with objective judgment, but the elegiac tone dominates the judicial. "Lockhart allowed his fidelity to govern his detachment."

31   HOLCOMB, ADELE M. "Turner and Scott." Journal of the Warburg and Courtauld Institutes, 34, 386-97.
      Scott regarded the illustration of his work as a concession to popular taste, and he disliked Turner as personally uncouth. However, they shared "an adherence to the Romantic mystique of place," and their collaboration enhanced the "brief supremacy" of real landscape illustration over the more traditional idealized conceptions, such as those of Delacroix.

32   IMBERT, HENRI-FRANÇOIS. "Conjectures sur l'origine scottiene du titre de Rouge et Noire." Revue de Littérature Comparée, 45, no. 3 (July-September), 305-22.
      In the first chapter of Waverley Scott contrasts the heraldic colors of "gueles" and "sable" to explain historical changes in modes of conflict. This may have been the source of Stendhal's title. The heroes of both novels must choose between two colors which represent their destiny. Scott's first chapter deals with other subjects of interest to Stendhal: the choice of a title, the problem of narrative distance, and the embodiment of the lessons of history in fictional form. However, where Scott veiled history in

1971

a romantic mist, Stendhal sought a more direct critique of contemporary society.

33 JACOBSON, SIBYL. "The Narrative Framing of History: A Discussion of Old Mortality." Journal of Narrative Technique, 1, 179-92.
The frame of Old Mortality raises themes relevant to the entire work--the transformation of fact into artifact, the preserving power of memory, and various attitudes toward death. While the narrative frame distances the reader, the details of the action give the novel immediacy. This double perspective emphasizes the simultaneous development of Morton's consciousness and the limitations imposed on it by the world. He must achieve a balance between private and public demands while maintaining the law of humanity.

34 LAS VERGNAS, RAYMOND. "Pour le bi-centenaire de sa naissance: une gloire europienne, Walter Scott." Les Annales Conferencia, 249 (July), 3-18.
As the most prestigious writer of the nineteenth century, Scott left an intellectual testament in a new freedom to depart from the imperatives of classicism and to place confidence in particular truths.

35 LEGOUIS, ÉMILE. "La Fortune littéraire de Walter Scott en France." Études Anglaises, 24, no. 4 (October-December), 492-500.
Reprint of 1933.B19.

36 LEVER, TRESHAM. "Sir Walter Scott and the Murder of Porteous." Blackwood's Magazine, 310 (August), 212-24.
Captain Porteous was innocent of murder, and he was used unjustly by the city fathers of Edinburgh. Scott sacrificed historical accuracy for dramatic effect in telling Porteous' story in The Heart of Midlothian, a justifiable artistic liberty, but now Porteous' reputation should be restored.

37 LOCHHEAD, MARION. "Abbotsford--A Dear Green Place." Edinburgh Scotsman (14 August), supplement p. 6.
Scott was deeply concerned with the planting around Abbotsford and "spent as much care on his plantations as would have been full-time work for most men." He loved trees for the sake of both present and future generations.

*38 LOTT, NELDA J. "The Tragedies of Scott, Lamb, and Coleridge: Their Elizabethan Heritage." Ph.D. dissertation, University of Southern Mississippi, 1971.
An abstract by the author appears in Dissertation Abstracts International, 32 (1972), 5189A.

39 LOW, DONALD A. "Scott on Burns." <u>Burns Chronicle and Club</u>
    <u>Directory</u>, 3rd ser. 20, 14-20.
        Scott's assessment of Burns was colored by his own so-
    cial and literary assumptions. He regarded Burns as in-
    spired but lacking self-discipline. While his literary
    instinct admired Burns's poetry, his social and moral con-
    science condemned him for self-indulgence and lack of honor.
    Scott's middle-class Tory prejudices stood in the way of an
    objective appraisal of both Burns and Byron.

40 _____. "Scott's Lost Love." <u>Scots Magazine</u>, N.S. 95, no. 5,
    442-50.
        Although Scott acknowledged the social and economic
    barriers between him and Williamina Belsches, he probably
    cultivated romantic fantasies of overcoming them. The
    character of Matilda in <u>Rokeby</u> reflects some of Scott's
    bitterness about losing her to William Forbes, the success-
    ful suitor whom Lady Jane Belsches actively encouraged.
    Scott's love for Williamina may have been the source of
    much of his ambition and of his decision to publish the
    Waverley Novels anonymously.

41 _____. "Walter Scott and Williamina Belsches." <u>Times Literary</u>
    <u>Supplement</u> (23 July), pp. 865-66.
        Scott never recovered from the shock of losing Williamina
    Belsches to a rival suitor. Includes previously unpublished
    letters and Williamina's poetry notebook.

42 McNEIL, NORMAN L. "Origins of 'Sir Patrick Spens,'" in <u>Hunters</u>
    <u>and Healers: Folklore Types and Topics</u>. Edited by Wilson
    M. Hudson. Publications of the Texas Folklore Society,
    No. 35. Austin: The Encino Press, pp. 65-72.
        Scott suggested that the ballad "Sir Patrick Spens" was
    based on a thirteenth century quarrel between Scotland and
    Norway over Margaret, the granddaughter of Alexander III,
    known as the "Maid of Norway." She was both a princess of
    Norway and heir to the Scottish throne.

43 MacQUEEN, JOHN. "Scott and His Scottish Contemporaries."
    Edinburgh <u>Scotsman</u> (14 August), supplement p. 3.
        Scott lacked sympathy with the Calvinist spirit, and he
    was not interested in the industrial revolution, North
    America, or India. These sympathies and subjects were
    covered by his contemporaries, James Hogg in <u>Private Mem-</u>
    <u>oirs and Confessions of a Justified Sinner</u>, and John Galt
    in <u>The Entail</u>.

1971

44 _____. "Scott and Tales of My Landlord." Scottish Studies,
15, 85-97.
Scott as improving landlord and modern agriculturalist
found much of importance in his voyage round Scotland in
1814. The dedication of the first series of Tales of My
Landlord shows the importance of this voyage. Scott's concern with the continuity of past and present extended to
the land itself, but despite his faith in progress, he
could not "embrace every feature of the new world."

45 MAXWELL, IAN R. "Abbotsford: The Way Back?" Educational
Magazine, 28 (August), 300-302.
Abbotsford stands as an appropriate symbol for Scott's
"richness of spirit" as well as his questionable "taste for
sham Gothic." He introduced the historical spirit into fiction by showing people rooted in time and place, and he
wrote most effectively of public life rather than of "the
privacy of passion."

46 MAKHAL'SKAYA, N. "Val'ter Skott. K 200-leityu so dnya rozh-
deniya pisatelya" [Walter Scott. On the 200th Anniversary
of the Writer's Birth]. Literatura v shkole, 4, 88-92.
Scott brought socio-historical analysis to European literature and combined it with the writer's ability to create
a colorful and unique world. He demonstrated the historical
collisions of social forces and the dependence of the individual upon historical events. As a Tory he feared revolutions and democracy, but in his best novels he is on the
side of the people.

47 MILLER, KARL. "King Walter." Listener, 85 (15 April), 486-88.
Edgar Johnson's biography of Scott is faulty on Scots
history and dialect and leaves out too many important anecdotes. It fails to give an accurate account of the many
contradictions inherent between Scott's politics and his
"sweet democratic fictions."

48 MUNBY, A. N. L., ed. Poets and Men of Letters. Sale Catalogues of Libraries of Eminent Persons, Volume I. London:
Mansell with Sotheby Park-Bernet Publications, 85-97.
Reproduces the catalogue of the sale of Scott's manuscripts in August, 1831. The lot also included a collection
of autograph letters. The auction proceeds did not go to
Scott but to the creditors of Constable & Co.

49 NIKOLYUKIN, A. "Val'ter Skott v Rossii" [Walter Scott in
Russia]. Moskovskii Komsomolets (15 August), p. 7.

Marx reread Scott's novels several times, and Pushkin admired Scott's use of Shakespearean traditions and of historical realism. Gogol called him "a great genius," and in A Hero of Our Time Lermontov has one of the main characters read a Scott novel before participating in a duel. Scott's works have been translated by famous Russian writers; a new complete 20-volume edition was recently published in Russia.

50 NYE, ROBERT. "Some Preliminary Observations Concerning Sir Walter Scott." Edinburgh Scotsman (14 August), supplement p. 1.
Although Scott's inventiveness was vigorous, he had "a tendency to the verbose, the affected, or the obscure." The structure of his novels suggests a "creative ambiguousness" between the subject of conflict and the kindly style. His genius is embodied in the Scottishness of his visual imagination and of his language and in the "peculiar companionable insight" he brings to this indigenously Scottish material.

51 ORLOV, S. A. "Russkie druz'ya Val'tera Skotta" [Walter Scott's Russian Friends]. Moscow Literaturnaia Gazeta (11 August), p. 14.
Scott's Life of Napoleon shows his admiration for the courage of the Russian people during the 1812 war. He was acquainted with the Kosack hero Matvey Platov, and he admired the Russian hero and poet, Denis Davydov, with whom he corresponded. English critics who stress Scott's Toryism have concealed his interest in Russia.

52 PARKER, WILLIAM MATHIE. "An Edinburgh Man. A Journey Round the Capital in the Steps of Sir Walter." Scots Magazine, N.S. 95, no. 3 (June), 234-41.
A survey of Scott's Edinburgh and the places in the city where he lived and worked.

53 PARSONS, COLEMAN OSCAR. "Foreword" to The Two Drovers: A Short Story. Westwood, New Jersey: The Kindle Press, pp. i-x.
Scott uses a combination of historical, fictional, and legendary sources in "The Two Drovers." To heighten the narrative, he includes Scottish folklore and superstition and his own "tragic consciousness of man's lot on earth," which was developed by the bankruptcy and the death of his wife.

54 PEASTON, MONROE. "The Liberals and the Enthusiasts: Sir Walter Scott's Old Mortality Reconsidered." Religion in Life, 40, 547-56.

1971

>   In Old Mortality Scott questions the fate of the liberal
> man in a time of religious enthusiasm. Balfour demonstrates
> the link between religious enthusiasm and violence, while
> Kettledrummle, Macbriar, and Mucklewrath reveal the pre-
> tentious, single-minded, and insane versions of Covenanter
> fanatics. Morton's story seems to indicate that there is
> no place for the liberal observer in a world of extreme
> conflicts; he cannot help being drawn into them, and he is
> usually unable to effect any immediate change.

55   PETROV, RUMEN. "Pred 200-godisninata ot rozdenieto ne Voltar
>   Skot" [Walter Scott's 200th Anniversary]. Bibliotekar:
> Durzhavna Biblioteka Vasil Kolarov, 18, no. 6, 39-40.
>   Russian writers such as Pushkin and Lermontov admired
> Scott, and he was one of the favorite authors of Marx. As
> a true realist, Scott depicted the struggle for Scottish
> independence. Despite his own conservative views, he gave
> an accurate account of British historical forces. Scott
> was first mentioned in the Bulgarian press in 1875, and
> his novels have been translated into Bulgarian since the
> end of the nineteenth century.

56   PIKOULIS, JOHN. "Scott and Marmion: The Discovery of Iden-
>   tity." Modern Language Review, 66, no. 4 (October), 738-50.
>   The Introductions in Marmion give the poem a double fo-
> cus--on Marmion and on Scott as his "diminished heir." They
> draw parallels between the themes of the poem--guilt, the
> occult, war, and national identity--and the emotional pres-
> ence of the poet. The narrative illuminates and deepens
> the poetic autobiography in the epistles, and this link
> provides a "close correlation between the parts of the poem
> and the interpenetrating realities which vivify it."

57   POYNTON, ORDE. "Observations on the First Edition of Waverley."
>   Private Library, 4, no. 2 (Summer), 85-92.
>   Supports Pope-Hennessey's contention that Waverley was
> half finished when James Ballantyne saw it in 1810. Scott
> wrote the second half in 26 days, and consequently it con-
> tained far more misreadings and printing errors. Offers
> several additions to the defects listed in Greville Worth-
> ington's Bibliography of the Waverley Novels (London: 1931).
> See 1933.B1 and 1948.A1.

58   RAPPAPORT, S. "Sir Walter Scott Bicentenary: Isaac of York
>   and Rebecca." Jewish Affairs (26 September), pp. 41-45.
>   In Ivanhoe Scott fought against anti-Jewish prejudice
> through his favorable characterization of Rebecca and his
> understanding attitude toward Isaac. He sympathizes with

Isaac as a victim and admires his feelings of resistance. Scott makes Rebecca into "an ideal figure of true Jewish womanhood" and a "paragon of virtue." He uses these two characters as touchstones by which the Normans and Saxons may be judged. Ironically, they represent the Christian values of love and sacrifice, which are absent from the chivalric code.

59 REBOLO, LUÍS DE SOUSA. "No centenário de Sir Walter Scott." Colóquio, 3, 70-73.
      Edgar Johnson's biography of Scott presents a rich and complex personality. Scott inherited the rationalism of the previous generation, and he understood the importance of industrialism. But he sought a decorative, heraldic refuge from his fear that traditions and old cultural values might be lost.

60 REIZOV, B. "Istorija i vymysel v romanax Val'tera Skotta" [History and Fiction in the Novels of Walter Scott]. Izvestiya Akademii nauk S.S.R. Seriya literatury i yazyka, 30, 306-11.
      Scott created a new form of literature by dissolving the barrier between history and literature. His novels depend on the relativity of truth, which allows the reader to sympathize with characters holding divergent views. He believed that moral awareness and certain ruling passions remain as constants in human nature. In the course of historical progress, these will merge class limitations in the common interests of society. This dream of a future unity without conflict pervades all Scott's work. Translated: 1974.B20.

61 ROGOV, V. "Val'ter Skott." Detskaya Literatura, 8, 44-46.
      Although he is often regarded as a writer for children, Scott was actually a complicated and contradictory artist. Even in the novels devoted to Scotland's struggle for freedom, he stood for compromise, peace, and political tolerance. Although he feared rebellion, he believed the people create history. Scott was the first writer to accept this premise.

62 RUBENSTEIN, JILL. "The Defeat and Triumph of Bourgeois Pacifism: Scott's Fair Maid of Perth and The Fortunes of Nigel." Wordsworth Circle, 2, no. 4 (Autumn), 136-41.
      Scott associates chivalry with violence and middle-class values with civil peace, and pacifism becomes a moral value which flourishes best in a bourgeois milieu. Through an act of imagination, a character may reject some or all of

the prevailing cultural standards of his time. In <u>The Fair
Maid</u> none of the characters achieves this imaginative re-
finement of consciousness. However, in his renunciation of
violence and his acceptance of burgher standards, Nigel
attains a moral and imaginative victory.

63   <u>   </u>. "Symbolic Characterization in <u>The Lady of the Lake</u>."
<u>Dalhousie Review</u>, 51, no. 3 (Autumn), 366-73.
    In <u>The Lady of the Lake</u> Scott uses the characters to
represent various historical forces coming into conflict,
which anticipates his technique in the Waverley Novels.
Roderick Dhu embodies both the vitality and the destructive
anarchy of the old order. King James represents law, order,
and a sophisticated civilization, and the hunting motif
associated with him suggests his moral development through
the poem.

64 RUSS, JON R. "A Possible Source for the Death Scene in Arnold's Tristram and Iseult." <u>Victorian Poetry</u>, 9, no. 3
(Autumn), 336-38.
    Arnold may have been familiar with Scott's "Thomas the
Rhymer" and used Scott's version of the death of Tristram
and Iseult in Part III as the framework for his own poem's
climax.

65 SARIEVA, LYUBA. "Background and Character in Scott: <u>Quentin
Durward</u>." <u>Godisnik na sofijskiya universitet. Fakultet po
zapadni filologii</u>, 64, no. 1, 293-335.
    Scott unifies historical background, characterization,
and narration into an expression of moral values. He pro-
jects the qualities of the characters onto the physical
setting and uses historical details to account for personality traits. Scott's own values emerge through direct commentary and literary allusions, which link the novel with
the humane ideals of his own time.

66 S.[COTT], R. E. "Unknown Portrait of Sir Walter Scott."
<u>Transactions of the Hawick Archaeological Society</u>, Session
1971, 20-21.
    Describes a lithograph portrait of Scott, located in
Hawick Museum, presumably by Elliot Aitchison, a stocking-
maker by trade and an amateur artist. According to Corson,
the lithograph was printed in the 1820's. No other copies
are known to exist.

67 SICILIANO, ENZO. "Non scherzare su Robin Hood" [Do Not Jest
With Robin Hood]. <u>La Stampa</u> (22 September), p. 3.

Scott is too often perceived as a writer for young
people. In the Waverley Novels he described the tragedy of
Scotland. He showed the value of physical courage in the
medieval period giving way to intellectual and bourgeois
values. Scott analyzed the past from the critical position
of the present, and his detached irony reveals his favorable
attitude toward bourgeois reality.

68   SIMMONS, JAMES C. "The Novelist as Historian: An Unexplored
      Tract of Victorian Historiography." Victorian Studies, 14,
      no. 3 (March), 293-305.
          In the 1830's and 1840's reviewers attacked Scott's lack
      of intellectual substance and historical inaccuracies.
      These charges led to a change in the form of historical fic-
      tion. Writers such as Bulwer Lytton, Harriet Martineau,
      Edward George Howard, and Charles Macfarlane avoided charges
      of frivolity by concentrating upon factual rather than
      imaginative material. They attempted to instruct their
      readers through accuracy and scholarship, and in so doing,
      they broadened the range of romantic historiography. Re-
      printed: 1973.B48.

69   SIMPSON, JOHN M. "The Father of Nationalism." Edinburgh
      Scotsman (14 August), supplement p. 2.
          Scott's works provide an artistic justification for
      Scottish nationalism and express the hope "that what makes
      Scotland Scotland need not be lost." The whole range of
      his characters, both rich and poor, heroic and unheroic,
      conveys what Scott saw as "the essence of things Scots."

70   SKINNER, BASIL C. "Monuments to Scott." Edinburgh Scotsman
      (14 August), supplement p. 6.
          Reviews the Scott exhibitions and other events for the
      bicentenary. The various images of Scott include publicizer
      of Scotland, recorder of historical tradition, writer of
      high literary stature, and important figure in the romantic
      and nationalist movements.

71   SMITH, JANET ADAM. "Redgauntlet: The Man of Law's Tale."
      Times Literary Supplement (23 July), pp. 863-64.
          Redgauntlet is "permeated by ideas of law." The charac-
      ters and plot reflect Scott's concern with the law's nature
      and its limitations. The novel considers law in its facets
      as a Scottish institution, a profession, a philosophy, and
      as the preservation of civil order.

72   SPEAIGHT, ROBERT. "The Journal of Sir Walter Scott." Contem-
      porary Review, 219 (October), 205-10.

1971

   Scott's <u>Journal</u> gains poignancy from the accident that
he started it just before the bankruptcy and the death of
his wife. It shows Scott as a man who found zest in every-
day things, but it does not explain why Scott kept his
partnership with Ballantyne a secret.

73 ____. "Scott and the Biographers." <u>Ariel: An International</u>
   <u>Review of English Literature</u>, 2, no. 3, 16-26.
   Lockhart concentrates on Scott the man, his values and
his human relationships. Edgar Johnson's biography makes
up for this deficiency and chronicles Scott's artistic
growth. He treats Scott seriously as a writer and frees
himself from the clichés of traditional Scott criticism.

74 SROKA, KENNETH M. "Fact, Fiction, and the Introduction to the
   Waverley Novels." <u>Wordsworth Circle</u>, 2, no. 4 (Autumn),
   142-52.
   Scott's introductions attempt to assert a balance between
the real world and the world of imagination, a balance
necessary for both individuals and societies. Scott argues
in these introductions that fiction provides pleasure by
allowing the reader to expand his limited experiences and
to indulge his repressed primitive instincts.

75 STEWART, ALASDAIR M. "Sir Walter Scott and Sir James Skene of
   Rubislaw." <u>Aberdeen University Review</u>, 44, no. 1 (Spring),
   68-71.
   Skene loaned Scott some German books in 1794, and their
friendship lasted until Scott's death. It was especially
comforting to Scott in the years after the bankruptcy. At
the age of ninety, shortly before his death, Skene experi-
enced a psychic phenomenon in which Scott appeared to him
and they "had a quiet talk."

76 SUTHERLAND, ROB. "The 'Shirra' and the Wordsworths at Melrose."
   Edinburgh <u>Scotsman</u> (14 August), supplement p. 4.
   When William and Dorothy Wordsworth visited Scott in
1803, he took them on a tour of Melrose Abbey, which had
become a tourist attraction after the publication of <u>The</u>
<u>Lay of the Last Minstrel</u>. In 1822 Scott persuaded Lord
Montague to repair the Abbey, which was in danger of col-
lapse. Scott himself supervised the work, and his last
visit took place just before he left for Italy, when he
accompanied Robert Burns's son to Melrose.

77 THOMPSON, PAUL V. "Suppressed Names in Swift's Letters, 1735."
   <u>Notes and Queries</u>, 216 (February), 52-55.

In Scott's first edition of Swift's Works (1814) he included in his "Corrigenda et Addenda" certain names omitted in Deane Swift's 1768 edition of twelve letters between Jonathan Swift and his cousin, Mrs. Martha Whiteway, written in 1735.

78 TREVOR-ROPER, HUGH. "Address to the Sixty-third Annual Dinner of the Edinburgh Sir Walter Scott Club." The Edinburgh Sir Walter Scott Club Annual Report.
Scott was a man of his time who found "romantic charm" in what the previous generation regarded as "the relics of barbarism." His mind combined Augustan rationalism, British patriotism, and love for the traditional life of Scotland. He created "a new literary form and a new historical philosophy," and he provided Scotland with a new identity which reconciled the antipathy between Saxon and Celt. Reprinted: 1971.A13.

79 _____. "Sir Walter Scott and History." Listener, 86 (19 August), 225-32.
Scott's best novels (from 1814 to 1819) changed the study of history. He could "see the past on its own terms" and sympathize with it without indulging in mere nostalgia. He believed that history must be judged in a context composed of the totality of its culture, and this attitude markedly influenced the historical writing of Carlyle, Ranke, and Macaulay.

*80 VERES, GRIGORE. "Un scriitor popular: Walter Scott." Cronica, 6 (August), 9.
Cited in the Annual Bibliography of English Language and Literature (London: Modern Humanities Research Association, 1973), XLVI, 484, item #8495.

81 VERNON, J. JOHN. "Walter Scott, Defending Counsel, Hawick Horse-Dealer on Trial." Transactions of the Hawick Archaeological Society, Session 1971, 17-19.
Describes a trial held before the High Court of Justiciary in July, 1800 in which Scott successfully defended one George Elliott, horse-dealer in Hawick, charged with dealing in forged banknotes.

82 WAGENKNECHT, EDWARD. "In Praise of Sir Walter." Studies in the Novel, 3, no. 1 (Spring), 103-107.
Scott's "provincialism," rather than his politics and his "complete decency," are responsible for his decline in popularity. The present generation dislikes dialect, disdains history, and is exhausted by "Scott's eighteenth

1971

century ponderousness." Partially a review of 1969.A3 and 1970.A5.

83 WAITE, VIRGINIA. "With Scott in the Land of Brigadoon." Saturday Review, 54 (13 March), 37-39 and 102.
    Scott's "picture in words of the country he loved" may still be recognized in the Border Country. Visiting places in the area associated with him recaptures his multi-faceted life as laird, lawyer, financier, collector, and novelist.

84 WARD, WILLIAM S. "Contemporary Reviews of the Major Poems of Sir Walter Scott: A Supplementary List for the Years 1805-17." Bulletin of Bibliography, 28, no. 3 (July-September), 81-83.
    Supplements the annotated list of contemporary reviews in Corson, 1943.A1.

85 WEINSTEIN, MARK A. "Imagination and Reality in Romantic Fiction." Wordsworth Circle, 2, no. 4 (Autumn), 126-35.
    Both Austen and Scott use the term "imagination" pejoratively in opposition to "understanding." They assume the existence of an objective reality which may be discovered through experience by the protagonist. Scott's characters succeed when they attain a realistic understanding of their own perpetually changing societies. They fail when they "project imaginative visions onto contemporary reality."

86 WOOD, G. A. M. "The Great Reviser; or the Unknown Scott." Ariel: A Review of International English Literature, 2, no. 3, 27-44.
    A collation of the available texts of the Letters of Malachi Malagrowther on the Currency indicates that Scott revised copiously and added considerably to his proof-sheets. The revisions show "Scott the novelist" improving the work of "Scott the writer of economic tracts." The textual history of Redgauntlet also reveals a series of changes between manuscript and printed volume. Scott read proof from memory in a creative process of embellishing his original thoughts. Partially reprinted: 1973.B53.

87 _____. "Sir Walter Scott and Sir Ralph Sadler: A Chapter in Literary History, Part IV." Studies in Scottish Literature, 8, no. 4 (April), 253-64.
    Publication of the Sadler Papers was delayed by Scott's slowness, printing problems, and a missing copy sheet. The "cavalier treatment" of the manuscripts reflects the careless editorial procedures of this period and the fact that no one accepted final responsibility for the quality of the

editorial work. Reviewers condemned the inaccuracies and omissions in the text. <u>See</u> Part I, 1969.B43 and Parts II and III, 1970.B24, B25.

88 WOOD, HARRIET HARVEY. "Scott and Jamieson: The Relationship Between Two Ballad Collectors." <u>Studies in Scottish Literature</u>, 9, nos. 2 and 3 (October-January), 71-96.
    During their long friendship, Scott did Jamieson many favors, particularly in regard to Jamieson's search for a suitable position. They quarreled after Jamieson failed to be appointed as Keeper of the Advocates' Library, a post for which Scott had recommended him.

89 WRIGHT, AUSTIN. "Minstrel of the Scottish Border: Sir Walter Scott--Two Centuries Later." <u>Carnegie Magazine</u>, 45, 238-40.
    Scott's career was "one of the most amazing success stories in literary history." In spite of the obvious flaws in his novels--inaccuracies, superficial heroes and heroines, contrived plots, padding--Scott managed to convey the liveliness and charm of the past and the romance of Scotland. His comic figures, like Chaucer's, represent "God's plenty."

1972 A BOOKS

1 ANDERSON, W. E. K., ed. <u>The Journal of Sir Walter Scott</u>. Oxford: Clarendon Press, 858pp.
   This definitive edition includes a Preface explaining editorial principles, a long critical introduction, a tabular condensation of the events covered by the <u>Journal</u> with the parallel progress of Scott's works, extensive notes, appendices, maps of Edinburgh and the Abbotsford area, and a detailed index. The editor has attempted to provide an accurate version of the manuscript plus notes "which in effect expand the work into a day-by-day biography of Scott's final years."

*2 DYER, CALVIN R. "Setting and the Search for Justice in Four Waverley Novels of Sir Walter Scott." Ph.D. dissertation, Indiana University, 1972.
    An abstract by the author appears in <u>Dissertation Abstracts International</u>, 32 (1972), 6925A.

*3 GREEN, AUBREY. "Technique and Style in Selected Waverley Novels of Sir Walter Scott." Ph.D. dissertation, Texas Tech University, 1972.
    An abstract by the author appears in <u>Dissertation Abstracts International</u>, 33 (1973), 4345A.

1972

*4   JANSSEN, JUDITH M. "Scott's Use of Setting as a Narrative De-
      vice in the Waverley Novels." Ph.D. dissertation, Univer-
      sity of Kentucky, 1972.
          An abstract by the author appears in <u>Dissertation Ab-
      stracts International</u>, 33 (1973), 5127A.

*5   LACKEY, LIONEL C. "Plausibility in the Romantic Plot Construc-
      tion of Scott's Novels." Ph.D. dissertation, University of
      South Carolina, 1972.
          An abstract by the author appears in <u>Dissertation Ab-
      stracts International</u>, 33 (1972), 2332-33A.

*6   MASSMAN, KLAUS. <u>Die Rezeption der historischen Romane Sir
      Walter Scotts in Frankreich (1816-1832)</u>. <u>Studia Romanica</u>,
      24. Heidelberg: Carl Winter, 117pp.
          Cited in "The Romantic Movement: A Selective and Criti-
      cal Bibliography for 1973," <u>English Language Notes</u>, 12,
      supplement to no. 1 (September, 1974), 75.

1972 B SHORTER WRITINGS

1   AMBROSE, MARY E. "'La Donna del Lago': The First Italian
      Translations of Scott." <u>Modern Language Review</u>, 67, no. 1
      (January), 74-82.
          The large number of Italian translations of Scott's nar-
      rative poetry indicates a widespread and lasting popularity.
      The most important was a verse translation of <u>The Lady of
      the Lake</u> by Giuseppe Indelicato, which received wide and
      generally favorable critical attention.

2   ARA, PEDRO. "Walter Scott y los 'deliciosos horrores' de
      Edimburgo." Madrid <u>Los Domingos de ABC</u> (10 September),
      supplement pp. 32-39.
          Recounts a walking tour of the Old Town of Edinburgh and
      recalls the body-snatching scandals of Scott's time. The
      medical students were obliged to procure cadavers for ana-
      tomical study from murderers or thieves who dug up freshly
      buried bodies from nearby cemeteries. This took place in
      the area where Scott lived before he moved to Abbotsford.

3   BARBÉRIS, PIERRE. "De l'histoire innocente à l'histoire im-
      pure: entretien avec Pierre Barbéris." <u>Nouvelle Revue
      Francaise</u>, 238 (October), 248-64.
          Scott was successful in France because Frenchmen saw
      their own problems reflected in English history, and because
      readers were tired of psychological novels. (Deals with
      Scott only peripherally).

4 BELL, ALAN. "Scott Manuscripts and the Collector." Manuscripts, 24, no. 1 (Winter), 44-47.
   The two most important collections of Scott manuscripts
   are owned by the Pierpont Morgan Library and the National
   Library of Scotland. All his manuscripts are in a fluent,
   regular handwriting which "displays a general indifference
   to the niceties of letter-formation and punctuation."
   Scott's later letters reflect his physical deterioration.
   There are many forgeries of Scott letters by Alexander How-
   land Smith, but the forgeries are easily detectable.

5 BOSWELL, GEORGE W. "Villainy in Scott's Fiction." University
   of Mississippi Studies in English, 13, 31-42.
   Many of Scott's villains are only partially evil. When
   he tried to repeat a similar villainous character he generally failed; Lady Glenallan, for example, is an inferior
   copy of Lady Ashton. Scott shows the potential for evil
   even in good characters, and he never uses a villainous
   protagonist. Scott most scorned ambitious greed, and many
   of his villains embody public evil on the private level.

6 BRIGGS, K. M. "Folklore in Nineteenth Century English Literature." Folklore, 83, 194-209.
   Scott was "steeped in folk traditions." In the novels
   he usually explained country superstitions in rational
   terms. However, in the short stories the magic sometimes
   remains unexplained, although it does not demand the
   reader's credulity.

7 CLARK, ARTHUR MELVILLE. "Sir Walter Scott, P. R. S. E.   A
   Bicentenary Tribute to 'A Borderer Between Two Generations.'"
   Royal Society of Edinburgh Yearbook, Sessions 1969/70 and
   1970/71, pp. 1-14.
   While Scott admired the color of the past, he was at
   home with "the new civility" of the present and did not
   wish to replace it. Traces Scott's connection with the
   Royal Society of Edinburgh, particularly his term as President. At Abbotsford Scott included all the modern conveniences inside and the advances of scientific farming outside.
   His Edinburgh contemporaries regarded him as practical,
   forward-looking, and interested in scientific matters.

8 CLEMENTS, FRANCES M. "'Queens Love Revenge as Well as Their
   Subjects': Thematic Unity in The Heart of Midlothian."
   Studies in Scottish Literature, 10, no. 1 (July), 10-17.
   When viewed as a dramatization of the revenge theme, The
   Heart of Midlothian appears as a unified novel. Evil re-
   sults from a desire for vengeance, and good derives from

1972

tolerance or forgiveness. The interview between Jeanie and the Queen demonstrates how the desire for revenge must yield to reason.

9 CRAWFORD, THOMAS. "Introduction" to Selected Poems of Sir Walter Scott. Oxford Paperback English Texts. Oxford: Clarendon Press, pp. vii-xix.
   Folk poetry and ballad were the strongest influences on Scott's development. The long poems synthesize national sentiment, local description, and antiquarian detail, but they often read like narratives about to turn into novels. His major successes are the shorter occasional poems or songs, which are best when they express either robust action or elegiac sadness.

10 DEAN, DENNIS R. "Four Notes on Scott." Studies in Scottish Literature, 10, no. 1 (July), 51-53.
   Notes concern: 1) a six line variant reading for The Field of Waterloo; 2) Scott's remarks on education in a speech on 1 October, 1824; 3) a toast offered by Scott at a meeting of the Society of Scottish Antiquaries in the fall of 1824; and 4) new information on Scott's trip to Ireland in 1825.

11 FAULKNER, PETER. "A Roman Camp in a Fourth Author?" Notes and Queries, 217 (October), 381.
   The Spiritual Quixote (1773) by Richard Graves may have been the source for similar scenes in Bage's Hermsprong, Scott's Antiquary, and Peacock's Crotchet Castle in which an antiquary labels archaeological remains as Roman and is then challenged by another character. See 1966.B19.

12 FINLEY, GERALD E. "J. M. W. Turner and Sir Walter Scott: Iconography of a Tour." Journal of the Warburg and Courtauld Institutes, 35, 359-85.
   In 1831 Turner travelled to Scotland to view firsthand the scenes for a projected illustrated edition of Scott's poetry. He spent over a month sketching in the areas of Abbotsford, Loch Katrine, and the Highlands. This period is documented in Robert Cadell's Abbotsford Diary, extracts from which are included. Despite his initial reluctance and his ill health, Scott extended every courtesy to Turner.

13 GARSIDE, P. D. "Scott, the Romantic Past, and the Nineteenth Century." Review of English Studies, N.S. 23 (May), 147-61.
   Scott's view of the past grew out of the intellectual milieu of late eighteenth century Edinburgh and the thought of the "philosophical" Scottish historians. His medieval

novels repudiate the barbarity and grossness of the Middle
Ages while affirming the importance of acting within one's
historical context. Scott's conservatism was intellectually
based in his respect for the enlightened eighteenth century
ideal of degree and ordered prosperity.

14 GOODIN, GEORGE. "Walter Scott and the Tradition of the Political Novel," in The English Novel in the Nineteenth Century:
Essays on the Literary Mediation of Human Values. Illinois
Studies in Language and Literature, No. 63. Urbana and
London: University of Illinois Press, pp. 14-24.
    In his defense of Old Mortality, Scott offered a "drama-
tic principle" of plot construction, in which the reader
must gather the meaning from dialogue. This dramatic principle allows the author to represent both sides in a political controversy. It results in the uncommitted hero, who
is exposed to strongly committed minor characters. Discusses Old Mortality in terms of three patterns: the
"double-victim" plot, the "New Comedy" plot, and the "romance" plot which celebrates the ideals of a past age.

15 GUEST, ANN M. "Imagery of Color and Light in Scott's Narrative
Poems." Studies in English Literature, 12, no. 4 (Autumn),
705-20.
    Scott uses color to emphasize natural detail, to drama-
tize scenes of battle and pageantry, to establish mood, and
to provide appropriate background for the supernatural. In
characterization he uses color to convey the shadings of
good and evil and the effects of passion in both heroes and
villains. Color also helps to provide a poem's structural
unity. Scott's appreciation of painting and of natural
beauty shaped his use of color in the narrative poems.

16 HOLMAN, C. HUGH. "Nigel and the Historical Imagination," in
The Classic British Novel. Edited by Howard M. Harper, Jr.
and Charles Edge. Athens, Georgia: University of Georgia
Press, pp. 65-84.
    Setting The Fortunes of Nigel in the reign of James I
gave Scott many opportunities to contrast old and new ways,
chivalry and capitalism. Under the comic tone of the novel
lies the tragic irony of the historical moment. Nigel's
passivity emerges directly from Scott's view of shaping social forces and from his belief in the permanence of human
nature and of the moral order.

17 HOOK, ANDREW. "Introduction" to Waverley. Harmondsworth:
Penguin Books, pp. 9-27.
    Waverley established the historical novel and confirmed
the novel as the dominant literary form. It unites the

1972

elements of Romance with the novel of manners and the
Bildungsroman to present a study of the dangers of the romantic temperament. Scott advocates compromise and the
values of the Scottish Enlightenment, and the restored
Tully-Veolan symbolizes the assimilation of historical
divisions.

18 HOWELL, ELMO. "Faulkner and Scott and the Legacy of the Lost
     Cause." Georgia Review, 26, no. 3 (Fall), 314-25.
        The "idea of the Lost Cause" inspired both Faulkner and
     Scott. They were Tories who loved the romance of lost
     causes but returned to the modern world. Both wished to
     preserve what is culturally distinct in a region threatened
     by "a more powerful commercially minded neighbor." Faulk-
     ner's romantic treatment of Southern history contrasts to
     Scott's more common sense approach, and Faulkner's undis-
     ciplined mind and unsteady inspiration make his the lesser
     achievement.

19 HUGHES, G. R. "Sources Wanted." Notes and Queries, 217 (May),
     184.
        Requests the sources of two quotations from Scott which
     deal with poetry and rhyme.

20 JACK, R. D. S. "The Novel and Scott," in his The Italian In-
     fluence on Scottish Literature. Edinburgh: Edinburgh Uni-
     versity Press, pp. 213-31.
        Scott had an early interest in Italian language and lit-
     erature, and his novels make many references to Italian
     culture. He was influenced by the model of Ariosto in both
     form (flexibility combined with narrative control) and con-
     tent (the mixture of realism and romance). However, he
     tended to stereotype his Italian characters as Machiavel-
     lians. Considers the influence of Scott on Tommasso
     Grossi's Marco Visconti.

21 KIELY, ROBERT. "Waverley" in his The Romantic Novel in Eng-
     land. Cambridge, Massachusetts: Harvard University Press;
     London: Oxford University Press, pp. 136-54.
        The Waverley Novels reveal a conflict in Scott's mind
     between imaginative individualism and the demands of actu-
     ality. However, in Waverley Scott retreats from the serious
     implications of this conflict "between the irrational urges
     of a romantic sensibility and the demands of an ordered so-
     ciety." Edward Waverley escapes moral responsibility by
     regarding his romantic adventures as an unreal dream. His
     ultimate rejection of Jacobitism is analogous to Scott's
     rejection of a total dependence on the imagination.

22   LASCELLES, MARY. "Jane Austen and Walter Scott: a Minor
      Point of Comparison," in <u>Notions and Facts: Collected</u>
      <u>Criticism and Research</u>. Oxford: Clarendon Press,
      pp. 230-46.
         Scott's imagination was drawn to a system of order and
      justice outside society, whereas Austen's mind acknowledged
      only the order of the ordinary social world. Her poor and
      dependent heroines are invariably rescued by a good mar-
      riage, one of the regular and probable conditions of life.
      Scott's portionless heroines, such as Lucy Bertram in <u>Guy</u>
      <u>Mannering</u>, also resolve their problems within the complex
      framework of law and society. However, the happy ending to
      Lucy's conventional dilemma requires the intervention of
      Meg Merrilies, the representative of a "polity outside so-
      ciety," an alternative which Austen's imagination did not
      encompass.

23   _____. "Scott and Shakespeare," in <u>Notions and Facts: Collec-</u>
      <u>ted Criticism and Research</u>. Oxford: Clarendon Press,
      pp. 179-95.
         Essentially the same argument as 1961.B9 with some minor
      verbal revision.

24   _____. "Scott and the Art of Revision," in <u>Notions and Facts:</u>
      <u>Collected Criticism and Research</u>. Oxford: Clarendon Press,
      pp. 213-29.
         Essentially the same argument as 1968.B24 with some minor
      verbal revision.

25   _____. "Scott and the Sense of Time," in <u>Notions and Facts:</u>
      <u>Collected Criticism and Research</u>. Oxford: Clarendon Press,
      pp. 195-212.
         Revision of 1961.B10. Includes some additional material
      on <u>Redgauntlet</u>, but excises analysis of "Wandering Willie's
      Tale," incorporated in 1968.B24 and 1972.B24.

26   LAWS, G. MALCOLM, JR. <u>The British Literary Ballad: A Study</u>
      <u>in Poetic Imitation</u>. Carbondale: Southern Illinois Univer-
      sity Press, 192pp., passim.
         Treats Scott's "questionable" practices as an editor in
      improving various ballad texts and passing some of his own
      compositions as traditional material in the <u>Minstrelsy</u>.
      The emphasis is primarily on the evolution of the literary
      ballad as conscious imitation after Percy and Scott.

27   McCLATCHY, J. D. "The Ravages of Time: The Function of the
      <u>Marmion</u> Epistles." <u>Studies in Scottish Literature</u>, 9,
      no. 4 (April), 256-63.

1972

The introductory epistles in <u>Marmion</u> develop the relationship between time and the imagination. Their couplets
and conversational tone contrast to the ballad measure and
romantic tone of the narrative to emphasize a sense of
relativity. The poem as a whole concerns the efforts of
the imagination to redeem time, an anticipation of the
theme of the novels.

28   MACK, DOUGLAS S. "Preface" and "Introduction" to <u>Memoir of</u>
      <u>the Author's Life</u> and <u>Familiar Anecdotes of Sir Walter</u>
      <u>Scott</u> by James Hogg. Edinburgh and London: Scottish Aca-
      demic Press, pp. vi-xviii.
          Although Lockhart objected to Hogg's <u>Familiar Anecdotes</u>
      as an insult to Scott, many passages reveal Hogg's admira-
      tion and affection. His approach is frank and deeply mov-
      ing. Lockhart has characterized him unfairly as a fool and
      probably invented some of the less than flattering anecdotes
      about Hogg in his own <u>Life of Scott</u>. Includes a history of
      the text.

29   MULLENBROCK, HEINZ-JOACHIM. "Scott und der historische Roman:
      Aspekte der neueren Forschung." <u>Die Neueren Sprachen</u>, 11,
      660-69.
          <u>The Heart of Midlothian</u> illustrates how Scott integrates
      moral themes with his treatment of history. He relates the
      nature of justice in the novel to its historical particu-
      lars, and he parallels the development of Jeanie Deans with
      historical-cultural transformations. Scott demonstrates
      that the nature of our humanity directly depends on our
      spatial and temporal environment. Includes a review of
      recent Scott criticism.

30   MURDOCH, J. D. W. "Scott, Pictures, and Painters." <u>Modern</u>
      <u>Language Review</u>, 67, no. 1 (January), 31-43.
          Scott used his knowledge of the visual arts in his por-
      trayal of both landscape and emotion. He had an eye for
      the picturesque but little aesthetic judgment. He bought
      portraits for their historical interest and emotional ap-
      peal, distrusted academic connoisseurship, and was "a de-
      termined popularist in art."

*31   NELSON, CAROLYN C. "Patterns in the 'Bildungsroman' as Illus-
      trated by Six English Novels from 1814 to 1860." Ph.D.
      dissertation, University of Wisconsin, 1972.
          An abstract by the author appears in <u>Dissertation Ab-</u>
      <u>stracts International</u>, 33 (1973), 3597-98A.

32 NIELSEN, JØRGEN ERIK. "Sir Walter Scott." <u>Notes and Queries</u>,
217 (March), 108.
Lists six texts published in Danish translation under
Scott's name and requests additional information on them.

33 PARSONS, COLEMAN OSCAR. "Sir Walter Scott--Yesterday and Today." <u>Proceedings of the American Philosophical Society</u>,
116, 450-57.
Scott scholarship and criticism falls into six phases:
1) the contemporary critics and reviewers; 2) the biographical and bibliographical activity after Scott's death; 3) the
defensive tone of the 1871 Centenary; 4) the important
textual work between 1890 and 1932; 5) the 1932 Centenary
leading to the letters and new biographies; and 6) the
present revaluation of Scott as realist and historical
novelist.

*34 PHILIPPIDE, AL. "La centenarul lui Walter Scott" [At Walter
Scott's Centenary], in <u>Consideratii confortabile</u>, Volume II.
Bucharest: Editura Eminescu, pp. 88-91.
Cited in the <u>Annual Bibliography of English Language and
Literature</u> (London: Modern Humanities Research Association,
1974), LXVII, 469, item #8363.

*35 REESE, THEODORE I., III. "The Character and Role of Guenevere
in the Nineteenth Century." Ph.D. dissertation, Brandeis
University, 1972.
An abstract by the author appears in <u>Dissertation Abstracts International</u>, 33 (1973), 5138-39A.

36 RIGOTTI, GIUSEPPE. "Walter Scott non si legge piu" [Walter
Scott is Not Read Any Longer]. <u>Fiera Letteraria</u> (21 May),
p. 15.
Until the last quarter of the nineteenth century, Scott
was formerly popular all over the world. Readers were fas-
cinated by the elegant style and aristocratic spirit of the
novels. In Italy during the first half of the nineteenth
century, many publishers offered both elaborate and modest
editions of Scott. Now, however, only one or two titles of
Scott are even included in the Oxford Classics, and con-
densed versions of <u>Ivanhoe</u> are regarded as appropriate
children's books.

37 ROBINSON, K. E. and PHILLIP ROBERTS. "Sir Walter Scott and
John Bell of Newcastle-on-Tyne: Some Unpublished Correspondence." <u>Yearbook of English Studies</u>, 2, 130-38.
Sixteen letters between Scott and John Bell, the Newcastle bookseller and antiquarian, are reprinted from the

1972

Robert White Collection in the University Library at Newcastle-on-Tyne. The letters concern Border antiquities and
Scott's election as an Honorary Member of the Newcastle Antiquarian Society.

38   RUBENSTEIN, JILL.   "The Dilemma of History: A Reading of
      Scott's Bridal of Triermain."   Studies in English Litera-
      ture, 12, no. 4 (Autumn), 721-34.
          The tripartite narrative and temporal structure of The
      Bridal of Triermain reflects two of Scott's recurring
      themes: the emergence of moderation through time, and the
      necessity to reconcile discordant qualities in the mature
      individual as well as in the mature society.   The Arthurian,
      medieval, and eighteenth century stories and their three
      narrators demonstrate a growth from a somewhat corrupt ro-
      manticism to a capacity for self-knowledge seized from a
      decadent society.

*39   SCHUELER, ROBERT A.   "Functions and Purposes in the English
      Historical Novel of the Nineteenth Century."   Ph.D. disser-
      tation, Duke University, 1972.
          An abstract by the author appears in Dissertation Ab-
      stracts International, 34 (1973), 1253-54A.

40   SHIPPS, ANTHONY W.   "Sir Walter Scott's Quotations."   Notes
      and Queries, 217 (August), 305.
          Identifies quotations from Charles Morris' "The Toper's
      Apology" and John Logan's "Ode on the Death of a Young
      Lady."   See 1944.B13.

41   SIMPSON, DAVID and ALASTAIR WOOD.   "Introduction" to Thoughts
      on the Proposed Change of Currency by Walter Scott and Two
      Letters on Scottish Affairs by John Wilson Croker.   Shannon:
      Irish University Press, pp. v-xxv.
          National pride is the basic emotion of the three Malachi
      Malagrowther letters.   Scott objected to penalizing the
      Scottish banking system by financial legislation designed
      to remedy English banking problems.   His real concern was
      not economic but political, an appeal to national sentiment.
      The Government was forced to back down and villified Scott,
      but he was praised for his victory in Edinburgh.

42   SPEAIGHT, ROBERT.   "Sir Walter Scott."   Essays by Divers Hands,
      N.S. 37, 108-21.
          Scott's greatness lies in his kinship with Shakespeare
      and in his "tragic sense of life."   His style often posses-
      ses the "casual and yet musical rhythm" of Shakespearean
      prose.   Scott took liberties with history but kept his

situations psychologically plausible; he should be admired for his realism as well as his romance. Presented in the Don Coloma Memorial Lecture, read 3 December, 1970.

43   SPINK, GERALD W. "Sir Walter in Yorkshire." Studies in Scottish Literature, 10, no. 2 (October), 103-20.
      Reviews Scott's friendship and correspondence with John Morritt of Rokeby and surveys Scott's other correspondents in Yorkshire and the many references to Yorkshire in the novels. Morritt was one of the few to whom Scott openly acknowledged the authorship of Waverley, and Lockhart dedicated the Life to him.

44   STAVES, SUSAN. "Don Quixote in Eighteenth Century England." Comparative Literature, 24, no. 3 (Summer), 193-215.
      Waverley reveals Scott's awareness of Cervantes. The beginning of the novel imitates Don Quixote's reading, and Scott uses the idea of the literary Quixote "to create the romance which he sees as the most authentic realism."

*45 STINE, PETER W. "The Changing Image of Mary Queen of Scots in Nineteenth Century British Literature." Ph.D. dissertation, Michigan State University, 1972.
      An abstract by the author appears in Dissertation Abstracts International, 33 (1972), 733-34A.

46   THOMSON, FRED C. "'With all Deliberate Speed': A Source in Scott." American Notes and Queries, 11, No. 3 (November), 38-40.
      Scott uses this phrase in Rob Roy, and the context links it with the common legal idiom of the day. The phrase probably existed in eighteenth century Chancery law.

47   WARD, WILLIAM S., comp. "Scott, Sir Walter," in his Literary Reviews in British Periodicals, 1798-1820: A Bibliography. With a Supplementary List of General Articles on Literary Subjects. Volume II. New York and London: Garland Publishing, 480-90.
      Lists the contemporary reviews of Scott's works from the Minstrelsy through The Abbot. Appendix A also includes three pages of general (non-review) articles on Scott.

48   WATERSTON, ELIZABETH. "Galt, Scott, and Cooper: Frontiers of Realism." Journal of Canadian Fiction, 1, no. 1, 60-65.
      Galt's Bogle Corbet (1831) turns away from Scottish subjects to explore life in Colonial Canada. In this novel Galt reacted against the Waverley pattern in several other ways. His protagonist and heroine differ from the Waverley

1973

types, and he explores a probable situation and uses first-person narration. Galt uses setting anti-romantically and does not neatly resolve his plots "in the Sir Walter Scott manner."

1973 A BOOKS

1 BELL, ALAN, ed. <u>Scott Bicentenary Essays: Selected Papers Read at the Sir Walter Scott Bicentenary Conference</u>. New York: Barnes and Noble, 354pp.
    A selection of papers from the conference held 15-21 August, 1971 and sponsored by the Institute for Advanced Studies in the Humanities of the University of Edinburgh. Includes 24 essays plus a list of papers read at the conference but not reprinted in this volume.

2 MacKERCHAR, E., comp. <u>Wit and Wisdom from the Waverley Novels: 366 Quotations</u>. Folcroft, Pennsylvania: Folcroft Library Editions, 31pp.
    Provides a quotation for each day of the year. Most are short one-sentence proverbs and are identified only by the title of the novel in which they appear.

3 MAYHEAD, ROBIN. <u>Walter Scott</u>. British Authors Introductory Series. Cambridge: Cambridge University Press, 142pp.
    Scott's "appetite for the complex and contradictory" results in a relish for ambiguity and a mixed degree of success. In <u>Waverley</u> he acknowledges that change involves loss and waste. <u>The Heart of Midlothian</u> explores the complexities of justice. In <u>Guy Mannering</u>, <u>Redgauntlet</u>, and <u>The Antiquary</u> he fails to separate matters which deeply interested him from more superficial concerns. <u>Rob Roy</u>, <u>Old Mortality</u>, and <u>The Antiquary</u> reflect Scott's preoccupation with the idea of prudence. Partially reprinted from 1956.B10; 1969.B28; and 1973.B37.

4 OMAN, CAROLA. <u>The Wizard of the North: The Life of Sir Walter Scott</u>. London: Hodder and Staughton, 396pp.
    A sentimental biography which intentionally avoids critical discussion of Scott's works. Although the "Preface" acknowledges Lockhart's inaccuracies, the body of the volume incorporates many of them, such as his account of Scott's last words. Includes an Appendix on "Who Was Lady Scott" which discourages the persistent rumor that she was the illegitimate daughter of Lord Downshire.

1973 B SHORTER WRITINGS

1   ALBRECHT, W. P.   "An Unpublished Letter by Sir Walter Scott."
    Notes and Queries, 218 (February), 47-48.
        Prints a letter not included in Grierson's edition writ-
    ten by Scott to his neighbor, James Pringle of Torwoodlee,
    in the winter of 1830.   The letter, which is now owned by
    the University of Kansas Library, concerns a change in the
    road passing by Abbotsford.

2   ALLENTUCK, MARCIA.   "Scott and the Picturesque: Afforestation
    and History," in Scott Bicentenary Essays.   Edited by Alan
    Bell.   New York: Barnes and Noble, pp. 188-98.
        Scott's essays "On Landscape Gardening" and "On Planting
    Waste Lands" reveal that he saw landscape both visually and
    connected to historical associations.   At Abbotsford he
    wished to combine the picturesque and the utilitarian, and
    his plans for the grounds were influenced by the works of
    Sir Uvedale Price and Henry Seton Stewart.   He used trans-
    planting to bring the future within his grasp "by leaping
    over the slower processes of time and history."

3   ANDERSON, W. E. K.   "The Journal," in Scott Bicentenary Essays.
    Edited by Alan Bell.   New York: Barnes and Noble, pp. 80-
    86.
        Scott's unintentional omissions in the Journal reveal his
    mind moving faster than his hand.   His misspellings indicate
    that he wrote what he heard himself dictating in his head,
    and they often reflect the vowel sounds of a Scots accent.
    The Journal confirms Scott's generosity and courage and re-
    markable diligence.   It reveals few details about other
    people, as he resolved to refrain "from all satirical com-
    position."

4   BAKERMAN, JANE A.   "The Popinjay: A Comment on the Romance,
    A Reading of Old Mortality."   Indiana English Journal, 7,
    nos. 1-3, 31-40.
        Scott's villains, or Fate Figures, are destroyed by their
    inability to reconcile commitment to a cause with their
    selfish monomania.   Unlike the villains, the heroes are
    aware of choices; their reevaluation of motives and deci-
    sions deepens their characterizations.   The hero is passive
    but self-aware, while the Fate Figure is active but not
    self-aware.   The conflict between them dramatizes Scott's
    favorite theme, the individual's moral responsibility to
    confront and evaluate the forces of the historical moment.
    In Old Mortality both Claverhouse and Burley function as
    Fate Figures, but Burley's active attempt to remake the

times shows him to be the most dangerous. Morton's renunciation of Burley and compassion toward Evandale measure
his growth in understanding.

5   BEATTIE, WILLIAM. "Scott," in <u>Scott Bicentenary Essays</u>. Edited by Alan Bell. New York: Barnes and Noble, pp. 1-17.
     Scott wrote "the prose of a professional man" and under-
stood the difference between style and mannerism. His poems
reflect great metrical virtuosity as well as a strong feeling for "the movement and sound of people." He introduced
poetry into the novel and possessed a profound awareness of
the psychology of character and motive. He actualized the
past through the strength of his language.

6   BELL, ALAN. "Scott Manuscripts in Edinburgh Libraries," in
<u>Scott Bicentenary Essays</u>. Edited by Alan Bell. New York:
Barnes and Noble, pp. 147-59.
     Surveys the manuscripts of Scott's major works in Edin-
burgh libraries and relevant material at the Scottish Record Office. Provides the main categories of the Abbotsford
and Walpole collections at the National Library of Scotland.
Other collections concern Scott's business and military activities, his legal career, and his family. Newly acquired
items include the Ashestiel Manuscript, Scott's letters to
Constable and Cadell, the papers of Cadell, and the letters
of the Ballantynes.

7   BITTON, LIVIA G. "The Jewess As a Fictional Sex Symbol."
<u>Bucknell Review</u>, 21, no. 1 (Spring), 63-86.
     The Jewess is "the perennial sex-object of literature"
and plays a triple role of virgin, lover, and mother.
Scott's Rebecca is subjected to the conventional literary
separation from the Christian male (Ivanhoe) to whom she is
devoted and retires in dignity at the end of the novel to
"a form of Jewish convent invented by Walter Scott."

8   CLUBBE, JOHN. "After Missolonghi: Scott on Byron." <u>Library
Chronicle</u>, 39, 18-33.
     Scott admired Byron as a poet but regretted the scandals
caused by his behavior. To assist Thomas Moore in writing
his biography of Byron, Scott gave him the letters he had
received from Byron as well as a memorandum of recollections
of Byron (printed here). Scott's discussions with Moore un-
doubtedly influenced the biography, and he was pleased with
Volume I. He regarded Byron as a "transcendent genius
flawed by moral lapses."

9 _____. "Byron and Scott." <u>Texas Studies in Literature and Language</u>, 15, no. 1 (Spring), 67-91.

Byron and Scott understood each other's worth and each judged the other's work perceptively. Although they were regarded as literary rivals, jealousy did not spoil their friendship. Scott's anonymous review of Byron in the <u>Quarterly</u> of October, 1816 revealed the differences in their temperaments, but its generosity and sympathy meant a great deal to Byron. Although there was little or no reciprocal literary influence between them, there are many similarities, particularly in their use of romantic irony.

10 COONEY, SEAMUS. "Scott's Anonymity--Its Motives and Consequences." <u>Studies in Scottish Literature</u>, 10, no. 4 (April), 207-19.

Enumerates ten reasons for Scott's anonymity culled from his letters and prefaces and from anecdotes. His moral rationale is connected to modesty and unpretentiousness. He also affirmed an inexplicable connection between his anonymity and his ability to write. Anonymous authorship liberated him from his inhibitions and his social mask and allowed him to create a series of new personalities, primarily in the introductory sections of the novels.

11 CRAIG, DAVID. "Scott's Shortcomings as an Artist," in <u>Scott Bicentenary Essays</u>. Edited by Alan Bell. New York: Barnes and Noble, pp. 101-14.

Scott was more of a catalyst than an active contributor to the literary tradition, and it is remarkable that so faulty a writer could have been so popular. Quotes a series of parallel passages from Scott and other writers to demonstrate Scott's inferiority.

12 DAICHES, DAVID. "Scott and Scotland," in <u>Scott Bicentenary Essays</u>. Edited by Alan Bell. New York: Barnes and Noble, pp. 38-60.

Scott's ambivalent attitude toward history derives from two sources: his youthful exposure to romantic tales, and his exposure to the historians of the Scottish Enlightenment. He was by temperament a mediator, and his attitude to the Union of 1707 combined both nostalgic and progressive reactions. He regarded change as a part of history and realized that social and historical forces could effect changes in human nature.

13 DEAN, DENNIS R. "Scott and Mackenzie: New Poems." <u>Philological Quarterly</u>, 52, no. 2 (April), 265-73.

Uses circumstantial evidence to attribute to Scott the prologue and to Mackenzie the epilogue of <u>Helga; or, the</u>

Rural Minstrels, a controversial play which closed after
one performance on 22 January, 1812. Scott never acknowledged his composition (printed here), which is "mediocre
poetry" and "tarnished by its association with a disastrous
play."

14 DRESCHER, HORST W. "Walter Scott: Tales of My Landlord. The
Black Dwarf and Old Mortality," in Der Englische Roman im
19. Jahrhundert: Interpretationen. Edited by Paul Goetsch,
Heinz Kosok and Kurt Otten. Berlin: E. Schmidt, pp. 22-35.
The Tales of My Landlord affirm the national unity of
Scotland transcending political and religious factionalism.
In The Black Dwarf Scott tried unsuccessfully to create a
personification of primitive demonic forces. In Old Mortality he linked narrative technique and historical event
through Morton, who mediates between past and present. Although he exaggerated the fanaticism of the Covenanters, he
presented most of the other characters as products of their
social and historical environment.

15 ELBERS, JOAN S. "Isolation and Community in The Antiquary."
Nineteenth Century Fiction, 27, no. 4 (March), 405-23.
Refutes the general critical opinion that The Antiquary
is deeply flawed by lack of a coherent structure. The
novel is organized through a "series of thematic contrasts
between isolation and community." It contrasts man cut off
from the social body to man linked to social organization
through sympathy and tradition. The rescue scene in chapters 7 and 8 exemplifies this theme, since the success of
the rescue depends upon links of communication and connection which bind together the entire community.

16 FINLEY, GERALD. "Turner's Illustrations to Napoleon." Journal
of the Warburg and Courtauld Institutes, 36, 390-96.
Turner's illustrations to Scott's Napoleon, commissioned
by Cadell in 1832, are unified and highly dramatic. They
are primarily landscapes, with a few human figures included
as mere "pictorial embroideries." Turner's pictures reveal
that he shared Scott's admiration for Napoleon.

17 GORDON, CATHERINE M. "Scott's Impact on Art." Apollo, 98
(July), 36-39.
The artistic treatment of Scott's subjects followed
trends in popular taste. The initial interest in landscape
soon gave way to anecdotal subjects and a narrative mode.
The majority of these are comic or sentimental.

18   GORDON, ROBERT C. "Scott Among the Partisans: A Significant
     Bias in His Life of Napoleon Buonaparte," in Scott Bicenten-
     ary Essays. Edited by Alan Bell. New York: Barnes and
     Noble, pp. 115-33.
         In his Life of Napoleon Scott views the irregular sol-
     diers and partisans as an heroic patriotic militia and a
     force for conservatism. He tampered with the evidence to
     defend the character of the Spanish irregulars, who were
     actually undisciplined and primitive. This bias severely
     qualifies the image of Scott as a believer in progressive
     Enlightenment ideals.

19   HAGGIS, D. R. "Scott, Balzac, and the Historical Novel as
     Social and Political Analysis: Waverley and Les Chouans."
     Modern Language Review, 68, no. 1 (January), 51-68.
         Balzac saw himself as a kind of modern Walter Scott, and
     Scott helped Balzac to discover the historical novel as a
     tool for the political and social analysis of recent so-
     ciety. Both Waverley and Les Chouans concern a moment of
     historical transition and question the permanence of the
     new order. They share other similarities in historical
     perspective, the characterization of individuals and groups,
     and the structural role of hero (Waverley) and heroine
     (Marie de Verneuil).

20   HART, FRANCIS R. "Limits of the Gothic: The Scottish Ex-
     ample," in Racism in the Eighteenth Century. Edited by
     Harold E. Pagliaro. Studies in Eighteenth Century Culture,
     No. 3. Cleveland, Ohio and London: Press of Case Western
     Reserve University, pp. 137-53.
         Scott uses several archetypal Gothic elements in the
     Waverley novels--"the macabre-picturesque ambience, the
     definitive character relationship, the hereditary curse."
     These are more fundamental than the historical particularity
     of the settings, which are essentially timeless. Scott's
     fanatics and outlaws represent "a demonic element in the
     human inheritance," and his plots become "patterns of ex-
     orcism" in which the conscious exorcises the preconscious.

21   _____. "Scott and the Novel in Scotland," in Scott Bicentenary
     Essays. Edited by Alan Bell. New York: Barnes and Noble,
     pp. 61-79.
         Identifies five traditions of Scottish fiction: 1) the
     Blackwoodian group; 2) the later Scottish romancers; 3) the
     novelists of the Highlands; 4) the theological warfare of
     Kailyard and anti-Kailyard; and 5) the twentieth century
     mythmakers. Scott shares with the last group a sense of
     the importance of concilation, "cultural humility and ironic
     romance."

1973

22   HENNELLY, MARK M. "Waverley and Romanticism." Nineteenth
     Century Fiction, 28, no. 2 (September), 194-209.
          Waverley exemplifies "common epistemological strains in
     Romantic poetry and prose fiction," the elements of Romance,
     myth, and dialectic as defined by Harold Bloom, Northrop
     Frye, and Albert Gérard. The novel coalesces Romance and
     Realism as Waverley is transformed from pariah to messiah
     who rehabilitates the ravaged kingdom, represented by
     Tully-Veolan.

23   HEWTON, AINSLIE. "A Comparison of Sir Walter Scott's 'The Eve
     of St. John' and Zhukovsky's Translation of the Ballad."
     New Zealand Slavonic Journal, 11 (Winter), 145-50.
          Zhukovsky's translation maintains formal fidelity to
     Scott's original in stanza form and vocabulary. However,
     Zhukovsky makes the Baron more noble and the Lady more ro-
     mantic. His knight is "more earthly and earthy" than
     Scott's enigmatic Sir Richard of Coldinghame. Although
     Zhukovsky's version is "more spectacular and dramatic"
     than the original, it does not reach as high a standard.

24   HOLT, R. F. "Achim von Arnim and Sir Walter Scott." German
     Life and Letters, N.S. 26, no. 2 (January), 142-60.
          In Die Kronenwächter, which appeared three years after
     Waverley, Arnim intended to analyze history in its relation-
     ship to the development of the German people. He wished to
     "assert the force of myth," and so saw little value in at-
     tention to detail and surface historical content. This
     treatment of history in fiction differs markedly from
     Scott's, and the difference is consistent with their respec-
     tive views of history.

25   HYDE, WILLIAM J. "Jeanie Deans and the Queen: Appearance and
     Reality." Nineteenth Century Fiction, 28, no. 1 (June),
     86-92.
          In the interview scene in The Heart of Midlothian the
     Queen was not completely converted on the spot by Jeanie's
     eloquence, but she was inclined to give Jeanie the pardon
     for practical political reasons. However, Jeanie's elo-
     quence provided the Queen with the "moral encouragement" to
     do this. Scott thus remains true to the historical situa-
     tion while creating a "powerful fictitious scene."

*26 JAMES, GLENN JOSEPH. "Walter Scott and George Eliot: A Common
     Tradition." Ph.D. dissertation, Emory University, 1973.
          An abstract by the author appears in Dissertation Ab-
     stracts International, 34 (1973), 4207A.

27   JOHNSON, EDGAR. "Scott and the Corners of Time," in <u>Scott Bi-</u> <u>centenary Essays</u>. Edited by Alan Bell. New York: Barnes and Noble, pp. 18-37.
        Scott was a "Tory progressive" and a rationalist with a deep respect for tradition. He did not fear change, and he respected technological progress and human dignity. He saw the past as "the matrix in which the present had been formed." His "revolutionary insight" was his simultaneous emphasis on what is uniform in human nature and what is culturally determined. His "essential theme" concerns the individual caught at "corners of time" where large, impersonal forces clash in history. Reprinted: 1973.B28.

28   _____. "Scott and the Corners of Time." <u>Virginia Quarterly</u> <u>Review</u>, 49, no. 1 (Winter), 46-62.
        Reprint of 1973.B27.

29   JONES, STANLEY. "Sir Walter Scott's Quotations." <u>Notes and</u> <u>Queries</u>, 218 (November), 424-25.
        Identifies the source of a Scott quotation as Hawthorn's song in Act I, scene 2 of Bickerstaffe's comic opera <u>Love</u> <u>in a Village</u>. See 1944.B13 and 1973.B47.

30   JORDAN, FRANK. "Scott and Wordsworth; or, Reading Scott Well." <u>Wordsworth Circle</u>, 4, no. 2 (Spring), 112-23.
        The narrative methods of Scott and Wordsworth force the reader to become his own narrator. Wordsworth's reader must actively piece together the parts of the poem. Similarly in Scott's novels after <u>Waverley</u>, the amount of authorial commentary diminishes, requiring an increasingly dramatic and participatory narrative technique.

31   KATONA, ANNA. "The Impact of Sir Walter Scott in Hungary," in <u>Scott Bicentenary Essays</u>. Edited by Alan Bell. New York: Barnes and Noble, pp. 271-82.
        Scott's influence in Hungary began in the 1820's; it led to the creation of the Hungarian historical novel and stimulated interest in popular poetry. He was admired for his pictures of popular life and for the moral basis of the novels. Jósika created Hungarian fiction by adapting the methods of Scott to his native Transylvanian subject matter.

32   KEMP, MARTIN. "Scott and Delacroix, with Some Assistance from Hugo and Bonnington," in <u>Scott Bicentenary Essays</u>. Edited by Alan Bell. New York: Barnes and Noble, pp. 213-27.
        Delacroix's changing attitude toward Scott reflects his intellectual development. Delacroix's "romantic antiquarianism" was stimulated by his work with Hugo on the costumes

1973

for <u>Amy Robsart</u>. However, after 1830 as he moved toward
Realism, he painted fewer Scott subjects and criticized
Scott's novels as boring and monotonous. In his later
paintings of Scott themes, Delacroix concentrated on passions rather than historical details.

33 KOSKENLINNA, HAZEL M. "Setting, Image, and Symbol in Scott and
Hawthorne." <u>ESQ: A Journal of the American Renaissance</u>,
19, no. 1, 50-59.
Hawthorne and Scott both transformed the actuality of
landscape in their descriptions; Hawthorne also borrowed
Scott's link between landscape and historical associations.
They use wilderness scenes as natural background with symbolic overtones, and they share several characteristic
image patterns. Scott's work helps to link Hawthorne with
the European literary tradition.

*34 LAZU, ELENA. "Opera lui Walter Scott în Romania." <u>Analele
Universității</u>, 22, 141-50.
Cited in the <u>1974 MLA International Bibliography</u> (New
York: Modern Language Association, 1976), I, 111, item
#6762.

35 LIGOCKI, LLEWELLYN. "The Imitators and the Imitated: Scott,
Ainsworth, and the Critics." <u>Papers of the Bibliographical
Society of America</u>, 67, no. 4, 443-46.
Ainsworth's works differ from Scott's in both method and
aesthetic viewpoint. Scott used history indirectly and concentrated on fictive characters and events, while the characters and events of historical record are central to Ainsworth's method.

*36 LOW, MARIE E. D. "Self in Triplicate: The Doctor in the
Nineteenth Century British Novel." Ph.D. dissertation,
University of Washington, 1973.
An abstract by the author appears in <u>Dissertation Ab-
stracts International</u>, 34 (1973), 2638A.

37 MAYHEAD, ROBIN. "The Problem of Coherence in <u>The Antiquary</u>,"
in <u>Scott Bicentenary Essays</u>. Edited by Alan Bell. New
York: Barnes and Noble, pp. 134-46.
<u>The Antiquary</u> is unified by a prevailing note of John-
sonian pessimism. A feeling of futility surrounds many of
the episodes in the novel. Scott was aware of the novel's
disparate materials, and the idea of tragic or absurd as-
sortments of things becomes a recurring principle of organization. <u>The Antiquary</u> offers "a sombre vision underlying
much extravagant comedy." A revised version with essentially the same argument appears in 1973.A3.

38   MILLS, NICOLAUS. "Sir Walter Scott and Fenimore Cooper," in
     his <u>American and English Fiction in the Nineteenth Century:
     An Antigenre Critique and Comparison</u>. Bloomington: Indiana
     University Press, pp. 32-51.
         Both <u>Rob Roy</u> and <u>The Prairie</u> reflect "the tension between
     two opposed ways of <u>life</u>." Rob and Natty value personal
     honor over money, and in their wish to perpetuate a doomed
     way of life they demonstrate their uncompromised heroism.
     However, they cannot cope with the complexities of civiliza-
     tion. In direct contrast, the world of Frank and Middleton
     reflects society's ability to create order and to unite two
     cultures. These heroes acknowledge society's need to recog-
     nize the culture it threatens to destroy.

39   MITCHELL, JEROME. "Operatic Versions of <u>The Bride of Lammer-
     moor</u>." <u>Studies in Scottish Literature</u>, 10, no. 3 (January),
     145-164.
         Discusses operas by Adolphe Adam, Michele Carafa, Luigi
     Rieschi, Ivar Frederik Bredal, and Alberto Mazzucato. None
     of these compares favorably to Donizetti's <u>Lucia di Lammer-
     moor</u>, which emphasizes the love story, eliminates Scottish
     local color, and avoids the weaknesses of previous versions.

40   OCHOJSKI, PAUL M. "Waverley Ueber Alles--Sir Walter Scott's
     German Reputation," in <u>Scott Bicentenary Essays</u>. Edited by
     Alan Bell. New York: Barnes and Noble, pp. 260-270.
         Scott's reputation in Germany was "hardly exceeded" by
     any other foreign writer, and he exerted an enormous influ-
     ence on German literature. While critics occasionally gave
     adverse notices to the novels, Scott was adored by the read-
     ing public. The Waverley Novels stimulated many German sub-
     literary imitations by hack writers, some of whom affixed
     Scott's name to their works.

41   PHILLIPSON, N. T. "Scott as Story-Teller; An Essay in Psycho-
     biography," in <u>Scott Bicentenary Essays</u>. Edited by Alan
     Bell. New York: Barnes and Noble, pp. 87-100.
         Scott's autobiographical exercises, particularly the
     "Ashestiel Memoir," reveal that he was deeply concerned
     with his identity and that he possessed strong needs to
     compensate for an absent father and for his lameness. He
     fulfilled these needs as a child by storytelling and as a
     man by compulsive writing.

42   PITTOCK, JOAN. "Scott and the Novel of Manners: The Case of
     <u>Saint Ronan's Well</u>." <u>Durham University Journal</u>, N.S. 35,
     no. 1 (December), 1-9.
         In <u>Saint Ronan's Well</u> Scott attempts to fuse novel and
     romance. The plot mingles satire, intrigue, melodrama, and

1973

tragedy. The setting and epigraphs give the story a context of social convention, and the action proceeds through a series of social occasions typical of the novel of manners. The melodramatic story contrasts to the emphasis on decorum, and the novel succeeds in exploring the middle ground between realism and romance.

43   REDPATH, THEODORE. The Young Romantics and Critical Opinion, 1807-1824. New York: St. Martin's Press, pp. 35-39.
     Deals with Scott only peripherally, mainly in his role as one of the founders of the Quarterly Review and as a critic of Byron.

44   RIESE, TEUT ANDREAS. "Sir Walter Scott as a Master of the Short Tale," in Festschrift Prof. Dr. Herbert Koziol zum Siebzigsten Geburtstag. Edited by Gero Bauer, Franz K. Stanzel, and Franz Zaic. Wiener Beiträge zur englischen Philologie, No. 75. Vienna: Wilhelm Braumüller, pp. 255-65.
     Scott's short tales are often well constructed and economically written. When they are integrated into novels, they provide functional thematic contributions, not mere padding. The Chronicles of the Canongate and "Wandering Willie's Tale" are Scott's "most significant contributions to the art of short fiction." His skill with the short narrative may have developed from his early acquaintance with ballads and folktales.

45   RUFF, WILLIAM. "Deceptions in the Works of Scott; or, Lying Title-pages," in Scott Bicentenary Essays. Edited by Alan Bell. New York: Barnes and Noble, pp. 176-87.
     A survey of "bibliographical ghosts, American and French piracies of [Scott's] works, 'spurious' title-pages, lying dates and the like." Real harm came from title pages from Scott's own printers which carried deceptive information about the numbering of editions. These made Scott think he had more money than he actually did and thus contributed to his financial downfall.

46   SHIPPS, ANTHONY W. "Sir Walter Scott." Notes and Queries, 218 (August), 298.
     Varselstegnet is a translation of The Omen (1825) by John Galt.

47   _____. "Sir Walter Scott's Quotations." Notes and Queries, 218 (August), 297.
     Identifies quotations from The Universal Songster, including a song by Bickerstaff, Young's "The Instalment," and Samuel Rogers' "To. . . ." See 1944.B13 and 1973.B24.

48   SIMMONS, JAMES C. The Novelist as Historian: Essays on the
        Victorian Historical Novel. Studies in English Literature,
        No. 87. The Hague: Mouton, 66pp.
            The development of the historical novel after Scott re-
        flects the widespread Victorian taste for historical fic-
        tion, the desire for fiction that would edify, and a
        deepening historical consciousness. In the first part of
        the period, the historical novel developed as an imitation
        of and then a reaction to Scott. After 1850, interest in
        the historical romance declined. Includes reprints of
        1968.B39 and 1971.B68.

49   SIMPSON, JOHN M. "Scott and Old Norse Literature," in Scott
        Bicentenary Essays. Edited by Alan Bell. New York: Barnes
        and Noble, pp. 300-13.
            Scott read about Norse literature all his life and used
        this knowledge in his writing. Although he collected some
        primary source material, he was mainly limited to unreliable
        secondary authorities. He used saga material in his essays
        on "Chivalry" and "Romance," and his "Abstract of the Eyri-
        biggia Saga" (1814) was a "pioneering step" into the Ice-
        landic Sagas.

50   SKINNER, BASIL C. "Scott as Pageant Master--The Royal Visit
        of 1832," in Scott Bicentenary Essays. Edited by Alan Bell.
        New York: Barnes and Noble, pp. 228-37.
            The finding of the Regalia, the founding of the Celtic
        Society, and the 1821 Coronation provided Scott with ideas
        for the Royal Visit. Although the preponderance of the
        tartan element drew satire, the ceremony involving the
        Honours of Scotland was more discreet and successful. Scott
        related his ceremonial arrangements to historical tradition
        and was pleased by the national fervor the visit produced.

51   WELSH, ALEXANDER. "Contrast of Styles in the Waverley Novels."
        Novel, 6, no. 3 (Spring), 218-28.
            Scott used a mixed style--high for the protagonists and
        historical figures and low for lower ranks and comic charac-
        ters. Like Shakespeare, he distributed high and low styles
        according to genre and social class. The low style vital-
        izes the serious action, and comic relief mocks it. Dialect
        often signifies impertinence and functions as ironic de-
        flation.

52   WOOD, E. H. HARVEY. "Scott's Foreign Contacts," in Scott Bi-
        centenary Essays. Edited by Alan Bell. New York: Barnes
        and Noble, pp. 238-59.
            Scott had an instinctive suspicion of foreigners, and
        his closest friends were British. He had a few close

foreign friends, including Washington Irving, Henry Weber, and Vladimir Davydoff. However, "the essential man" remained remarkably untouched by foreign influences.

53 WOOD, G. A. M. "The Manuscripts and Proofsheets of Redgauntlet," in Scott Bicentenary Essays. Edited by Alan Bell. New York: Barnes and Noble, pp. 160-75.

The manuscripts and proofsheets of Redgauntlet demonstrate that Scott revised extensively. The novel's textual history shows "a jostling multiplicity of variants, both substantive and accidental." Scott left many minor decisions to the discretion of his copyist, and he accepted many of Ballantyne's suggestions. He did extensive revision during the printing of the first edition and made more changes in the Magnum Opus edition of 1832. Partially reprinted from 1971.B86.

54 _____. "Scott's Continuing Revision: The Printed Texts of Redgauntlet." Bibliotheck, 6, 121-98.

The first edition of Redgauntlet contained many errors, some of which Scott corrected in the collected edition of 1827. For the Magnum Opus edition he added new material separate from the text and made extensive stylistic revisions. The collations demonstrate that Scott used an interleaved copy of the 1827 octavo reprint to work on the Magnum Opus edition, and this became the printer's copy text. Includes list of collations.

55 WOOD, HARRIET HARVEY. "A Scorpion in the Post: John Gibson Lockhart Through His Letters." Cornhill Magazine, 180 (Autumn), 114-32.

Lockhart's letters reveal humor, vitality of mind, and his characteristic bent for satire. Scott cautioned him against indulging this love of satire, especially in Blackwood's, but Lockhart did not always heed Scott's advice.

56 ZUG, CHARLES G., III. "Scott's 'Jock of Hazeldean': The Recreation of a Traditional Ballad." Journal of American Folklore, 86 (April-June), 152-60.

Scott rewrote and renamed "Jock of Hazeldean" and even made him a member of his own clan. A century later the ballad was collected from the oral tradition in America with almost all Scott's alterations intact. His early ballad imitations were exercises in narrative poetry, but "Jock of Hazeldean" (1816) demonstrates his increasing skill in folksong.

1974 A BOOKS

*1   BAILEY, THOMAS CULLEN. "The Late Novels of Sir Walter Scott."
      Ph.D. dissertation, Washington University, 1974.
          An abstract by the author appears in Dissertation Ab-
      stracts International, 35 (1975), 6089A.

*2   DARLEY, WILLIAM DUANE. "Sir Walter Scott and the Historical
      Novel: Intellectual Values and Definitions of a Genre."
      Ph.D. dissertation, Wayne State University, 1974.
          An abstract by the author appears in Dissertation Ab-
      stracts International, 35 (1975), 4509A.

*3   DOUCETTE, FRANCIS DANIEL. "Origins and Patterns of Chivalrous
      Generosity and Self Denial in the Works of Sir Walter
      Scott." Ph.D. dissertation, Harvard University, 1974.
          Cited in Comprehensive Dissertation Index 1974 Supplement
      (Ann Arbor, Michigan: Xerox University Microfilms), IV,
      555.

4   HARTVEIT, LARS. Dream Within a Dream: A Thematic Approach to
      Scott's Vision of Fictional Reality. Bergen: Universitet-
      forlaget; New York: Humanities Press, 264pp.
          Scott's vision of reality derives from his divided alle-
      giance to the romantic and prosaic. Although firmly ground-
      ed in a specific social milieu, his characters can transcend
      it in a solitary quest and gain a moment of epiphany. Es-
      pecially during moments of national crisis, the Waverley
      Novels may shift from the "daylight world" of the novel of
      manners to the "twilight realm" of the marvelous. Includes
      chapters on The Heart of Midlothian, Waverley, Guy Manner-
      ing, Old Mortality, and Redgauntlet.

*5   PILKEY, JOHN DAVIS. "Walter Scott's Fiction and the British
      Mythographic and Ethnological Movements." Ph.D. disserta-
      tion, University of Kansas, 1974.
          An abstract by the author appears in Dissertation Ab-
      stracts International, 36 (1975), 908A.

1974 B SHORTER WRITINGS

1   ALLEN, WALTER. "What Is a Short Story?" Listener, 91
      (28 March), 405-406.
          Scott's "The Two Drovers" (1827) is "the first modern
      short story in English." The short story is distinguished
      from the novel by being rooted in a single perception or in-
      cident. It has origins in oral and folk tales and was
      shaped during the nineteenth century.

1974

2 ANDERSON, W. E. K. "Scott," in The English Novel: Select
Bibliographical Guides. Edited by A. E. Dyson. London:
Oxford University Press, pp. 128-44.
Surveys the most important critical studies and commen-
taries and divides them into three groups: 1) the catholic
critics, who like all the Scottish novels; 2) the puritans,
who accept only The Heart of Midlothian and the short
stories on the basis of formal unity; and 3) the unbeliev-
ers, who dismiss Scott entirely.

3 BUCKLEY, JEROME HAMILTON. Season of Youth: The Bildungsroman
from Dickens to Golding. Cambridge, Massachusetts: Harvard
University Press, pp. 8-9.
Waverley is not a real Bildungsroman, because Scott does
not develop the initiation theme. He gives only sketchy information about his hero's childhood, and he subordinates
his mental and moral growth to places, historical events,
and other characters.

*4 BURKE, JOHN JOSEPH, JR. "The Literary Imagination and the
Problem of History." Ph.D. dissertation, University of
California at Los Angeles, 1974.
An abstract by the author appears in Dissertation Ab-
stracts International, 35 (1975), 5389A.

5 CARNIE, R. H. and M. F. MORAN. "Sir Walter Scott and the
Maitland Club." Studies in Scottish Literature, 12, no. 1
(July), 51-61.
Scott was admitted to membership in the Maitland Club of
Glasgow in 1829; although he never attended a meeting, he
maintained a lively interest in the Club's affairs. Reprints twelve letters written from 18 June, 1828 to 2 August, 1829 between Scott and John Kerr, one of the Club's
founders. The letters reflect "that love of and interest
in things Scottish characteristic of the legal and literary
life of this period."

6 CLIPPER, LAWRENCE J. "Edward Waverley's Night Journey."
South Atlantic Quarterly, 73, no. 4 (Autumn), 541-53.
The form of Waverley imitates both the romance quest and
the hero myth, "using timeless patterns of symbol and arche-
type" in a primarily psychological drama. When he leaves
Tully-Veolan, Waverley experiences psychic disintegration
and the loss of identity. When he returns from England to
"redeem the lost Eden of Tully-Veolan," he retreats to sta-
bility, compromise, and balance. Scott thus rejects the
psychological insights of the traditional hero myth and appeals to his nineteenth century readers who feared the sur-
render to irrational forces.

7   COONEY, SEAMUS. "Scott and Progress: The Tragedy of 'The
    Highland Widow.'" Studies in Short Fiction, 11, no. 1
    (Winter), 11-16.
        Lukács is inaccurate when he argues that Scott did not
    directly reflect on historical necessity. In "The Highland
    Widow" the narrator simultaneously acknowledges the right-
    ness of change and pities those who cannot accommodate them-
    selves to it. Scott unifies individual and political
    themes, the effect of excessive mother-love and the effect
    of social change. This combination of historical analysis
    and emotional engagement demonstrates that Scott's art was
    directly concerned with the problem of historical necessity.

8   COWLEY, MALCOLM. "The Heart of Midlothian." Horizon, 16,
    no. 3 (Summer), 106-109.
        Scott's romances of chivalry are suitable for children,
    but the Scottish novels should appeal to more sophisticated
    readers. Scott inspired later novelists, such as Joyce and
    Faulkner, to do for their own lands what he did for Scot-
    land. A revival of interest in Scott would center on the
    democratic and realistic aspects of his work. Includes a
    plot summary of The Heart of Midlothian, the author's favor-
    ite among the Scottish novels.

9   GARSIDE, P. D. "A Legend of Montrose and the History of War."
    Yearbook of English Studies, 4, 159-71.
        Dugald Dalgetty symbolizes modern warfare, and through
    him Scott demonstrates the advantages, disadvantages, and
    amorality of professional armies. He uses warfare to define
    the nature and values of the several societies in the novel
    and shows each to be deficient. The novel warns of military
    callousness and the vulnerability of society to military
    force. However, Scott's optimism manifests itself in the
    survival of Menteith and Dalgetty, the aristocratic and
    bourgeois components of the new Scotland.

10 GORDON, ROBERT C. "The Year of Scott's Birth: A Question Re-
    considered." Notes and Queries, 219 (May), 163-71.
        It is impossible to establish with any certainty whether
    Scott was born in 1771, as claimed by Corson and most biog-
    raphers, or in 1770, as claimed by Arthur Melville Clark.
    There is much evidence for both dates, and dogmatism remains
    unjustified. The correspondence between H. J. C. Grierson
    and James Glen from 1932 to 1935 indicates a definite un-
    certainty about the birth date. See 1970.A2, B5.

11 HAFTER, MONROE Z. "The Spanish Version of Scott's Don Roder-
    ick." Studies in Romanticism, 13 (Summer), 225-34.

1974

Scott's <u>Vision of Don Roderick</u> was translated into Spanish in 1829 by Augustín Aicart. He attempts to depict as
noble, Spain's role in the conquest of America, which Scott
had severely criticized. He also defends the monarchy and
reduces Scott's praise for Spain's British allies. Aicart
wrote less as a translator than as a patriot, affirming the
conservative values of Spanish Romanticism under Fernando
VII.

12 HAGGIS, D. R. "<u>Clotilde de Lusignan</u>, <u>Ivanhoe</u>, and the Development of Scott's Influence on Balzac." <u>French Studies</u>, 28,
no. 2 (April), 159-68.
Several similarities of situation and episode suggest
Balzac had <u>Ivanhoe</u> in mind when writing his early novel
<u>Clotilde de Lusignan</u>. However, at this early stage in his
career he was interested primarily in history as decorative
setting. His later historical novel, <u>Les Chouans</u>, provides
a critical perspective on the past. As Balzac reflected on
Scott's work, he progressed from merely imitating him to
incorporating Scott's influence into his own mode of historical fiction.

13 _____. "Fiction and Historical Change: <u>La Cousine Bette</u> and
the Lesson of Walter Scott." <u>Forum for Modern Language
Studies</u>, 10, no. 4 (October), 323-33.
Balzac learned from Scott "how a novel might be made to
express a judgment on men, events, and the process of history." Like <u>The Bride of Lammermoor</u>, Balzac's novel traces
the fortunes of a family and contrasts past and present.
Balzac's reappearing characters suggest the continuity of
history and help to create the illusion of a real society
actually existing through time.

14 HAHN, H. G. "Historiographic and Literary: The Fusion of Two
Eighteenth Century Modes in Scott's <u>Waverley</u>." <u>Hartford
Studies in Literature</u>, 6, 243-67.
<u>Waverley</u> should be read in terms of eighteenth century
historiography and theories of fiction. The novel's conflicts dramatize the Enlightenment concept of history as a
struggle between the forces of reason and unreason, and
Scott's introductory remarks suggest the Augustan idea of
the uniformity of human nature. Scott developed the historical novel from the coincidence of his own eighteenth
century taste with the demand of the reading public for
novels which would provide entertainment and a simplified
moral universe.

15 IRWIN, FRANCINA. "Lady Amateurs and Their Masters in Scott's Edinburgh." Connoisseur, 187, 230-37.
  Deals with Scott only peripherally. After The Lady of the Lake promoted tourism and the search for the picturesque in the Trossachs, landscape painting became increasingly popular. One of the most notable instructors, Alexander Nasmyth, led sketching expeditions into the countryside.

16 ISER, WOLFGANG. "Fiction--the Filter of History: A Study of Walter Scott's Waverley," in his The Implied Reader: Patterns of Communication in Prose Fiction from Bunyan to Beckett. Baltimore: Johns Hopkins University Press, pp. 81-100.
  Translation and revision of 1964.B6. The argument remains essentially the same.

17 LEVINE, GEORGE. "Politics and the Form of Disenchantment." College English, 36, no. 4 (December), 422-35.
  Scott's novels show "the qualities of individual human goodness" withstanding the pressures of history, religion and politics. He carefully keeps Waverley away from violence, and hence from guilt, so he can retreat into decorum and forgiveness when he discovers the nature of reality to be "practical, reasonable, sensible." This implied faith in the coexistence of order, power, justice, and landed property results in an incoherent sense of reality and an incoherent narrative form.

18 MACINTYRE, LORN M. "Scott's Story of Invernahyle." Blackwood's Magazine, 316 (August), 142-53.
  Scott became interested in the Highlands through Alexander Stewart of Invernahyle, a client of his father. Both Edward Waverley and the Baron Bradwardine show traces of Invernahyle's courtesy, chivalry, and gallantry. Scott may have learned Invernahyle was not the committed Jacobite he first appeared, but Scott remained true to the romantic version of the noble Highlander.

19 PICKERING, SAM, JR. "Evangelical Readers and the Phenomenal Success of Walter Scott's First Novels." Christian Scholar's Review, 3, no. 4, 345-59.
  Scott's correct morality and use of historical settings recommended the Waverley novels to Evangelical Christians, who regarded history as less harmful than fiction to the imagination. In the first chapter of Waverley Scott deliberately separated himself from sentimental romances and Gothic and fashionable novels. Later he demonstrated the errors resulting from Waverley's too imaginative education

and modeled his development on the parable of the Prodigal Son.

20 REIZOV, BORIS G. "History and Fiction in Walter Scott's Novels." <u>Neohelicon</u>, 2, nos. 1-2, 165-75.
    Translation of 1971.B60.

*21 SPEER, RODERICK STANBERY. "Byron and Scott: The Waverley Novels and Byron's Life and Works." Ph.D. dissertation, University of Pennsylvania, 1974.
    An abstract by the author appears in <u>Dissertation Abstracts International</u>, 36 (1975), 331A.

22 STEPHENSON, WILLIAM A. "Two Notes on Sir Walter Scott's <u>The Antiquary</u>." <u>Studies in Scottish Literature</u>, 11, no. 4 (April), 250-52.
    Scott places Oldbuck's dinner party on Tuesday, 17 July, when the time lapse has been a week from the opening scene, set on Tuesday, 15 July. Scott's geographical details indicate that the novel takes place in Fifeshire, rather than in Forfarshire, where most of the critics have placed it.

23 STUART, ALICE V. "Scott and Wordsworth: A Comparison." <u>Contemporary Review</u>, 224 (May), 251-54.
    A comparison of Wordsworth's "Fidelity" to Scott's "Helvellyn," both written to commemorate the same faithful dog, shows characteristic differences in temperament, approach, and technique. "Fidelity" is intentionally plain and reflects Wordsworth's love of mountain scenery. "Helvellyn" reveals Scott's empathy for the dog as well as his love of place names and chivalric pomp.

24 SWAMINATHAN, S. R. "Keats's 'Epistle to Reynolds' and Scott's <u>Marmion</u>." <u>Notes and Queries</u>, 219 (September), 333-34.
    The name Cuthbert de Saint Aldebrim in line 44 of Keats's "Epistle to Reynolds" alludes to Saint Cuthbert of Lindisfarne, whose cloister is described in <u>Marmion</u>. Keats's description of the castle in Claude's painting echoes Scott's Lindisfarne Abbey, which combines heathen and Christian architecture. In lines 45-46 of his poem, Keats recalls Scott's Abbess of St. Hilda.

25 WILLIAMS, IOAN. "Inspiration and Inhibition in the Novels of Walter Scott," in his <u>The Realist Novel in England: A Study in Development</u>. London: Macmillan; Pittsburgh, Pennsylvania: University of Pittsburgh Press, pp. 25-40.
    Scott wanted his novels to resolve the conflicts between the determinist and idealist views of character. He suggests

that individual fulfillment may be found only through adaptation to historical circumstances, and his passive heroes exemplify the moral value of the individual who exchanges his right to selfish action for the protection of society. <u>Waverley</u> is typical of the other novels in its want of proportion and its failure to integrate theme, action, and narrative method.

26   ZUG, CHARLES G., III. "Sir Walter Scott and George Thomson, the Friend of Burns." <u>Studies in Scottish Literature</u>, 12, no. 1 (July), 33-50.

    Thomson sent Scott traditional tunes and encouraged him to compose verses for them. This stimulus led Scott to insert songs into the narrative poems and novels. Like Burns, Scott used the music as "a kind of charge for his creative battery." However, the collaboration between Scott and Thomson did not result in Scott's best work, although it made him realize the value of interpolated songs.

1975 A BOOKS

1   BRADLEY, PHILIP. <u>An Index to the Waverley Novels</u>. Metuchen, New Jersey: Scarecrow Press, 695pp.

    An index whose purpose "is to locate persons, things, places, words, phrases, proverbs, etc., which appear in the Waverley Novels, and also to arrange a number of persons by trade or profession, and of things by subject." Covers the novels, the shorter prose works, Scott's notes, and all introductory material written by him.

2   MAXWELL-SCOTT, WALTER. <u>Abbotsford</u>. Melrose: privately printed, 16pp.

    A new edition of 1952.A2 revised by James Corson, Honorary Librarian of Abbotsford.

*3   MAYORKAS, MARYHELEN. "Minstrels and Minstrelsy: Their Function in the Works of Sir Walter Scott." Ph.D. dissertation, New York University, 1975.

    An abstract by the author appears in <u>Dissertation Abstracts International</u>, 36 (1975), 3657A.

*4   SULKES, STANLEY. "The Code of Hospitality in the Waverley Novels: A Study of Sir Walter Scott's Fiction." Ph.D. dissertation, University of Cincinnati, 1975.

    An abstract by the author appears in <u>Dissertation Abstracts International</u>, 36 (1976), 6122A.

1975

1975 B SHORTER WRITINGS

*1   BROWN, RAYMOND LAMONT. "Sir Walter Scott and the Man From
      Hell." Scotland's Magazine, 71 (March), 15-16.
           Cited in British Humanities Index, January-March, 1975
      (London: The Library Association, 1975), p. 127.

 2   CALDER, ANGUS. "Introduction" to Old Mortality. Harmonds-
      worth: Penguin Books, pp. 7-46.
           Scott accelerates historical events to give his novel a
      sense of rapid movement, and at the same time he establishes
      the social context in full detail. He uses dialogue to ex-
      pose the central conflicts. Morton's humanistic rhetoric,
      the language of the British ruling class, expresses the
      public strengths of Scott's own day. The language of some
      of the other characters exposes the limitations of these
      values. The narrator's ultimate commitment is to simple
      happiness in this world, an elusive quality in a novel
      dominated by death.

 3   CHANDLER, ALICE. "Chivalry and Romance: Scott's Medieval
      Novels." Studies in Romanticism, 14, no. 2 (Spring),
      185-200.
           The medieval novels should not be judged by purely re-
      alistic standards. They take place in a mythical and alle-
      gorical realm and glorify the virtue of altruism, manifested
      in chivalry for the few and loyalty for the masses. They
      concern the conflict between self-interest and chivalry and
      demonstrate the importance of honor in a society bound by
      loyalty. These novels exist in a world ordered by Provi-
      dence, and the hero must make a leap of faith to accept
      this Providential control which transcends rational under-
      standing.

 4   GARSIDE, PETER D. "Scott and the 'Philosophical' Historians."
      Journal of the History of Ideas, 36, no. 3 (July), 497-512.
           As a student in the eighties and nineties, Scott was ex-
      posed to much "philosophical" history through his teachers
      Dugald Stewart, Baron David Hume, John Bruce, and A. F.
      Tytler. His membership in the Speculative Society and his
      early connection with Jeffrey and the Edinburgh Review gave
      additional scope to his interest in "philosophical" history.
      The intellectual atmosphere of Edinburgh, especially among
      the lawyers, was permeated by "philosophical" history and
      the concern with the development and progress of social
      institutions.

5   KARP, WALTER. "The Golden Age of Edinburgh." <u>Horizon</u>, 17, no. 4 (Autumn), 10-23.
    "Old and New Edinburgh coalesced in the person of Walter Scott." He was both a man of the Enlightenment and of the violent traditions of Scottish nationalism. Deals with Scott only peripherally.

6   LAMONT, CLAIRE. "Literary Patronage in Late Eighteenth Century Edinburgh." <u>Scottish Literary Journal</u>, 2, 17-26.
    The legal profession in Edinburgh constituted a social and intellectual élite, and many members of the Faculty of Advocates cultivated an interest in Scottish literature. Typical of this group was Alexander Fraser Tytler, Lord Woodhouselee (1747-1813), who assisted John Black, John Leyden, and William Tennant. He corresponded with Burns and helped him with publication problems. Tytler and his father William also took a deep interest in the preservation of earlier Scottish literature.

7   _____. "A Note on Gaelic Proverbs in <u>Waverley</u>." <u>Notes and Queries</u>, 220 (February), 64-66.
    Scott often indicates a Gaelic speaker by his use of traditional proverbs. Many of these appear in Donald Macintosh's <u>A Collection of Gaelic Proverbs and Familiar Phrases</u> (1785), which Scott owned. The second edition, edited by Alexander Campbell, appeared in 1819. It contained several Gaelic toasts not present in the original edition and all of which had appeared in <u>Waverley</u> (1814).

8   _____. "The Poetry of the Early Waverley Novels." <u>Proceedings of the British Academy</u>, 61, 315-36.
    The poetry in <u>Waverley</u>, <u>The Antiquary</u>, <u>The Heart of Midlothian</u>, and <u>The Bride of Lammermoor</u> shows little of the carelessness of Scott's narrative verse. His mad singers offer their hearers information from an unlikely source, and the hearers must be matured by tribulation before they can learn to listen meaningfully. Scott's lyric voice is deliberately impersonal and self-effacing. His songs represent a kind of common utterance linking various layers of society, and they suggest the conflicting emotions which may exist simultaneously in a single mind. They express Scott's values of action and living life to the full. Material is from the Chatterton Lecture on an English Poet, read 17 November, 1975.

9   McCOMBIE, FRANK. "Scott, <u>Hamlet</u>, and <u>The Bride of Lammermoor</u>." <u>Essays in Criticism</u>, 25, no. 4 (October), 419-36.

1975

> Scott envisioned Ravenswood as a kind of quiet, sensi-
> tive, contemplative Hamlet as portrayed by the actor Kemble.
> Both Ravenswood and Hamlet must choose between betrayal of
> the self through action or betrayal of the past through in-
> action. Like other Romantic heroes, Ravenswood possesses
> Hamlet's tortured soul but lacks his sense of isolation in
> an alien world. He is "a latter-day Hamlet . . . though
> enlightened by the humane rationalism of a later age."

10 MACINTYRE, LORN M. "Scott." Blackwood's Magazine, 318 (July),
 28-29.
 A poem in praise of Scott as "the greatest bankrupt."

11 MAXWELL, J. C. "A Scott Echo in Don Juan, X. 71. 2." Notes
 and Queries, 220 (September), 394.
 This line in Don Juan was intended by Byron to be a deliberate echo of stanza 47 of Scott's "William and Helen."

12 MORGAN, PETER F. "Lockhart's Literary Personality." Scottish
 Literary Journal, 2, 27-35.
 Lockhart eulogises Scott as an exemplary combination of
 virtue and genius but also describes him as the victim of
 a boundless imagination, which was partially responsible
 for his failure as a businessman. Lockhart characteris-
 tically turns Scott's defeat into "the triumph of duty over
 inclination." His admiration for the two qualities of
 balance and passionate effusion in Scott's writing parallels
 the combination of feeling, principle, and reserve in Lockhart's own literary personality.

13 POSTON, LAWRENCE. "The Commercial Motif of the Waverley
 Novels." Journal of English Literary History, 42, no. 1
 (Spring), 62-87.
 Scott regarded commerce as "a potentially creative force"
 but distrusted the unregulated working of the commercial
 instinct. In the Waverley Novels he uses commercial transactions as a moral index and contrasts "the old order of
 honor and the new order of credit." He values a world
 where these are not mutually exclusive and where the commercial spirit may be assimilated rather than scorned by
 the old aristocracy. Includes an extended discussion of
 The Fortunes of Nigel.

14 _____. "Uriah Heep, Scott, and a Note on Puritanism."
 Dickensian, 71 (January), 43-44.
 Andrew Skurliewhitter in The Fortunes of Nigel has several similarities to Uriah Heep in David Copperfield. Both
 characters begin in humble circumstances, attain relative

prosperity, and are finally revealed as villains. They resemble each other in physical appearance and in the hypo-
critical affectation of humility.

15 RANCE, NICHOLAS. "Introduction" and "The Historical Novel
    after Scott," in his <u>The Historical Novel and Popular Poli-
    tics in Nineteenth Century England</u>. New York: Barnes and
    Noble, pp. 11-62.
        Scott was the first to write national history by writing
    of popular life. He combined "the alternative responses to
    rapid change" in the objective portrayal of history in the
    Scottish novels and the escapism of the medieval novels.
    These latter inspired the "historical romance industry" of
    Ainsworth, James and Lytton, but they failed to grasp
    Scott's technique of depicting popular life. By the 1860's,
    Scott was attacked for factual inaccuracy, and the histori-
    cal romance was regarded as primarily appropriate for
    children.

16 STEPHENSON, WILLIAM A. "A Scott Echo in <u>Don Juan</u> XIII, 37-38."
    <u>Notes and Queries</u>, 220 (September), 394.
        Byron's metaphor of frozen champagne applied to Lady
    Adeline Amundeville was borrowed from Scott's review of
    <u>Childe Harold's Pilgrimage</u>, Canto IV, published in the
    <u>Quarterly Review</u> of April, 1818.

17 WEINSTEIN, MARK A. "An Echo of Mrs. Bennet in <u>Waverley</u>."
    <u>Notes and Queries</u>, 220 (February), 63-64.
        Bailie Macwheeble's reaction to Waverley's announcement
    of his intended marriage echoes Mrs. Bennet's reaction to
    Elizabeth's announcement that she is going to marry Mr.
    Darcy.

<u>1976 A BOOKS</u>

1 ALEXANDER, J. H. <u>Two Studies in Romantic Reviewing: The Reviewing of Walter Scott's Poetry, 1805-1817</u>, in <u>Romantic
   Reassessment</u>. Edited by James Hogg. Salzburg Studies in
   English Literature, No. 49, part II. Salzburg: Universitat
   Salzburg, Institut für englische Sprache und Literatur,
   201pp.
       Some of Scott's reviewers treated his poems merely as
   examples of traditional genres, but others recognized the
   originality of the form. They generally accepted historical
   inaccuracy but objected to the antiquarian elements. They
   regarded his medieval subject matter as a continuation of
   the medieval revival of the last twenty years. Many reviews

1976

paid detailed attention to plots and gave high praise to
Scott's natural descriptions. Includes a discussion of the
critical reception of each of the poems as well as a survey
of general evaluations of the poems as a group.

1976 B SHORTER WRITINGS

1   ALEXANDER, J. H. Two Studies in Romantic Reviewing: Edinburgh Reviewers and the English Tradition, in Romantic Re-
assessment. Edited by James Hogg. Salzburg Studies in English Literature, No. 49, part I. Salzburg: Universitat
Salzburg, Institut für englische Sprache und Literatur,
pp. 135-37, 167-80, 202-14.
Jeffrey admired Scott's poems for their lack of affectation or timidity. However, he objected to the Lay and
Marmion because their subjects were insufficiently digni-
fied. Includes analysis of Jeffrey's reviews of these two
poems and the extent to which his work was adapted by several other reviewers. Scott was "the Edinburgh's most
prominent literary contributor apart from Jeffrey." His
treatment of the translations of Amadis de Gaul by Southey
and Rose is marked by scholarship, critical perception, and
personal concern. His reviews of Godwin's work are distinguished by "a unique balance and sanity."

*2 DARST, DIANE WASSMAN. "Napoleon in Romantic Thought: A Study
of Hazlitt, Stendhal and Scott." Ph.D. dissertation,
Columbia University, 1976.
An abstract by the author appears in Dissertation Abstracts International, 37 (1976), 1142A.

3   DOUBLEDAY, NEAL FRANK. "Wandering Willie's Tale," in his
Variety of Attempt: British and American Fiction in the
Early Nineteenth Century. Lincoln and London: University
of Nebraska Press, pp. 49-60.
"Wandering Willie's Tale" demonstrates Scott's skillful
use of vernacular narration and his strong feeling for the
period. Willie as narrator is completely distinct from the
author, so interest focuses on the events of the tale, not
on their influence on the narrator's psyche. The tale has
its basis in popular folklore, but Scott transmutes several
elements of traditional diablerie for his own purposes.

4   FRYE, NORTHROP. The Secular Scripture: A Study of the Structure of Romance. Cambridge, Massachusetts and London:
Harvard University Press, 131pp., passim.

Like Dickens, Scott writes "on the boundary of serious fiction and romance." The Waverley Novels use traditional romance elements but also parody them. Scott's beleaguered virgins typify the mythical goddess-heroines of romance. Other romance motifs in his work include the lost identity of the heir, the mirror image or twins, the descent into an outlawed society, the animal or inarticulate human companion, and the transformation of the past.

5 GORDON, ROBERT C. "Scott and the Highlanders: The Non-fictional Evidence." Yearbook of English Studies, 6, 120-40.
   Scott admired the loyalty and tenacity of the Highlanders and considered them a potential military asset. However, he deplored their superstitions when they interfered with military effectiveness. He believed in their right to bear arms and to be let alone. Scott hoped to see a "new heroism" in the Highlands which would combine the peaceful pursuit of agriculture with a state of unregimented but effective military readiness.

6 GOSLEE, NANCY M. "Romance as Theme and Structure in The Lady of the Lake." Texas Studies in Literature and Language, 17, no. 4 (Winter), 737-57.
   Like Renaissance versions of Arthurian romance, The Lady of the Lake develops the connected themes of testing the hero and building political unity. James V learns that he must exert both personal and political control and avoid escape into the realm of romance. He redefines romance to reinforce his benevolence and sovereignty. Through the characters of minstrel and bard, the narrator redefines his own role as he learns to control the anarchic forces of history and art and integrate them into his romance-fiction.

7 HOGG, GEORGE. "Malachi Malagrouther 150 Years On." Scottish Bankers Magazine, 68 (May), 33-36.
   The First and Second Letters called in strong terms for resistance to English attempts to interfere with the Scottish banking system. They hinted of both martial and political rebellion. The Third Letter avoided emotional appeals and reaffirmed support for the Government, but by then many opponents of the projected legislation had been embarrassed by Malachi's ill-timed appeal to romantic violence.

8 KESTNER, JOSEPH. "Jane Austen: The Tradition of the English Romantic Novel, 1800-1832." Wordsworth Circle, 7, no. 4 (Autumn), 297-311.

1976

Deals with Scott peripherally. Scott shared with Austen, Ferrier, Edgeworth, Galt, and Mitford an awareness of writing fiction in a period when the novel was being redefined. In the Scottish novels, he de-emphasized plot in favor of manners and a circumscribed locale, a shift in focus typical of the fiction of this period. The Romantic novel explored its restricted location through the issues of education and law, especially the entailed estate. It often intentionally eliminated the authorial voice and gave preeminence to character through dialogue and dialect.

*9   McCOMBIE, FRANK. "The Completion of The Bride of Lammermoor." Notes and Queries, 221 (October), 454.
     Cited in British Humanities Index, October-December, 1976 (London: The Library Association, 1976), p. 139.

10   SCOTT, PAUL HENDERSON. "The Malachi Episode." Blackwood's Magazine, 320 (September), 247-61.
     In the "Letters of Malachi Malagrowther" Scott was concerned with both the immediate issue of the currency question and the larger problem of the relationship between England and Scotland. He resented government interference in Scottish affairs and the attempt to destroy the remaining differences between the two kingdoms. The letters "amount to a coherent statement of the philosophy of Scottish nationalism" and are its first modern manifesto. Scott's primary motives for writing them lay in his deep national feeling and in his cautious attitude toward change.

11   SUTHERLAND, KATHRYN. "Walter Scott and Washington Irving: 'Editors of the Land of Utopia.'" Journal of American Studies, 10, no. 1 (April), 85-90.
     Scott's Jonathan Oldbuck and Irving's Jonathan Oldstyle resemble each other in more than name, and there are parallels in the uses of the personae of Tales of My Landlord and the History of New York. The similarities between the works of these two writers more likely result from "kindred minds" than from direct imitation.

12   WEINSTEIN, MARK A. "The Creative Imagination in Fiction and History." Genre, 9, no. 3 (Fall), 263-77.
     As the philosophy of history changed from an emphasis on objective fact to a view of the historian as imaginative creator, the historical novel also developed to view the protagonist as a "hero of thought" who uses reason, imagination, and dream to reconstruct the past. Scott accepted the distinction between the novel as fiction and history as fact. His fiction assumes the existence of an objective

reality; the protagonist discovers it only through struggle, but the narrator uses it to demonstrate the continuity of present and past. Thus Waverley's growth occurs only when he observes the real world accurately and begins to reflect upon it. Also deals with Thackeray, Faulkner, Pynchon, and Mailer.

*13   ZEKULIN, N. G. "Turgenev in Scotland, 1871." Slavonic and East European Review, 54 (July), 355-70.
    Cited in Humanities Index, 3, no. 4 (March, 1977), 170.

14   ZUG, CHARLES G., III. "The Ballad Editor as Antiquary: Scott and the Minstrelsy." Journal of the Folklore Institute, 13, no. 1, 57-73.
    Scott used his knowledge as an antiquary to take editorial liberties with ballad texts, a practice regarded as acceptable in his time. He believed that ballads deteriorate in the course of oral transmission. To preserve their quality, he adopted the editorial procedures of conjectural emendations and the fusion of variants to form a complete text. He also tinkered with the text to improve metre and rhyme, eliminate anachronisms, and restore original story lines.

1977 A BOOKS - NONE

1977 B SHORTER WRITINGS

1   ANON. "The Blackwood Papers." Blackwood's Magazine, 321 (April), 273-74.
    The Blackwood Papers at the National Library of Scotland comprise a record of nearly 150 years of Blackwood's Magazine and its publishers. Among the archives is Henry Mackenzie's unpublished review (1817) of Scott's Tales of My Landlord.

2   ROLLYSON, CARL E., JR. "Faulkner and Historical Fiction: Redgauntlet and Absalom, Absalom!" Dalhousie Review, 56, no. 4 (Winter), 671-81.
    Redgauntlet and Absalom, Absalom! share many similarities. Both take place in a period a few decades after an historical crisis which is "a still remembered but rapidly retreating past." Darsie Latimer and Quentin Compson must define themselves in relation to the past, and each is helped by a secondary character who represents the new order and brings the protagonist to a "cumulative and progressive" assessment of the past. Each novel contains a

1977

short story paradigmatic of the hero's efforts to deal with his past. However, whereas the conclusion of <u>Redgauntlet</u> redeems the past by synthesizing it into the present, the conclusion of <u>Absalom, Absalom!</u> retreats away from the past to a vision of a grim future.

*3   SULTANA, DONALD E. "Introduction" to <u>The Siege of Malta Re-discovered: An Account of Sir Walter Scott's Last Novel and His Last Journey</u>. London: Chatto and Windus. Due for publication in 1977.

4   TREVOR-ROPER, HUGH. "England and Scotland: 1707-1977." <u>Listener</u>, 97 (3 March), 260-61.

Although Scott was a romantic conservative, he recognized the advantages of the Union and sought through his novels to create a Scottish identity which could coexist with it. He gave to the Highlanders and to Scotland's pre-Union past a "romantic patina," and he created a myth to mend "the broken continuity of Scottish history." This synthetic myth allowed the Scots to be proud of their national identity while at the same time they used the advantages of the alliance with England.

Index

The Correspondence of Sir Walter
    Scott and Charles Robert
    Maturin, 1937.A2
Corrigan, Eileen M., 1965.B5
Corson, James Clarkson,
    1939.B2, B3; 1942.B3, B4;
    1943.A1, B9; 1944.B3;
    1945.B4, B5; 1946.B6;
    1955.B4; 1956.B2, B3;
    1957.A1; 1962.B3; 1963.B6,
    B7; 1969.B7-B9; 1970.B5;
    1971.A8; 1975.A2
"The Course of Realism in the
    English Novel from Addison
    and Steele through Sir
    Walter Scott," 1934.B12
Cowley, John P., 1943.A2;
    1953.B3
Cowley, Malcolm, 1974.B8
Craig, David, 1958.B5;
    1961.B4; 1973.B11
"Craignethan Castle," 1964.B16
Crawford, Thomas, 1965.A1;
    1969.B10; 1970.B6; 1971.B15;
    1972.B9
"The Creative Imagination in
    Fiction and History,"
    1976.B12
Crépet, Jacques, 1932.B39
A Critical History of English
    Literature, 1960.B4
"The Criticism of Gulliver's
    'Voyage to the Houyhnhnms,'
    1726-1914," 1941.B6
"Critics of The Bride of
    Lammermoor," 1938.B25
Crockett, W. S., 1932.B42, B43;
    1940.B4
Croker, John Wilson, 1940.B3
Crowley, John, 1950.B3
Crowl, Samuel Renninger,
    1970.A3
Cruttwell, Patrick, 1957.B6
"'Cumnor Hall': The Analogue
    of Scott's Kenilworth,"
    1934.B26
Cunliffe, Walter R., 1936.B6
Cunninghame, A. T., 1932.B44
Curious, 1940.B5
Curle, James, 1932.B45, B46;
    1937.B5

Curry, Kenneth, 1971.B16
Cusac, Marian H., 1969.A5. See
    also Hollingsworth, Marian
    Everett
Cuthbertson, Stuart, 1937.B6

D

D., A. E., 1942.B5; 1943.B10, B11
Daiches, David, 1948.B4;
    1951.B2; 1956.B4; 1958.B6;
    1960.B4; 1964.B3; 1965.B6;
    1966.B5; 1968.B7, B8, B11;
    1971.A9, B17; 1973.B12
"The Dalrymple Legend in The
    Bride of Lammermoor,"
    1943.B24
"Daniell (Thomas, William, and
    Samuel)," 1951.B4
Dargan, E. Preston, 1934.B7
Darley, William Duane, 1974.A2
Darst, Diane Wassman, 1976.B2
"The Date of a Scott Letter,"
    1967.B24
"The Date of Sir Walter Scott's
    Birth," 1970.A2
Davie, Donald, 1961.A1, B5;
    1968.B9, B10
Davis, Nelson V., 1957.B7
"The Dead Hand: Dickens and
    Scott," 1943.B18
Dean, Dennis R., 1972.B10;
    1973.B13
"The Death of Alasco,"
    1966.B15
"The Death of Catherine in The
    Monastery," 1933.B26
"The Deaths of Glossin and
    Hatteraick in Guy Mannering,"
    1945.B12
"The Defeat and Triumph of
    Bourgeois Pacifism,"
    1971.B62
"Defoe and Scott," 1941.B26
Defoe, Daniel, 1941.B26;
    1944.B12
Dekker, George, 1967.B8
"A Deletion in Scott's 'Private
    Letters of the Seventeenth
    Century,'" 1969.B27

Hollingsworth, Marian Everett, 1964.A2. See also Cusac, Marian H.
Holman, C. Hugh, 1951.B7; 1972.B16
Holmes, John Haynes, 1933.B18
Holt, R. F., 1973.B24
Holthouse, E. H., 1946.B8
Home, Alec Douglas, 1967.B14
Hood, F. C., 1969.B17
Hook, Andrew D., 1967.B15; 1969.B14; 1972.B17
House, Jack, 1962.A1
The House of Desdemona, 1963.B9
Howarth, Robert Guy, 1938.B10; 1971.A14
Howell, Elmo, 1972.B18
"How the Waverley Novels Were Produced," 1933.B24
Hudson, Charles M., Jr., 1943.B16
Hughes, G. R., 1972.B19
"Hugh Henry Brackenridges Epistel on Sir Walter Scott," 1963.B27
"The Humanity of Scott," 1932.B12
Humphries, Walter R., 1956.B7
Hutchison, Robert, 1932.B90
Hutton, W. H., 1932.B91
Hyde, William J., 1973.B25

I

"Ichabod Crane's Scottish Origin," 1968.B26
"Ideals and Idealism in the Waverley Novels," 1960.A2
Ignoto, 1943.B17
"The Illustrations of Sir Walter Scott," 1971.B27
"Imagery of Color and Light in Scott's Narrative Poems," 1972.B15
"Imagination and Reality in Romantic Fiction," 1971.B85
Imbert, Henri-François, 1971.B32
"The Imitators and the Imitated: Scott, Ainsworth, and the Critics," 1973.B35

The Implied Reader, 1974.B16
"Incident in Sir Walter Scott's Journal," 1936.B1, B6
"Indebtedness of the Southern Novel to the Waverley Novels," 1940.A2
"In Defence of Rob Roy," 1968.B18
"An Index of the Supernatural, Witchcraft, and Allied Subjects in the Novels, Poems, and Principal Works of Sir Walter Scott," 1966.A1
An Index to the Waverley Novels, 1975.A1
"The Influence of Grillparzer on The Heart of Midlothian," 1945.B13
"The Influence of Scott," 1932.B17
"The Influence of Scott and Cooper on Simms," 1951.B7
"The Influence of Sir Walter Scott on the Vocabulary of the Modern English Language," 1948.A2
"In Fortsetzung Bagehots," 1936.B4
Inglis-Jones, Elisabeth, 1959.B5
"In Honour of Waverley," 1932.B157
"In Memory of Scott," 1933.B37
"The Inns of Scott," 1935.B25
"In Praise of Sir Walter," 1971.B82
"In Praise of Sir Walter Scott," 1933.B12
Insh, G. Pratt, 1937.B12
"The Interest of Scott's Public in the Supernatural," 1943.B25
"Interleaved Copies of Scott's Poems," 1941.B41
"In the Land of Guy Mannering," 1932.B63
Introduction to the English Novel, 1951.B9
Irving, Washington, 1947.B5; 1965.B15; 1968.B26; 1976.B11
Irwin, Francina, 1974.B15
"Isaac D'Israeli and Scott," 1964.B14; 1965.B16

Iser, Wolfgang, 1964.B6;
1974.B16
"Isolation and Community in
The Antiquary," 1973.B15
"Is Thy Servant a Dog," 1945.B3
"Istorija i vymysel v romanax
Val'tera Skotta," 1971.B60
The Italian Influence on Scot-
tish Literature, 1972.B20
Italy, reputation and influence,
1937.B21; 1967.B4; 1968.B34;
1972.B1, B20
Ivanhoe, 1932.B158; 1940.B18;
1941.B24; 1953.B5, B6;
1955.B5; 1959.B10; 1960.B16;
1961.B16; 1962.B4, B13;
1968.B14; 1969.B22; 1971.B58;
1973.B7
"Ivanhoe," 1932.B158
Ivanhoe, "Afterword," 1962.B13
"Ivanhoe and Simms' Vasconselos,"
1941.B24
Ivanhoe, "Foreword," 1962.B4
Ivanhoe, "Introduction,"
1953.B5; 1969.B22
Ivanhoe, "Preface," 1959.B10;
1968.B14

J

J., W. H., 1932.B94; 1938.B11,
B12; 1939.B9, B10; 1940.B15,
B16; 1941.B18; 1943.B18, B19
Jack, Ian, 1958.A3; 1963.B14;
1965.B10
Jack, James William, 1933.A6
Jack, R. D. S., 1972.B20
Jackson, (Mrs.) Nevill,
1932.B93
Jackson, Wilfred S., 1938.B18
"A Jacobite Refugee Mystery,"
1951.B14
Jacobitism, 1932.B4, B89;
1951.B14; 1966.A2; 1970.B6;
1974.B18
Jacobson, Sibyl, 1971.B33
Jaloux, Edmond, 1932.B94
James Fenimore Cooper the
Novelist, 1967.B8
James, Glenn Joseph, 1973.B26

"James Hogg's Familiar Anecdotes
of Sir Walter Scott,"
1936.B22
James, Louis, 1963.B15
Jamieson, M. E., 1932.B95
"Jane Austen: The Tradition of
the English Romantic Novel,"
1976.B8
Janssen, Judith M., 1972.A4
"Jeanie Deans and the Queen,"
1973.B25
Jeffares, A. Norman, 1969.B18
Jefferson, D. W., 1969.B19
"Jeffrey, Marmion, and Scott,"
1951.B1
"The Jewess as a Fictional Sex
Symbol," 1973.B7
"J. M. W. Turner and Sir Walter
Scott," 1972.B12
"J. M. W. Turner's Illustrations
to the Poets," 1966.B9
"John Banim, ein Nachamer Walter
Scotts," 1936.A7
John Dryden: Some Biographical
Facts and Problems,
1940.B26
John Gibson Lockhart, 1935.B10;
1954.B6
"John of Skye, Sir Walter
Scott's Piper," 1948.B5
"Johnson and Scott: A Greek
Inscription," 1939.B23
Johnson, Edgar, 1956.B8;
1963.B16; 1964.B7; 1965.B11;
1968.A2; 1970.A5
Johnston, Arthur, 1964.B8
Johnston, George Burke, 1950.B5
Johnston, Reginald F., 1932.B96
John Wilson Croker, 1940.B3
Jones, Dorothy Wooten, 1940.A2
Jones, Stanley, 1973.B29
Jones, W. Powell, 1940.B17
Jordan, Frank, 1965.A2;
1968.B23; 1973.B30
Journal, 1933.B16; 1936.A9;
1938.A3, B14; 1939.A1;
1940.B41; 1941.A1, B5;
1946.A1; 1950.A3; 1956.B9;
1965.B2; 1971.B1, B7, B72;
1972.A1; 1973.B3
"The Journal," 1973.B3

Orlov, S. A., 1971.B51
Orrick, James, 1932.B131
Osborn, J. M., 1940.B26
Osgood, Charles Grosvenor, 1935.B11
"'Ossian,' Scott, and Cooper's Indians," 1969.B16
Ostrowski, Witold, 1964.B15; 1965.B17
"De Oudste Nederlandse Vertalingen van Scott's Romans," 1959.B4
"Our Debt to Scott Today," 1932.B50
Owen, E., 1938.B25
Owen, Walter, 1937.B20

P

The Paradox of Scottish Culture, 1964.B3
Parker, William Mathie, 1932.A15, A16, B132–B134; 1933.A4, A5, B24; 1934.A2, A3, B15; 1935.A3, A4, B12, B13; 1936.A2, A3; 1937.A1, B21–B23; 1938.B26; 1939.B15, B16; 1940.B27–B29; 1941.B28–B30; 1943.B22; 1944.B13; 1946.A1; 1950.A3; 1951.B14; 1952.B8; 1954.B8; 1955.B10; 1956.B12, B13; 1957.B20, B21; 1958.B9–B11; 1959.B10; 1960.B12; 1962.B18, B19; 1966.B17; 1967.B18; 1969.B32, B33; 1971.B52
Parrott, T. M., 1944.B14
Parsons, Coleman Oscar, 1932.B135; 1933.B25–B30; 1934.B16–B18; 1942.B13, B14; 1943.B23–B30; 1945.B12–B14; 1962.B20; 1964.A4; 1966.B18; 1967.B19; 1971.B53; 1972.B33
Partington, Wilfrid, 1932.A26
"The Passing of Sir Walter Scott," 1933.B16
Paterson, J. H., 1965.B18
Patten, John A., 1932.A27
"Patterns in the 'Bildungsroman' as Illustrated by Six English

Novels from 1814 to 1860," 1972.B31
Patterson, Richard F., 1936.B19
Paul, Adolf, 1934.A4
Paul's Letters to His Kinsfolk, 1946.B1
Pearsall, Robert B., 1951.B15
Pearson, Hesketh, 1954.A1; 1960.B13
Peaston, Monroe, 1971.B54
Peckham, Morse, 1962.B21
"Pepper and Mustard: The Dandie Dinmont Terrier," 1932.B55
Perés, R. D., 1932.B136
Perth and Sir Walter Scott, 1932.A5
"Peter's Letters to His Kinsfolk," 1940.B27
Peterson, Clell T., 1962.A3; 1967.B20
Petrov, Rumen, 1971.B55
Pettet, E. C., 1952.B9
Peveril of the Peak, 1932.B100; 1939.B6; 1946.B4
P-G., H., 1940.B30
Philippide, A1., 1972.B34
Phillips, Lawrence, 1932.B137; 1934.B19; 1935.B14, B15; 1936.B20; 1937.B24; 1938.B27–B31; 1939.B17–B21; 1940.B31, B32; 1941.B31–B36
Phillipson, N. T., 1973.B41
Philoscotus, 1939.B22–B24; 1940.B33, B34; 1941.B37–B39
Pickering, Sam, Jr., 1974.B19
Piggott, Stuart, 1966.B19
Pike, B. A., 1966.B20; 1968.B32
Pikoulis, John, 1971.B56
Pilkey, John Davis, 1974.A5
The Pirate, 1946.B13; 1957.B14
Pittock, Joan H., 1957.B22
"Plausibility in the Romantic Plot Construction of Scott's Novels," 1972.A5
"A Plea for the Waverley Novels," 1944.B8
Poe, Edgar Allan, 1932.B39; 1936.B16; 1938.B22; 1951.B12; 1966.B10; 1969.B31; 1970.B14
"Poèmy Val'tera Skotta," 1970.B18
"Poe's Conception of the Grotesque," 1966.B10

"Poe, Scott, and 'The Murders
in the Rue Morgue,'"
1936.B16
"Poe's Orang-outang," 1938.B22
"Poe's Reading of Anne of Geierstein," 1951.B12
"Poe's Use of the Name Ermengarde in 'Eleanora,'"
1970.B14
"Poet, Romancer, and Man of Law,"
1932.B56
poetry, 1932.A8, B16, B52, B88,
B176; 1934.A1; 1936.A1, A8,
B10; 1937.B28; 1938.B15;
1940.B11; 1941.B7, B28;
1942.B9, B20; 1945.B14;
1949.B7; 1950.B11; 1952.B7;
1955.B9; 1960.B9; 1961.B5;
1962.B1; 1964.B10; 1967.B21;
1968.A8, B21, B42; 1969.A8;
1970.B18; 1971.A14, B15, B84;
1972.B9, B15; 1975.B8;
1976.A1
The Poetry of History, 1947.B7
"The Poetry of Scott," 1932.B16
"The Poetry of Sir Walter
Scott," 1932.B176; 1950.B11;
1952.B7; 1961.B5; 1971.A14
"The Poetry of the Early
Waverley Novels," 1975.B8
Poets and Men of Letters. Sale
Catalogues of Libraries of
Eminent Persons, 1971.B48
Poets, Patriots, and Lovers,
1933.B23
"Point of View and Structure in
The Heart of Midlothian,"
1961.B12
Poland, reputation and influence,
1934.B11; 1936.B14; 1964.B15;
1965.B17
"The Polite Letter-Writer,"
1943.B10
"Political and Protest Songs in
Eighteenth Century Scot-
land," 1970.B6
politics, 1932.B117; 1933.B17;
1949.B1; 1950.A1, B3;
1961.B17; 1970.B11, B26;
1971.B13, B46, B47; 1974.B17
"Politics and the Form of Disenchantment," 1974.B17

Politics and the Press, c. 1780-
1850, 1949.B1
Politics in English Romantic
Poetry, 1970.B26
Pollin, B. R., 1970.B14
Polwarth, Lord, 1968.B33
Pope-Hennessy, Una, 1932.A28,
B138, B139; 1933.B31;
1948.A1
"The Popinjay: A Comment on the
Romance," 1973.B4
"Pop, Op, and Black Humor,"
1968.B36
"Portrait of Sir Walter,"
1935.B5
Portrait of the Scott Country,
1968.A4
"The Portraiture of Sir Walter
Scott," 1932.B127
Portugal, reputation and in-
fluence, 1951.B17; 1971.A15
"A Possible Source for the Death
Scene in Arnold's Tristram
and Iseult," 1971.B64
Poston, Lawrence, 1975.B13, B14
Poston, M. L., 1943.B31
Potter, Lee H., 1955.A1;
1969.B34
Pottle, Frederick A., 1945.B15;
1969.B35
"Pour le bi-centenaire de sa
naissance," 1971.B34
"The Power of a Magic Pen,"
1932.B59
"The Power of Memory in Boswell
and Scott," 1945.B15;
1969.B35
Power, William, 1932.B140
"Poyais Cacique: An Imposter,"
1940.B5
Poynton, Orde, 1971.B57
Praviel, Armand, 1932.B141
Praz, Mario, 1937.B25; 1956.B14
"Pred 200-godisninata ot
rozdenieto ne Voltar Skot,"
1971.B55
"President Eliot on Sir Walter
Scott," 1932.B57
Price, J. Arthur, 1933.B142
Price, Lawrence Marsden, 1953.B12
"A Prisoner's Escape, Scott and
Dumas," 1940.B15

Pritchett, V. S., 1944.B15;
1947.B8
Private Letters of the Seven-
teenth Century, 1939.B16;
1947.B3; 1969.B27
Private Letters of the Seven-
teenth Century, "Introduc-
tion," 1947.B3
"A Problem in Editorial
Method," 1941.B5
"The Problem of the Scottish
Poet," 1936.B10
"Proofreading Lockhart's
Scott," 1961.B7
"The Prose Style of Sir Walter
Scott's Waverley Novels,"
1968.A1
"'Proud Maisie' und die Lyrik
von Sir Walter Scott,"
1968.B42
"Proverbs in the Waverley
Novels of Sir Walter
Scott," 1954.A2
"Providence, Fate, and the His-
torical Imagination in
Scott's Heart of Midlothian,"
1955.B6; 1968.B15
Punzo, Franca Ruggieri,
1969.B36
Pushkin, Aleksandr Sergeevich,
1940.B42; 1965.B8
"Pushkin and Sir Walter Scott,"
1965.B8

Q

Quare, 1938.B32, B33
Quarterly Review, 1943.B1, B12;
1944.B1; 1964.B1; 1973.B43
Quayle, Eric, 1968.A7; 1969.B37
"'Queens Love Revenge as Well as
Their Subjects': Thematic
Unity in The Heart of Mid-
lothian," 1972.B8
"Quelques remarques sur Stendhal
et les héroines de Walter
Scott," 1966.B1
Quentin Durward, 1932.B101;
1935.A1; 1955.B8; 1960.B12;
1963.B2; 1970.A1; 1971.B65

Quentin Durward, "Afterword,"
1963.B2
"Quentin Durward and St. Ronan's
Well," 1932.B101
Quentin Durward, "Preface,"
1960.B12
"Quentin Durward: The Astrolo-
ger's Expedient," 1935.B18
"Queries from Scott's Abbot,"
1939.B17, B28
"Queries from Scott's Anne of
Geierstein," 1936.B2, B20
"Queries from Scott's Antiquary,"
1937.B1, B24, B26, B27, B33
"Queries from Scott's Betrothed,"
1941.B14, B31
"Queries from Scott's Black
Dwarf," 1939.B18
"Queries from Scott's Bride of
Lammermoor," 1938.B18, B27,
B41
"Queries from Scott's Chronicles
of Canongate, 'Highland
Widow,' and 'Two Drovers,'"
1941.B32
"Queries from Scott's Fair Maid
of Perth," 1936.B8; 1941.B33
"Queries from Scott's Fortunes of
Nigel," 1940.B22, B31
"Queries from Scott's Heart of
Midlothian," 1938.B12, B17,
B28, B44; 1939.B9, B11
"Queries from Scott's Ivanhoe,"
1938.B29; 1939.B19, B30
"Queries from Scott's Legend of
Montrose," 1939.B20
"Queries from Scott's Old Mortal-
ity," 1938.B30
"Queries from Scott's Pirate,"
1940.B2, B16, B30, B32, B35,
B39
"Queries from Scott's Quentin
Durward," 1941.B3, B34, B42
"Queries from Scott's Redgauntlet,"
1935.B9, B14, B22, B24;
1941.B10, B35, B37
"Queries from Scott's Rob Roy,"
1938.B7, B31; 1939.B4, B10
"Queries from Scott's Talisman
and 'Aunt Margaret's Mirror,'"
1941.B16, B36